W9-DFF-331

DECORATING *with* PAINT

ABOVE Many shades of stippled red glaze, plus tinted varnish, create a gorgeous depth of lacquered colour which is particularly glamorous lit up at night.

PREVIOUS PAGE Artist John Fisher paints cut-out portraits in the style of the old 'silent companions' sometimes seen standing in a corner, or in front of the fireplace, in paintings of rooms from Jacobean times onwards. By using photographs, he was able to portray a vivid likeness of me.

DECORATING *with* PAINT

How to Create Decorative Surfaces with Trompe l'Oeil, Stencil, Spatter, Marble, Lacquer, Stipple and Sponge Techniques

JOCASTA INNES

Harmony Books/New York

CONTENTS

CONTENTS

INTRODUCTION

When I first began writing about decorative paint finishes five years ago, the subject was one of limited interest. Apart from exclusive decorating firms, which incorporated a discreet use of decorative techniques like dragging and marbling into their house style, and a few little-known centres for instruction in 'fantasy' finishes along the lines of the Isabel O'Neil studio in New York, hardly anyone seemed to have heard of those outlandish phrases I used to drop experimentally, such as 'scumble' or 'rag-rolling'. I had been on the trail of tinted glazes or 'transparent paint', especially in its DIY application, for several years – in fact, ever since the day I found a couple of painters racing up and down ladders, putting lilac glaze over dove-grey, in a house that I was visiting. I felt this was a discovery that ought to interest everyone who had become bored with flat emulsion and gloss white, and I was sure that if they could be shown how distinguished and attractive distressed or broken colour could look, and how subtly it could be used to remedy the sort of problems most DIY decorators face, there could hardly fail to be some response. Despite my faith in the subject, I was as astonished as anyone else when my first book, *Paint Magic*, found itself in the best-seller list.

Decorative painting was already sophisticated in ancient Egypt, as shown in this tomb painting of hunting fowl in the marshes at Thebes.
Tapestries have always been luxuries, but cheaper alternatives have existed – painted canvas hangings or 'water works', like this ravishing seventeenth-century example from a Gloucestershire manor house.

The ideas in my book were not new – nearly all discoveries in interior design are re-discoveries – and all I had done was to research the decorative techniques I found most appealing and describe how to apply them. The real innovation was in telling an old story to a new audience – the sophisticated end of the DIY market. The fact that stylized marbling and graining are found on Mycenaean pottery of 2200 BC shows just how old the story is. In ancient Egypt, where timber was scarce, realistic fake graining, complete with knots and characteristic figuring, was being produced by the Third and Fourth Dynasties. Egyptian furniture was painted, gilded and stencilled. Fresco decoration, where a range of lime-resistant colours were applied to wet lime plaster, was highly developed by Roman times, as the murals at Pompeii show.

Specialized paint effects went in and out of fashion through history in response to the predominant mood in interior decoration, which, in its turn, was affected by broader cultural trends and the economic climate. By the time I came to write about them, decorative finishes had been generally out of favour for almost a century, though a robust vernacular tradition of graining and marbling persisted in pub décor. My own explanation for the success of the decorative paint revival is that it has coincided with a growing appetite for colour and pattern in reaction to the bland neutrality of 'Scandowegian' (shorthand for Scandinavian-influenced design) and the ascetic sparseness of the Modern Movement, which between them inhibited delight in colour and texture in favour of 'form'.

The idea adopted most enthusiastically of all has undoubtedly been the tinted glaze. Manipulated while still wet, glazes can be used to create a dizzy array of textured effects from pintucks to crushed velvet, while achieving a soft, 'see-through' quality far removed from the thick, brash, opaque colour of modern miracle paints.

ABOVE *Painted 'architecture' was already a recognised decorative device for framing murals by 79 AD, when the Hall of Mysteries was painted in Pompeii.*

LEFT *The Entrance Hall at Saltram, grand and formal, illustrates how closely the eighteenth-century neo-classicists followed the classical system of sub-dividing wall spaces to create a 'framework'.*

For centuries, the use of glazes has been standard academic practice among painters for building up flesh tints, deepening shadows and generally adding depth or luminosity to paint colours. It was John Fowler, the most inventive British decorator of this century, who pioneered the decorative uses of 'transparent paint', as he called it. Combining the delicate film of colour in a tinted glaze with the grainer's traditional techniques for imitating wood, such as stippling, combing and mottling, he opened up a wealth of fascinating possibilities. Subtle rather than showy, this transparent overpainting lent a delicate ambiguity of tone which softened and enlivened all colours, even notoriously risky interior colours, like red. Layering different transparent colours over each other gives an almost infinite range of possible effects, and a richness of nuance matched only by the exquisite fabrics of that master colourist, Fortuny, coloured with layer upon layer of transparent dye. As Gerard Manley Hopkins wrote gratefully: 'Glory be to God for dappled things.'

Not all the comments on the rash of speckled, sponged, ragged, dragged and marbled surfaces which appeared some five years ago were favourable. Rumbles of discontent emanated from the élite of professional specialist painters, who felt that all this amateur activity, with half-trained art students and eager beginners muscling in, was lowering standards and giving special finishes a bad name. Nevertheless, despite criticism and the suspicion that this new enthusiasm for special finishes might be short-lived, the notion of using paint decoratively is not only still with us, but livelier and more inventive than at any time since the mid-nineteenth century.

This book aims to show how paint finishes have developed. The state of the art has gone from strength to strength: the discreetly distressed finishes in fruit-sorbet colours that once seemed so novel are now the norm, while today the more adventurous are creating effects of much greater intensity, with richer colours and bolder patterns. However, as soon as you introduce strong colour and pattern in one area of a room, for example richly textured and coloured walls, the other room elements – ceiling, floor, woodwork, doors – cry out for similar treatment. White ceilings, white woodwork and close carpeting in plain colours, standard ingredients of interiors a decade ago, provide such a negative surround to rich wall schemes that the whole room becomes unbalanced.

It should come as no surprise, then, that leading decorative painters today receive as many commissions for special floors, ceilings and woodwork schemes as they do for walls. The late Geoffrey Bennison was a recognized master of this kind of polychromatic approach, piling on effects with a simultaneous grasp of both the detail and the broad sweep. Jean and Mark Hornak, two of the most imaginative decorative painters, developed some of their most exciting ideas under Geoffrey's guidance; marbled woodwork containing the sudden visual surprise of boldly striped 'agate', a painted ceiling showering flowers as vividly precise as those in a Dutch still life, subtly wood-grained doors and shutters which stencil artist Mary MacCarthy then elaborates with marquetry designs inspired by seventeenth-century Dutch furniture. These effects, splendid taken singly, are quite breathtaking when matched with equal bravura in wall finishes, curtains, furnishings, floors and lighting.

Another decorative trend which is emerging strongly, and which gives today's rooms a more energetic, virile look, is the use of boldly patterned graining on doors and woodwork. In keeping with the current vogue for Biedermeier furniture, decorator Victoria Waymouth has designed a room with immaculate blond sycamore graining on all the woodwork, dramatized by a sleek black fillet which echoes the customary Biedermeier inlay of ebony or ebonized fruit wood. The same house runs a gamut of spectacular grained finishes, each chosen to complement a particular room – pale ivory 'camembert box', streaked with silvery grain marks, is used for one room, mahogany for double doors with gilt mouldings, burr maple for an amazing casket-like bathroom. The magic of such expert finishes is that they give a convincing and luxurious look to the most unprepossessing, if practical, materials like fibreboard, chipboard and ply.

Another effect which is becoming popular imitates the time-weathered patina of painted walls seen in Italy, where earthy ochres and siennas blend into each other to create a warm overall glow. This is a look that can be achieved by various different means and methods. I have seen a whole range of techniques used – colour rubbed in finely like rouge, thick colour sanded off to leave a freckle embedded in the surface, pink plaster with artificial cracks crayonned in and then varnished with orange shellac to give a burnished sheen, or watercolours worked on in layers. Another way to give walls patina is with traditional materials, now unexpectedly fashionable again. The extraordinary 'antiqued' finish invented by Jim Smart, doyen of the trade, uses dry colour over gesso and French chalk. Distemper – another revival – combines whiting and glue size for a powdery texture which is fragile compared with modern vinyl emulsions, but gives wonderful chalky colours. Designer and antique dealer, Leonard Lassalle, finds distemper an ideal wall finish in the old beamed houses in his part of Kent. He uses odd muted lilacs, grey-greens and ochre-yellows, and sometimes paints a wall black as a background to a dramatic painted wall design in egg tempera, based on early crewel-work (see pp. 96–7, 112–3).

For a real showstopper, however, murals and trompe l'œil (painted decoration so realistic as briefly to deceive the eye) are hard to beat. Not since the Renaissance have so many clients commissioned so many ambitious wall decorations, and a showpiece painted by one of the famous 'muralisers', such as Lincoln Taber, Ian Cairnie or Richard Shirley Smith, is an international status symbol. Clients may choose a mural of a romantic Italian garden or an exotic jungle scene to surround an indoor swimming pool, a stylized oriental landscape for a stairway, or the ruins of Petra for a bathroom. But painted illusion need not be so elaborate. One of the simpler notions, a 'sky' ceiling, painted blue with drifting white clouds, is so much in demand that a decorative painter could easily make his living on skies alone, were it not for the back troubles which follow too much ceiling work. Painted 'stone-work', or rustication, is a favourite finish for entrance halls, lobbies and stairwells, as it gives an air of architectural consequence to uninteresting or awkward spaces. The grandest solution of all for walls that are in the wrong place is to dissolve them visually with a huge mural suggesting a classical panorama or a wooded landscape.

It is not mandatory to be a millionaire, with teams of specialist painters at your command, to enjoy such painted spectaculars; gifted amateurs can achieve great effects with time and patience. However, labour-intensive schemes such as that designed by Carlo Briganti for the room of a Parisian client are probably best avoided. He devised an intricate collage of tiny brown and tawny painted paper strips, inspired by pretty nineteenth-century straw-work called Tunbridge Ware, and it took four workers five months to paste down each strip of paper individually over the four walls.

If you cannot own a glorious old tapestry, the eighties solution is cheap and cheerful – paint one. Or, if that seems too onerous, steal a motif or two from it and stencil them onto your walls.

Stewart Walton (whose artwork illustrates this book) created a rich overall wall pattern for his own house, based on motifs from an oriental rug (see p. 108). Painted in soft colours, which vary in intensity just like an irregularly faded rug, the pattern keeps growing as time permits. Similarly, the wall design in my own kitchen grew in fits and starts, and almost everyone who came to the house helped by adding a panel or two. The bold curvaceous pattern is based on a Jacobean wall design I saw in an Essex pub, and each panel has been painted freehand, resulting in a pleasing, and human, irregularity (see p. 20).

Art critic Roger Fry, founder of the Omega group, wrote an article in 1917 called 'The Artist as Decorator' in which he imagines the artist turned house-painter. 'Now our artist may be able, merely out of the contrast of two or three pure colours applied in simple rectangular shapes, to transform a room completely, giving it a new feeling of space and dignity or richness. In fact he can underline as it were the actual proportional beauty of the architecture or counteract its architectural defectiveness.' I like to imagine the reverse of that situation, where the house-painter dares to turn decorative artist, but Fry's observations on the potency of colour and its ability to transform still stand.

As Jim Smart is fond of saying: 'A room that has been properly painted needs no furniture.' This is not to say that marbled dados, sky ceilings and ragged walls would compensate for living in empty rooms, but it serves to dramatize the importance of colour and texture as the sovereign remedies for the imperfect rooms in which most of us live.

ABOVE *Flamboyant gilded and painted chairs designed by William Burges show how a Victorian genius re-interpreted traditional decoration.*

RIGHT *William Burges was one of the few great English architects to use colour uninhibitedly, and this room designed around his furniture shows nineteenth-century polychrome decoration at its most dazzling.*

1

EXPERIMENTING WITH PAINT

PAINTABILITY AT HOME

IN MY OWN LONDON HOUSE

You might reasonably suppose that the most excitingly decorated homes would be those belonging to decorative painters themselves. People who do not earn their living by the brush assume that an expert marbler, like one of the Hornaks, must live surrounded by panels of golden sienna or white Sicilian marble, and that someone with as many skills as Susan Williams, who used to run the Colefax Studio, would have covered every inch of furniture with some lavish fantasy finish. With a few notable exceptions, the last place most painters feel inspired to work on is their own home. What strikes the amateur as challenging and fun is more often a busman's holiday for professionals who cannot help automatically costing out their brushwork, and often feel disorientated when left to their own devices, without a decorator or client imposing restrictions.

For my sitting room I devised my own rubbed-in effect, aimed at giving a fresco texture. The blue 'framing' sharpens up an amorphous space and ties in with a stencilled frieze, giving the room a sort of logic. In my bathroom I used greyed pastel colours with a honeysuckle stencil, to which greater definition is given by painted bands.

RIGHT *Based on a Williamsburg colour, the warm blue in my study was 'dirtied' with both burnt and raw umber. The blinds were hand-painted to pick up the carpet design.*

ABOVE *A detail of the frieze, cribbed from an Indian textile design, enlarged and re-coloured. The fat rope stencil was added later.*

AUTHENTIC DECOR
PETER THORNTON
THE ART OF COLOUR DECORATION BY J.D. CRACE

Ian Cairnie, one of the more imaginative trompe l'œil artists, admits that he goes to pieces if he is not given a stylistic framework. He can paint a brilliant pastiche of a Claude Lorraine landscape or a Dutch flower painting in a few days. But, in his words, 'if you asked me to paint something in my own style I'd still be there weeks later, not knowing where to begin. I need to be given a style in which to paint.'

Many decorative painters admit to fantasies about how they would like their own homes to look, but this transformation rarely takes place. Lack of time is one excuse. Then there is the curse of sheer perfectionism, which comes of producing work to the highest standards in luxurious and beautiful surroundings. 'I'm such a perfectionist', says stenciller Mary MacCarthy, the owner of a small, pretty cottage in Norfolk, 'that everything has to be exactly right or I can't live with it. So I look at blank walls and tell myself how wonderful it will be when I finally get round to it.'

Like Mary MacCarthy, I find it hard not to give a guilty start and become apologetic when I am asked if my house is covered from top to toe 'with all those wonderful painted finishes you write about'. Seeing, analysing, and writing about so much excellent decorative work makes it easy to become over-critical, and too mindful of all the shortcomings (unfinished areas, ideas that need further development) to take in the overall effect of your own home. But when I suddenly see my place with new eyes, after a few days away somewhere, I realize all over again that it has a special atmosphere, a look of its own, and that this is due more than anything else to colour and pattern achieved with paint.

One lesson I learned in turning the dilapidated ruin I stumbled upon six years ago into the tolerably complete state it has now reached, is that an adventurous deployment of painted effects and finishes is the cheapest, most effective solution to decorating problems given that the ideal solution is usually too expensive to carry out. For instance, all the original wide, elegant cornices characteristic of Regency interiors had disappeared, except for a battered stretch left in the front hall. It would have been better practice architecturally to restore them because the proportions of period rooms depend on such details, but the cost was prohibitive so I was obliged to try and achieve a similar visual balancing act by other means. Painted or stencilled friezes, painted lines and stencilled borders in contrasting colours help to restore the balance as well as making a decorative point in their own right. I am just beginning to realize, however, after seeing some of the latest developments in painted and decorated ceilings, that for this ruse to work fully, the painted treatment needs to be extended over the ceiling as well.

The house was a near derelict shell when I bought it; ghetto-like poverty overtook Spitalfields when the silk-weaving industry collapsed in the early nineteenth century. My reason for buying it was the most persuasive one possible. I was homeless, had next to no money, and it was available, central and cheap. Even so, by the time it had been re-roofed, the windows re-made, ground floors replaced, and the back extension completely rebuilt, there was a large hole in my bank account. On the advice of friends with experience of rehabilitating 'squats', my young daughters and I began by colonizing the top floor. The moment any cash came my way, I put it towards reclaiming the cold, empty, desolate rooms below, employing tradesmen to do the skilled work, like plastering, while I, and such skilled and unskilled helpers as I could recruit, worked at those time-consuming jobs that are feasible for amateurs: burning-off thick crusts of old paint on the woodwork, pulling out nails, patching holes, sanding, filling, scraping, priming and painting.

John Fowler always recommended, and I endorse this, that you should never do anything to a new place till you have lived in it for six months. In that way you discover things not immediately apparent, but important for intelligent redecorating: how the light falls, which rooms are sunlit and at what times, how the layout of the building works or fails to work, and what arrangements of furniture are possible. Yet anyone who has lived on a building site knows how passionately one craves an oasis of order, colours instead of endless plaster dust, textures and the illusion, at least, of a proper room. The moment the plaster had dried (and sometimes before, which has led to an unpremeditated 'old palazzo' look on the walls downstairs), I rushed in with my paints and my ideas about colour. Should anyone wonder how far I follow my own precepts, let me say that there is not a square foot of the building, except perhaps for a ceiling or two, that has not had its paint-work teased about in some way or other.

It is not that I cannot let well alone, but that I keep trying to make 'well' better. I belong to the 'organic' school of decorators, who insist that rooms and colour schemes should be allowed to grow. I find blueprint rooms, where everything has been planned on the drawing-board, unsympathetic, and as uncomfortable and constricting as clothes that are too tight. I find certain colours strongly suggest themselves for particular rooms after a while, but the great usefulness of paint techniques like glazes and washes is that they allow you to have second and third thoughts even after the colour is on the walls, if the result is not what you want – unlike wallpaper. The thundery blue which covers everything in my study except the ceiling, was a proprietary paint in a grey-blue shade which I tinted down with ultramarine stainer. On the walls, however, as often happens, the colour which looked so pretty over a small area misbehaved and looked oppressively dark, its matt surface sucking in every ray of light. Sponging over a paler version of the original colour, lightened with white, was helpful, as was shining-up blue painted woodwork with varnish, but the saving grace of the room proved to be the wide frieze (a pattern copied from the border of an Indian cotton bedcover) painted round the room just beneath the ceiling in warm peachy colours. Blue curtains overloaded the colour yet again, so I stepped up the stencil with a second band of colours, a fat red and yellow rope, underlining the first.

I try to use paint, whether in a plain colour or as a pattern, architecturally, to help define space and correct imbalance. The blue lines that divide the walls of my sitting room, which has cloudy pinkish walls (strong red glaze rubbed to the merest veil of colour over a smooth silk vinyl), are perhaps the most successful example. The room began rosy, which was pleasant enough but rather nondescript. A stencilled frieze round the top of the walls unbalanced the room completely, emphasizing its odd shape and leaving great yawning spaces below. The idea of running coloured bands round to give the walls more definition was inspired by photographs of an apartment in New York. It took two days to complete, from measuring out to the final painting of a second layer of khaki glaze over the first blue glaze which had a softening, ageing effect – at first it looked too much like gift wrapping. The room still needs what I call 'thickening up', but the lines have helped to anchor it visually.

The most fashionable finish in my house, the low key rustication of the front hall and staircase, is the only one original to the house. I uncovered the design, printed in sepia and off-white on thick parchment-textured paper, as I scraped off the usual palimpsest of later papers, varnishes and other rubbish deposited over a century and a half. The paper was beyond rescue, so I simply copied it in paint, liking it for its demure neo-classicism and curious to see how well the original de-

ABOVE *The hand-painted block motif in my kitchen is based on one I found in an old pub. I think of it as a painted version of a 'friendship' quilt because friends add bits now and then.*

RIGHT *The very restrained painted 'stonework' in my hall reproduces the original Regency wallpaper design. The mural uses a Greek vase motif found on a matchbox cover while on holiday in Rhodes.*

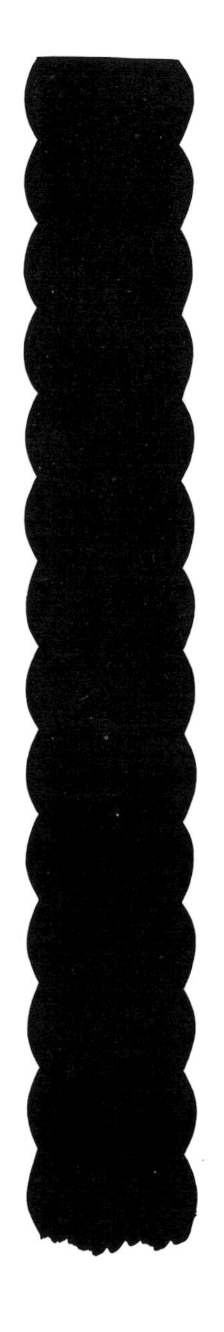

corators had understood their building. Most people take to it at once, but what makes it work for me is the flash of colour beyond in a mural of running figures, which is an enlarged version of the picture on a tiny matchbox picked up on holiday in Rhodes. It was not the only Regency paint finish that I uncovered. Two more, which I decided not to reproduce, also turned up: the sitting room was stencilled with brown anthemion borders on blue paint, and one of the upstairs bedrooms was sponged in a wild medley of red and green over creamy-white, making huge wavy stripes of colour that I found decidedly unsettling.

Nearly all my furniture is junk, and much of it is painted, either to disguise its lowly origins, or change its character to suit a room, or sometimes just to try out an idea. Professional decorative painters dislike painting furniture as a rule because they cannot make a profit out of work that takes days to achieve the superlative finish needed if painted pieces are to sell. For the DIY painter with a decorative urge, on the other hand, painting furniture is a picnic, a small-scale operation that you can take up and leave off as you please and that gives just enough scope for trying out new ideas. I have experimented with nearly every style of furniture painting, from Adam's neo-classicism (to be avoided unless you are prepared to make a meticulous job of it – bodged Adam is bad news) to ethnic or folksy. My most successful pieces, I think, are those to which I gave a 'printed' look with a tiny overall stencil, or in one case (a good idea by the way) a lino-cut copy of a sixteenth-century fabric printing block.

My bedroom is the one room in the house that owes nothing to paint. The walls are stapled over with striped cotton shirting, discovered in a great bolt in the basement of a wholesale fabric shop in London's Brick Lane. I bought 50 metres at 50p a metre, which gave me more than enough to 'wall' the room completely, stapling the cotton over thin wadding straight onto the plaster, make quilted curtains to match, and still have enough left over to run-up sheets and a duvet cover one day. But it would not be my room if signs of my ruling obsession had not begun to creep in. First, I painted the four-poster bed, made out of deal by an American friend, furniture designer and craftsman Jim Howett. Painted and varnished many times for an old japanned look, it will acquire gilded decoration one of these days. Then I painted the bedside trolley black with gold lining, and finally I have yielded to a sudden impulse to transform the overmantel mirror, perhaps because I find its prim Adam shape provoking. I have decided to give it a polychrome treatment. Most mornings I add another colour element, picking out a moulding, or glazing a red to a maroon, and almost every night I look at it critically and decide to change it all again. But that is the way decorative painting goes as soon as you break with tradition and try for something personal and different. There are few decorative painters I respect more than Graham Carr, and I have Graham's word for it that the only way to get something right is to be prepared to get it wrong, not just once or twice but for as long as it takes to attain that flow of certainty, the conviction that you have achieved the revised but definitive version. If John Fowler was prepared to paint a room out and start again, half-a-dozen times if necessary, in order to realize the vision in his mind's eye, why should we lesser visionaries be too proud?

A splendidly handsome rope border can be built up from three separate stencils, first the background, then the zigzags in contrasting colours to suggest shading.

2

COLOUR AND PAINT

CREATING COLOURS

FOR VISUAL EFFECT

When colour is so sumptuous and pleasurable, as well as cheap and accessible, it puzzles me that so many people still approach colour in decorating with such misgivings. Instead of revelling in this inexpensive luxury and taking inspiration from all the colour expertise that surrounds us in shop windows, posters, magazines and clothes, they are paralysed by fears that colour is too hot to handle without professional training – as if it were necessary to be a chef to cook, or a Wine Master to appreciate a glass of claret. Although some people do seem to be born with an extra sensitivity to colour, just as others may have perfect pitch, colour sense, like any other sense, can be strengthened and sharpened simply by using it. Besides, you do not have to be a great, innovative colourist to put together attractive and successful decorating schemes.

One colour plus white is an easy formula which always looks effective, especially with a sophisticated colour like this pale terracotta. Note how it is carried over onto the ceiling. Cold and warm colours of similar value make restful painted stripes. This is one of the easiest finishes to do, thanks to masking tape.

To cultivate your colour sense you should begin by training yourself to *look*, with an assessing eye. When some colour effect attracts your attention, apple blossom maybe, or regimental uniforms, try to see it in relation to the other colours present. It is understanding how colours affect each other that makes for confidence in using them. It is not just the pink and white of the blossom to which your eye responds, but the blue of the sky, the sombre tone of the bark, the medley of greens in the leaves, even the tiny spark of yellow in the stamens. As Bauhaus colour theorist Josef Albers concluded: 'Colour is the most relative medium in art.'

To get an impression of the overall colouring of a scene rather than the detail, try half-closing your eyes until the subject is almost a blur. Taking in the colouring – which colours, in what proportions – is not much more complicated than figuring out what ingredients comprise the flavour of a particular dish. It soon becomes an automatic response, and it is this mental store of colour relationships that good colourists draw on all the time.

Subjective Colours

Everyone has a personal colour harmony, a combination of colours which they find most pleasing. Johannes Itten, another famous colour theorist, defined this personal selection as 'subjective colour' and he was emphatic that identifying and using our subjective colours does more than make our environment more attractive. 'To help a student discover his subjective forms and colours is to help him discover himself.'

That only sounds far-fetched if you have never progressed beyond the childhood idea of one 'favourite' colour. Even that can be a useful point of departure. If you are drawn to one colour, like red, in your clothes or furnishings, you inevitably begin seeing other colours in relation to red when you decide, for example, what coloured shoes to wear with a red dress. You will know, too, that there are many colours or tones which can be classified as 'red'. You may put two or three colours together with your red dress one day which make the dress sing out in a way it has not done before, and you have the indefinable feeling that something has clicked into place.

Using your subjective colours in your immediate surroundings is not just pleasurable, it is therapeutic, just as living among alien colours, or neutral chromatic tones, can be strangely depressing. Itten believed that 'colours are forces, radiant energies which affect us positively or negatively whether we are aware of it or not.' He carried out an experiment on some of his students in which they were kept first in a blue-green painted room, then in a room painted orange-red. They began to feel cold in the blue-green room when the temperature dropped to 59 degrees, while in the orange-red room they did not complain of the cold until the temperature had dropped a further 5 degrees, or in some cases 7 degrees. Orange-red is unconsciously perceived as the colour of warmth.

Colours do not have to be 'colourful' in the obvious sense – bright or strongly contrasting – to have an emotional effect or a psychological importance. Some people are drawn to muted, subdued shades, just as some painters like to work with a muted palette.

Rules and Theories

I never refer to colour systems, like colour wheels or charts, when I am thinking about the colours I might combine in a room. I do not know any decorators, or decorative painters, who do, though artists like Alan Cuthbert find a knowledge of colour theory and principles helpful as well as fascinating. What Alan Cuthbert does consciously, many other colour-minded people probably do unconsciously, registering impressions of interesting, subtle, or beautiful colour mixtures without stopping to analyse what made them memorable. Very often, when you do analyse a particularly successful colour combination it does in fact conform to established principles.

The study of colour is a complex science, but you will find it a great help when experimenting with paint colours if you are at least familiar with the basic rules and terms, however obvious. Colour begins, literally, with hue. The hue – red, blue, mauve – *is* the colour, the element that differentiates it from all others. The 'tone' or 'shade' of a colour refers to the degree of lightness or darkness. If the colour or hue is blue, for instance, the blue tones will be all those shades that result from adding increasing amounts of white, or lightness, or increasing amounts of black, or darkness, to the original pure blue. Pigment is the substance itself, the raw material of colour, which is sometimes derived from natural materials, sometimes from chemical processes. Many pigments have an undertone of another colour that is hard to identify. Two full-strength blues may look quite similar, but when you add white to both and compare the pastel shades, the different undertones show up clearly. The most useful way to classify colours for decorating purposes is to group them into 'warm' and 'cold' categories, but there are warmer versions of cold colours, and vice versa.

The Colour Tribe

Red, blue and yellow are the three primaries with which we are all familiar. Primary means first, or original, and the almost infinite number of colour permutations – around a million identifiable shades, according to Alan Cuthbert – all derive from this trio, plus black and white. Some decorative painters, and colour mixers like Cyril Wapshot, use only these five basic colours to make all the other colours that they need. In some ways this is a convenience – you need carry only five tubes of pigment around with you – but it can take longer to mix colours than would be the case with a wider range, and some painters feel it gives cruder, less controlled results. Secondary colours are produced by mixing two of the primaries (orange from yellow plus red, purple from red plus blue, green from blue plus yellow). But it is the tertiaries, made by mixing the primaries with secondaries (red plus orange giving orange-red, blue plus green giving blue-green), and the tones or shades obtained by lightening or darkening them, which really supply the sort of colours decorators use. The further a colour is from a primary, the less vivid it is and the easier to combine with other colours of the same intensity. Vivid hues are exciting, especially when used together, but generally they are too challenging to live with in any quantity. The tones or shades obtained by lightening, darkening or intermingling colours are much less visually demanding. It is these colours that decorators value most.

When the colours are arranged as they are on our artist's palette, another and very important relationship emerges – the complementaries. The colour opposite any given colour on the palette is its complementary – the complementary of the primary red is secondary green, that of tertiary blue-purple is tertiary orange-yellow.

Complementary colours balance each other visually. Physiologically, we seem to need this colour balance. This, at least, is one way of explaining why if you look hard at any colour for about twenty seconds and then look at a plain white or grey sheet of paper, the complementary colour immediately appears as an after-image. (See our colour boxes with grey centres on p. 32.) Grey works as well as white because it is chromatically neutral.

The arrangement of colours on our artist's palette demonstrates an important colour relationship. The colour opposite any given colour on the palette is its complementary – the complementary of the primary red is secondary green, the complementary of tertiary blue-purple is tertiary orange-yellow. A knowledge of complementary colours is invaluable when balancing a colour scheme.

For decorating purposes, the value of complementaries is in balancing a colour scheme. Just suppose that a room has become overwhelmed by, say, blue-purple. You could immediately rectify matters by introducing a flash of orange-yellow. This may sound crude as a decorating scheme, and in fact you would be more likely to use paler tones of purple like mauve or lavender (whose complementary would be a similarly lightened tone of orange-yellow), but it provides a useful pointer when hunting for the colour that will irradiate a scheme that feels unbalanced and lifeless. Not merely the direct complementary, but also colours adjacent to it on our artist's palette will marry happily – in the case of lavender, this will include all those colours from yellow-green to brown-red, or rather their paler versions – almond green and salmon pink.

Mixing equal amounts of complementary paint colours always gives grey. Mixing a little of one colour into a lot of its complementary has a softening effect, which is useful to know if you need to dull or soften a bright paint colour without altering its tone.

Colour Values

Talk of colour values sounds pretentious, but it helps to know what the term means because an understanding of colour values is important to the success of close combinations of colours, as in a stencilled pattern. If you have ever tried to work out sympathetic colours for a three-colour border, and found one colour 'jumped' out at you restlessly, it is because you got the colour values wrong. Value in this context means vividness or intensity, and the secret of a pattern or blend which 'lies flat' and knits together harmoniously is to use colours of similar value. The stripes which decorator Nemone Burgess painted on the walls of her bedroom are an example of colours which work together. They are restful rather

Primary colour on a white ground jumps out at you and looks strident over a large area. By bringing the colour values closer, darkening the background and softening the motif colour, the pattern 'lies flat'. Adding the complementary colour in more or less equal quantities has a similar balancing effect and enriches the pattern.

than restless stripes, because the colours used are of the same value. If either colour were a few degrees brighter, it would seem to be advancing while the other was receding, and this would be disturbing when repeated throughout the room.

One way of working out whether colours are of approximately the same value is by imagining them photographed in black and white. Colours of similar intensity will come out as similar tones of grey. If you stencilled red flowers on a white ground and photographed them, the flowers would be almost black in relation to the ground. Maximum contrast of this kind will always look 'jumpy' on walls, though a fabric designer might like the excitement that this creates. Wall patterns, even on the limited scale of a border, work best where no one colour predominates, so to make this idea work you would need to raise the ground colour value to, say, a warm buff colour, and 'knock back' the flowers. You could do this either by mixing the red with green or raw umber to give a softer red, or by framing the red flowers with green leaves, since red and green juxtaposed neutralize each other. This would also make a more satisfactory, richer looking pattern.

Another example comes from my own house. The mid-blue lines, painted to form a 'frame' for the pink walls of my sitting room, looked too hard and emphatic. The blue was too intense for the soft transparent background because these colours are of different tonal values. 'Dirtying' the blue with thin washes of raw umber, burnt umber and a little burnt sienna, rubbed on with a rag, unevenly for speed, produced a dull blue-green close to the colour of weathered copper. This was not only closer in value to the pink but, because of the green tone, was nearer to being the straight complementary of the pink, and as a result the walls and painted framework settled down harmoniously as if made for each other.

The Family of Tones

As you experiment with mixing colours you will find some that are immediately attractive, others that are odd but interesting and some that are frankly depressing or displeasing. Fortunately for those of us who need guiding through the colour jungle, this vast range of colours has been winnowed over the centuries by decorators, painters and other colour-minded people. It is not easy to define what makes a 'good' colour; most decorators have their own favourites (see pp. 34–5, 38), but they all recognize a good colour even if it lies outside their personal range of preferences, which suggests that 'good' is not a purely subjective judgement. Broadly, I would define a good colour as one interesting enough to look at in its own right, positive enough to allow other colours to be played off against it, but subdued enough to remain a background to furnishings, pictures, possessions and people.

Now and then, a good colour becomes a fashionable decorating trend, and you see it so often that it begins to look jaded. Apricot is an outstanding recent example, with terracotta, in its paler shades, a close second, and currently mauve is coming up strongly. But the caprices of fashion do not alter the fact that good colours are classic decorating colours, and for this reason anyone interested in developing their colour sense should study them and see how they perform. The easiest way to do this is to leaf through decorating magazines, noting which colours look most effective. Recently, I saw photographs of a house where the bedroom had been painted, unexpectedly, in a moody but wonderful violet-grey, mixed to match thunder-clouds seen over the moors outside. Relieved by vivid patchwork, shiny old wood, lots of pictures and personal treasures, this colour, which might not normally be thought of as a 'bedroom colour', had strength and character, and immediately

An optical reflex which suggests an unconscious need to find a balance in colours. If you stare hard at each coloured square in turn, the complementary colour will appear over the neutral grey centre.

joined my mental file of attractive colour possibilities.

Among the few colours which are 'good' just as they come are the earth colours – ochre, raw and burnt sienna, raw and burnt umber, Indian or Venetian red – which are always satisfying, especially for exteriors, though even then most painters would modify them a little. There are others: indigo is a particularly good blue, as is cerulean, and Naples yellow, lemon yellow and Paynes grey also fall into this category.

However, a 'good' decorating colour is usually one which has come about by mixing several colours in varying proportions. Often, though not always, it is called a 'dirty' colour, dirty here signifying approval, and denoting a softening and mellowing of the original hue which is close to the effect of time. Ambiguity of tone, I think, is a common feature of most good colours in decorating. Blues will have a brownish or greenish cast, greys a violet or pearly tinge, pinks a greyish-brown tone, while yellows may be greyish or pinkish. Just why this makes them more effective as decorating colours is a little mysterious, but to anyone sensitive to these nuances – and this is where a developed colour sense leads you – the difference between one of these complex colours and a simpler one is almost palpable.

This brings me smack into my next point, which is that if you care enough about 'good' colours to want them around you, you will almost always have to mix them yourself. The commercial paint ranges are short on good colours, except in the paler neutral shades. Decorative painters do use them, but mostly for convenience as a base on which to apply their transparent paint effects. Graham Carr, for instance, used a commercial red as a base for the obelisk bookcases in his open-plan room, knowing that he could mix up a colour in glaze which would combine with the red base to give just the effect he wanted. It would have wasted time, and used up a great deal of tinting colour, to mix up the red base, as is the case with any strong colour. Transparent paint, as we shall see, solves many problems.

Some specialist paint firms pride themselves on marketing good colours, others will match a colour swatch for you. If you despair of being able to mix colours successfully, this could be your answer. Nothing, however, gives the same flexibility as taking your courage in both hands, getting a selection of tinting colours, and mixing up your own. As we all know, there is many a slip between colour sample and painted room; if you mix you can correct the colour on the spot.

Beginners in colour-mixing, as in cookery, need recipes. Knowing that you are on the right colour path makes all the difference. It also means that you know what ingredients – that is, tinting colours – to stock up on. Decorating colour formulas are something of a trade secret, information painters prefer to keep to themselves. I am grateful for the generosity with which many of them have shared their favourite formulas.

FAIL-SAFE COLOUR SCHEMES

I know from experience that some people take to the notion of mixing their own colours and building up their own colour schemes with no difficulty at all. For those who are less confident, it can be reassuring to know that there are many reliable basic colour schemes for rooms which always look attractive, and are easy to live with. Once you have got the basics together, adding experimental touches becomes easy and fun.

Painters know about the chemistry, and performance of colour because this is their special field of study. Analysing the 'palette', how much of which colours are used by your own favourite artist, can give helpful pointers when choosing a colour scheme.

Neutral rooms

The best neutral room schemes are costly looking. Use stone colours – putty, beige, greys and buffs – ranging in tone from the interesting off-whites to slate-greys, tobacco-browns and sepia. All these colours blend together easily in a room, are undemanding background shades for pictures, flowers and furniture, and create a cool, calm effect. The main problem with neutrals is that they can look drab. The remedy is to concentrate on textures – rough like matting, stone and wood, shiny like marble, lacquer, silk and satin, or soft and furry like velvet. For contrasting colour, add shiny black, dull red, or a bunch of cushions in mauve, pink or greeny-yellow. The best colours in standard paint ranges are neutral shades.

Monochrome rooms

Taking a favourite colour, and working through tones of it for the wall colour, furnishings and fabrics in a room, can give a surprisingly rich effect. It is important to mix warm and cold tones to keep it lively, and some contrast of texture will help too. A subdued use of pattern will prevent monotony. This monochrome effect is a popular one right now, and designers like Tricia Guild use it as the basis of a 'co-ordinated' look. Rooms like these look good with walls given a decorative paint finish in two tones, for instance dragged in mid-blue over light blue or ragged in terracotta over palest pink. For contrast, try small doses of the complementary colour in its paler shades.

Greyed-pastel rooms

Colour theorists often suggest taking colour ideas from flowers, but I feel this is risky because a growing flower needs to be seen in relation to its foliage. Dried flower colours, on the other hand, are softened to the point where they harmonize beautifully to form what Graham Carr calls 'old, dirty colours'. If you want to use many colours in a room successfully, you could try sorting out a packet of pot-pourri into its basic colours and using these as a starting point. Greyed or dirty pastels consort very happily together, and create a pretty, nostalgic effect. Try to introduce a few darker tones for strength, like the maroon of dried red rose petals or wallflowers, or the room may become too prettified. The drab green of dried leaves is another obvious, and safe, contrast colour.

White-plus-one-colour rooms

This is hardly original but it always works and looks fresh and appealing. Except for a young girl's bedroom, I would steer clear of brilliant white with a pastel colour; interesting off-whites (see p. 35 for details of what the experts use) plus tones of one sophisticated colour such as pale blue, brick-pink or violet-grey, would look more elegant and grown-up. The disadvantage, of course, lies in keeping it reasonably clean. It is essentially a country cottage look.

GOOD COLOURS AND HOW TO USE THEM: WHAT THE EXPERTS SAY

Mark Hornak is the son of another well-known decorative painter, Jean Hornak. Despite having been to art school himself, he says roundly: 'I find art students can't mix colours; most of them have never heard of burnt umber. They don't seem to have been taught to appreciate the earth colours, all those subdued hues which look so wonderful in room schemes. If you ask them for a yellow, they will hand you a chrome yellow, something that hits you in the eye. They'd never think of using a subtle yellow, like raw sienna. I don't like the colours that come from aniline dyes, like the chromes or viridian green. I'd always mix a little burnt sienna into viridian to kill it slightly. If I wanted a brighter yellow, I'd probably mix ochre with lemon yellow, maybe a little raw sienna, too. Beginners should start with a limited range – your five basic colours will do – extending it gradually into the brighter colours.

'The colours that hover between warm and cold are the good colours for me. We've been using a dark, dark green on some furniture, which is like the dark green you get on French coffee cups, almost black in some lights. It is one of those colours that have such depth you never get to the bottom of them.

'One of the most useful decorating colours is a good off-white. You can't buy one ready-mixed. The John Fowler formula was black, lemon-yellow, raw umber and maybe a little raw sienna mixed into white. I might use black, plus raw and burnt umber with white. My wife, Rosie, sometimes paints a whole room in different shades of this off-white; it looks not boring but lively, creating its own light and shade.

'Of course, there are lots of ways of arriving at the same colour, or coming close to it. I might make up an apricot using Windsor red, burnt sienna, spectrum yellow, raw sienna and white. If I wanted a dirtier colour, I would add raw umber. But you could get a similar apricot using quite different colours. I like to add a little black to my greens and blues; it gives them character. Ivory black is better than lampblack because it is transparent. But of course the way to get real depth of colour is with glazes, one colour on top of another, like the Old Masters used to do. There's nothing to beat transparent colour. We usually use a glaze over white, or off-white, to get that effect of reflected light shining through, but if you scumble, using a paler glaze over a darker colour, you get some really intriguing effects.

'You must like the colour yourself, that's important. Also, when you are mixing colours you should never see them in isolation – a decorating colour doesn't mean anything on its own, but only in relation to everything else in the room.'

Graham Carr also had an art school training, but really began learning about colour while working for John Fowler, accompanying him around country houses and the National Trust's historic buildings. Almost any detail of a Carr interior provides instruction as to how you can make surfaces more interesting with paint.

'I'm a great mixer. The only colours I don't use are clear, clean colours – pastels. I like dirty colours; to live with colours I think they have to be dirty but that may be because I love colours to look old, as if they had always been there. I don't stick to a few basic colours – I like to have lots of different yellows and reds, for instance, and I mix them up to get what I want, rarely the same mixture twice running. I use oil colours rather than stainers because I don't think stainer colours are as pure. I try to stick to historically correct colours for old rooms. I use the same colours in modern rooms, adapting them to suit or mixing in something a bit surprising. It's a question of going with, rather than against, the building.

'A good colour should act as a background to a room. You need to study what light does to it, and what that colour does for the people who live with it. If I want cheering colours, I keep to hot oranges, yellows and reds, but of course I mix in lots of other colours to make them more interesting.

'For a good off-white, I'd mix raw umber and black into white to get a pale stone colour, which is what off-whites really are. For a good blue, I'd start with cobalt, add a little black and just a touch of scarlet lake to warm it. I don't like ochre, it's too dead and flat. I prefer raw sienna – it's got

The 'before' and 'after' pictures of our painted transformation scene. 'Before' is a typical no-colour room – neutral and lifeless. 'After' shows how much more complete the same place looks when surfaces have been brought to life with colour and texture: ragged walls, a limed fireplace and grained door, dragged woodwork, a combed floor and a frieze stencil, based on the classic Greek key design and using colours related to the room scheme.

more life to it. For a yellow, I'd start with lemon-yellow, add raw sienna and a touch of vermilion. A good yellow should not be too green, or too hot. For a warm red, I'd probably use vermilion and scarlet lake for brightness, then burnt sienna and burnt umber to knock it back again.

'Transparent colour is what it's all about, really, because the great thing about transparent colour is that you can build it up to any shade you want. The red walls in a study I painted were coloured up with two shades of red glaze, one on top of the other, followed by a tinted varnish to give a real depth, like lacquer.'

Nemone Burgess has been a decorative painter for over twenty years, and taught herself by 'doing it'. She paints anything from chinoiserie-style patterns on walls to sky ceilings, or frivolous trompe l'œil shell decoration on a wooden lavatory seat. It is noteworthy that her colour range is rather different from the two male painters.

'I find myself using, and liking, a lot of mauve, aubergine, grey and yellow – a Chinese yellow, which is quite sharp. I have to say that I am personally bored with those canteloupe and peach colours that everyone loves at the moment, though of course I use them if that's what the client really wants. If I am working on something like a chinoiserie design I take my cue from the old hand-painted wallpapers and use all the colours of the rainbow. But for the usual paint finishes the following colours, in different combinations, are the ones I use most at the moment.

'If I were painting a mauve or aubergine finish, I might start with a grey or mauve undercoat which I would tint myself. I use stainers mostly for tinting; the stainer range has a wonderful Bordeaux purple which I use a lot and a violet which is good. I don't mix glazes to an exact formula; the amount of commercial glaze I use depends on the sort of finish I want. I use more when I need a "globby", stippled look, and less when I want the surface to be very flat and thin.

'To mix a grey I would use blue with a little black and maybe a dash of red oxide to enliven it. I tend to add a little black to any red colour I mix. My favourite earth colour is a terracotta. Terracotta has masses of blue in it, much more than anyone would think. I mix mine with blue, black, Bordeaux purple, and red oxide.

'Some painters always seem to go for strong, positive colours. I tend to stay with the wishy-washy ones, maybe because they are easier to live with and clients like them.'

TRANSPARENT PAINT: GLAZES AND WASHES

You will be aware by now that the paint used by the experts is unlike the commercial paints sold over the counter, which are fast-covering and therefore opaque. For convenience, it is often referred to as transparent paint as its translucent quality is immediately striking. Decorative painters use some commercial paints, but the 'special effects' which are their stock-in-trade are largely based on decorative manipulation of transparent paint to create effects which they could never achieve with the commercial panoply of gloss, semi-gloss or alkyd, matt or silk-finished emulsions.

Transparent paint has two outstanding properties. It allows colour to be introduced as a delicate film, so sheer that the colour beneath shines or 'grins' through. Over pale colours transparent paint adds colour with very little loss of luminosity, because light rays are reflected back from the base colour underneath. The delicacy and radiance of transparent colours used in this way are flattering to any room, particularly those problem rooms that are too dark or small. Alternatively, applying one colour over another, or perhaps three slightly differing tones of one colour on top of each other, you can build up colours that are richer, livelier and softer than any opaque paint could achieve. Transparent colour seems to dissolve surfaces and contours which is why it can do two apparently irreconcilable things: open out small spaces, and make large objects look less substantial.

The other property of transparent paint, which makes it the decorative painters' favourite medium, is that it takes impressions very readily. It can be patterned with rags, sponges and brush bristles to create complex textures unlike any others.

Given these attractions, it is hardly surprising that transparent paint and its uses became something of a trade secret. As soon as it was realized, however, that anyone could get hold of these materials and produce very creditable effects of their own without special training, decorative paint finishes became the new discovery in home decorating.

There are in fact several different forms of transparent colour in common use. In my experience, the type which is based on a proprietary transparent oil glaze is easiest to handle, and consequently the one that amateur decorators invariably settle for.

Glazes

Artists have used glazes since oil colour first became popular (Van Eyck is credited with the invention of oil painting) because transparent films of colour allow subtle effects in modelling, highlighting and building up flesh tints. An artist's glaze is usually composed of oil colour mixed with linseed oil and turpentine, or white spirit. The linseed oil adds strength and dries to a tough, durable film, while the solvent thins the mixture and speeds drying time. Decorative painters do make use of artists' glazes like these on occasion, but they usually add matt or eggshell varnish to the mixture to speed drying and give 'body' to what is otherwise a very fluid, fragile mixture while wet. Len Pardon, whose virtuoso graining and marbling is shown in Chapter 3, often uses this type of glaze and his recipe is given in our Glaze Box.

Ready-made glazes, formulated specially for decorative painting over large areas like walls, are produced by specialist paint firms (see suppliers index). These come in varying consistencies but they all have substances like wax and drying agents added to make them hold decorative impressions clearly, dry faster (they are touch-dry within between four and eight hours as opposed to four days for the artists' mixture) and give a durable finish which does not need to be varnished for protection. However, most painters cover glazed walls with varnish just to be on the safe side.

Commercial glazes come uncoloured. In theory some can be used straight from the can with added tinting colour, but used in this way they dry to a rather thick, gummy texture which makes the decorative effects look coarse, 'like jam on bread' as Colefax-trained Susan Williams describes it. They are invariably used in a 'let down' form, thinned with white spirit. Enough commercial glaze should be used to hold marks clearly and encourage your mixture to stay wet, or 'open', for as long as possible, but not so much that it adds its own texture to the final finish. Relying on the commercial glaze to do the job for you is the mark of an amateur, but if you are inexperienced you will find a generous proportion of commercial glaze decidedly helpful. Start with the beginner's recipe in our Glaze Box, and progress to the more diluted recipes as you get more experienced.

Commercial glaze plus tinting colour plus white spirit gives completely transparent colour, which looks delicate and pretty in the paler pastel shades but can look 'jammy' when the colour is quite strong. Imagine a vivid coloured nail lacquer, and you will get the idea. Most pro-

Three swatches of the same colour showing the different effects of opaque paint, transparent glaze and a transparent wash.

fessionals, like Graham Carr and Nemone Burgess, add a varying amount of white undercoat or eggshell (mid-sheen) paint to their glaze mixture, at least one tablespoonful, to soften the colour slightly and make it a little cloudier.

How to mix a glaze

Use a white plastic paint kettle, because white shows up your glaze colour best, and a long-handled artists' brush with a good clump of firm bristles (a hogs'-hair brush, about 25 mm wide, would be fine) to keep your hands clean and disperse the colour effectively. Mix up tinting colours (artists' oil colour or commercial stainer colours – see suppliers index) separately in a white bowl, and use an old spoon to transfer colour to the kettle. Keep a few sheets of white paper handy for testing the colour (though you can use the wall itself if you rub the colour off again immediately with a rag dampened in white spirit); you will also find lots of old rags (old sheets are good for this) are invaluable.

Start by pouring commercial glaze plus white spirit into the kettle in the proportions given in the recipe you have chosen. Add the solvent to the glaze gradually, and stir with the brush to mix well. If you are using white undercoat or eggshell, mix it with the glaze before pouring in the white spirit. Half a litre of this mixture will be enough to glaze a small-to-average sized room, but it is better to make too much rather than too little. The extra glaze can always be kept in a screw-top jar for touching up purposes later on. Remember where possible to label the jar with the colour formula, because even a rough guide to the colours used is very helpful if you ever want to mix up that precise colour again. Another advantage of white paint kettles is that they come in standard sizes so you can estimate quantities at a glance.

It is impossible to be precise about the amount

This colour sample shows the different quality of transparent glaze with and without the addition of a white undercoat.

of pigment or stainer you will need, but if in doubt, use small quantities. Put a good squeeze of the main tinting colour into your bowl, then add proportionately smaller amounts of the other colours. Tip in a little of your mixed-up glaze base, stir very thoroughly with the long-handled brush, and then try a brushstroke on the white paper. Almost certainly it will be too light. Go on adding more of the prepared glaze mixture from the kettle, stirring each time and testing, until you have attained the right intensity. You may find this happens before you have used up the prepared glaze mixture, in which case you will need more colour, but scaled down to the quantity of glaze left. If you have used up all the glaze and it is still too light, add more of the glaze mixture, mixed up separately as before. You may be lucky and hit the shade you want quickly, but more often than not you will have to spend an hour or so getting it exactly right. Professionals expect to put time into this stage of the game, so do not be discouraged.

If you have mixed up a colour and do not feel quite happy with it, brush the colour thinly over a sheet of paper and let it dry. Glaze colours tend to settle down as they dry, and a larger expanse once dried will look softer than a small brushstroke when wet. If it is too dark, add more of the basic glaze mixture. If it is the right intensity but too vivid, add some of the complementary colour, first diluted in white spirit. If it needs to be toned down still further, try adding some raw umber which softens and mellows any colour, ageing it instantly. If, however, this is not the effect you want, and a clear shade is required, you have the choice of either lightening and softening it with white, which will take it towards a pastel colour, or shading it with black or one of the in-between greys, which will 'kill it' a little. Take Mark Hornak's tip and use transparent ivory black, but go slowly because a little can make a great difference to the more transparent pigments.

Colour on colour – variations on the glaze theme

In most cases professionals glaze with a pale colour over a white base. 'It's so much easier to ask the painters to do it all white,' Nemone Burgess explains. And white, with its reflectiveness, is often the best base colour for many glaze effects. But one variation, which is popular because it makes for a very rich tone of any given colour, is the use of a pastel or mid-tone colour for the base coat, which is then glazed over in a darker tone. It does not matter if the base colour is slightly out – too cold or too dull – because the glaze can be mixed to correct this. Mark Hornak's pyjama-stripe dragging (see p. 53) shows the difference between blue glaze over white and blue glaze over pale blue.

Amateurs could steal a march on the professionals, I feel, by trying out different colours on top of each other, burnt sienna over green, for instance, or lilac over grey or beige. The most

This is the sort of kit a decorative painter might carry about – artists' colours, specialist brushes, graining combs, glaze, a steel rule, sponge, scalpel, varnish and gold size. For amateurs, small is sensible to begin with. Note the curious graining gadget on the right for making knots and heartwood markings.

extraordinary, subtle colours can be arrived at in this way, as you can prove by experimenting on coloured boards.

One subtlety Nemone Burgess uses regularly consists of brushing a milky glaze over a terracotta base to reproduce the fine bloom you see on unglazed flowerpots. Paler glazes over dark colours can create attractive opalescent effects, and can also be a godsend if your wall colour turns out to be too bright. Brushing a pale glaze over the top is the quickest way to 'knock it back'.

Washes

Washes are another form of transparent paint used in decorative painting. They are soluble in water. There are various forms of water-based paint, but in practice decorators usually prefer gouache, acrylic colours, old-fashioned distemper (if available) or thinned-down standard flat emulsions, all 'washy' when thinned.

Colour diluted in water and thinly applied is called a wash. It is just as transparent as oil glaze but it has a freshness and purity which colours in oil cannot match, since the oil itself has a yellowing effect. Also, it dries to a matt, powdery, fragile finish, which is appealing, like a fine cotton lawn as opposed to a fine silk gauze. Colours which might look too rich when applied as a glaze look excellent in a wash. The difference is not striking, but it is noticeable. The warm earthy colours on my landing are painted with gouache sealed with matt varnish, and I think they have a better, drier texture than if they had been coloured with a glaze which would have fattened them up to something more like chocolate and toffee. The two problems with a wash colour finish are firstly that it is trickier to apply, since what we are talking about is virtually coloured water, and secondly even when sealed with varnish it is less durable.

The medium used most often for colour-washing walls is gouache colour, most intense of the water-based colours. When distemper paint

A good example of how colour which would blaze in an opaque paint becomes soft and glowing when ragged with transparent glaze over a white base. A shiny varnish adds sparkle and protection.

RIGHT *A demonstration in the use of complementary colours to balance a colour scheme. The vivid mauve of the walls could have been overwhelming without the accents of its complementary colour, yellow, but together they are a sophisticated combination.*

was commonly available it was popular with decorators like John Fowler for colourwashing because it contains enough whiting, or powdered chalk, to give a delicious powdery texture when dry. He used it thinned with water to create surfaces of rustic spontaneity and charm, the 'old cottage wall' look. Gouache, applied over a base of matt emulsion or vinyl, gives a similar texture, though it is less powdery.

Thinned flat emulsion used on its own has something of the wash quality, but the colour is never as luminous because of the 'plastic' content of modern convenience paints. Poster colours are also used by some painters, but mainly for graining and marbling. Another water-based paint which is used a great deal is acrylic colour, which dries almost immediately and can be overpainted without dissolving, but it would be expensive used over a large surface. Acrylics are used for stencilling as a rule, where their drying speed is a great advantage.

Applying a wash

The texture of the base coat of a wash finish is important – watery colour will not adhere readily to a smooth silky base, though the addition of a little Unibond or Copydex adhesive, or even a squeeze of washing-up liquid, can help. It is best to start with a surface as close as possible to the quality of blotting paper. Standard matt emulsion undercoat or acrylic primer is sold through builders' merchants and some DIY stores, and dries to a gritty finish, which may need smoothing off with sandpaper.

You will need a large soft brush, like those sold for pasting wallpaper, to apply the wash colour, and a second soft-bristled brush like a painter's dust brush (see suppliers index) for picking up trickles and drips, and for 'softening' streaks and over emphatic brushmarks. Spread plastic sheets or newspaper over carpets if they come close to the wall to prevent spatters. Keep some soft rags handy for mopping up trickles on paintwork. Clear matt varnish is best for sealing a watercolour finish and most painters prefer the least yellow product (see suppliers index). Use a separate brush for applying varnish. A white plastic paint kettle is again useful for mixing up the wash.

To mix up the wash colour put a good squeeze of gouache into your kettle, plus a tablespoonful of standard white emulsion to give it body. Add water gradually, mixing it very thoroughly indeed because a streak of undissolved watercolour makes a very big mark on a wall. Test the wash on white paper. When the colour is right, try the wash on the wall (you can always wipe it off again with wet rags). It will almost certainly start trickling down, but try catching the trickles with your dust brush and smoothing them into the coloured area. You need to move fast, using your brushes lightly, to achieve a softened effect. If the wash still seems to be streaming off, try adding a spoonful of Unibond adhesive, but no more than one level tablespoon per half litre.

For maximum colour variation and a 'dappled' effect, some painters like to apply wash colours in two successive coats. The first coat of colour is applied loosely over a white ground, covering the surface unevenly so that the colour build-up is intense in some spots, yet next to nothing in others. When this coat is perfectly dry, a second coat of colour is brushed on top, again loosely and unevenly. Streaks and splodges should be smoothed into the base colour with the softening brush. This finish suits pale, glowing colours best – all the dull pinks and warm yellows through to apricot and cantelope.

A second wash coat needs to be sensitively applied so as not to shift the first. An isolating coat of matt varnish can help here. All water-based wall finishes should be given a final coat of matt varnish to protect them.

Glaze Box

Beginners' glaze recipe

50% commercial oil glaze
50% white spirit
tinting colour
1 tablespoon of white oil-based paint, like undercoat or eggshell, can be added per ½ litre to soften the hard-edged effect.

Standard glaze recipe

25% commercial oil glaze
75% white spirit
tinting colour
1 tablespoon undercoat or eggshell white paint per ½ litre.

Len Pardon's all-purpose glaze recipe

1 part raw linseed oil (slows drying but makes for a harder finish when dry)
1 part white spirit
1 part clear matt varnish
For a softer effect, add up to 1 part white undercoat.

Mark Hornak's standard glaze mixture

1–2 parts white undercoat (depending on how much opacity or transparency is required)
1 part commercial oil glaze
1 part white spirit
2 tablespoons raw linseed oil
artists' oils for tinting.

Graham Carr's glaze

Graham Carr frequently uses a glaze made up with no transparent paint at all. His work for the National Trust taught him to steer clear of anything containing linseed oil, which has a yellowing effect on colours in time. His thinned undercoat glaze will not discolour but takes some practice to handle as it 'goes off' much more quickly. Depending on how much opacity he wants from the glaze colour, which in turn depends on the finish and the colours he has in mind, Graham uses between 10% and 30% standard white undercoat, making up the rest with white spirit and using artists' oils to arrive at the colour he wants. A glaze of this sort is not transparent like commercial glazes, but any colour underneath shows through slightly and a distressed finish will of course reveal more.

3

A L L T H E T E C H N I Q U E S

PAINTING THE WALLS I

M A S T E R I N G T E X T U R E

Although transparent paint is, in itself, attractive as a wall finish, its true appeal lies in the way it can be manipulated while wet to create a wonderful variety of effects. These subtle textures, suggestive of natural substances like stone, marble, foliage and feathers, seemed to be just what everyone was looking for five years ago or so. They were disenchanted with the dead 'plastic' surface and unmysterious colours of commercial paints, and although wallpaper offered an alternative, it seemed to be restricted to sub-William Morris florals and calico sprigs. It was inevitable that the more adventurous DIY spirits should cast about for something new, which would allow more control over the end results. Instead of frightening off the inexperienced, the challenge of experimenting with unfamiliar techniques has encouraged a newly independent approach. People are not afraid to take chances and make mistakes if they think they may end up with the house they have always envisaged.

A coarse stippled effect gives walls a texture almost like hessian, while lively under-the-brush work with dragging below the dado rail provides a handsome background to pictures and knick-knacks.

I see this refusal to be satisfied with other people's colours and designs as a minor but significant aesthetic revolution, and a healthy reaction against those 'off-the-peg' designs shown in glossy house-style catalogues. With a little perseverance you can find not only the right colour, but the precise shade you have in mind. You can go on to create as much or as little texture and pattern on your walls as you like, from a diaphanous veil of watercolour to the richest of stippled glazes covered with tinted varnish, giving you what Mark Hornak calls 'a colour you can fall into'.

I have included only one finish in this book which is technically demanding: the gesso and dry colour 'antiqued' finish invented by Jim Smart. Although impractical for most households, some of you may like to try it as it is very distinguished. Otherwise most of these decorative finishes are encouragingly straightforward, although they are usually best tackled by two people working in tandem unless you are very experienced, or the wall surfaces are small. Practise on a board until you are familiar with the one you have chosen and then launch off on the window wall. Imperfections are least visible here, and windows also provide a handy natural break in the strenuous business of applying the glaze and texturing it before it dries or 'goes off'.

Preparation

Preparing a room for decorating simply takes time and patience. All painters have yarns about walls which were filled and rubbed down time and again until the surface was flawless and as flat as plate glass. Of course such perfectionism is unrealistic, but high standards of preparation do show in the end. Those professionals who bother most about details also tend to be the most deft, expert and successful. You must therefore balance the satisfaction of working on clean, smooth surfaces against how much time you can spare and how long you need your decorating to last.

Minimum preparation requires the following: all surfaces must be dusted and washed down with a weak solution of a grease-cutting cleaner like sugar soap (tops of doors and window-frames need special attention as grime and dust accumulate here); cracks, holes and chips in the plaster should be filled with standard or fine surface filler, sanded back until smooth and level when dry, and touched in with undercoat or base coat to seal it before painting; one, or preferably two coats of base paint, lightly rubbed down when dry with medium or fine grade sandpaper to remove grit, hairs and trickles, and then quickly brushed over with a dust brush. The ideal base paint for most finishes is an old-fashioned, oil-based eggshell, or mid-sheen paint, as this is smooth and non-absorbent. It is, however, a slow, heavy paint to brush out evenly and many people find that a silk vinyl emulsion, which has similar qualities, is easier to handle.

The commonest mistakes amateurs make are not sealing in the filler adequately (which leaves streaks of colour in your glaze finish because it is so much more absorbent) and not bothering to rub the walls down after applying the base coats. It is surprising how much dust settles on paint as it dries. If you are worried about cutting through the base paint at this stage – which can easily happen with vinyls – use a fine grade wet-and-dry paper and very light pressure.

However carefully you go, some glaze always smudges onto the ceiling or cornice and over the adjacent woodwork. Do not try to avoid this as it will inhibit your style. You can touch the smudges out later, or, if you are redecorating the whole room, you should paint the ceiling first (any subsequent smudges can be touched out) but leave the woodwork at the primer stage until you have finished. While the glaze is still wet, it can be easily rubbed off woodwork with a rag dampened with white spirit, but be careful not to smudge your wall finish.

Tools and Materials

These are the basic tools that you will need – the special tools for specific finishes are listed in the practical sections that follow.

Good quality housepainters' or DIY brushes should be used for applying base paint and glaze. A 75 mm brush is a good all-purpose size, but you will find a wider one helpful when applying glaze (this should be kept separate). Use a special varnishing brush for applying final varnish and clean it well with white spirit, then soapy water. For mixing colours a smaller brush is useful, a standard 12 mm painters' brush at a pinch, but preferably a firm bristled artists' brush with a long handle. Two or three of these will save time in cleaning, as you will need a clean brush each time you experiment with a new colour. It is good practice to knock a brush hard against something solid before use, just to shake off the clinging debris of old paint. I sometimes rake them through with a wire brush if they look clogged.

White plastic paint kettles are cheap, light and handy. White sets off your own colour well, and they come with lids to keep glazes and other preparations overnight.

Your step-ladder should be light, strong and aluminium for manoeuvrability and safety.

Buy a large keg of white spirit, at least 1 litre. Nothing is more exasperating than running out of this essential solvent.

For mixing colours I often use small foil containers sold for freezers, which can be thrown away after use; otherwise, use saucers or bowls. Keep a box full of empty jamjars with lids for odd mixing purposes – you can never have enough. A couple of old metal spoons are useful for adding small quantities of this and that.

You will need a large supply of old rags for mopping and cleaning up, best made from torn-up, worn-out old sheets, and plenty of waste-paper – old newspapers or lining paper is fine – for testing colours and brushing out remaining paint and glaze before cleaning your brushes.

Tints

Tinting colour comes in various forms and any specific requirements are listed separately with the instructions for the finish. Professionals tend to use artists' oil colours for tinting because the colours are more finely differentiated and stable, but universal stainers, available in tubes in most DIY shops, have the advantage that they can be used for tinting both oil- and water-based paints. The range of colours available is always improving. They are also very intense and are economical to use.

Glazes

Ratcliffes, Craig and Rose, and Bolloms all produce a basic glaze preparation to which you add colour and solvent. Bolloms's glaze is the thickest in texture and most prone to yellowing, while the Craig and Rose Luxine Glaze is generally considered the most delicate (which can make it harder to control) and least likely to yellow with time. A 1-litre can of any of these will go a long way – enough to cover two or more average size rooms, depending on the glaze recipe (see p. 47).

OVERLEAF

1 *Ragging in a subdued blue (ultramarine, indigo, a little of both umbers, a speck of black) over off-white gives an elegant crushed velvet texture.*

2 *Starting with two tones of green, warm over cold, Mark Hornak spattered on off-white, brown-black and golden yellow to create an old endpapers look.*

3 *This example of sponged-on colour uses five contrasting colours, but because they balance each other visually, the effect is not overpowering.*

4 *Rag-rolling in spaced out stripes over gentle ragging in a sharp, rich yellow gives a dramatic moiré effect.*

5 *Mark's dragging, done with a chopped-away brush. Note the different results when the thundery blue is dragged over white, and then over pale blue.*

6 *An under-the-brush finish creates spontaneous, 'painterly' effects, best in good colours like this mellow red.*

1

2

3

4
5
6

RAGGING

Ragged effects are achieved by pressing soft bundled-up rags into wet glaze in a constantly changing direction to make a flowing pattern with the look of damask or brocade. It can be played down until it is simply texture – I have seen rooms in which a creamy glaze was ragged over off-white to look like parchment – or stepped up dramatically using contrasting colours or two layers of slightly different coloured glazes. Nowadays, the favourite colouring is a soft apricot glaze over off-white. This is warm and pretty but needs some colour contrast.

Materials

For soft lint-free rags you can use old torn-up sheets, or industrial cloth, which is particularly favoured by painters for its crisp prints and absence of fluff. For different effects there is a whole variety of materials that you can try for added texture, such as well-washed hessian, crumpled plastic bags, paper or chamois leather.

Method

This finish is easier with two people. Starting in one corner, the first person brushes on a strip of glaze, about 30 cm wide, or whatever seems manageable, from top to bottom. The glaze need not be brushed out absolutely smoothly, but it should cover the base coat and be sufficiently even to allow the ragged prints to register clearly. When the glazer gets half way down the wall, the second person hops up the ladder and begins ragging into the wet glaze. The rag should be bunched up in one hand, tight enough to make a controllable wodge, but loose enough to give a busily folded pad – it is the folds that print the patterning. Simply press the pad into the glaze, changing the direction of your hand all the time and covering the area of wet glaze. While the second painter is ragging from the middle to the bottom of the wall, the first painter should be up the ladder brushing glaze onto the next strip. The strips should overlap just a little, but not so heavily that the glaze colour builds up as a stripe.

You will rapidly discover how much pressure to put on the pad in order to obtain distinct but not heavy-handed impressions and a soft flow of colour. Stand back from time to time to check that your work is fairly even – it will look more even as it dries. 'Skips', where the glaze is thin or the ragging indistinct, can be touched in lightly with the glaze-wet rag. Areas where the glaze has built up are best rubbed off carefully with a rag dampened with solvent, and then glazed and ragged over again, feathering in where the new glaze hits the first glaze coat. As a rule, however, the minute you hang pictures and replace the furniture, small unevennesses recede and become unnoticeable.

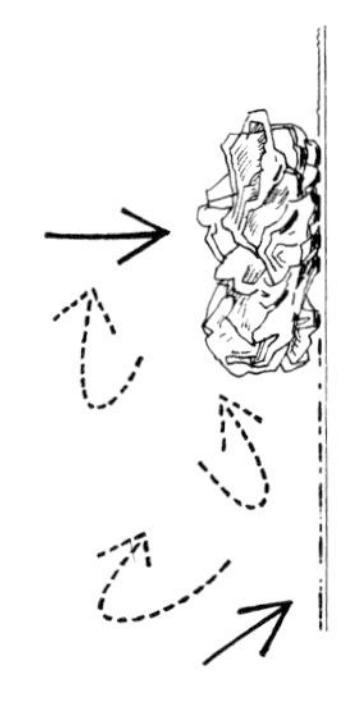

Ragging prints the marks of crumpled fabrics into wet glaze. Use a variety of fabrics for different effects – chamois leather, cheesecloth, gauze, industrial cloth, well-washed cotton and linen. As cloths become saturated with glaze, they should be replaced. Folds need rearranging frequently, too, to avoid repetition. Change the direction of the prints continually when ragging to avoid monotony.

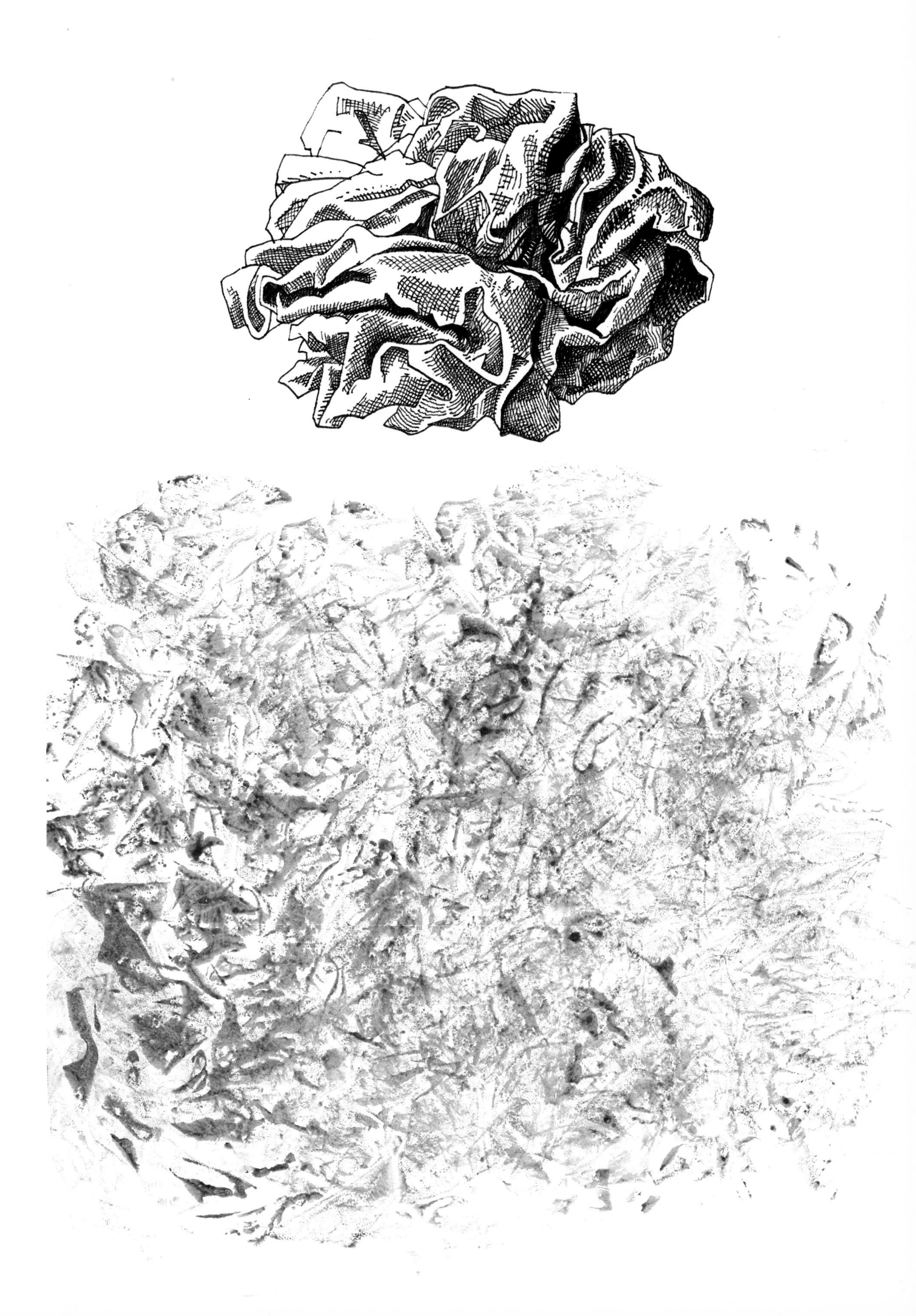

ABOVE LEFT *A lot going on here in the 'special effects' line – two kinds of marbling, fake panels in two tones of sharp yellow, coarsely dragged over white inside the panels and more finely dragged over yellow for the surrounds. The panels are further indicated by painted outlines in shades of grey.*

LEFT *A close-up of the same walls showing the vigorous brushiness of a dragged finish, and also how it consorts urbanely with an elegantly mounted and framed drawing.*

ABOVE *The remarkable yellow associated with Colefax and Fowler owes its depth and vibrancy to at least three coats of differently toned yellow glazes applied over a standard margarine-yellow base. Two coats of tinted varnish bring it up to a lacquer brilliance.*

RAG-ROLLING

Method

The same *modus operandi* applies, but here the rags are bunched into a shape like that of a small muff, and rolled up the wet glaze from bottom to top with the merest overlap where one roll-up meets the next. This effect looks more directional, almost stripey but not quite, because the surface of the roll changes in use. In all ragging processes the rags themselves will need changing occasionally as they become clogged with glaze. You should either re-bunch, or swap them for a new supply.

RAGGING PLUS ROLLING

Mark Hornak used a vivid yellow to demonstrate this one for us (see p. 53 for colour illustration, and p. 47 for the Hornak glaze recipe).

Method

For this finish, which is again best done by two people, a strip of wet glaze is first ragged lightly and quickly with scrumpled kitchen paper or tissue paper, just enough to give it a mottled look. Then, using a roll of soft muslin bunched into a little bolster about 20 cm long, roll a stripe up the mottled and still-wet glaze to create a rather formal, moiré effect. Then move onto the next strip of wet glaze, mottling and then rolling another stripe about 13 cm away from the first. The chief problem with this highly decorative finish is keeping the verticals lined up. Mark Hornak suggests pencilling guidelines on the wall before glazing, using an HB pencil which will not show under the glaze finish.

DRAGGING

This is less popular than ragging because it is hard to get slick vertical pin-stripes without a great deal of practice, but it looks crisp and elegant, especially in eighteenth-century rooms. The character of dragging changes with the type of brush used, since the finish consists of deliberate brushmarks made by dragging bristles through wet glaze.

Materials

To get a very fine striping, use a fairly wide fine-bristled brush, such as a varnish or paper-hangers' brush. Worn-down bristles will give rougher, less regular stripes which some people prefer.

Method

As with all glaze work, it is important to keep a speedy rhythm going, one person laying on the glaze, the other dragging, to prevent the glaze hardening or 'going off'. If the glaze is applied in narrow strips, and includes a fair amount of commercial oil glaze, this problem should not occur. If it does, the solution is to rub off the dry patch and re-glaze. A good rule to remember is do not stop until you reach a corner, which gives a natural break.

Dragging a high wall is usually done in two movements, from the top down as far as you can reach, then from the bottom to meet the top section, feathering off the meeting point to blend the dragged stripes together. It is almost impossible for amateurs to avoid a slight build-up of colour at the top and bottom of each dragged strip where your brush pressure changes slightly. Wiping the brush clean on a rag and very gently re-brushing over these areas can help to even out the colour, but it must be done straight away

In rag-rolling, a sausage of rags is rolled up or down wet glaze to create a directional effect, which is more forceful than simple ragging. Mark Hornak combines the two for interest (see p. 53).

KEW
GARDENS
LUTYENS Country Houses
Houses and Gardens
by E.L.Lutyens

BRIAN DAVIS
NEW YORK BOTANICAL GARDEN
PRINT GALLERY/APRIL 10 · MAY 9, 1981

before the glaze 'goes off'. If you find it difficult to keep a steady vertical brushstroke going while descending a ladder, you have one explanation for why most decorative painters prefer to keep dragging as a finish for woodwork, where surfaces are altogether smaller and more controllable.

MARK HORNAK'S DRAGGING FINISH

Mark Hornak's father used to lament the good old days 'when dragging was so much more virile'. This dashing effect is Mark's attempt to put back some of its lost vitality.

Materials

To get bold stripes, Mark chopped a whole row of bristles off a paper-hangers' brush, leaving a much thinned but even row of bristles. Thin bristles clump together when you brush paint on with them. But to make the stripes still heavier he went a step further. The glaze was poured onto an enamel plate with a slightly convex bottom to it, so that as he drew the brush through the glaze it picked up more colour on the outer bristles and less in the middle. Hence the 'thick, thin, thick, thin' effect across the wall.

Colourways

To soften the bold striping a little, it was painted tone on tone – a moody blue over a pale blue background. The background colour was made by tinting white eggshell (or vinyl silk) with permanent blue, ultramarine and a little raw umber to give a warm light blue, like a sunny day. Mark used artists' colours for tinting the oil-based eggshell – but remember to use a colour that dissolves in water if painting with a water-based vinyl.

FAKE LACQUER

Stippling is often used by painters to build up a fake lacquer effect. The deep glowing colour and smooth shiny surface looks chic and dramatic, especially at night, reflecting back lamplight.

Preparation

A very high standard of preparation is needed for this finish to look good, as grit, dust and other flaws really stand out on a high-shine surface. The painters I have talked to all have their own ways of achieving this particular finish. The most elaborate method uses differing tones of water-colour with a sealing coat of matt 'guard', or wallpaper seal, in between each wash, finishing with two coats of tinted varnish, stippled on. This gives extraordinary depth of transparent colour, but 'took for ever', according to decorative painter Carolyn Benson.

Fake lacquer can, however, be done more simply. The colour needs to be extra transparent, so the glaze mixture should have very little white undercoat added to it. A little clear matt varnish in the glaze will help counteract the thickness of the commercial glaze preparation. Two or three layers of glaze are applied in the usual way, each tinted to a slightly different tone. A blue-red glaze over a warmer orange or brown-red glaze looks richer and more interesting than if one glaze is mixed up to combine all these tones. Take great care to brush on the glaze smoothly, then stipple it closely with a soft brush to even out the colour and eliminate any brushmarks. All brushes need extra careful cleaning between sessions. A professional stippling brush, made of badger hair, comes into its own for fake lacquering as it has a comparatively large bristle surface. Unfortunately, these brushes are so expensive that many painters make do with what they can find in the

PREVIOUS PAGES *Stippling is a simple way of giving an almost imperceptible, suede-like bloom to any tinted glaze colour, like the acid yellow carried over all the surfaces shown here.*

Perfect dragging is difficult to achieve on large surfaces like walls, but makes an interesting surface on woodwork and furniture. Many professionals use worn-out standard brushes rather than a dragging brush, as shown here, for built-in variety.

LEFT *An under-the-brush finish in a 'dirtied' soft blue gives just enough wall texture to carry the bravura bed-head treatment of stripes, frills and gilt corona.*

ABOVE *Carried over the cupboard wall in a large 'panel' which ignores the placing of doors, the lively finish 'fades out' a lot of boring joinery.*

BELOW *A close-up of the brushy finish, applied over a white base after the surround has been masked off. When the glaze dries, the tape is peeled off, leaving neat edges.*

way of a soft flat-bristled brush – clothes brushes, shoe brushes or painters' dust brushes, for example. You should allow sufficient time between applying glaze coats for the previous coat to dry hard – preferably overnight.

The final varnish is vital to the lacquer look and it must be applied smoothly and evenly, with as few brushmarks as possible. There should be no 'skips' or bare patches. The varnisher should avoid going back over the same patch too often because the uneven build-up of varnish creates slight variations of colour as well as texture, at least on walls at right angles to the light source. Apply one or even two coats of shiny varnish – this can also be tinted if further modification to the colour is needed after glazing. Some painters use standard gloss varnish, slightly thinned down or mixed with eggshell polyurethane, while others go for the 'high deep gloss' of old-fashioned carriage varnish.

STIPPLING

Method

This is a straightforward finish to apply, feasible for one person working alone – if you are strong and speedy. Wet glaze is brushed on a strip at a time, and then distressed with the tip of a soft-bristled brush. Stab the bristles gently into the glaze to break up the colour into a myriad of dots. It is a useful way of softening any rich, strong colour to give a suede-like texture. It also breaks up the 'gummy' look of undoctored commercial glaze.

Try applying a richly-coloured glaze over a base colour just a couple of tones paler. The texture is not pronounced, but you have only to compare a stippled and unstippled patch to see how a broken surface glaze enriches and softens the whole effect.

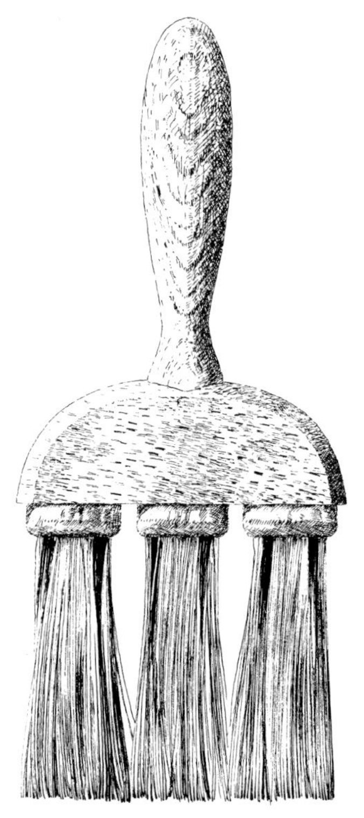

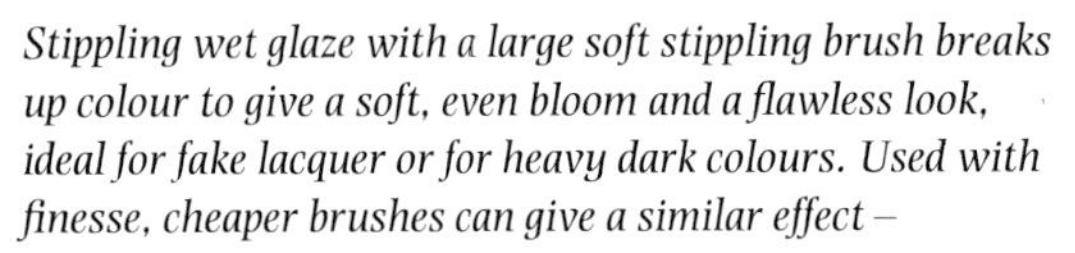

Stippling wet glaze with a large soft stippling brush breaks up colour to give a soft, even bloom and a flawless look, ideal for fake lacquer or for heavy dark colours. Used with finesse, cheaper brushes can give a similar effect – a dust brush or shoe brush as shown above would be a fraction of the price. Apply with even pressure at right angles to the wall surface.

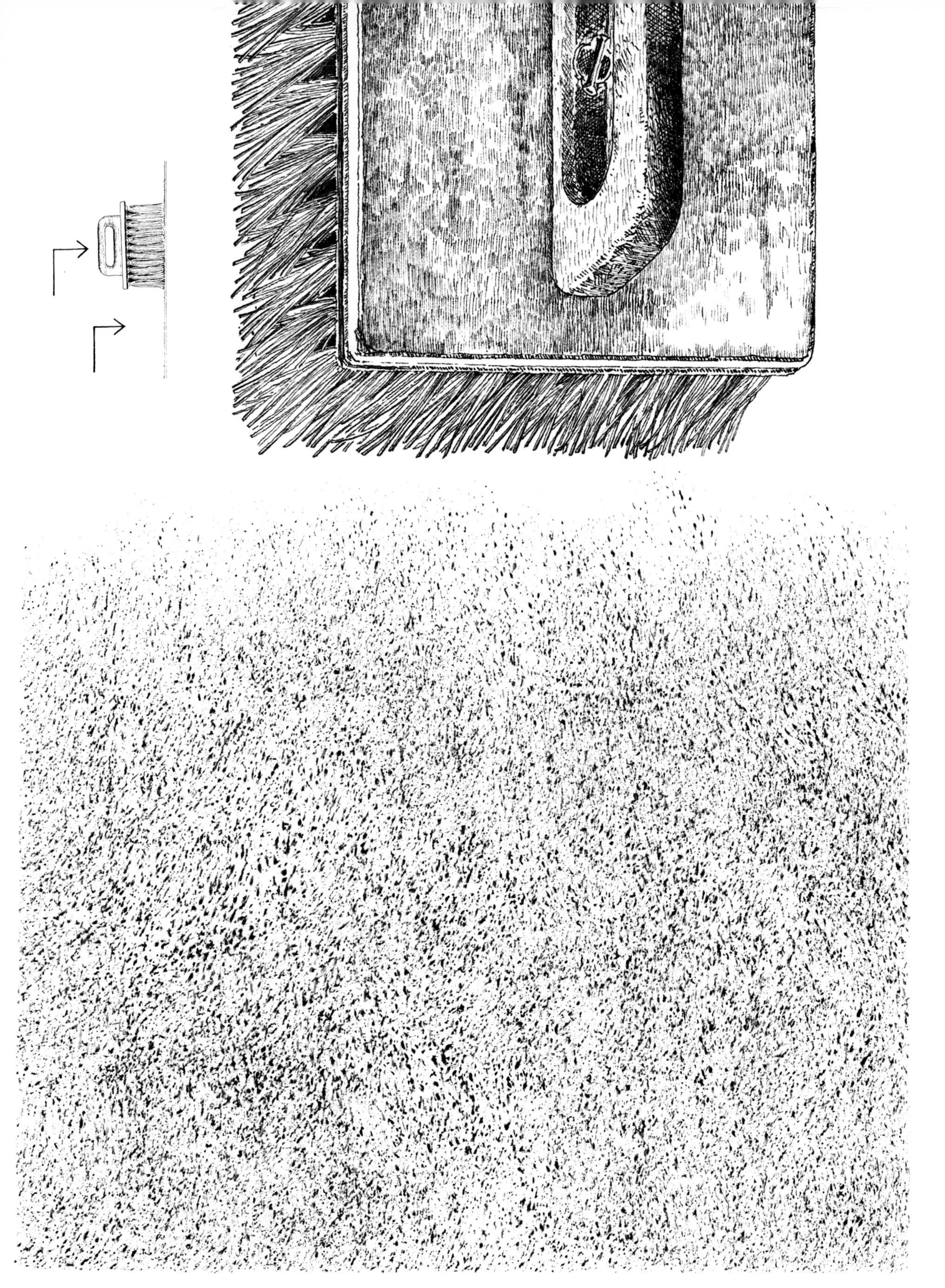

MARBLING

Marbling in paint can be done on any surface providing it has been properly prepared, which means primed, filled, undercoated, fine-filled, and then given two coats of eggshell. Whatever you do, don't do any filling in the eggshelled surface or the colour will soak in and leave a mark in your marble.

Materials

Len Pardon, a maestro of marbling, uses what he calls basic glaze for marbling. This is made with equal parts of raw linseed oil, white spirit (not turps substitute which is less refined) and ordinary white undercoat. In a room where the air is moving this will dry in twenty-four hours, and I mean twenty-four hours, not overnight. A fan heater gives the right air movement. If you need to dry it faster, or if the room is damp, the addition of some matt varnish in proportions of roughly 1 breakfast cup to $2\frac{1}{2}$ litres of glaze will speed drying time.

Len always uses regular artists' oil colours to colour the glaze and to paint with, rather than universal stainers whose colour is less permanent. The brushes you will need are: a white hogs'-hair filbert (size 30) for applying oil colour, a lining fitch for taking colour off, and a Whistler Lilyduster which has tapered bristles for softening. You will also need a goose feather, a soft white rag and white spirit.

Method

Countless varieties of marble are quarried in the hills of Siena in Italy. *Broccatella* is Len's favourite.

The colours most commonly found in marble from this area are raw sienna, yellow ochre, burnt umber, ivory black, burnt sienna and a little blue. For *broccatella*, use raw sienna, ochre, burnt umber and ivory black. The glaze consists of 1 part each of white spirit, white undercoat and raw linseed oil, well mixed.

1) Brush the glaze on evenly. With a white hogs'-hair filbert (No 30) and a squeeze of raw sienna, form a strata in the glaze, adding yellow ochre over and around the sienna, as shown.

2) Immediately after this stage, dip the brush tip into burnt umber, then into black, and paint in angular veinings, together with crossed veins.

3) Rag the whole surface lightly with a crumpled cotton rag.

4) With a badger softener, or dust brush, soften the whole surface by holding the bristles at right angles to the surface and brushing gently in all directions to create a suffused, opaque finish.

5) With the tip of a goose feather dipped first in white spirit, then in ivory black, go lightly over the veins with colour to accentuate their depth. Then, using white spirit only, put in the fine crystalline fractures. Finally, soften again.

Professional marblers use a goose feather to put in veining because it breaks up the colour naturalistically. Hold the goosefeather loosely, like a diviner's rod.

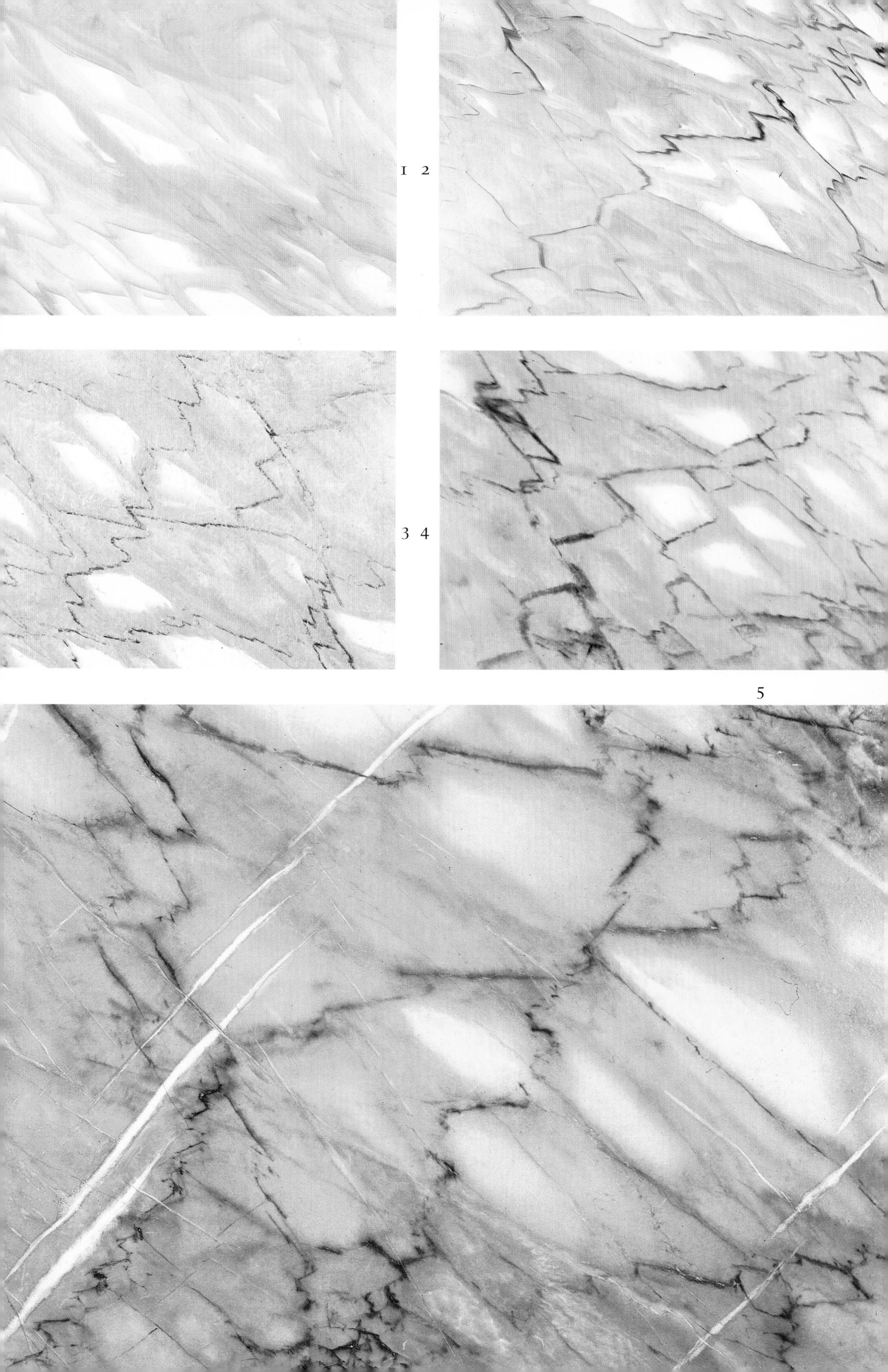

1 2
3 4
5

SPATTERING

Wonderfully complex colour effects can be built up on any surface by spattering – or raining dots of different coloured paints over a coloured or neutral base. Spattering is easy enough to do, but requires a certain judgement as to which colours to combine, and how heavily to spatter them. It also makes a lot of mess, as some flicked colour always ends up where it is not wanted. A room which is to be spattered needs to have everything masked off but the walls, unless the rest of it is to be painted over later. The trade usually keeps spattering for furniture and fireplaces for this reason, but it can make a spectacular wall finish.

Materials

Flat emulsion, tinted with stainers or gouache colours, is a good medium to use as its opacity helps the tiny spots to stand out instead of blending in as they tend to do with a transparent paint.

Method

The simplest spatter finish is done by flicking two or three colours onto a plain flat emulsion base in a suitably neutral shade. A safe guide when assembling colours is to stay within tones of one colour, but add some off-white for lightening and blending, and a very fine spatter of near-black (or the darkest tone of the predominant colour) to sharpen it all up at the end. Speckled stone colours are particularly effective.

Thin the emulsion with water – but not too much. Test the consistency by flicking against the wall experimentally (it can be wiped off again with a wet sponge). The spots should be quite fine and should stay put without turning into blots or trickling off. If they all start running, add more emulsion.

When spattering large areas, like walls, painters use a standard decorating brush, 50–75 mm in size, which they dip in the paint and then rap sharply against a piece of wood held in the other hand, so that spots of paint rain onto the nearest surface. This is a quick way of spattering large surfaces, but it needs rehearsing first on lining paper or a spare wall to get the knack of it. How far you stand from the wall, how hard you knock the brush, how much paint you take up on the brush – all these factors affect the result.

For closer control, usually over small areas, you can spatter effectively using a short stiff brush like a stencil brush, flicking your forefinger upwards over the bristles in a quick staccato movement. This gives finer spatters which can be aimed very precisely, but you need to stand closer to the surface itself.

MARK HORNAK'S SPATTER FINISH

This is a de-luxe version of spattering, aiming at the depth of colour of fine old marbled endpapers. A cool blue-green base of tinted eggshell was first lightly ragged with a transparent glaze in a darker, yellower green. Crumpled paper was used to mottle the wet glaze. First, an off-white (almost a cream, as pure white on green looks blue) was used, then a bitter chocolate brown-black, and finally a light, uneven spatter of golden yellow made with a higher proportion than usual of ochre gouache to white emulsion (see p. 52).

A light freckling of shiny gold looks rich on some spattered finishes. This can be achieved by mixing bronze powder (obtainable from artists' suppliers in various shades) into gum arabic, a watery adhesive which will fix the drops of metallic powder without dulling its brilliance, as oil-based media or varnishes do.

Spattering colours over a coloured base (which can be sponged, stippled or ragged for interest) allows you to arrive at a colour gradually with scope for correction at any stage. Fun to do if you do not have to worry about making a mess. Excellent on small items like lamps, frames and trays, and currently very fashionable. Over a large surface spattering is done faster by striking a colour-loaded brush (not too much) sharply against a stick.

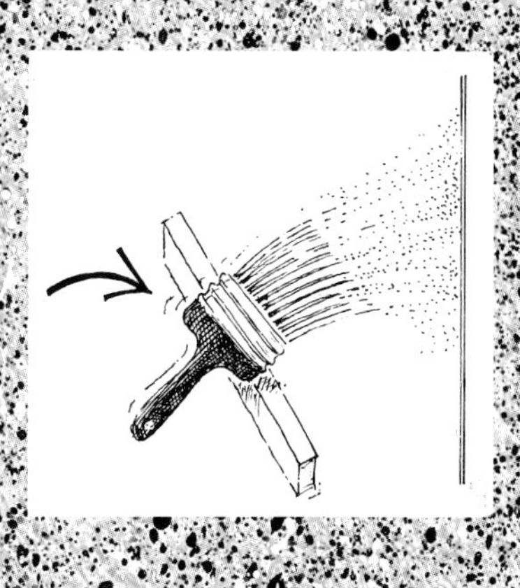

RIGHT *One of the most talked about special finishes ever – ridgy gesso, fluffed over with powder colour and accented with wax. Unique, expensive and definitely* not *washable, this finish demands sumptuous furnishings.*

FAR RIGHT *Bravura marbling in grey-white and* rouge roi *colours, plus discreet trompe l'œil mouldings, gives flat walls and surfaces a look of Second Empire splendour in the champagne bar of the Sheraton Park Tower, Knightsbridge.*

ABOVE *A close-up, showing how convincing well-painted trompe l'œil details can be.*

UNDER-THE-BRUSH

This is a finish decorative painters might well use on their own walls. It is the freest and most painterly, its looping brushmarks creating a soft but highly textured surface. To subdue the busy pattern, painters tend to use a more opaque glaze than usual, that is, one where white undercoat predominates over commercial glaze. The proportions are somewhere between 2 to 1 and 1 to 1, depending on the colour used and the effect wanted. (For the sample board, see p. 53. Mark Hornak used a 2 to 1 mixture.)

Method

After the wet glaze is applied (two people are needed to paint a wall larger than 2.5 × 3.0 metres), it is distressed in a 'series of upward and downward flying curves, a sort of controlled chaos'. Mark Hornak uses a standard 75 mm paint brush. The stylishness of this particular finish consists in snapping off the ends of the curved brushmarks, at both the start and the finish of each stroke, so that they form little rainbows without blurred or trailing ends.

For those who prefer a more gentle effect, Mark suggests softening the surface with a badger blender or dust brush while the glaze is still wet. To make this finish completely matt, cover it with a final coat of extra pale, dead flat varnish.

SPONGING ON

Technically by far the easiest decorative finish to apply, sponged-on colour – which can be in the form of glaze, or thinned emulsion – makes for a mottled texture which can be crisp or blurred, depending on whether it is done over a white base or a coloured one. A clear pastel colour sponged onto a white base looks fresh and pretty, a cheering finish for a kitchen, bathroom or 'cottagey' bedroom. By using sophisticated colours, complex effects can be achieved. Sponging is a finish beginners can have fun with, as there is no problem with keeping the glaze wet.

Materials

An ocean sponge, in a size which fits comfortably into your hand, is the only special equipment needed. You should also have a flat plate to put the colour onto, and waste paper for testing prints.

Method

Sponging with a standard glaze mixture gives softer, transparent prints. First wring out the sponge in white spirit to soften it, then take up some glaze and experiment on paper until you get the right amount of colour. Pat the paper lightly – the prints should be clear, not splodgy.

Sponging with emulsion, which can be tinted with gouache or stainer, or used straight from the tin, gives stronger, opaque prints. You may want to thin the emulsion with a little water to make softer marks. Wring the sponge out in water before use – it should be just damp, not wet.

For one-colour sponging simply start at a corner and dab sponge prints over the wall surface. Sponging usually looks more attractive if the prints are applied randomly, leaving a varying amount of background colour showing through. Change the sponge round from time to time to vary the marks it makes.

When sponging in two or three colours it is best to leave more base coat showing through on the first colour. The finished effect should combine areas where the colours are mingled. Stand back now and then while applying second and third colours to judge the effect – add more colour if you are not satisfied with the balance.

Under-the-brush is the painters' paint finish, the song of the brush as it were. Great for rough walls, it may look like organized chaos initially, but it comes together the moment you hang a picture up, or when allied to characterful furnishings. The secret of under-the-brush is to keep the brushed arcs moving in different directions, but snap them on and off at the start and finish of strokes to avoid indecisive blurs.

SPONGING OFF

Method

This is really a rapid way of breaking up the surface of a standard emulsion paint to give a little texture. Use an ocean sponge again to give an irregularly blotched surface. The emulsion should be thinned a little with water, and brushed on a strip at a time. Then go over the wet paint with the sponge, dabbing at it to shift the paint around and mottle it. You may need to rinse the sponge out in clean water occasionally to clear off excess paint. Emulsion brushed on in this way dries to a slightly richer texture than usual, and makes a good background for stencils.

NEMONE BURGESS'S SQUARE SPONGE PRINTS

The overlapping gold-leaf squares which make up the background of Japanese screens gave Nemone Burgess the idea for this finish.

Method

A standard synthetic sponge is used to make the prints, overlapping at all the edges to suggest the effect of gold leaf. Foam sponges will give even prints, while holey, synthetic sponges will give more textured prints. Again, sponging with glaze will give softer prints than sponging with thinned emulsion. Nemone used a soft greyed-yellow with the gold leaf in mind, but it would look effective in almost any soft colour.

For the best results pour the glaze into a flat dish or a large foil freezer container, so the sponge can pick up colour evenly all over. Test on paper each time you renew the colour. Then simply press sponge prints across the wall, row after row, overlapping each print about 12 mm all round. Finish with clear matt varnish.

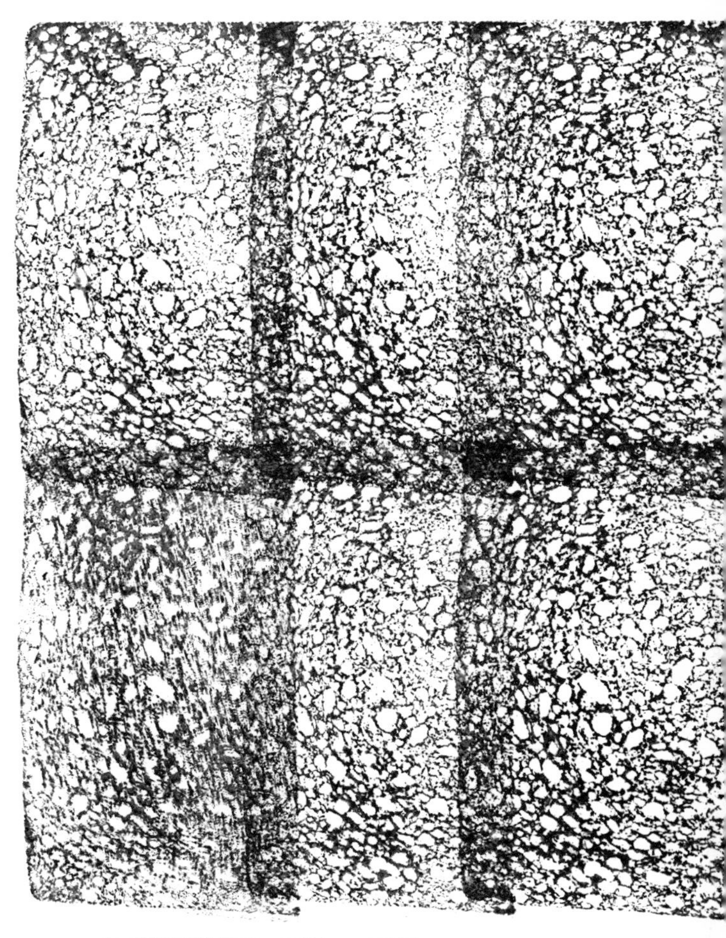

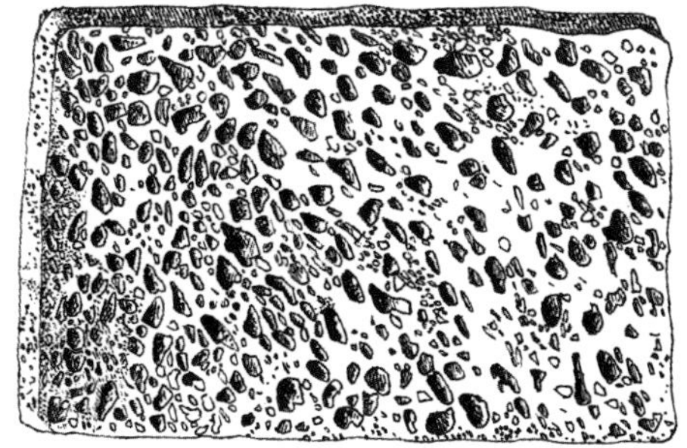

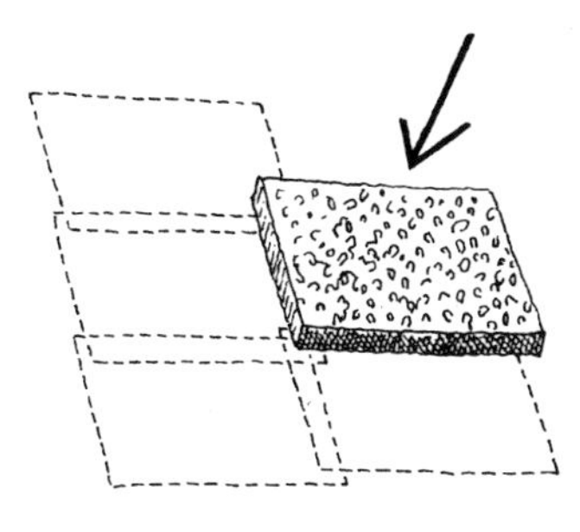

LEFT *Sponging is fun because you do not have to hurry to beat the drying time of wet glaze, and because you can step up the total colour effect gradually. Sponging can be sparse and naïve looking, or dense as in a pointilliste painting. For blurry effects, use a dampened sea sponge.*

ABOVE *Nemone Burgess discovered this offshoot of sponging which could look magnificent built up to suggest overlapping gold leaf, or just making quiet abstract shapes in a modern room. Press a synthetic sponge into wet glaze, overlapping prints to create a regular grid.*

GESSO AND DRY COLOUR

This is a truly virtuoso finish, not for beginners, though you might like to adapt some of the techniques and effects involved. Jim Smart invented it for its 'antiqued' appearance and extraordinary texture – at once ridgy and rough due to the brushed-out gesso, and deliciously soft and powdery due to the French chalk and dry colour. The toughest challenge it presents to an amateur is getting the gesso to the right consistency. If you are prepared to experiment until you master this, the rest is feasible.

I should add, however, that the uses for this finish are limited; by its very nature it can neither be sealed to protect it nor can it be washed to clean it.

Materials

You will need the following tools and materials: five 1-kilo bags of whiting and 1 kilo of rabbit skin glue granules (from artists' suppliers); 1 kilo of French chalk; dry powder colour in the shade you want – paler shades look best, but expect the powder colour to appear a couple of tones lighter on the wall than in the jar; a large hogs'-hair brush, preferably rounded like an old-fashioned painters' sash tool, for applying the gesso – the rounded clump of bristles will pick up more gesso; something soft and fluffy for applying the French chalk and dry colour, like a shaving brush, powder puff or cotton wool; several sheets of fine sandpaper; a very large double boiler arrangement or *bain-marie* for cooking up the gesso and keeping it warm; and a large bowl or bucket, preferably metal, not plastic.

Method

Tip 500 g of rabbit skin glue granules into the top of your double boiler, add 4.5 litres of water, and mix with a wooden spoon. Stand this in the bottom of the double boiler and heat the pan slowly, stirring the glue mixture till the granules are dissolved – do not rush this part. When the glue is hot and lump-free, turn the heat down a little, and tip 1 kilo of whiting into a large bowl or bucket. Stand this beside you and begin slowly crumbling handfuls of whiting into the glue. If you can sieve the whiting, so much the better. The object of this is to eliminate air bubbles and lumps, both of which could cause the gesso finish to crack later. Continue feeding whiting into the glue until it shows above the surface, then stir gently but firmly with a long-handled wooden spoon until you get a thick white mixture. The problem at this juncture is knowing if you have enough whiting in your glue to give a gesso mixture which is neither too thick, which means it will set too hard too fast, nor too thin, which means it will not stick fast enough to the wall surface.

The test is whether a layer forms on the surface after a period of gentle heating and stirring. It should form a skin, rather like jam, and develop a slightly brownish colour. A little gesso pressed between two fingertips should be tacky – not exactly sticky, just clinging. If all this fails to happen add more whiting, stir, and slowly heat again. Getting the gesso right can take up to an hour, but it should not be hurried, and the heat beneath the double boiler should be moderate only.

Having got the gesso to the right consistency, take the double boiler over to the wall surface. It is best to begin on the window wall, which is against the light. Dip the sash tool into the gesso and, at the top right-hand corner, quickly begin brushing down over the entire wall surface, keeping the brushstrokes going in the same direction. The gesso leaves a ridgy texture. Try to keep the coat even, moving quickly to avoid a pile-up, and roughing the surface with the brush

1, 2

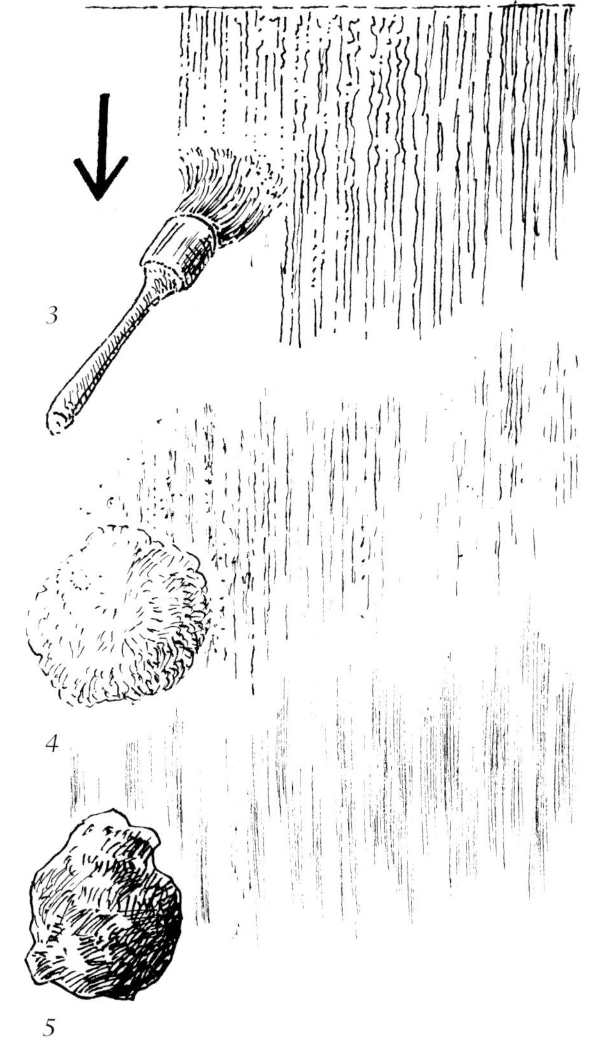

3

4

5

tip if it shows signs of hardening off. If the brushmarks get too heavy it means that the gesso is cooling too much and needs heating up gently again. Ideally, the *bain-marie* should be kept on a platewarmer to maintain an even temperature, but gesso must *never* boil.

Gesso brushed on like this will not take very long to dry hard. By the time all four walls have been covered, the first section will be ready for the next stage, which is less arduous and more intriguing.

Tip some French chalk into a saucer, and begin dusting it over the gesso surface, going with the grain or brushmarks, to coat it with this fine slippery substance. The chalk makes the dry colour cling more evenly – French chalk is dusted over wooden dance floors to make them slippier. When you have covered the entire wall surface, pick up some of the dry colour on a soft cloth or cotton wool, and stroke it over the gesso, again following the brushmarks. Start in a hidden corner so as to practise the next sequence of actions before embarking on the entire room. First chalk, then dry colour, then – and this is surprising perhaps – go over the whole surface with fine sandpaper, again with the grain. Magically, this softens and refines the colour, as well as slightly smoothing the surface. The final touch, which is optional but gives a certain relieving sparkle to the gentle bloom of this finish, is to take a ball of beeswax and rub it lightly down the gesso ridges here and there.

FAKE FRESCO

There are many different ways of achieving the fresco effect, but they all seem to follow naturally after the gesso and dry colour look since their appeal has to do with a similarly dry, 'lean' finish on walls, and a gentle bloom of chalky colour. True fresco, used for painting walls from ancient

1 *Rabbit skin glue being warmed until it dissolves in a* bain-marie.

2 *Whiting being sieved in, a handful at a time.*

3 *A round sash tool holds more gesso and makes ridgy brushmarks.*

4 *Fluffing on dry colour with cotton wool, a powder puff or a soft brush, again following the ridges.*

5 *Rubbing beeswax along the ridges.*

Fine abrasive paper, rubbed down the brushmarks, will smooth and soften the colour.

RIGHT *Colourwashing in a soft, greyed, raw sienna makes an ideally unobtrusive but charming background to the cottage style – rush matting, stone flags and precise stencilling – of this tiny hall in the country.*

ABOVE *Ragging can look formal, an impressive foil to a handsome Victorian fireplace, dark picture frames and a strongly patterned Chinese pot. Here the colour is picked up in the marbled skirting board.*

BELOW *Years ahead of everyone else, this classic example of the faded fresco effect, decorated with 'grisaille' saplings, was designed by John Fowler for a small summerhouse.*

times, was the technically demanding process of applying colour to wet lime plaster, a patch at a time. Colour and plaster integrated as the patch dried to create an extremely durable surface with a peculiarly dry texture. The colour has a beautifully luminous quality.

Because true fresco is so exacting to do – mistakes are almost impossible to paint out – there is little demand for it today, even among the more sophisticated. Sometimes described as the 'crumbling palazzo' finish, the fake fresco look is still in the experimental stages, with all the more innovative decorative painters trying various approaches and combinations to suggest the real thing. It looks both old and ageless and gives great distinction to any room.

RUBBED-IN COLOUR:

This is my own version of the fresco effect, which has the charm of being immensely easy to do as well as giving characteristically diaphanous colour. As so often happens, I stumbled on the method accidentally (rubbing a mistaken glaze off a board), and though my own use of it has been successful, I feel it could still be improved upon.

Preparation

It is essential to have a slippery base coat – vinyl silk proved satisfactory in my case, but eggshell would probably be better. Any filling in of the wall surfaces needs to be thoroughly touched in, or sealed, with repeated coats of paint because the 'soak in' of colour is very pronounced, like great streaks and bruises, where the wall suddenly becomes porous. Slightly rough areas in the wall surface are less problematic because although the finish will reveal these, they do not look as ugly as they would on a shiny lacquer finish, but merely 'rough and old'.

Method

Use a mixture of solvent, commercial glaze and stainers plus a small amount of undercoat for the glaze, and tint it up to a very strong version of the desired colour. You need to have a very intensified version of your chosen colour as it will look much paler once it has been rubbed in. For the cloudy rose colour in my sitting room I mixed a tone close to mahogany red. The effect of a deep colour teased and rubbed to a pale blush is not the same as the pale blush colour thickly applied. The rubbing action not only makes the colour transparent, a mere film, but makes it settle a little irregularly. I used some dry powder colour in my mixture, which does help to give a 'lean' powdery look, but is a nuisance to use as the powder tends to settle at the bottom of the mixture and needs constant stirring to keep it dispersed. Experiment on a board coated with the same base paint till you get the colour right.

Application is simplicity itself. Using old rags, rub the colour quickly and firmly onto the wall, dispersing it as far as it will go while maintaining the right degree of colour. A circular polishing motion seems to work best, and it is very good exercise! The finish dries to a tough, washable surface with a very slight pearly sheen. To make it more matt, cover with extra pale, dead flat varnish.

ANCIENT RUBBED-AWAY COLOUR:

This is my own name for an effect which is highly unorthodox, but is worth mentioning because it makes walls, even new plasterwork, look as if they had been standing for thousands of years. It makes a splendid base for further painted decoration, like the mural in my own house. It would also enhance one of the sophisticated multi-layer stencils. An interesting feature of the finish is that while it looks rough and grainy, the wall surface will in fact emerge silky-smooth, an ideal surface for paint.

Method

The colour on the walls is what remains after 90 per cent of the paint has been sandpapered off, so you need to start with a very intense colour. I used a deep brownish-red made from a red matt emulsion tinted up with stainers. It looked like cocoa powder. It was put on very roughly with a roller, just covering the wall area with strips of dark red, spiking off in every direction. When dry, I went over it with sandpaper, coarse and then medium grade, rubbing really vigorously until all that was left was a fine glow of apricot, shading into red. It had a fascinating 'ancient' texture when examined closely where the darker red had been rubbed into all the little imperfections you find in any wall surface. The amount of colour in this finish depends entirely on how thoroughly you sandpaper. From time to time, stop to check the effect, standing back a few feet, because you might like more colour left, or a slightly more evened-out effect.

DEMI-SECCO:

This effect is achieved by applying a watery gouache colour over a 'thirsty' textured wall.

Materials

The base coat should be old-fashioned distemper, made from whiting or chalk, glue size and a preservative such as alum. This can be obtained in some circumstances from the Society for the Protection of Ancient Buildings (SPAB) who keep stocks of it for the restoration of old buildings. Oil-bound distemper is available commercially: it is less powdery than the classic distemper but much more durable.

Method

Mix up the wash using a little of the base coat and a lot of water, tinting with gouache colours. One colour brushed over a distempered wall will look charmingly natural, slightly dappled where the brushstrokes overlap. For a more antique, sophisticated look, try using two or three sympathetic washes of colour, dappling them irregularly over the walls and softening the overlaps a little with a dry brush. Not for the timid, this finish can look magnificent. Sealing with extra pale, dead flat varnish helps to prevent the powdery colour rubbing off, but the colour will look fresher without it.

"Scumbling technically involves using darker washes or glazes over paler colours, or paler washes or glazes over darker colours to create a chalky, fresco effect.

Designer Annabel Grey arrived at this technique almost fortuitously. One of her first commissions after leaving the Royal College textile department was a set of painted curtains. The curtains seemed to need more

painted effects to go with them, so Annabel designed a mural scheme for the whole room, taking her inspiration from the shapes and decorations of Etruscan and Roman pottery fragments. She knew exactly the effect she wanted: 'A matt, dull surface . . . old, not terribly intruding, quiet', and the method she used to achieve this was inspired by her work with textiles.

'Because I'm used to painting on fabrics with pigments which need a lot of dowsing with white if they aren't to look garish, I often end up with a chalky finish. I like that look, the colour just coming through the white. So that's how I did this room. When I wanted, say, a faint pink, I painted on a fierce, blinding red, and then put white on over that till I'd cooled it right down to a whisper. It was done by trial and error and instinct.'

In this way, her areas of tinted emulsion in violent fauve colours of orange, purple and red shine through a layer of thinned emulsion to emerge in the most subtle, ghostly fashion, quite distinct from each other but with all their heat tempered, as blocks of purest chalky pastel colour. More than anything, it reminded me of ancient wall painting in churches, uncovered from layers of later lime-wash. What gives her muted decorations their special chic is the decisive contrast supplied by touches of Plaka gold and crisp black.

Annabel's work on this elegant, distinctive room led directly to her being commissioned to design murals for the refurbishing of Marble Arch and Finsbury Park underground stations. ”

COLOURWASHING

This finish derives from the weathered colour of rural buildings, and the special charm of earth colours which were once vivid, but have faded over the years. Anyone who has been struck by the beauty of Suffolk pink, or the bleached ochre and mellowed red oxides of Provence, will have noticed that exterior paints fade unevenly, and it is this finish that colourwashing attempts to reproduce – but indoors. Unlike 'under-the-brush', which is done with an oil-based glaze and looks distinctly textured, colourwashing uses water-based colour and aims for floating, uneven effects. It remains one of the prettiest treatments for cottage interiors. Any colour can be applied in this way: yellow through to apricot, pink and soft brick-reds, all give an incomparably warm, glowing look, while clear pale blue and green seem delicate and luminous.

Materials

The ideal base for colourwashing is a white distemper-type paint, as this has the right absorbent powdery texture. Oil-bound distemper is still available (see suppliers index), less powdery than the classic distemper but tougher and washable. Standard white matt emulsion can be substituted, too. Choose an off-white shade in preference to brilliant white, which has a blue cast to it that shows through a coloured wash. Whichever base paint you use, apply enough coats for the surface to look thick and evenly white – unevenness must come with the colour.

Method

The wash is made by tinting a little of the base coat paint with gouache colours, stainers or powder pigment. Powder pigment should not be used to colour oil-bound distemper because the powder does not dissolve properly when oil is present. It helps the powdery look, however, when mixed with standard emulsion, so you may like to experiment with it, but make sure you dissolve the powder first in water, grinding it with a pestle and mortar if necessary to refine the particles. The tinted paint is then diluted heavily with water to make a wash. When very watery, the colour is purer, but the wash trickles and is difficult to handle. Adding more paint makes it easier to manage but gives a more opaque, pasty colour because of the white content. As with most of these finishes, a little experimentation and rehearsal pays off.

Colourwashing is done in two stages to maximize the dappling of colour. Using a large bushy decorating brush (125 mm size), brush the coloured wash out in all directions, deliberately keeping it a little uneven so that some of the white base shows through in patches. Keep a second dry brush handy for catching the worst trickles of colour and softening them. When the first wash coat is quite dry, go over the walls again in the same loose, every-which-way fashion, covering the white surface this time and allowing colour to build up where several layers have been superimposed. It may look wild at this stage, but it will come together as it dries.

Because of the washy colour and uneven application, this is the finish that reflects back most light from a pale base. It has an unpretentious charm everyone likes, ideal for rustic settings.

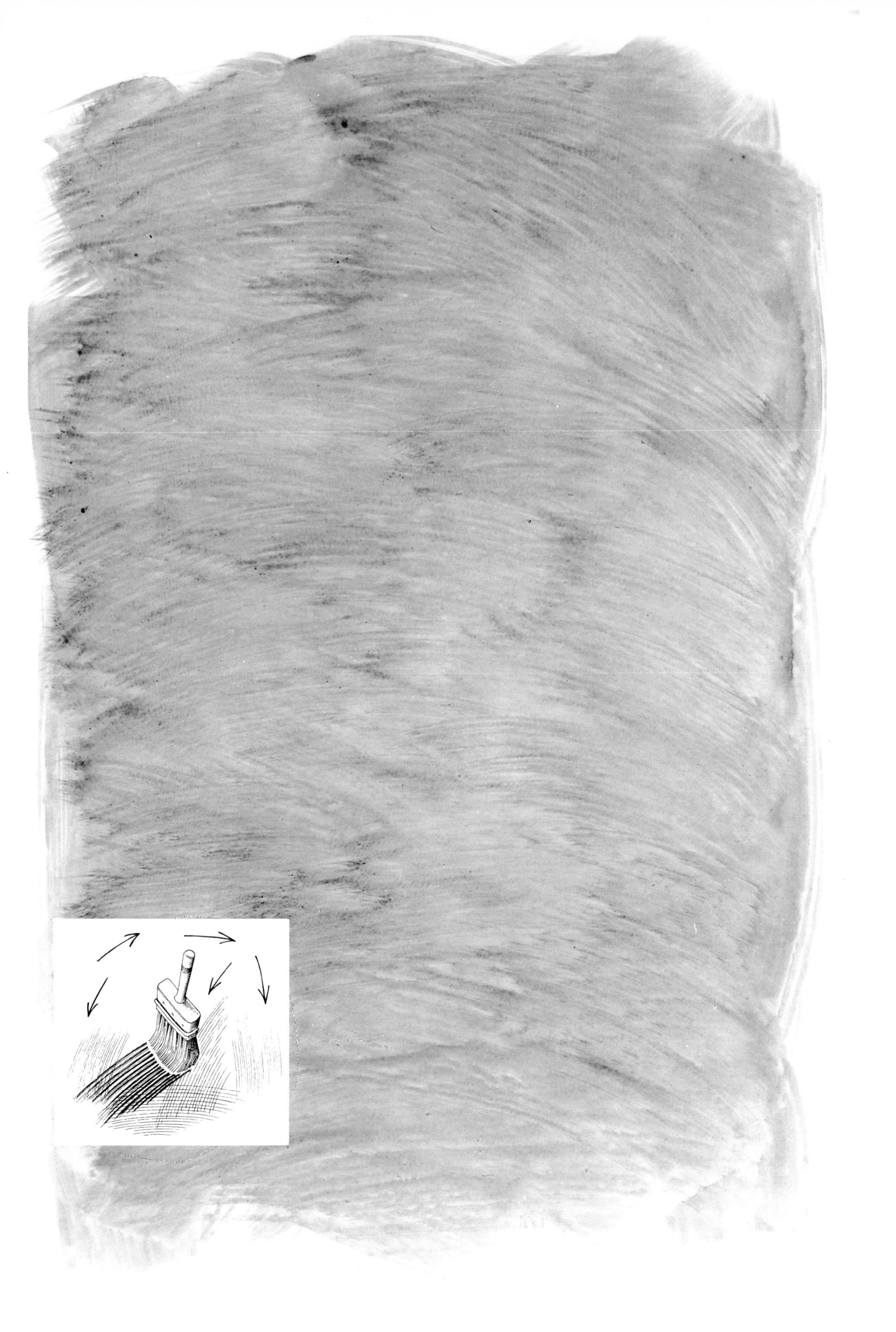

4

ALL THE TECHNIQUES

PAINTING THE WALLS II

MASTERING PATTERN

Painting patterns on your walls by hand may seem a long way round when there are so many wallpapers to choose from, but anyone who covets a completely individual room will feel the results more than repay the time and effort involved. As with all painted decoration, the charm of painted pattern is that it can be tailor-made for your room. And of course you can have as much or as little of it as you want, from a discreet border to intricate, multi-layered stencilling covering the entire wall. If you live in an old house you might consider a stunning, but essentially simple harlequin pattern inspired by Florentine frescos. A cottage with uneven walls and low ceilings is the perfect setting for the primly charming stencil motifs that are derived from the American provincial tradition. A glum north-facing room can be made dazzling when decorated with the bold shapes and fauve colours associated with the Omega Workshop. Pattern need not be applied with a brush. It can be stamped, rolled or sprayed onto walls, using stencils or even an old cotton lace curtain to create a design.

Charleston Manor, home of Bloomsbury figures Vanessa Bell and Duncan Grant, is packed with examples of their exuberant decorative work. The colours sing, the textures breathe, the patterns look dashed on – it all has that casual vitality which amateurs never quite achieve. This is one of my favourite stencils ever, fresh and subtle, an updated Paisley.

Pattern appeals, I think, to a very basic human desire to impose order in a chaotic universe, and pattern-making must be one of the most ancient decorative impulses. It seems likely, from the universality of certain basic pattern rhythms – waves, spirals, zigzags – that pattern-making evolved from the repetition of mystic or magical symbols. We no longer recognize the original meaning of most of the patterns we use, but in view of the persistence of certain motifs perhaps their archetypal power registers at a subconscious level.

Pattern is decoration in its purest form, a repetition of aesthetically pleasing shapes which make surfaces rich and lively to look at without demanding the mental attention you would give to a picture. Most people find patterned walls easier to live with than picture-walls – and more satisfying than plain or textured walls. Pattern allows you to introduce more colour, but above all it involves movement, a dynamic rhythm of colour and shape which activates what would otherwise be static. Sophisticated patterns usually try to disguise the 'repeats', but I suspect that the repetition is one reason for the power of pattern. It is the visual equivalent of calming, repetitive sounds such as ticking clocks, heart beats and breaking waves.

Trying to invent new patterns is largely wasted effort. Even the greatest designers, like William Morris, were content to work with traditional elements, developing and refining them, introducing new colour combinations and reinterpreting old themes. Save your originality for colour and arrangement, and borrow motifs from any source that appeals to you. As stenciller Felicity Binyon firmly states, 'Inspiration is everywhere once you start to look.'

Old tiles, pottery, wrought iron grilles can all supply motifs for pattern-making. Spend an hour or so in a museum, sketching ideas that can be adapted for your own decorative use.

CRESSIDA BELL'S LEAF STAMP

This is one of those brilliantly simple ideas that someone else always thinks of first. Cressida Bell cut a leaf shape out of plastic foam and, dipping it into a vivid cerise matt vinyl emulsion, printed a whirling shower of leaves all over her bedroom walls.

If you copy this idea you should remember to vary the direction of your leaf prints – to keep them lively make them overlap or spiral round. Keep on printing after the colour begins to wear thin, because the contrast of colour and texture this gives is very attractive. Cressida could not resist adding squiggles to her leaves here and there with a gold felt-tipped pen. If you follow suit, be prepared to invest in several pens as the gold runs out quite rapidly.

THE DECORATIVE RUBBER STAMP

Derived from blockprinting on fabric, this idea comes via George Oakes of Colefax and Fowler, who stamped little green sprigs on the bathroom walls of his country cottage to create an innocently charming effect. I found my motifs in old Indian textiles, and they are reproduced here, drawn to scale, for anyone to copy them. They can be turned into rubber stamps by any reasonably enterprising rubber stamp manufacturer for a modest price. Varying your pattern with stamps in two different sizes, as George Oakes did, will give your pattern twice as much liveliness.

Materials

There are a number of different types of paint that you can use: acrylics are handy, but they tend to dry rapidly; Plaka water-based paints are quite easy to use, but take care not to smudge them; printing inks pick up and print nicely, but, again, take care not to smudge them while they are drying; signwriters' colours (see suppliers index) behave well and dry fast. Keep a small pane of glass handy for spreading colour onto; a flat plate will do just as well.

Method

You can pencil lightly where you propose to stamp, but I do not think it is necessary for most patterns. A simple grid looks best, alternating large and small motifs, and staggering each row so that the motifs are spaced halfway between those in the rows above and below. A painted ribbon of the same colour neatens up wall edges prettily.

Anyone who has used a commercial rubber stamp will know just how to set about printing patterns. The only things to watch out for are taking up too much paint on the stamp, which creates a blurred impression, and allowing the colour on the plate or glass to dry up. If it does, add a few drops of water or white spirit, depending on the base of your paint.

All these designs, inspired by old textile blocks, would reproduce well as decorative rubber stamps.

STRIPES

Broad stripes in clear, gentle colours, like the ones shown in Cressida Bell's flat, are tranquilly decorative, easy to do and suit most rooms. Cressida used standard matt emulsion, tinting and mixing until she got the right colour values for her stripes.

Method

A plumb line and masking tape make easy work of getting the stripes tidy and vertical. Remove excess adhesive from the tape by attaching it to another surface, then peeling it off before fixing it to the next wall. This avoids fall-out when you finally remove it. In rooms with coved or pitched ceilings, such as attics, the stripes can be taken up over the ceiling for a tented effect.

ABOVE *A repro Georgian fire surround, picked out in a pale orange colour, was inspired by an Omega Workshop piece (Vanessa Bell was Cressida's grandmother).*

LEFT *A simple leaf shape and oddments of coloured emulsions produced this riot of colour in her bedroom.*

RIGHT *Cressida Bell's painted stripes are wider and the colours are warmer than Nemone Burgess's (see p. 24), but they work to make a gentle yet striking background to her own stunning prints.*

CRESSIDA BELL

FREEHAND PATTERN BLOCKS

When painting my kitchen walls, I decided not to translate the pattern into stencils, which would have given a regular effect, preferring the variety of a freehand approach. The blocks of pattern, repeated over the wall, make a very positive impact (see p. 20).

Method

Marking out beforehand is less critical with rectangular blocks. I pencilled in key vertical and horizontal lines and cut a template the size of the blocks. A steel rule and plumb line always make marking out easier. I added the ground colour, a dirty ochre yellow (I mixed in some turmeric for a laugh – it worked), to standard white emulsion, thinned with water to a milky consistency, and brushed it on roughly to give an aged look. The red and black pattern blocks are painted in acrylic colours, also thinned slightly with water, and applied with stubby artists' brushes. The walls were finished with two coats of yacht varnish, the toughest varnish available, which sealed the decoration against the steam and smoke of kitchen life.

HARLEQUIN DIAMONDS

Bold designs like this were often used for the walls of late medieval Italian palaces and castles, especially in Florence, where they would have been painted in fresco. This dries to a fine matt surface, leaving the colour clear but soft – the use of standard opaque paints would make such patterns appear too harsh. Leonard Lassalle used his favourite technique of pure artists' pigment over oil-bound distemper which gives much the same effect (see p. 112). Anyone trying a design like this should follow suit. For the detailed painting, such as the frieze over the bookcases and the witty trompe l'œil cat, Leonard used his other favourite medium – egg tempera (see p. 111).

Method

Geometric patterns need rather careful measuring and marking out in pencil or chalk before painting. Diagonals are tricky because a line which is only a couple of degrees out at the base of a wall will have wandered noticeably further afield by the time it reaches the top. And when you are using three transparent washes of colour, mistakes can only be rectified by painting out with the white base and starting all over again. Note Leonard's use of white between the coloured diamonds; it helps to soften the contrast between two strong complementary hues. You might perhaps try this design in the delicate pastel colours of the traditional harlequin costume – you would not need the white buffer zone for this, but care should be taken to keep the colour values similar. It would be a good idea to research some actual examples – ballet designs, paintings of masquerades or carnivals, for instance.

STENCILLED PATTERN

Stencilling has become deservedly popular since designers such as Cile Lord in America and Lyn Le Grice in Britain pioneered the revival of this ancient decorative craft almost a decade ago. These two, in their turn, owe a great deal to the inspiration of a remarkable lady, Janet Waring, who tracked down surviving examples of early nineteenth-century stencilling in New England and recorded them in a classic book – *Early American Stencils* – published in the thirties.

Stencils are creativity without tears, a simple and straightforward means of adding pattern to walls, floors, furniture and fabric. They have been used since the time of the pharaohs, at least. A stencil consists, essentially, of a decorative cut-out in some paint-proof material (for example, leather, thin metal, oiled card or paper and acetate) through which paint can be brushed, sponged, sprayed or dabbed onto the surface beneath. Their first use was to speed up the process of repetitive decoration – an early form of mass-production. Ironically, their popularity today stems largely from a reaction *against* mass-production. People like their stencilling to look a little irregular, perhaps unevenly coloured, for that very reason. Wallpaper firms are producing papers with a stencilled look, but hand-painted stencilling still has more class.

It is possible, given skill and patience, to reproduce any design with stencils, even filigree patterns of such complexity as Mary MacCarthy's bravura stencilled 'marquetry'. The bold foliage and colouring of Jacobean crewel-work can be recreated on the walls of a cottage bedroom, though this may involve using more than thirty separate stencils. Elaborate patterns take longer to build up, simply because they require more stencils – one per colour. The process itself

A chinoiserie stencil designed by Stewart Walton. Try it in gold on dark painted furniture, or in colour on walls.

Leonard Lassalle uses egg tempera, one of the oldest and toughest of painting media, for these strong, colourful murals inspired by Tudor and Jacobean crewel work. They make vivid settings for the virile oak furniture in which he specialises. Against a dark ground, Leonard first paints in the design with white distemper, later applying egg tempera colours which he mixes himself.

BELOW *A close-up detail shows the loose, confident nature of this technique; nothing is fussy or worked over.*

remains the same and is largely mechanical, although artistic judgement obviously comes into the choice of colours and arrangement of motifs. In keeping with the current tendency towards polychrome decoration, the trend in stencilling is towards greater intricacy, with whole teams of decorators working for weeks to give walls ravishing subtleties of pattern and colour. There is nothing to prevent you from aiming at a similar effect, building up the pattern over the course of months by adding to it in spare moments.

Beginners, impatient for results, can now choose from quite a good range of pre-cut, or ready-to-cut, stencils. There is even a small but thriving shop devoted entirely to the craft (see suppliers index). These stencils are mostly in simple folk style, with florals predominating. Lyn Le Grice, however, has recently added some sophisticated chinoiserie-inspired designs to her range of stencils.

All the same, it is a pity not to try designing and cutting your own stencils because mastering the simple principles of this technique puts a useful decorative tool at your fingertips and makes so many more effects possible.

SIMPLE STENCILS :

Simple does not necessarily mean 'naive' in the style of the early American folk designs. Both Cressida Bell's fleur-de-lys stencil on a stone-coloured ground and Graham Carr's striking blue chinoiserie stencils (see p. 108) are simple in the sense that they use only one colour and one motif, spaced out on a grid. These designs were inspired by old textiles, one of the richest sources of suitable motifs.

Others might include embroideries, heraldic designs or lace. Photocopying makes light work of enlarging designs to the right size for use on a wall.

The classic 'gul' or pine motif as seen on the cover, used on Kashmiri and later Paisley shawls, is here translated into a stencil for you to copy. Enlarge or reduce the size as required.

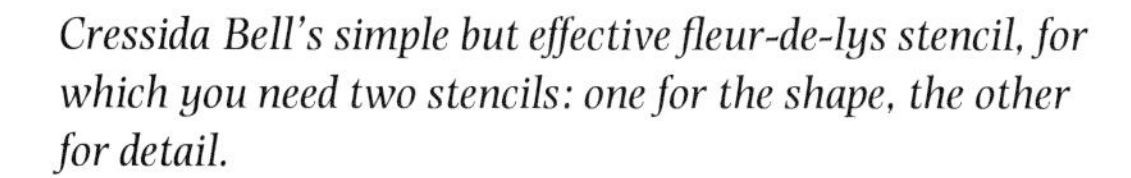

Cressida Bell's simple but effective fleur-de-lys stencil, for which you need two stencils: one for the shape, the other for detail.

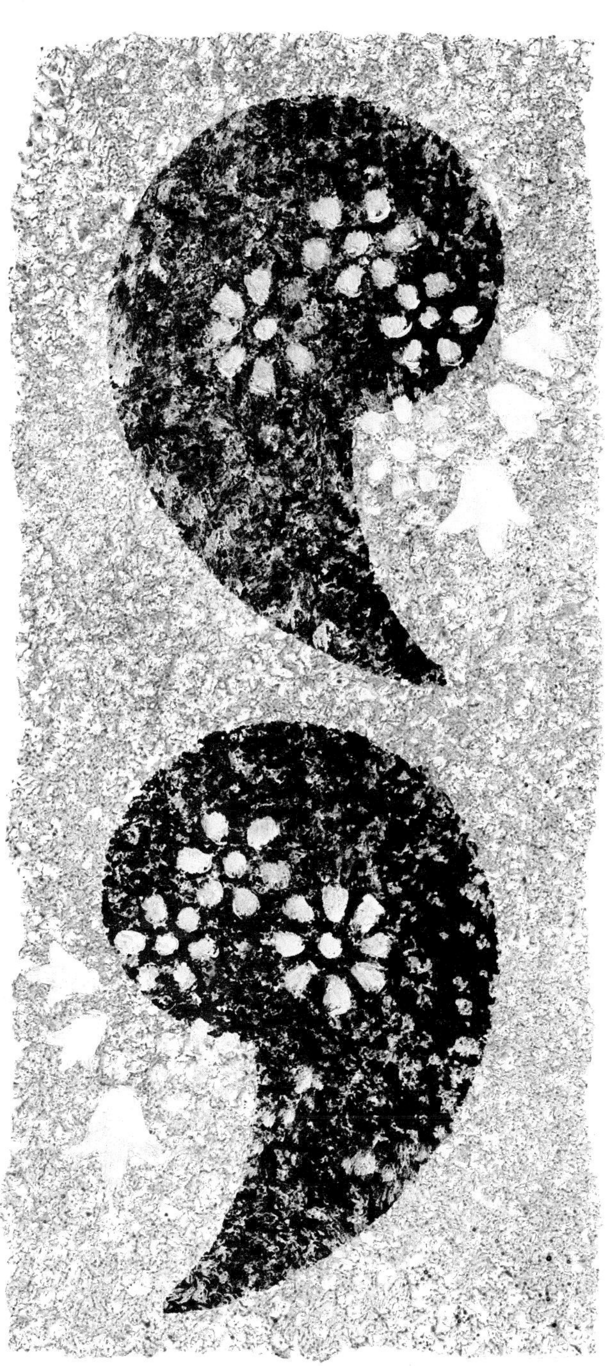

This stencil, based on the Charleston motif, contrasts springlike sprays of white flowers with roughly sponged 'comma' shapes beneath.

Graham Carr's stencilling is very distinctive. He likes to use large, loose motifs and sludgy colours, neatened off with painted bands. Tone and texture constantly vary, creating added vivacity. Graham has since washed over these walls in a drab yellow to make the room look warmer and more integrated.

When I described a stencil as a decorative cut-out, I was giving the simplest description possible; few shapes are both simple and decorative enough to be reduced to a single cut-out. A leaf or a cockle shell, perhaps, has impact as a silhouette, but most of the objects you might want to turn into stencils – flowers, birds, butterflies, trees and toys – need to be broken down further into visually and logically convincing elements. A rose silhouette looks much like a cabbage. To make it unmistakably a rose, the way the petals unfurl around the stamens needs to be indicated as simply and graphically as possible. You will note that the petals have to be stylized for the stencil to hold together. It becomes a series of petal-shaped holes connected to the body of the stencil by a web of little 'bridges'. These bridges, or 'ties' as they are called, are what you usually have to introduce when transferring patterns into stencils. As you can see from the rose stencil, the ties show in the finished effect as outlines. The image is one-dimensional, a characteristic stencil effect. A simple way to give the rose, or any other three-dimensional object, more roundness and greater naturalism is to shade it with a little darker colour. This does not have to be added carefully as if you were painting a portrait of a real rose – just a few touches rapidly applied will suffice. It is possible, by building up the rose with several separate stencils, to produce an entirely naturalistic flower – but the process would be so lengthy it would be easier to paint the rose freehand.

Materials

To make the stencil you will need stencil card or acetate (though thick varnished paper will do), tracing paper, carbon paper and a Stanley knife or craft knife, with several spare blades. Japanese stencils use ties of a single thread and are supremely naturalistic, but fragile.

The skill of designing a stencil lies in creating expressive but functional 'ties', which turn what would otherwise be a silhouette into a recognisable motif.

Method

To enlarge or reduce a pattern or motif, trace it and then have the tracing put through a photocopying machine. Using carbon paper, trace this onto your stencil board, or, if using acetate, put the clear sheet on top and use a Rotring pen or chinagraph pencil to trace round the shape. Cut round the stencil shapes as clearly as possible. It is best to do this on a waste sheet of plywood that you can score into, or a pane of glass. Leave a couple of inches of board or acetate round the cut-outs for strength because stencils have to be handled frequently. If the stencil is for a border, leave enough board to align the pattern against the cornice or ceiling. It is a sensible precaution to start by stencilling your pattern onto another piece of board which you can keep as a spare, in case the first one gets torn, or clogged with paint.

The best paints to use are fast drying to obviate smudging. Artists' acrylic colours dry almost instantly and the colour range is enormous. Many professionals, like Felicity Binyon and Liz Macfarlane, use signwriters' paints because they claim the colours are livelier and less 'plastic'. They also dry very quickly. What you use to apply the paint depends on the effect you want. You can brush the colour on using a brush with short, thick bristles; then use a stencil brush, with a stippling action, for shading. Alternatively, you can use only stencil brushes. A sponge is a very quick way of appplying the colour, although aerosol paint in cans, as used by Lyn Le Grice, is obviously the speediest and least tiring method. This, however, has the disadvantage of having to mask the surrounding surface.

Stencilled colour can be applied to most surfaces. Matt surfaces look best, although stencilling matt colour onto a shiny base gives a damask effect which can be very attractive. Opinions are divided as to whether the base colour beneath should be distressed or plain. There is a conven-

Use a sharp scalpel blade to cut your stencil; cutting at an angle gives a bevelled edge, the mark of an ace stencil cutter.

BELOW *Standing on this bedroom mantelpiece, beside a Quentin Bell sculpture, is a terracotta vase, decorated to match the room using acrylic colour and a glaze of polyurethane, white spirit and stainer.*

LEFT *Painted with a mixture of a signwriters' paint and eggshell, and then glazed, Botticelli's* Birth of Venus *covers one bedroom wall. The calico curtains and bedspread are painted with Procian's watercolour, their dyes and design achieved with a wax technique. Even the lampshade has been painted.*

tion that folk stencils of the early American variety, are applied onto plain, flat colour to keep the effect simple. I personally prefer the look of a lightly distressed background – sponged, stippled or colourwashed – for almost all stencilling.

Applying colour

Squeeze a little colour into a saucer. You need much less than you would believe possible. Work the brush bristles into the colour, and try it out on a sheet of waste paper. The best results are achieved with very little colour, worked to a fine film; thick colour looks clogged and tends to creep under the stencil. Complicated, fragile stencils may need to be fixed in place with masking tape or tacks to hold them steady, but simpler examples can usually be positioned with one hand while you stencil with the other. Again, practise on waste paper first. If your simple stencil requires two colours, one for a flower, say, and one for the leaves, you will find it easier to do these separately. Shading likewise can be added the second time around. By then you will be able to judge how your pattern is developing.

Registration of stencils

With any continuous pattern, like a border, you need to work out a way of ensuring that you begin a new section exactly where the last one ended. Clear acetate eliminates this problem, but on a stencil board you can either cut nicks in the stencil edge or arrange the stencil so that the pattern begins and ends on the same motif.

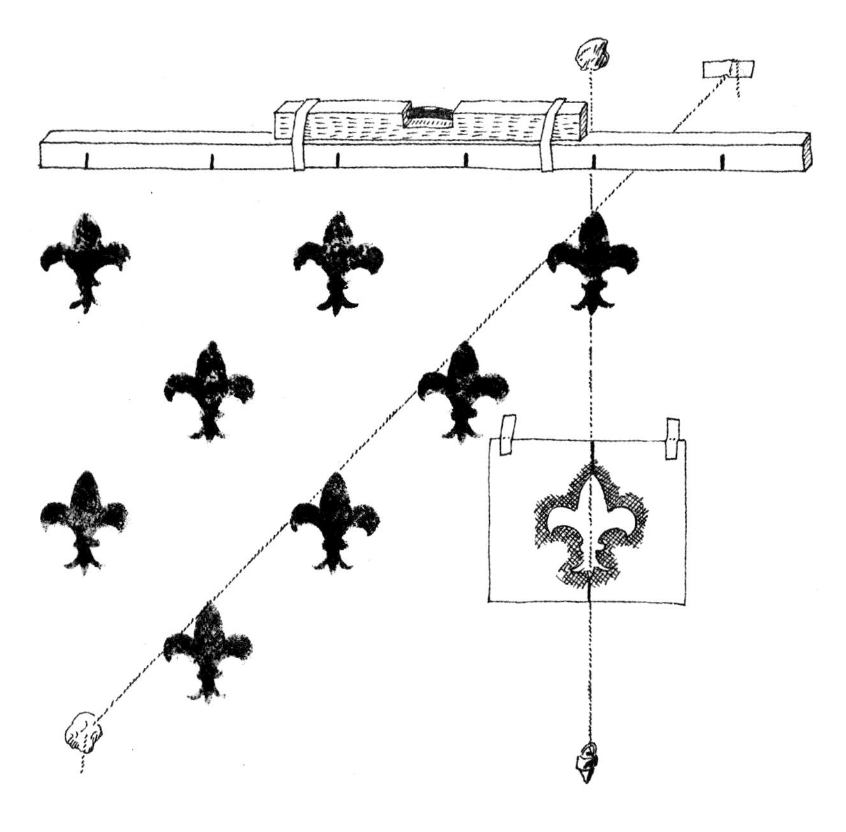

Elaborate stencils

If you want to reproduce a complex pattern like a rug design, which uses several colours, you will need several stencils. Stewart Walton liked the pattern of his sitting room rug so much he decided to use it as the basis of a stencil pattern for the walls. As you can see by comparing the original rug with the finished stencil (see p. 108), he has simplified the pattern and altered the colours. But the stencil retains the spirit and boldness of the handwoven rug. He cut five separate stencils, using one main motif from the rug. It would have been too much of an undertaking to try and reproduce them all. Having chosen his motif, he speeded up the process by plotting out his pattern on the largest sheet of stencil board available, cutting it out several times over to correspond with the way in which the pattern was to develop on the wall. This enabled him accurately to locate the motifs, and complete half a dozen at one go instead of having to measure and check each time as he would have done with a single-motif stencil. He cut two separate, smaller stencils for details, another large one for the bold outlines, and one more for the grid design which links the motifs together.

Stewart used acrylic colours for his stencil, diluted in a little water, to which he added some PVA adhesive (see suppliers' index) as a binder. The PVA allows the acrylic colour to be thinned down to a transparent solution without becoming too watery. To compensate for a simplified colour scheme, he rang the changes on his three basic colours, painting the motif red and details blue the first time, and then reversing the colour scheme the second time. For further variety he changed the texture of the stencilling as the mood took him, either stippling it with a brush, sponging it or ragging it. Tricks like these enrich the final effect for only a little more effort. Overlaying transparent colours on the principal motif also

Working out a grid for stencils on walls needs accurate measuring, but you can use primitive equipment – cotton and Blu-tack, string and a plumb line, or a wooden batten sectioned off at measured intervals. However carefully you measure, do not despise your 'eye' – not all walls are vertical, straight or flat.

This simplified motif, abstracted from an elaborately patterned rug, led via changes of colour to the richly patterned walls in Stewart Walton's own sitting room (see also p. 108).

FAR RIGHT *Not strictly painted, but too decorative to leave out – a tiny yellow painted bar-cupboard, the walls tricked out with black and white prints pasted onto the surface and framed with borders and bows sold through the National Trust.*

TOP *Very simple but effective, Cressida Bell's front hall with its fleur-de-lys motif in mauve-grey on creamy pink.*

CENTRE *Carolyn Warrender enjoys the demureness of early American stencil motifs like these, which she sells in her London stencil shop and combines in various colourways on the walls.*

BELOW RIGHT *More Graham Carr stencilling, bold and closely patterned in good 'dirty' colours. Here the base colour is warmer than before, the design consciously chinoiserie.*

BELOW *Details of Stewart Walton's rug (right) and the stencilled wall (left), showing how a change of colour can stretch the decorative power of a simple, repeated motif.*

SAMUEL JOHNSON, LL.D.

introduced a random effect where red over blue created mauve. If you did not want this surprise element, you could use an opaque mix of colour for the superimposed detail.

Stencilling a complex pattern over an entire room is not something to try and cram into a weekend. The realistic approach is to expect it to grow gradually, adding more as and when you feel like it. If you can enlist the services of a helper so much the better; stencilling is pleasant when it is convivial, and when you are enjoying your work progress always seems faster. Do not worry if the colours are not exactly the same each time. Busy stencilled schemes usually look more attractive with some colour variation. You do not want to go to all that trouble and end up with a wall finish that looks like wallpaper. Interior designer John Stefanides had the walls of his sitting room stencilled in imitation of old embroideries, which meant capitalizing on subtle colour variations. First, the background was distressed with patchily applied glazes; transparent colour was used for the stencils, and varied just a little to suggest fading. In some places the pattern was rubbed off slightly with wire wool to look worn. This may sound like a lot of work, but the effect of walls covered with beautiful old fabric is entirely convincing and much admired.

Large patterns like these cover the ground faster. The really laborious stencil schemes are those which reproduce small-scale motifs, especially regular ones. A trellis with climbing plants would be a standard example. These depend on exact measuring up and marking out, and careful execution.

However, one attractive effect can be obtained quite easily by stencilling with an oil-based paint on a matt emulsion surface, and then brushing a tinted wash over the whole surface. Oil repels water, so the colour wash builds up round the outer edge of the stencilled pattern, while hardly altering the stencil at all. Pale colours applied on a white base create an effect like old damask or brocade. Use a slightly thinned gloss paint to stencil with as this will emphasize the textural contrasts. Silky, rather than shiny patterns will emerge against a matt background.

Background for stencilling

Stencilling tends to be done on a pale ground, but it can look dramatic over a darker base. The simple way to do this is to stencil in a positive colour several tones darker than the ground colour – midnight-blue over pale red, for instance, or brown on bamboo. This gives something of a Toile de Jouy effect, distinguished without being too colourful. But if you want colour, like the vividness of an old chintz against a dark background, you must first stencil all the designs in white, and then stencil colour on top. Leonard Lassalle's crewel-style mural painting (see p. 96–7) shows how effective this can be, although this was painted freehand.

Mary MacCarthy has stencilled her bathroom with floral and leaf motifs in soft greyed pastels, bordering directly onto the thistle-pink plaster. This looks very attractive, and is a good idea to copy, but the plaster will need sealing with diluted Unibond to prevent grease marks showing – even fingerprints can be greasy.

Protecting stencils

Extra pale, dead flat varnish will protect any stencilled scheme without adding shine or altering the colours, and this is the most popular finish among professionals. It gives sufficient protection for walls which do not need frequent washing-down. The shinier grades of varnish, eggshell or gloss give more protection for bathrooms, kitchens and hallways. Toughest of all is yacht varnish, which definitely darkens and yellows the colours beneath. This can be a bonus, ageing everything instantly with an amber film. If you like this effect, but not the shine it builds up, yacht varnish can be rubbed over with fine wire wool to cut the gleam, but give the walls at least two coats of varnish first, otherwise you are liable to cut through the varnish itself to the paint beneath. Lubricate the wire wool by rubbing it on a bar of soap, and wipe the walls over afterwards with a damp rag.

Shading Stencils

Shading can bring stencilled patterns to life. Certain motifs can be greatly enhanced by a suggestion of 3-D modelling: fruit, flowers, architectural subjects, urns and columns, for instance. Shaded fruit and flowers can look effective without being done in naturalistic colours, and shading does not have to be stippled on with the realism of a Dutch still life. Lyn Le Grice shades a lot of her work with spray paint, which she focusses on the area in question from a distance, so that the spray is fine enough to control. This gives a professional smoothness almost like airbrushing. Liz MacFarlane and Felicity Binyon shade with stencil brushes, stippling colour where they want to suggest roundness. Architectural subjects are usually done in *grisaille* or monochrome, or sometimes stony colours such as grey, beige or black.

EGG TEMPERA

It is a striking feature of the current decorative scene that so many painters are being inspired to imitate or revive old techniques. In many cases they begin experimenting out of curiosity, but stay with these methods because they can achieve effects obtainable in no other way. Leonard Lassalle uses egg tempera, one of the oldest painting media of all, for his mural painting because he likes its 'gentle, transparent colours, like watercolour', plus the paradoxical fact that 'it gets harder and harder with time – it lasts for ever.'

It is possible to buy tempera-type paints in some artists' ranges, but being a down-to-earth Frenchman he prefers to make his own. The materials are of the simplest kind.

Materials

His recipe begins, jokingly, 'grab a chicken' – you *do* need a fresh egg. Break the egg in half, so you can use the rounder half as a measure. Separate the yolk from the white, and roll the yolk on newspaper gently to mop up any remaining albumen. Then, with care, break the yolk membrane over a jam jar so that the yolk itself drops in, but not the membrane. Add 1 half-egg measure of raw linseed oil and $2\frac{1}{2}$ measures of distilled water. Screw on the lid and shake vigorously until the contents form a creamy emulsion. At this point add Leonard's secret ingredient – a few drops of surgical spirit. This not only stops the egg going off, but helps it to dry faster. 'It took me six months to discover this', he said. Into the tempera base, Leonard mixes artists' quality powder pigments, which can be found in a good artists' suppliers and are the purest form of colour available. Egg tempera painting needs no varnishing. Small ceramic palettes, with round hollows in them, are good for mixing up colours.

For murals like his colourful crewel-type designs on a dark ground (see p. 96–7), a special underpainting is needed because the tempera colour, being semi-transparent, is lost on a dark base. Having sketched out the design, Leonard paints it onto the dark base in white oil-bound distemper. You could substitute white undercoat. Over a white base the tempera colours glow beautifully, and the whole effect on a dark ground has the dazzle of vibrant embroidery.

"Leonard Lassalle is an antique dealer and artist who specializes in Tudor and Jacobean furniture. He began by decorating his own shop in Tunbridge Wells because he wanted to get the right sort of setting for the furniture. Soon clients began asking him if he would re-create for them his simple but vibrantly coloured effects; walls boldly colourwashed with emphatic texture, vivid murals based on crewel work, Florentine-inspired interiors painted in strong lozenges of colour. He now spends as much time designing and painting rooms in his individual style as he does running his business. The Lassalle approach is refreshing, owing as much to his knowledge of French and Italian traditions (he buys a lot of his paint colours abroad) as to his painterly sense of what suits the heavily beamed farmhouses and cottages of Kent.

'I use an oil-bound distemper which comes in big tubs [see suppliers index] for the base coat on my walls. It is not an easy paint to use as it is heavy to brush out, but the way the brushstrokes cross makes for a texture which gives patination in the final result. I use pure pigment for colouring, dry artists' colours (see suppliers index), because I cannot find any other colour that has that vibration. Modern colours are dyes, whereas mine, if you look at them under the microscope, are tiny particles of real earth. I use ferrous colours like the oxides. In France and Italy you can buy very good colours which are used for staining cement. I mix my colours in water in a jam jar, adding a very little distemper and shaking long and hard to dissolve it. Then I tip some colour into a bowl and apply it to the wall using a wide, floppy-bristled brush which I keep wet. The powder pigment I use is very strong and the distemper soaks it up, so I have to check to see that it is diluted enough to give the degree of colour that I want. I also have an old rag in the other hand, which I use to spread the colour that I have brushed on, and soften it as necessary. Putting on the colour takes no time at all, maybe one and a half hours for a room 35 metres square.'

This method is designed to put character and colour

back into early houses, built before eighteenth-century urbanity and 'good taste' persuaded people to plaster over their stud beams and timbered ceilings. It is a 'peasant' look, virile and unpretentious, which is more appropriate to tough vernacular building than the suave, polished finishes like ragging and dragging. These suit rooms built in the neo-classical tradition and later. It has become standard practice to paint the plastered surfaces in beamed rooms white, or at the most, shell-pink. But rich, positive colours, brushed on casually in the Lassalle manner, not only make these rooms look more coherent, but are, I suspect, more historically accurate. Limewashing in white may have been the usual finish for old plaster in poorer dwellings, but colour and pattern were invariably introduced as soon as house-owners could afford display. Surviving fragments of early plastered infills in beamed dwellings are often painted with bold herringbone stripes or floral patterns in strong colours. ”

ROLLED-ON PATTERN

The easiest way to achieve this finish is with specially made rollers which are sold with detachable plastic roller heads. These are embossed with a variety of patterns, mostly floral. In many rural parts of Europe, colourwashed walls are still patterned in this way in imitation of wallpaper, which is either too expensive or too difficult to get hold of.

Colourways

Walls should be rolled in a darker tone of the base colour for the most telling effect: for example, gitane blue on a base washed over with a thinned-down pale blue colour. This looks attractive without being pretentious – something you should avoid if you want the full provincial nostalgia to show through. There is one exception to this rule: rolling white over a pastel colour gives a wonderfully frothy lace effect.

Method

Assemble the roller as shown on the pack, filling the container with standard matt emulsion. Begin rolling from the top of the wall downwards (if you roll across the wall, the paint will pour out of the container). Then repeat, immediately next to the first patterned stripe, and continue until the whole wall is covered. Some patterns require matching up at the seams – check by trying them out on a board – but most do not. Try to keep your rolling steady and straight; the odd wobble or swerve hardly shows in the final result, however. If you are concerned about this, use a plumb line as a guide.

Ordinary foam rollers, preferably the stiffer variety, can be cut with a scalpel to make bands of bold, African-looking pattern. Dip the roller in the paint (again standard emulsion is best, tinted with stainers if you wish) and then roll it on paper to remove the excess before applying it to the wall. The advantage of these rollers is that they can be rolled sideways as well, but they do run out of paint very quickly.

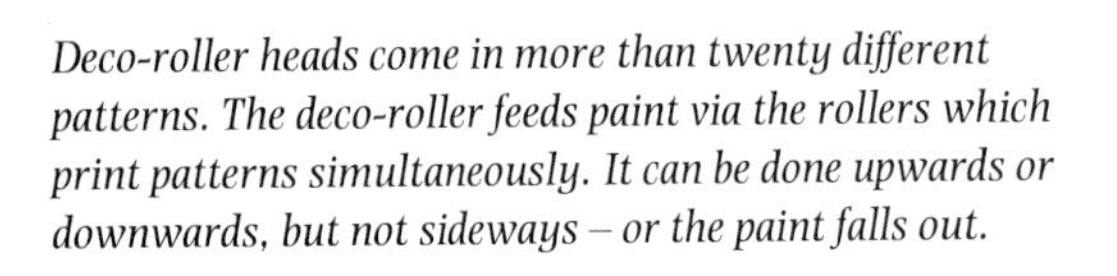

Deco-roller heads come in more than twenty different patterns. The deco-roller feeds paint via the rollers which print patterns simultaneously. It can be done upwards or downwards, but not sideways – or the paint falls out.

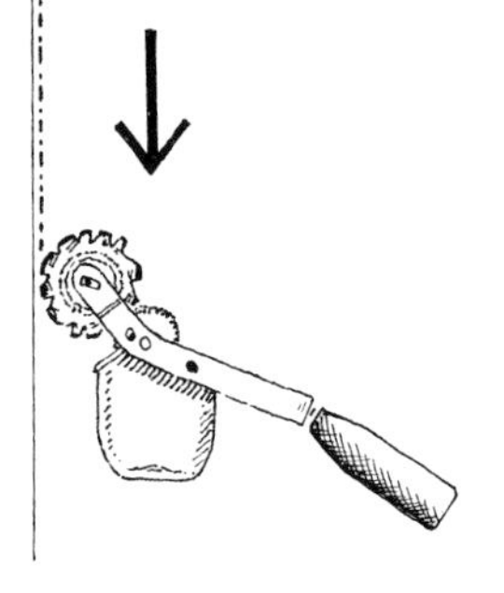

SPRAYED PATTERN

Dazzlingly easy and dashingly impressive, this finish can transform the walls of a small bathroom, for instance. Spray colour through a coarse cotton lace curtain, bought for next to nothing in street markets. The paint passes through the open mesh but not the finer woven pattern. It is hard to believe it will work, but it does, creating an instant brocade effect. Play this up by choosing suitable colours – sludge green on palest pink, brown on grey.

Materials

You can use the sort of spray paint sold for touching-up car bodywork (of which you will need several cans), and this comes in a huge range of colours, including metallics. The fumes are powerful, so work with the windows open and wear a mask. Alternatively, borrow or hire a spraying attachment which can be used with standard DIY paints.

Method

The lace can be tin-tacked or stapled in place each time – stretch it taut and close to the surface of the wall. Spray evenly, covering the whole piece of lace. It is as well to mask off each side with newspaper and Blu-Tack to catch paint. Eventually, the finer mesh in the lace will clog up with paint. One solution would be to get more than one length of the same pattern. If you are using a standard DIY paint, you can rinse out the lace in white spirit.

Spraying through lace can create wonderfully varied and opulent patterns on the surfaces beneath, almost without trying. Spray paints should be applied at the prescribed distance, with the surround masked off.

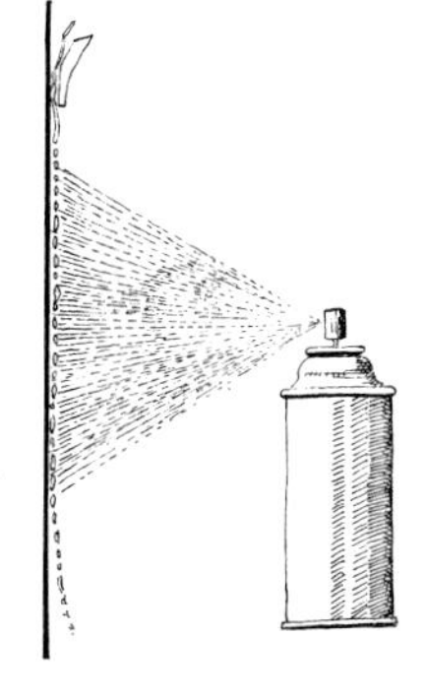

5

FINISHES FOR FLOORS,

PAINTING THE FRAME

CEILINGS AND WOODWORK

If pattern answers our need for ordered surfaces, a concern for proportion answers an equally powerful desire for ordered spaces. Ceilings that are too high, the unbalanced placing of windows, the bland results of stripping-out architectural elements – all these are vaguely disquieting, not so much positively wrong as not quite right. We feel comfortable in rooms with a clearly defined framework, with points of reference that allow us to orientate ourselves in a particular space. Just what module makes for the most convincing proportions, and why, is a mystery architects have pondered over since classical times. Probably it all comes back to that yardstick we all share, the human body. That wonderfully proportioned creation, the classical column, has three divisions – base, shaft and entablature – which can be seen as corresponding to legs, trunk and head. Traditional rooms have their walls sectioned off into three parts, like a column unrolled, and strike us as humanly-scaled however vast and palatial they may be. Rooms which are grounded with skirting and dado spell security, and a sense of place.

In an otherwise giddy space, a firmly painted cornice finishing off a cloudy-grey marbled wall makes room proportions manageable and supplies a visual 'framework'. Beautifully handled paint finishes make something elegant from an impossibly tricky hallway in a London flat – a lesson in how paint can make a silk purse from a sow's ear.

Not many people are lucky enough to live in classically-proportioned rooms, but there is a lot that can be done to rectify awkward spaces, restore harmony and introduce 'firmness'. (The classical objectives of architecture were summed up by the Elizabethan scholar, diplomat and architectural thinker, Sir Henry Wootton, as 'commodity, firmness and delight'.) Our eyes can be deceived: a painted line can stand in very satisfactorily for a dado, a stencilled frieze might substitute for a cornice, while high ceilings can be visually lowered and intrusive room fittings 'faded out' using nothing but artful paint.

Painted 'architecture' is one way of improving or correcting unsatisfactory proportions. Another, which has an equally respectable classical pedigree, is the use of colour to emphasize the three-dimensional aspect of a room, a box with a base and a lid as well as sides. The great designers, whether we are talking of Adam, Palladio or Mies van der Rohe, conceived of rooms in the round. The Adam library at Kenwood has a painted stucco ceiling and a carpet which picks up the ceiling design. The elaboration of these surfaces ensures that they are seen as continuous with the richly treated walls; substitute a plain white, flat ceiling and plain wall-to-wall carpet and the magnificent apartment falls apart. The same principle holds good in our own rooms. Enriching one set of surfaces – the walls, for instance – calls for a corresponding intensification of the others. One aspect of the decorative painting bonanza which has taken even the professionals by surprise is the number of commissions now received for painted ceilings, floors, and the elaboration of joinery and plasterwork which define the room space. The white woodwork and ceilings and plain fitted carpets that we are used to seeing are too neutral to be an effective surrounding for polychromatic patterned walls. In one way or another it is possible to apply most of the painting techniques that we have already discussed to the framework of the room. Wooden surfaces can be treated with stains and varnishes to create an array of wonderful effects – even the ceiling can become an excitingly patterned and textured element.

FLOORS

COMBING:

Combed colour gives floors a jolly, liquorice allsorts look. It is an easy finish to do and is popular with DIY enthusiasts. Rustic spaces, such as converted barns or lofts and big family kitchens, are ideal locations.

Materials

For the combs choose from a wide range of homemade equipment: a length of plastic with zigzag teeth cut into it; a rubber squeegee notched in the same way (this is particularly handy because of the handle); an Afro comb.

Method

It is easiest to comb plywood squares separately, laying them down afterwards, because then there is no problem keeping within the square. If you do comb your squares straight onto a floor, you will probably need to tidy them around the edges. Paint your floor in two stages – every alternate square the first time, the rest after the first squares have dried. Almost any paint can be used for a combed surface (including emulsion), but the base needs to be a little slippery to comb smoothly. Give it a coat of gloss or eggshell paint, or varnish it if the paint is matt. Pale colour mixtures, such as green on yellow or buff on white, are popular and attractive.

Paint on a coat of your top colour, evenly and thickly. Then with your instrument comb it across in straight lines, wavy lines, or art deco intersecting arcs. Combing allows the base colour to show through and over a floor area creates a subtle but definite build-up of texture. When dry, varnish as usual.

STAINS AND VARNISHES:

After years of wall-to-wall carpeting the pendulum is swinging the other way. The lively texture of bare wood floors, perhaps decorated with painted patterns, is popular again. Nothing looks more warmly dignified than a floor of solid, smoothly polished boards.

Preparation

Unfortunately, when you take up carpets you are more likely to find a patchwork of planking: partially stained, discoloured, peppered with nail holes and tack heads. Even so, it is astonishing how gratefully timber responds to a beauty treatment. The first step is to go over the entire surface with a sanding machine. The logical time to do this is after building operations and before the last stages of decorating because sanding covers every surface with fine dust. It is better to sand floors over lightly – just enough to remove the topmost layer – rather than to grind away until the wood looks quite new again, as was done in the sixties.

Method

Having cleared the decks, as it were, the next thing to decide is whether the floorboards need remedial treatment, and if so, what kind. Floors can be stained in a whole range of colours, they can be lightened by rubbing in paint, or even painted over completely and decorated with stencils, or combed patterns. If the timber is quite presentable but you feel the need for a little colour, a coloured varnish stain (see suppliers index) is the easiest solution. Being transparent the varnish stain allows the wood grain to show through, which is attractive. For deeper colour, apply more coats; alternatively, combine two different colours for an interesting effect.

A fashionable transparent grey finish could be a good way round the problem of scruffy old floorboards. Apply a diluted black stain and go over this with a matt varnish to which a little white paint has been added. It is important to start with the right black: as blacks are diluted, strong undertones of either red or blue tend to show up. A combination of both tones is best, giving a soft but warm grey. Stains can be either spirit- or water-based (see suppliers index). Test on spare wood until you get the right shade, remembering that the final white-tinted varnish will lighten the effect a little, softening and cooling the stain. Since woods vary so much, the only way to arrive at the best colour for your purposes is to experiment, trying different strengths of stain and varnish until you get the look you like. The more heavily figured areas tend to pick up more stain.

RUBBED-IN PAINT:

This gives a similar effect, especially if you use the off-white or greyish paints which people like for the bleached driftwood effect that they can impose on even the most gingery deal. The finish will not be so transparent, or quite so durable since stain penetrates deeper than paint even when the latter is rubbed into the grain. It is, however, a quick method of giving wood floors a cool, even look, and makes a very attractive background for stencilling.

"I get asked to do a painted floor from time to time, often by Americans. They seem to be more into slightly 'over the top' effects. I find it incredibly easy, like painting on a table – much easier than going up and down a ladder. The best thing to paint is a good old pine floor, cracks and all. Cracks are fine. What is important is to get off all the polish, stains and varnish – anything like that. The floor should be sanded over with a machine. I use oil colours and undercoat – it needs to be an oil-based paint because that is the only one which sinks into the wood. I would give it two coats of thin undercoat as a base, just enough to change the colour of the wood.

My inspiration for floor designs comes from historical examples: paintings, prints and sometimes from furniture. One floor I did was taken from the design on top of a Turkish box. The floor in my

own house is based on a marble one in an Italian palazzo. One should adapt any design to suit oneself. In a big room with lots of furniture you are best advised to go for a background colour – the floor doesn't want to be more important than the furniture. Looking at old pictures is a great help in evaluating this sort of thing. I usually use the natural colours of wood, stone and marble. My own floor scheme uses

marbled white squares set in a 3-D 'lattice' in shades of brown. The tawny sections are the original well-scraped floor boards.

I find it helps to think of a floor design as a painted carpet. It should be flat and decorative, but not too painterly. I start by finding the centre of the room, which is where the lines connecting the centre of the walls intersect. Then, depending on the pattern, I begin marking it out clearly with a pencil. You need to measure accurately. Then I mix up my colours and get down on my hands and knees and off I go. I use artists' brushes for fine detail and a decorating brush (small size) for filling in. When it is for a client, you go on until it is finished, varnish and all, but in my own place I kept adding bits when I felt like it, varnishing it as I went along. Varnishing is a bit of a drag, but you have to do it to prevent the paint being worn away – anything from three coats to ten, depending on how much time you have and how much wear the floor is going to get. From time to time, if the varnish seems worn, take everything out and clean the floor thoroughly and re-varnish. It should last for years and years. ”

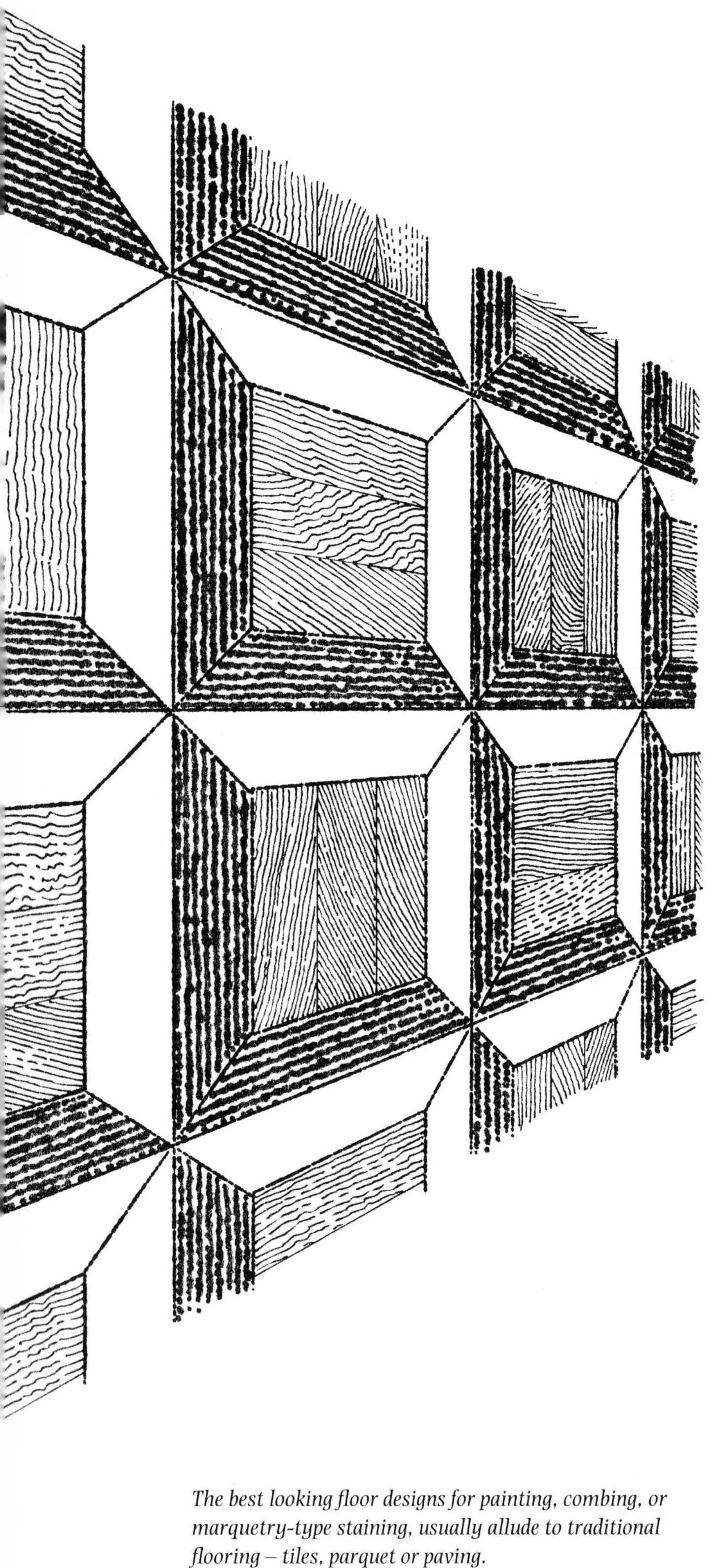

The best looking floor designs for painting, combing, or marquetry-type staining, usually allude to traditional flooring – tiles, parquet or paving.

Their geometric shapes look solid and coherent, extending over a floor space. They can either be painted onto smooth sheets of ply, or directly onto the floor boards ignoring the cracks, in the manner of Graham Carr.

LEFT *Cheeky, simple but effective, Cressida Bell's bathroom ceiling decoration is taken from the ideal* ad hoc *subject – the shower rose.*

RIGHT *Thanks to Paul Czainskis' masterful technique, a tiny disjointed space is transformed by the superb graining on the door, a painted marquetry floor and illusory stonework.*

ABOVE *The painted cornice and stonework, or 'ashlar', is stippled through stencils with a traditional grainer's mix of powder colour and stale beer.*

Preparation

The floor should be thoroughly scrubbed first with a de-greasing agent and left to dry. If this raises the grain too much, sand it lightly to smooth it.

Method

Almost any paint will do for rubbing in: emulsion, flat white (see suppliers index), eggshell or gloss. Thin the paint a little to make it easier to apply. Tint with appropriate colours. It can be put on in whichever way you find easiest: brushed on and then rubbed off, or rubbed in with a rag. To encourage the paint to soak in, coat the wood, leave it for a few minutes and then start rubbing off. This finish will need to be sealed in with two or three coats of matt or eggshell varnish – ideally dead flat, clear varnish which does not yellow.

STENCILLING:

There are stencilled floors in England dating from the seventeenth century, simple designs often centred on the family coat of arms. Stencilling has always been one of the easiest ways of adding colour and pattern to any surface.

The most acceptable design is one based on a carpet – with a border enclosing a central area stencilled on a regular grid. If this seems too ambitious, confine your stencils to a border around the edge of the floor and stain or paint the centre a solid colour. A neutral background, such as the rubbed-in finish, is very pretty stencilled in one colour – deep blue or burnt red, for example. The same colour and pattern can be repeated in a border on the walls.

Stencilled floors follow the same procedure as walls (see p. 94), but it makes sense to go for a tough paint. Signwriters' paints are good. Lyn Le Grice uses spray paints, which saves effort, but they can be tricky to handle as the paint often clogs up when the can is pointed downwards, and the colour tends to creep when it is sprayed at an angle. When spraying a border the skirting will need to be masked off, or re-painted later.

Thorough varnishing is essential, to prevent your work of art being rubbed away under passing feet. Depending on the colours, use flat, clear varnish, or a tough polyurethane, and give the floor several coats. Drying time is speeded if you leave a fan heater in the room, or the windows open in warm weather.

CHEQUERED PATTERNS:

Chequered patterns are the poor man's version of marble paving – at least if you tackle it yourself. Black and white lozenges painted over a plank floor in a hallway can look surprisingly convincing even though the floorboards may be gappy, and the painting quite casually done. Setting the chequers on the diagonal makes a hall look wider. In an old house the dim, matt effect of a non-shiny paint looks right, but for a crisper look substitute gloss and a shiny coat of varnish.

Method

Geometric patterns like these need accurate measuring. Mark off a long batten with your chequer intervals and use a smaller one, also marked off, to measure off the space between. No old floor is ever precisely square or rectangular with parallel sides. A solid-colour border, which can expand and contract to follow the walls, is the obvious solution. A magic marker gives clear outlines within which to paint.

For a black and white chequered effect, the whole floor should first be painted white. It does not have to be gloss; white emulsion will do provided you varnish it thickly at the end. Whatever colour combination you choose, paint the floor first with the lighter colour, then mark out the squares or lozenges, painting these with a pointed brush to outline the edges and a thicker brush to fill in the squares.

If you want to marble your squares see our section on marbling techniques (p. 68). If you are nervous of boldly dashing in veins, try Sally Kenny's playful ways of cheating to create a marbled effect (p. 166).

CEILINGS

COLOURWASHING:

The matt dapple of colour which colourwashing gives is very effective on ceilings. The Georgians and Victorians routinely coloured ceilings a couple of tones paler than the wall colour, a simple device which ties a room together without drawing attention to itself. If the walls have a brushy colourwash, the ceiling can be brushy to match (see p. 86 for colourwashing instructions). If the wall finish is discreet, you may want a softer ceiling look, which you can achieve by using two brushes – a wide paint brush to apply colour and a dry soft brush like the Whistler Lilyduster to soften out brushmarks while wet. To soften, move the bristles gently to and fro at right angles to the wet painted surface, teasing out the colour finely.

Limewashed ceilings were commonplace until World War II because apart from being cheap, limewash was considered hygienic, an antiseptic which also repelled insects. But as anyone who has restored an old house will know, old limewash has to be scraped or scrubbed off before any modern emulsion paint will adhere to a surface. So it is good to know that a newly available paint, called Keim after its German inventor, allows you to re-paint over a limewashed or distempered base. Keim paint is available, by post, in three formulations (see suppliers index). It is more expensive than the standard DIY paint but the manufacturers claim it provides a permanent finish.

Alternatively, if you live in an old, listed building you may again find the Society for Protection of Ancient Buildings can help you to locate actual limewash or distemper for restoration purposes.

STENCILLING:

If cornices are missing in an old house, it is a good idea to create some sort of visual replacement. Decorated walls which stop short abruptly when they hit the ceiling look unfinished. One solution is to stencil a border round the top of the walls, and then repeat the stencil round the ceiling, colourwashing the centre space in some pale shade keyed to the border colours or the wall colour. This is something I plan to do in my blue-painted study when I can escape from the typewriter, repeating the stencilled Indian motif border that goes round the walls. At present the white ceiling looks too much like a lid – unrelated to the room. Stencilling on a ceiling is done exactly as on any other surface, but is a little more back-breaking. Another cornice substitute has worked quite successfully in a spare bedroom and is less cruel to bad backs. A contrasting line is painted round the top of the wall. This line is echoed by a second line on the ceiling, set roughly where a cornice would reach to, and the centre space is colourwashed. The plain white area between the two painted lines becomes a 'negative' cornice.

One good reason for hanging upside down with a stencil brush is that a little decorative flair on a ceiling has great impact on our unaccustomed eyes, and makes an ordinary room re-

VERSAILLES
Irish houses & castles

LEFT *Handled with conviction, painted architecture together with a cloudy marbled finish gives a strangely shaped space an ordered, framed appearance.*

ABOVE *How to handle a painted moulding when it goes round a curved corner – positively and crisply.*

markable. A wreath of stencilled roses would transform a bedroom into a boudoir, while a severe architectural frieze would lend great dignity to a hallway or study. The style to aim for here is Puginesque – consult paintings of the period for ideas.

SKY CEILINGS :

The idea of painting ceilings to look like a blue sky, complete with drifting clouds, dates back to classical times; it is a decorative conceit everyone can respond to. 'Sky' ceilings are currently popular because they create an airy, romantic canopy for rooms that need a bit of interest aloft without going as far as *putti* and garlands. I have seen them in hallways and dining-rooms, and they look particularly attractive in high-styled bedrooms. Nemone Burgess recently painted one in her bathroom, only there the 'sky' starts halfway down the walls and dissolves the contours of the small room so that you seem to be looking up into luminous blue space. More often the sky is framed by a cornice and confined to the ceiling. No great artistry is needed to suggest a sky convincingly in paint but it is hard work painting overhead. Most painters try to rig up portable scaffolding – boards stretched between two ladders – so they can paint while lying on their backs.

Nemone Burgess paints skies over a creamy yellow base coat: 'This gives a lit-up look, like sunlight.' She uses a surprising range of colours – cobalt, ultramarine and cerulean blue, but also Paynes grey, orange and purple. She mixes them up with a little proprietary glaze, and quite a lot of white spirit: 'too much glaze can turn blues turquoise.' She describes her painting technique as 'rather like marbling overhead – I go zing-zing across the ceiling with my colour onto a dry paint surface, and then I stipple it out until it looks soft.' Having blocked in her sky and cloud shapes quickly and loosely with the overhead marbling, she then works up the ceiling a section at a time, adding more colour, stippling and softening, and standing back frequently to gauge progress.

Sally Kenny uses fewer colours over a white base – eggshell or vinyl silk. 'I'll use blue and white, of course, and greys and purple and maybe a little green. I brush the colours on in the ordinary way and then stipple over the colour, especially where two colours meet, so they seem to merge imperceptibly. When the paint is dry, I go all over it again with blue and white to bring it up where it needs dramatizing.'

Their skies are painterly, full of atmospheric effects, but a sky ceiling can work very well at a simplified level. Keep your cloud a skein rather than fat, nursery-rhyme puffs, and stipple out hard edges and colour demarcations. Do it in two stages, like Sally Kenny, to allow yourself time to ponder the overall effect. Then add white highlights, deeper blue depths, grey or green shading, and stipple again until merged. For reminders about cloudy skies, look at paintings by Constable, Claude Lorraine and Turner.

WOODWORK

FAKE MARQUETRY :

Cabinetmaker's marquetry consists of a decorative jigsaw of attractively grained wood veneers, cut and glued to a plain timber carcass to create patterns ranging from simple geometrics to the lavish rococo curlicues and floral motifs seen on seventeenth- and eighteenth-century Dutch pieces. On floors, the harder-wearing equivalent was parquet, *parquet de Versailles* being the most lavish with its use of precious woods and intricacy of pattern. Recently, many painters have been commissioned to paint 'fake' wood floors in patterns somewhere between elaborate marquetry and geometric parquet. Whole new floors of Canadian oak have been laid with invisible joins for the purpose. But common plank floors in reasonable condition look excellent given the same treatment, even when the cracks do show.

Fake marquetry is surprisingly easy to do and it dresses up small floor areas handsomely. Well-varnished and waxed, they last a long time, becoming weathered rather than worn-looking.

Preparation

Spend some time preparing the floor. Remove old tacks, hammer in loose nails and then sand over the boards to get a smooth, clean surface. A manual sander or power sander will do the job well – large machines can now be hired easily. After sanding, vacuum to remove as much dust as possible. Any noticeable holes can then be filled with toning plastic wood.

Method

Depending on the pattern you have chosen, you can either measure out the floor and pencil in the design, or make a template to draw round. When the shapes are clearly marked out, go over them with a sharp Stanley knife, cutting the outlines into the wood to a depth of about 3mm. This is to prevent colour seeping over the boundaries. Use spirit-based wood stains (see suppliers index) to colour in the marquetry. These come in a wide range of colours: light oak or teak, mahogany, Tudor dark oak, or black would give three nicely contrasting tones. Use a pointed brush for the outlines and fill in the rest with a painters' 25mm brush or a rag. Stain all the pieces of one colour first before going on to the next. Stains are best put on in the direction of the grain. If they dry patchily, go over them again.

Leave the floor for a day or two to dry, then vacuum again carefully to remove dust and hairs and give it three coats of eggshell or gloss polyurethane varnish. Begin varnishing in the corner farthest from the door. Thin the first coat with white spirit – about 3 parts varnish to 2 parts spirit – but thin the following coats less. If you sand the second coat of varnish, going with the grain and not rubbing too hard, and then wipe it over, your third coat will feel much silkier. Three coats of varnish is the minimum, and this is adequate on a small floor which does not get tramped over with muddy boots. Graham Carr has given a floor as many as ten coats of varnish. A spray attachment which will take varnish would make this job a lot easier, if available.

LIMED OAK GRAINING:

The neutral but textured look of 'limed oak' is a finish currently much in demand, according to virtuoso grainer Len Pardon. Details of his technique follow for you to try.

Preparation

The wood should be prepared as for marbling, with a white eggshell finish. You will also need steel combs (medium and fine), a sable brush and some rags.

Method

The colour Len uses is made from more or less equal quantities of raw umber, ivory black and Vandyke brown plus about half the total quantity of the other three in burnt umber (that is, 1 part each of the first three to $1\frac{1}{2}$ parts burnt umber). Mix them together with the glaze to make a deepish putty colour. Try it out on a white card to check.

A few painted lines can make all the difference to simply coloured walls. We took this idea from an old Swedish house, and painted the lines – not too precisely – in gouache colour 'fixed' with a little PVA *adhesive.*

Painted grisaille *cartouches, suggestive of carved ornament on French* boiseries, *add interest and prettiness. Here, they also have a practical function concealing a doorway.*

1

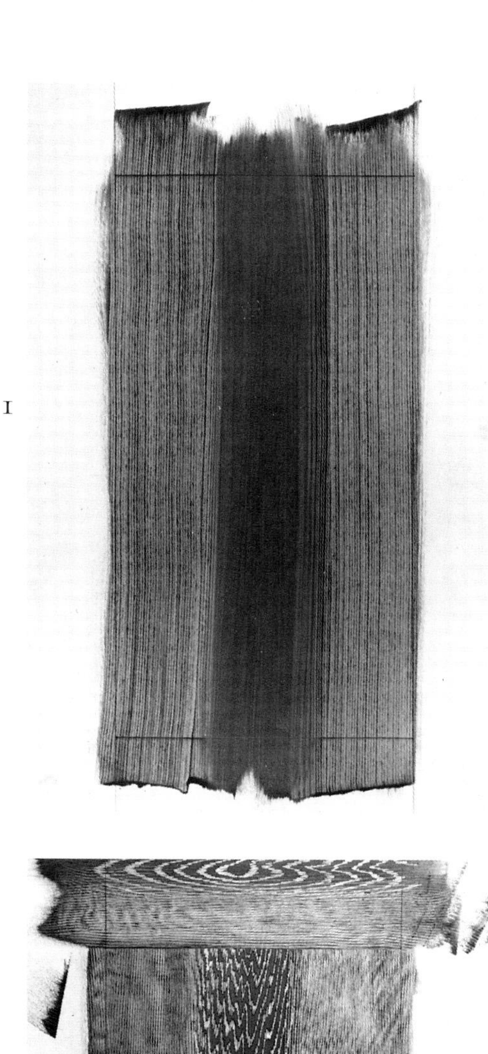

2

3

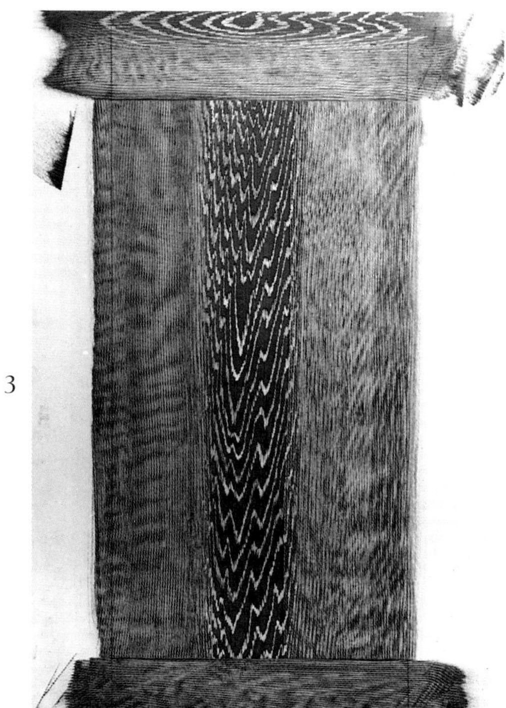

4

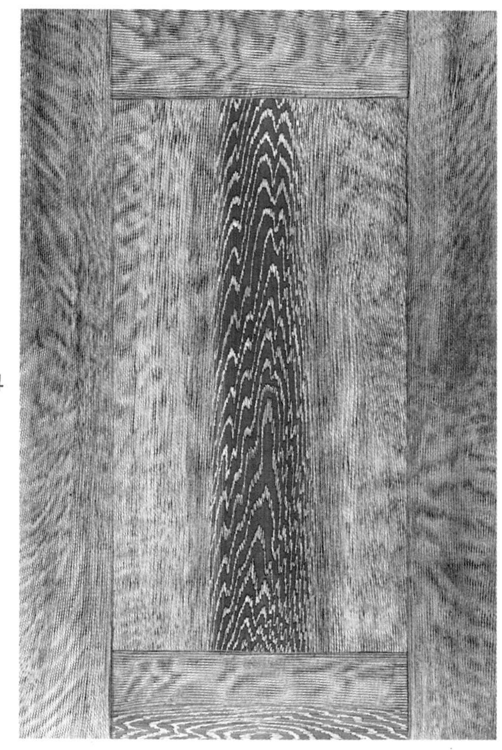

1 *Glaze brushed and combed over a door panel.*

2 *Heartwood being added in the central strip.*

3 *Liming colour applied and rag-combed over the horizontals.*

4 *Vertical stiles brushed and combed as before.*

5 *Completed door with quarterings and more heartwood.*

One of the prettiest examples of fake panels. Silk-ribbon blues in two tones, dragged and outlined in grey and off-white, subdivide a flat wall.

A dressier example of fake panelling, though no more difficult technically. Painted, distressed bands define and dramatize marbled walls in a tiny hallway.

Different ways of organizing surfaces by imposing painted panel shapes. Easiest to do are simple painted lines of varying thicknessess in watery colour. Alternatively, 3-D effects like traditional joinery can be created in monochrome. Dragged, combed or grained effects add texture and verisimilitude. 'Ashlar', or trompe stonework, is a matter of getting the shadows and highlights right, dovetailing where they meet.

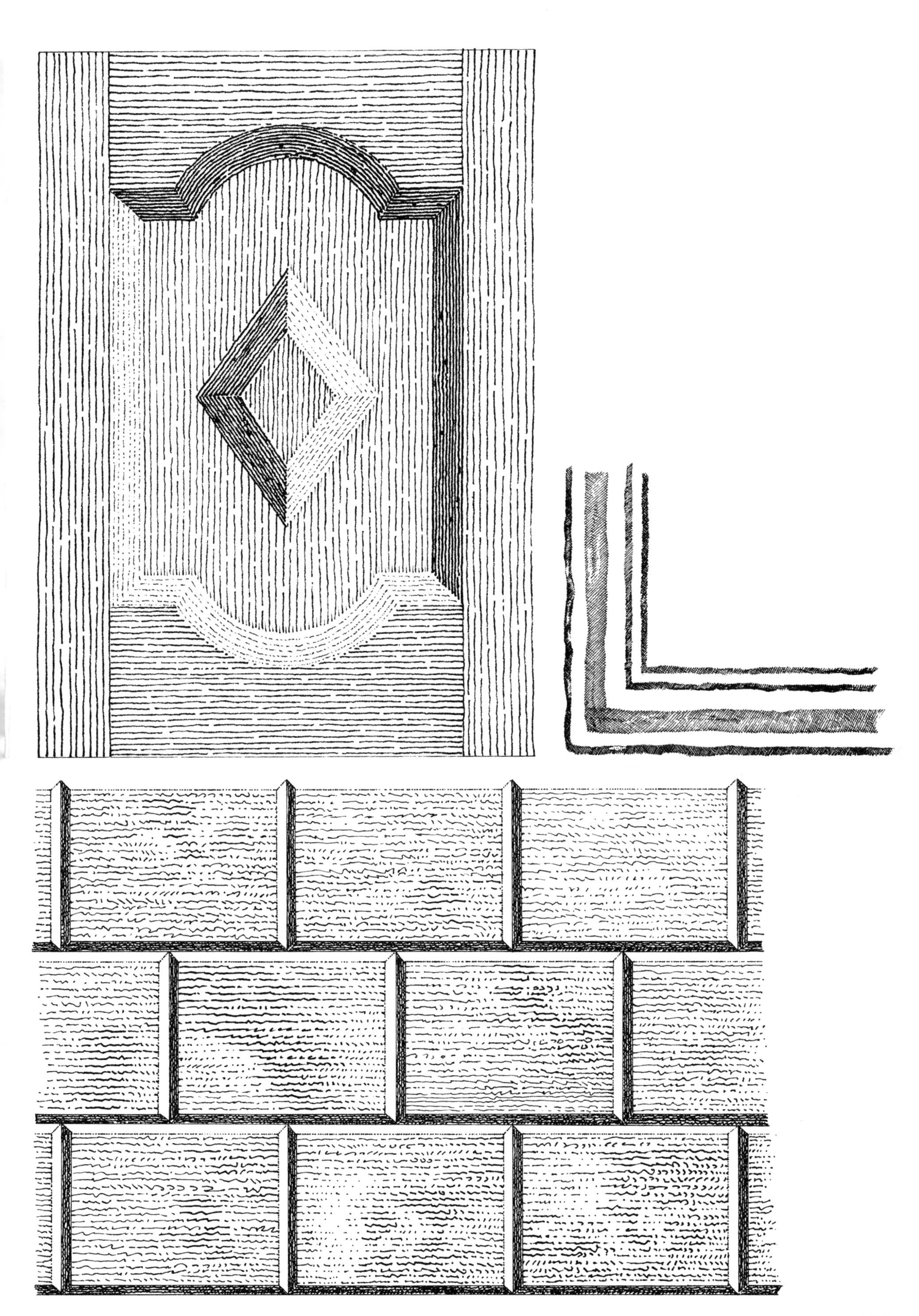

Painted by Stephen Calloway, who taught himself to do these finishes, a marbled architrave and onyx-style decoration on the door panels look dramatic framed in black and white.

Lavishly marbled, a solid wooden architrave takes on new and palatial dimensions.

Paint the door panel by panel or, if it is a long straight piece of wood like a skirting board, grain it section by section. Brush colour evenly over the panel. Stretch a rag tightly over the teeth of a steel comb and draw the wrapped comb, with even pressure, down both sides of the panel, leaving approximately 75mm of darker colour down the middle. Then, using combs without a rag, comb at a slight angle over the rag-combed area, first with a medium, then with a fine comb. Leave the strip down the middle. Using the pointed end of the sable brush, scratch typical oak sap markings in the dark strip of glaze. Hold the brush as if you were drawing or shading. Sapwood has zigzag markings – look at a real piece for guidance.

Quartering, where ripple marks occur across the grain (again, study a real piece of oak), is done differently. Instead of leaving the dark strip, as previously, the whole panel is rag-combed, and then combed again with fine and medium combs, aiming at a clean-looking but slightly more rippled finish. Quartering is done with the sable and the same glaze, warmed a couple of tones with a touch of burnt sienna. Load the brush, but do not make it too wet. Stroke out the excess on a card, then pinch the sable to a chisel shape which lets the colour flow through. Starting at the top, draw out quartered shapes tapering down to a fine line, and then repeat this halfway across the panel. Quartered oak is cut across where the sapwood is formed, and it is the varying rate of growth which creates the fascinating shapes.

FAKE PANELS

Where I live in the East End of London, there are several streets lined with early eighteenth-century houses, whose main rooms are entirely encased in original pine panelling. The rooms have low ceilings for their size, which dip pleasantly here and there. The old panels are full of gaps and cracks but, with the shutters closed, lamps glowing and a fire in the hearth, it would be hard to imagine rooms more delightfully cosy to sit in. Yet for all their simplicity and their oddities, they are effortlessly elegant.

The 'woodiness' of the rooms (some are painted, some stripped) is part of their special charm, but I think the real clue to their effect is their consistent development of a classical notion of good proportion in an eighteenth-century idiom. The panelling is regularly subdivided, with a chair rail running round at approximately door-knob level, echoed by a sturdy wooden cornice above. The strong horizontals that these make are then challenged by the rectangles of the panels above and below the dado, which set up a rhythm just varied enough to be interesting. It may be a trick of the eye, owing to the different planes of the panelling, but all these rooms seem more spacious than they actually are.

To install real wood panelling today would, sadly, be beyond the means of most of us. The appearance of it, however, is so easily suggested with paint that I constantly wonder why more people do not investigate what can be done with a little texture and some elementary trompe l'œil.

It is quite astonishing the difference that even flat painted lines, arranged in panel-like sequences, can make. These fake panel treatments provide a visual framework to which furniture, pictures and so forth can be related. This is particularly helpful when you are trying to make sense of the usual odd assortment of furniture that you tend to start off with in the early stages of setting up home. As soon as these painted divisions appear on the walls, it becomes inevitable that a chest of drawers or a sofa stands centrally beneath and that pictures and lamps are disposed in a logical way to either side, or grouped above.

PAINTED LINES:

The simplest fake panel idea (see p. 132) is purely notional and consists of nothing more than coloured lines painted on the walls like large picture frames. This effect can be deliberately formal and symmetrical, but it would work just as well, I think, with a looser arrangement. The lines here – not mathematically precise, please note – have been painted on freehand with a watery colour. I used gouache with a little PVA binder to prevent trickles, and two brushes: a pointed sable for outlining (you should lightly pencil in outlines beforehand), and a filbert for filling in.

FAKE PANELS WITH STENCILLED OUTLINES:

This effect can look traditionally folksy, or, in sophisticated colours like a dirty grey-green with sepia-coloured stencils, move up market. The 'panels' could be dragged with paint a couple of tones darker than the background colour of the walls, which would be enough to differentiate them. Their shape could be emphasized by a tidy frame of pointed leaves, as exemplified in a design by Graham Carr.

PAINTED PANELS:

The blue showroom at Colefax and Fowler's London offices (see p. 136), looks charming and intimate. This is partly due to the very successful colouring of pale subdued blues, and partly to the straightforwardly painted 'panels'. They give this small, irregularly shaped room character and warmth. Note once again how using darker tones of paint on the panels (which are dragged, as is the background) suggests the varied planes of wood panelling. The three-dimensional effect has been strengthened by adding two paler lines around two sides of each 'panel' and two darker lines round the other two sides. This minimal effect is enough to indicate light and shade, and relief. The dragging is done in the way John Fowler liked it, with a confident brushiness that looks spontaneous and lively in the best hand-painted tradition. If you want your drag painting to look classy, this, rather than the mechanical perfection of printed imitations, is the look to aim for.

False panels need not imitate woodwork. In a small but choice hallway (see p. 137), finished with a subdued, painterly marbling, the lines that dramatize and define the space are brushed on in a deliberately uneven fashion, suggestive of marble inlay, but not too seriously. Note how the effect is carried across the radiator below the shelf. The effect of the larger 'panels', with their curved corners, has a look of lighthearted romanticism without pretentiousness – the essence of John Fowler's style.

6

RESTORATION, DISGUISE,

PAINTING FURNITURE

AND TRANSFORMATION

Painted furniture is presently enjoying a general resurgence of popularity. People are finding that painted pieces fit especially well in the colour- and texture-conscious interiors of today. Paint is also the perfect camouflage for less distinguished furniture – either what the professionals call 'brown' (anything wooden but not antique) or all those purpose-made items in modern materials, which can be turned out cheaply and do not merit a second glance as they stand.

The term 'painted furniture' is vague enough to include anything from a valuable old chest with original painted decoration, to the tawdry pastel-and-gilt bedroom suites still produced for large department stores, or a bedside table or odd chair on which someone has slapped a coat of pink gloss paint. Once your 'eye' is in, it is not difficult to distinguish good from bad. Painted furniture is always worth another look – if it is of period shape and newly-painted, the paint may have been added to smarten up the original paintwork beneath, which can often be uncovered and re-touched.

One of Alex Galitzine's stencilled pieces, a simple old chest decorated with borders and posies in subdued 'old' colours. Above it, a rosemaling hatbox, painted in traditional colours by Ginty Watson.

Buying new painted furniture is expensive because of the man-hours taken to produce a well finished piece. It is a different story if you paint your own. Unless you cost your time, your hand-painted pieces will seem a remarkable bargain. And they can be worked at whenever you feel in the mood – which is not usually the case with a room. It is the ideal way to cut your teeth on the whole business of decorative painting; experimentation is easier, and the smaller scale makes the project less daunting and less tiring.

Restoration

Assuming it is solid and in good repair, a typical piece of 'brown' may only need to have the old finish removed to give a clean surface for paint. It is usually worth having furniture repaired professionally as it is exasperating to lavish time on making a piece look attractive if it functions badly.

If you find crude modern paint concealing an interesting old finish (this usually comes to light in chips and cracks), go carefully. I know someone who started work on a cupboard only to discover that she was rubbing off an original Burne-Jones painting with her wire wool. But modest pieces are often enhanced if you can uncover the original finish. I have been reasonably successful using paint stripper, wiping it away carefully with rags and using it on a small area at a time. Sally Kenny recommends acetone, or nail polish remover. It depends on the type of paint and varnish used originally. Sometimes it is only possible to salvage the hard, smooth priming – gesso in many cases – which painted pieces were given in previous centuries.

Painted detail can be put back – study any surviving decoration carefully first. Unless you are very sure of your brushwork, apply an isolating layer of white shellac – known as white polish – all over. This means you can wipe off mistakes and experiment safely. Make sure it is bleached shellac rather than orange shellac or button polish. These have orange tones that will alter any existing colours. For retouching use a slightly transparent paint (basic glaze with more undercoat and matt varnish than usual) and if in doubt, keep colours muted.

Transformation and disguise

Decorative painting really comes into its own as a means of disguising those useful but uninspiring pieces of furniture. Do not paint mahogany or any fine wood of good colour and markings. Oak is better stained and filled (see limed oak, p. 174) as its open grain looks wrong painted. Paint softwoods, and those spray-lacquered, knotty pieces of deal which look so sparkling when new but turn grey and sad with use. You can also paint kitchen and bathroom fittings or built-in cupboards.

Painted decoration should blend with your existing room. On the whole, special effects should be reserved for furniture that is attractive and interesting enough to play a star role; the best approach with yards of built-in cupboard doors might be to tone them in with the predominant room colour, perhaps breaking up the flatness with a lightly painted 'bamboo' moulding, or a plain line trim. You can have fun painting pieces with carved mouldings or decoration, barley-sugar pilasters, fretwork or knobs; or anything so plain that it can take a chic modern lacquer look, like spatter, for interest.

Preparation, Tools and Materials

The real craft of furniture painting lies in the preparation. While it may be sufficient for walls to look pretty, painted furniture is going to be used and needs to wear and handle well. If you have little time to spend on a piece but must have good results, your best bet is to give it two coats of undercoat tinted grey, dusty cream or snuff colour, and rub the paint down when dry so that the wood just shows through here and there. This way it will look old and worn, rather than the result of a skimped paint job – but it will not last very long.

Strip off any varnish using paint stripper and wire wool (use meths to remove French polish). Old paint need only be stripped if it is badly chipped or wrinkled. Otherwise simply rub the old paint back until smooth with the usual series of coarse, medium and fine grade abrasive papers. On bare wood – old or new – the first coat should be primer; on existing paint it can be undercoat. Any major filling should be done after priming as the primer highlights defects. The raw edges often found on built-in cupboard doors are best filled with a very tough substance such as car body filler and then sanded back until they are hard and smooth. Coarse grain may need overall filling for a really good finish. This is best done with gesso – traditional or acrylic (see p. 78). Professionals brush a coat of shellac, which is fast drying (an hour or less), over the filled and primed surfaces to seal them and stop the next layers of undercoat soaking into the porous filler.

The usual order of events for painting furniture is first primer, then undercoat, two coats of eggshell or flat oil paint, the decoration layer and two more coats of varnish. You should take it as axiomatic that every succeeding coat of paint or varnish, with the exception of the actual decorative ones, is better for being rubbed down. As the finish becomes smoother, the abrasive paper should be finer. On the last coats most professionals use papers lubricated with water (wet-and-dry) or soap to prevent scratching. Faithfully done, this sort of rubbing down produces a hard, smooth, thin but tough finish. A Colefax piece would probably undergo seventeen separate processes before completion, but no-one is obliged to take such pains. It is, however, worth taking some trouble over small, much-handled pieces like boxes or trays.

Since many thin coats produce a better finish than fewer thicker ones, professionals tend to thin most paints and varnishes down a little. Three parts paint or varnish to one part solvent would be about right. Brush with the grain for one coat and across it for the next to prevent brushmarks piling up. If the piece can be worked on in a dust-free environment, you will save time removing grit, dust, hairs and other fall-out which sticks to drying surfaces. You could always make a temporary tent from plastic sheeting.

It also saves time to keep certain brushes for certain jobs: an old brush for primer, a couple of standard brushes in small and medium sizes for undercoat and paint, and a couple of fine-bristled varnish brushes for putting on varnish and shellac. Keep the shellac brush separate and clean it with meths. You will want to add to these for specific tasks: hogs'-hair stencil brushes, a swordliner or lining fitch, a dust brush for dusting and softening, assorted artists' brushes (pointed, filbert or square) for painting different strokes or marks. Other useful tools might include a metal straight-edge knife, a craft knife with square blades, masking tape, lots of disposable foil containers for mixing colours, plus lidded jars for storing surplus glaze. You will also need a supply of lint-free rags.

Paints

As outlined above, for almost all furniture painting you will need primer, oil-based undercoat and varnish. The undercoat can double as top coat when tinted, but a flat white or mid-sheen paint, preferably oil-based, gives a more luxurious finish. Gloss paint is never used in polite circles on furniture except on nursery pieces, and even there it is better to built up a gloss with varnish on top of a mid-sheen or flat paint. If you find exactly

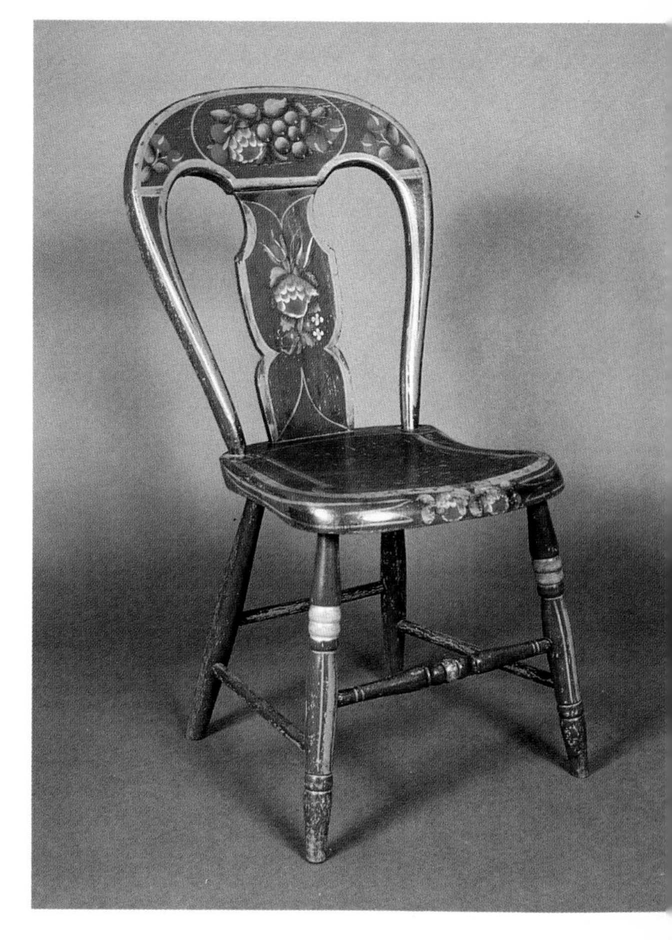

LEFT *An American, nineteenth-century dressing table set. The pale grey base contrasts with the red panels, lined and stencilled in gold in a style reminiscent of Hitchcock's chair decorations.*

RIGHT *One of a set of six, this richly decorated chair is dated 1820. Its croting and lavish yellow stripes bear a strong resemblance to the floral motifs of rosemaling pieces.*

LEFT ABOVE *Dated 1785, a Pennsylvanian dower chest painted with favourite folk motifs – hearts, tulips and vases – in traditional folk colours of red on blue.*

LEFT BELOW *Wonderfully vigorous and vivid, American folk graining at its best. The rope shapes are putty-grained in red with black loops on a white ground – proof that decoration can be technically easy but very stylish.*

the colour you want in a commercial range, buy that, but most professionals stock up on white paint and tint up their colours from these for each job. For dark colours, start with a commercial colour close to the shade, and modify with stainers or artists' oils.

Orange shellac and white polish are essential. There are various commercial glaze products, any one of which would do for furniture painting, or you can make up your own (see p. 47). Dead flat, extra pale varnish is very useful for adding to glazes as well as finishing non-shiny pieces. You will also need a gloss varnish. Clear polyurethane is easily available and quite tough; for really hardwearing surfaces use yacht varnish. Varnishes from the same product range can be intermixed to get just the degree of shine you want.

The above represents a basic paint kit for most purposes. Anything required specifically for a particular finish will be listed under that heading. Two other paints that you might find useful are red oxide metal primer (this is a cheap, handsome brown-red, which must be varnished to seal its 'tender' texture) and matt blackboard paint. This makes a useful black base but, like the red oxide, needs varnishing or waxing to give a surface – add a little brown or blue tint to the varnish to make the black more interesting.

Gesso

Gesso has been used for centuries to prime panels and to build up a flawless surface on furniture that is to be painted. In effect a surface primed with gesso has been covered with a very hard, fine skin of plaster. Despite the fact that preparing gesso is a bother, and handling it requires practice and judgement, the traditional form is still used in places like the Colefax and Fowler studio for fleshing out the ply and softwood used to make many small occasional pieces (see p. 78 for full details on making gesso).

For the amateur having fun with a few pieces, there is an effective modern substitute – acrylic gesso. This dries swiftly and needs no heating or mixing. It can be rubbed down to produce a surface almost as hard and uniform in texture as traditional gesso. But the old fashioned sort works out a lot cheaper.

Use a wide, thin varnishing brush to apply gesso. Six coats will build up a perfectly smooth surface, but with practice you can reduce the number to four, and for furniture priming fewer still may be adequate. Gesso is excellent for filling the surface of any open-grained wood before painting – the sort of wood that shows through as a finely ridged or crackled texture under endless coats of paint. Use fine grades of sandpaper for smoothing off the gesso. A final ivory smoothness is achieved by rubbing it over firmly, in a steady circular movement, with a soft old piece of sheet wrung out in water and folded into a smooth pad. Keep the pressure even, and do not linger too long in one spot because this smoothing is actually dissolving the top layer of gesso and spreading it out evenly. Before painting over gesso with oil paints it should be sealed with a coat of diluted shellac. Bear in mind that you are working with a transparent colour that cannot be painted out, so either stick to a simple effect or be prepared to shellac and paint it over if it goes wrong. Another possibility is to tint the gesso itself with gouache or powder colour, and finish with wax. Gesso takes a fine burnish.

Acrylic gesso is painted on in exactly the same way, and rubbed with fine abrasive paper until smooth. When rubbing down edges which have been gessoed, go carefully because they will be brittle and could chip off. If this happens, use a standard filler to patch them.

Since gesso acts as a primer, you start painting on it (after the shellac) with undercoat, and then go on to the usual oil-based paints. A gessoed surface is magnificent to paint on.

PAINTED FINISHES

All the decorative finishes used on walls can be transferred to furniture and look very attractive. The method is the same, so I will merely suggest some combinations which always work and look good.

DRAGGING:

Dragging, which is both neat and fine, is a formal finish which suits elegant furniture. Dragging over white (preferably off-white) gives subdued pastels, while dragging one colour over another can create wonderfully vibrant or subtle final shades. Dragging should follow the grain of the wood itself, travelling lengthways across table tops and drawer fronts, down table legs and dividing on frames, as on a door. Use a varnish brush to drag furniture, and the usual glaze, though it may look better slightly thinner. You could try artist Owen Turville's suggestion of dragging Plaka water paints, possibly adding Plaka medium for thickening. The only trim a dragged piece needs is lining – a thick and thin combination looks best – around drawer fronts, on table tops and so on.

STIPPLING:

Stippling gives furniture the same rich velvety bloom as it does walls. It is subtle, almost invisible except in close-up, but it makes a distinct overall contribution. Almost any strong dark colour on furniture looks better stippled. I also like it as a background to stencilling, tightened up with contrasting lines, or wide lines in the same colour. Stippling in a good colour will give any tacky furniture, provided you prepare it nicely, a new look of elegance.

SPONGING:

Sponging looks great in a strong colour, applied quite sparingly over a large, simple piece like a dresser or cupboard. It would be fun repeated over kitchen unit fronts too. In different colours, like peach and cream, tightly sponged prints could redeem every surface in a bathroom or bedroom. But please, if you have a decorative finish on the outside of cupboard doors, carry it over on the inside as well. Nothing looks meaner than opening a sleek, fancied-up door to be confronted with a bare blank inner face. Small details like these add a great deal of class.

SPATTERING:

Spattering on furniture is easier than on walls because you can take the item in question outside, where no masking off is needed. I find spattering goes nicely over sponging. If I want to finish a piece so that it tones with a room scheme or fabric using more than one colour, I might sponge it over fairly coarsely with the main colour. Then I would spatter on the others, plus a white or cream coat to soften, or a black one to sharpen it, until I liked the effect. The usual detail on this, too, is a lining trim, in the darker shade used. A spattered effect which suits spare modern pieces is achieved by pasting scraps of paper onto a dark base in a random fashion. The whole piece should then be spattered in toning colours. If you use dark grey as a base, spatter in granite colours – white, pale grey, black. When the paper is torn off, the shapes appear as abstract patterns.
It looks very lively, especially when given a deep, ultra-smooth, lacquer type finish.

Build up abstract patterns by pasting torn paper onto a coloured painted ground, and then spattering in toning shades. Removing some scraps at different stages gives varying degrees of contrast.

"Susan Williams used to run the Colefax and Fowler London studio with great verve, but she has since left to set up as a decorative painter on her own. Before her three and a half years at Colefax she did an art school training. A formidably competent young woman, and a perfectionist in her own line, she understands the complexities of her trade thoroughly – the sort of colour a client has in mind when they talk about a sharp yellow, how much 'lining' a piece can take and what paint to use, whether graining would look better done in oil or watercolour, how to achieve a good effect quickly. She is, in other words, that rare breed – a highly-trained, experienced and unflappable craftsperson.

Furniture painting and decorating at Susan's level tends to be a slow business, with most of the time being spent on preparation. Ten separate processes go into a standard, run-of-the-mill piece, but as many as seventeen may be necessary on a special item. A typical piece might start with primer, followed by gesso and filling. Then it will be rubbed down and given a coat of white polish, followed by undercoat and two coats of eggshell. A dragged glaze finish might be used together with any special decorating effects, followed by a thin coat of varnish. Finally, contrast lining might be added and then probably more varnish, a final smooth-over and perhaps a coat of wax.

A Colefax training encourages intelligent experimentation, and Susan has scores of less orthodox solutions tucked under that smooth head-girl appearance. For instance: 'If you are in a hurry with a piece, it is sometimes better to go for an effect which looks like a once-good finish that is now somewhat battered. A nice effect for some old wooden pieces simulates ebonizing, worn away at the edges and on the moulding. You just apply a couple of coats of matt black paint, and then wax the piece with fine steel wool, rubbing it down to the wood here and there, achieving a good sheen all over.' In the same spirit she suggests lining with a gold felt-tip pen. 'You can cut the tip with a scalpel to the shape you want. It doesn't look like real gold, but it makes a decorative effect and it is quite tough. I would just wax it over to protect it.'

Much of her decorative work is done with Liquitex acrylic colours, a technique she learnt at Colefax. 'You can get pearly colours with watercolour paints which you don't find with oils.' She

has used these for graining very grand bookcases in a burr maple finish, for dragging false panels in a soft terracotta, on furniture, and small knick-knacks. Adding acrylic medium, she says, delays drying long enough to create a distressed finish, providing you work fast. One discovery of Susan's is Dulux Weathershield, which she finds a very satisfactory paint to work with indoors. It has a fresco-like texture when thinned down, and is not gritty like many exterior paints. For graining she sometimes uses three worn-down brushes stuck to a piece of cardboard with masking tape. This gives an effect that is not too regular, or – a bogey word at Colefax – 'mechanical'.

She never has trouble mixing or matching colours, to which I can testify having watched her repeat a chintz fabric motif down to the slightest nuance of shading on a pair of painted lamp bases. She gave me the formula of the famous Colefax sharp yellow without even a pause for thought: a stock yellow undercoat, followed by a glaze of lemon chrome, raw sienna, raw umber and black. Raw umber and a tiny amount of black are present in almost all the firm's famously appealing colours. 'That started with John Fowler, I think. He liked raw umber with everything, and a little bit of black goes in as a matter of course.'

When hiring new painters for the studio, she went for people with some craft enthusiasm, like patchwork, or drying flowers, rather than those with art school qualifications. 'It takes a special sort of person to be able to paint the same little flower-stand or table a dozen times in a row, listening to *The Archers* on the radio, and doing each one as well as the one before.'

Her training method was simply to paint an item once, as a demonstration, and then let the class loose on a piece – having first sealed the surface with varnish so that errors could be wiped off. 'A new painter might do the same piece five times or more – and still get it wiped off again at the end of it all. But it is really the only way to learn. Doing it for "real" teaches you more about the whole business of decorating furniture than practising away on a board.' ❞

LINING

Painting a decorative line trim on a painted surface in one swift economical movement is a difficult trick to master. The experts agree that the only way to become a proficient liner is to equip yourself with a lining fitch, or a sword-liner, and a suitable thinned paint (basic glaze) and just practise on a smooth prepared board until you gain confidence. The special brush enables you to take up enough paint on the long bristles to allow quite a long line to be painted without needing to re-charge the brush. Well-painted lines add definition and a certain professionalism to a painted piece. But for those who just want to smarten up a painted table-top or box there are easier ways of getting an effect that is almost as good. Sally Kenny has never been able to master the lining technique, so she has devised various dodges which she passes on to you:

1) With a steel rule or straight-edge and a sharp scalpel blade, score the paint surface – lightly but enough to show – with two parallel lines as far apart as the desired width of your line. Then draw your sword-liner along and you will find that the paint stays inside the 'tracks'.
2) Use a felt pen, in a suitable thickness, and a ruler. Once varnished over or shellacked, this will look fine to anyone but a hawk-eye from the Colefax studio.
3) To line in negative, buy a role of 'pin' striping used on car bodies, stick that down, paint as usual, then peel off at the end to reveal a slick line of base colour.

Lines usually look best painted in a slightly transparent paint, expecially if they are more than a couple of millimetres thick. A little matt varnish, or indeed any varnish, helps the colour to flow smoothly. Alternatively, you could try the egg tempera mixture used by Leonard Lassalle (see p. 111).

VINEGAR GRAINING

Although you can use vinegar to imitate genuine wood grains of the bolder sort – oyster walnut, for example – it has a life of its own once you get started, and the random effects that can be made with a mere lump of putty are just as decorative. This is definitely a finish to have fun with, and can be used on a small-scale to enliven a bold, simple piece of furniture, or perhaps even on a large-scale for fake panelling. I vinegar-grained a cheap, self-assemble pine chair recently, and the transformation process took just three to four minutes' work. If you pay attention to the basic preparation, as I am always urging, and varnish carefully and well, your dresser, chest or chair will look like a collector's piece.

Colourways

The red oxide paint mentioned on p. 150 is ideal as a base colour for certain effects. A rich ochre yellow would look good too. Or, if you want to be different, black graining on grey would look dramatic.

Materials

To make the graining mixture, use powder pigments dissolved in standard malt vinegar, and add a little sugar (about 1 teaspoonful per $\frac{1}{2}$ litre) to help make it stick. The old provincial American grainers who used this domestic glaze tried all sorts of pattern-making tools – fans of pleated paper, dried corn cobs, crumpled paper and corks. You might like to experiment, too, but to start with the only other material you will need is a good lump of putty, kneaded and rolled into a cylinder for long, radiating shapes, or broken into stumps for stamping with.

Method

Dissolve your colour, vinegar and sugar together thoroughly. Try the mixture on a leg – it can be wiped off again easily with a damp cloth. The mixture will not coat the surface absolutely evenly, but it should more or less cover it. Once your mixture is right, brush it over one area of the piece at a time. Leave it to set for a minute or two, then begin making shapes with the putty. By stamping or rolling the surface, a wonderful variety of effects can be achieved, from complex spiralling shapes to seaweed-like blobs. Fan shapes can be created in the corners and circles in the middle of panels or drawers, with stamped shapes filling the spaces. It is one of those effects that should be spontaneous rather than laboured but try to take the shape of the piece into consideration. It only takes a minute to get the feel of this finish. As the graining mixture dries it will lose its sparkle, like a drying pebble. Do not worry – a coat of varnish or white polish will revive this at once.

ANTIQUING

Used in moderation, antiquing is a cunning device for dulling the brashness of new paint, softening decoration and ground colours into each other and suggesting something of the subtle patination that appears on a surface with time and use. The problem with this decorative trickery is that it is so quick and easy, and so immediately effective, that people do not always know when to stop as a quick look round the bedroom furnishing section of any large store will show you. Scrubbing burnt sienna glaze over the mouldings and into the cracks of your ivory-painted suite, so that it looks as though it had been dipped in treacle, is not the look to aim for. Sublety is the watchword.

Method

You can begin with the actual colours used to decorate the piece. Adding a little raw umber to most colours gives that slightly dusty, shadowed effect which makes colours look old. If this is not enough, try sponging over the whole piece with a thin wash of raw umber acrylic colour. As well as taking the other colours down a tone or so, it will settle into surface paint as darker flecks, which look natural and old. If using acrylic as a wash over oil paints, you can rub the colour in quite hard, repeating the process until you get the degree of duskiness you want. Raw umber dulls without dirtying, but it gives a cooler cast. For a warmer tone use burnt sienna in the same way, or a mixture of burnt sienna and raw umber. A spot of black can be tried too. But remember to use a light hand, and try the effect on the back of the piece or a leg until you are sure you have got it right. A final dodge is the addition of a little colour to the last coats of varnish, which thus become final layers of tinted transparent paint. Again, do not over-do it – the piece must not look *dirty*. Then gently rub down the second coat with wet-and-dry paper or fine steel wool to thin it here and there, which gives the surface a more natural appearance.

These are fast ways of cheating at an aged look. The slower, more controllable method is to mix up a glaze with raw umber and maybe a dot of burnt sienna. Brush this on, leave it for a few minutes until it is just beginning to set up, and then go over it with a rag, rubbing it away harder on the raised areas and the centre of panels and leaving more in cracks, carvings, and wherever dust might have naturally accumulated. Leave this to dry, and then cover the whole piece with matt varnish.

Powdered pumice or rottenstone (obtainable from cabinetmakers' suppliers) can be mixed into an antiquing glaze, which then takes on a dusty sheen.

TOP LEFT *'Before', 'after' and 'in-between' – three views of a cheap but sturdy chair which was painted with red oxide metal primer, then vinegar-grained, varnished and waxed. A finish with great possibilities.*

ABOVE *Two different ways with a cheap mass-produced table; overall stencilling for a contemporary look, stencils in metallic powders on black for a more classic effect.*

TOP RIGHT *David Linley and Matthew Rice mix natural wood colours with carefully controlled stained veneers for their range of elegant marquetry pieces inspired by Venetian vignettes.*

ABOVE *Using ferns as templates, and stippling in near-black over bare blond wood, this magnificent effect can be produced quite easily.*

FRENCH POLISHING

French polishing was originally developed as a finish for high-class furniture made of wood. In skilled hands it brought up the colour and figurings beautifully, as well as creating a deep, flawless sheen. Though its skilled application is still chiefly reserved for fine wooden pieces, it has a useful role as a relatively fast but impressively professional finish on painted surfaces. It should not be used on table-tops, or areas which might get wet, because damp produces cloudy marks on the shellac. Essentially, the technique allows many successive coats of fast-drying shellac to be superimposed quickly, without brushmarks, the polish being rubbed on with a 'fadge' or rubber. When polishing painted pieces, use white polish because this will not alter the decorating colours.

Method

To make a fadge, take a section of cotton wool, pour polish onto it, wrap it in a square of linen – linen is lint-free – and press it onto a piece of board to distribute the polish and work off the excess. Then dab a little linseed oil onto the base of the fadge to prevent it sticking.

Spread the polish evenly over the entire surface of the piece, and keep the fadge moving the whole time. The movements for applying it are ritualized, so practise them mentally before starting. For the first coat of polish, cover the surface in overlapping circular strokes, sweeping on and off the surface at the start and finish. Immediately afterwards, go over the surface again with figure-of-eight strokes. The last coat uses straight strokes, travelling in the direction of the grain beneath. Leave this coat to set up for about half an hour. You should apply four or five coats, allowing the shellac to harden at intervals. The piece should then be left for a day or more to harden thoroughly.

The last thing to be done to a French-polished surface is to remove any traces of linseed oil. Do this by dabbing the fadge in methylated spirits, and then rubbing it in straight strokes over the polished surface. If the meths dries out, add more. After a few minutes repeat this 'spiriting off'. If you want a real mirror finish, a special burnishing agent can be rubbed on, and you should follow the maker's instructions. For a duller finish, rub over the whole surface with the finest grade of wire wool dipped in furniture wax. In both cases, the final task is to buff the surface with a soft lint-free cloth.

For rubbing down French-polished surfaces in between sessions, use silicon carbide paper in a very fine grade.

GILDING

Water gilding, that is, real gold leaf floated onto clay bole, is gold at its most radiant. It is not really for amateurs, however; if you want that quality of gilding you should take a course in the craft. The expert consensus seems to be that amateurs achieve the best effects using transfer leaf. Applying transfer leaf is straightforward. The clever part comes when you apply certain chemicals to it afterwards to tarnish, discolour or slightly pit the surface, which dulls its garishness, ages it, and makes it look altogether more convincing. The degree of discolouration is optional – if you watch the process, you can wash off the chemical when you reach an effect you like.

Materials

Transfer leaf comes in various colours: Dutch metal is the nearest to gold; there is also silver and aluminium. The fine metal leaves are backed by waxy paper. Scraps of leaf 'skewings' can be used for patching, or for decorative finishes (see p. 165). Gold size, used for sticking down the gilding, is like a yellowy shellac – buy the fast-drying variety. Gilding looks better if you apply it over a coloured base, imitating the traditional clay bole bases for water gilding – Venetian red for gold, blue for silver and yellow ochre for either.

Method

The paint surface should be as smooth as you can make it, whether we are talking about a picture frame, a small stencil to be applied to a table-top, or bands of gilding on a turned chair back. Brush size carefully, in a good light, over the areas where you want to stick the leaf. Fast-drying size is usually ready in an hour, but check the instructions and test by touching it lightly – it should be just tacky, not sticky or wet. Then, picking up a sheet of transfer leaf, press it leaf-side down onto the size and rub it firmly from the back with your fingers. When you peel off the waxy paper, the leaf will remain with shreds hanging off. Leave these for now, and carry on over all the sized areas. You need to work fast to catch the size before it gets too dry. Finally, smooth down the leaf with cotton wool, removing all loose shreds. Any bad 'skips' will need patching – if the size is already too dry, apply more.

'PATINATING' ON METAL LEAF :

Most of these chemicals come in crystal form, so be careful of splashes when mixing up. Wear rubber gloves to prevent staining, wash off spills and work in a well ventilated room. Sally Kenny suggests using these chemical compounds over metal leaf, silver particularly, to suggest age and create a more interesting surface.

To tarnish silver leaf use potassium permanganate mixed with distilled water. Potassium sulphate mixed with distilled water will tarnish silver to an opalescent finish. Copper nitrate mixed with ammonium chloride and distilled water in the

Two methods of applying gold through stencils. Transfer leaf is most easily applied over designs previously stencilled with a mixture of gold size and a little colour. Metal powders are more tidily applied through the stencil itself onto a previously sized base to prevent seeping.

Hand-painted fabric in the form of cushions. Owen Turville painted all these with acrylic colours on calico or silk, sizing the cloth first with dilute acrylic medium. Some artists use Florentine, or Eliza Turck's fabric painting medium.

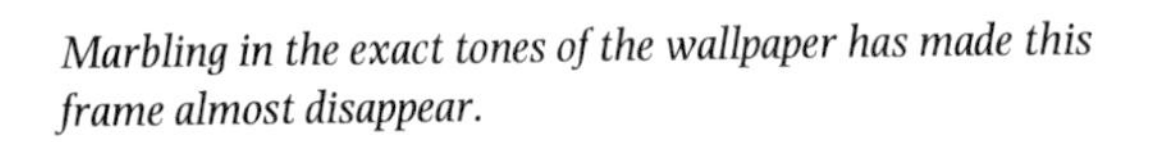

Marbling in the exact tones of the wallpaper has made this frame almost disappear.

This frame has been finished in porphyry spatter, while the tulips have been painted in tempera colour onto silk shantung in the style of nineteenth-century botanical painters.

This was an octagon of plain ply before painter Mark Ram turned it into a chinoiserie fantasy with a finish like old lacquer.

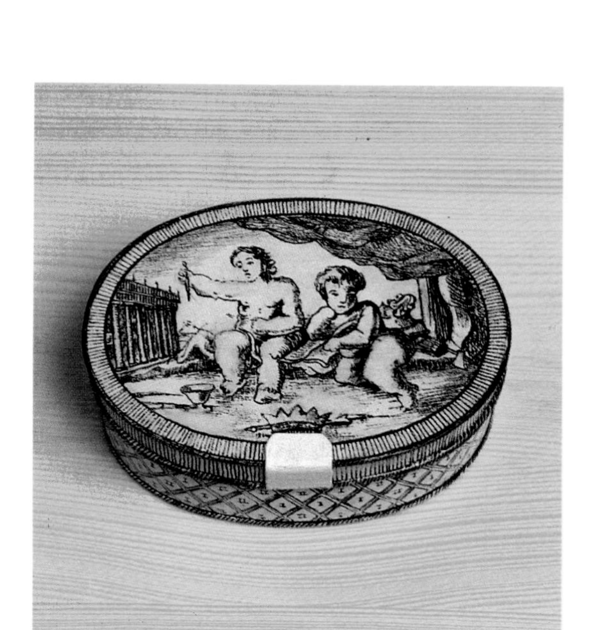

Old penwork pieces are so decorative they are immensely sought after today. Materials are simple: pen and ink. I did this little box as a holiday task.

Crackleglaze produces a complex decorative finish, like craquelure *on porcelain, or fine snakeskin. Plain tables can be transformed with this delicate finish.*

ratio of 1 part water to ½ part each of the chemicals will give metals a greenish, pitted look. Brush on the chemical you have chosen, wait until you see the right degree of reaction, then remove the chemical by flooding the surface gently with more distilled water and gently wiping it with cotton wool.

STENCILLING

Stencilling is a simple, attractive way of dramatizing or personalizing a piece of painted furniture. Stencilling on furniture is done in exactly the same way as stencilling on walls, or floors (see pp. 94–111, 126). The only point to emphasize is that when done on a small scale it needs to be more crisply and meticulously finished. The creative challenge comes in finding (or making) stencils appropriate to a particular piece, and in working out colours and an arrangement of motifs which underline its character and shape.

Stencilling in the folk style inspired by the Early American school looks best on simple pieces with a rustic air – dressers, blanket boxes, kitchen bits and pieces, or furniture for a child's room. Pre-cut stencils in this style are quite widely available. One mistake that people sometimes make is to go for too many colours, an over-naturalistic approach. This can look twee and fussy. Many old stencilled pieces were in fact painted in a limited colour range on dark or sludgy background colours. It is the *shapes* the stencil creates that make the decorative impact. For a sense of how such motifs would have been used one cannot do better than look through books on folk art (see bibliography) or at actual examples, like the ones in the American Museum at Claverton Manor near Bath. Old stencil motifs often seem vulgarized in modern interpretations because shiny paint has been used. They look most attractive when painted with a dry-looking matt paint over a lightly distressed background colour.

Alex Galitzine is a professional stenciller and decorative painter who especially enjoys working on furniture. She is a self-taught painter, disproving the notion that special training is essential. The actual stencilling of a piece takes her next to no time, but she may spend days thinking out the design if she is not working to a deadline. Her painting idiosyncrasy is to use tiny Humbrol enamel colours, of which she has a huge stock, for all her decorative work. Her affection for these enamels first began when she used them to paint chinoiserie-style pieces. They come in matt and gloss forms, and with these she can get virtually any effect she wants.

As stencilling adapts itself to more sophisticated furniture, it usually becomes more abstract. You have only to compare the stylized tulips in Mary MacCarthy's marquetry stencils with a folksy basket of tulips to see what I mean. On the richly-coloured pieces designed by William Morris's workshop, or the Victorian architect William Burges, stencils play an important but subordinate role, creating dense areas of continuous pattern surrounding painted panels.

Stencils for this sort of continuous pattern will have to be made yourself. Textiles, old and new, are an obvious source of ideas. The design I stencilled on a cheap coffee table as a demonstration piece was taken from one of the Victoria and Albert Museum's many Indian fabric printing blocks. The table is stencilled in a very straightforward style in inky-blue onto a greyish-yellow (see p. 156). Acrylics are good for an awkward object like a table as they dry so fast that there is no risk of smudging as you turn it round or upside down. Felicity Binyon and Liz McFarlane swear by Keep's Intenso colours for sign-writers, which are also fast drying. Stencilled finishes like these are adaptable: they can be used as discreet elaboration on a handsomely-shaped piece, or, conversely, they can make a mass-produced item look well-behaved enough

for company, yet unobtrusive. You can break up the patterning with solid-coloured mouldings, or ovals and circles (on top of a table, for instance) outlined by a fine line in the same colour.

GILDED STENCILS

Stencilling in gold looks effective if you do not overdo it. It can be done with transfer gold leaf, or with metal powders, onto fast drying gold size. I find it helps to give the surfaces a coat of shellac or varnish before adding gold, especially in the case of powders which infiltrate everywhere.

Method

Stencil the shapes onto the piece with the size, which should be tinted first with oil colour – this will help you to see where you have stencilled. When it is just tacky, with the stencil in place as before, press down your sheets of transfer leaf and peel off the backing. Cut the sheets close to the size of your stencil if it is small, and overlap them if it is large. Dull the gaudiness of new, metallic leaf by shading areas with a burnt sienna tinted glaze or adding lines in Indian ink – or both.

Metal powders look pretty if you dapple their colours a little, adding copper or silver to gold or bronze. The effect is much softer than transfer leaf. Use something like the foam applicators sold with eyeshadows to pick up the powder and press it onto the gold size. Do not overload the applicator, go slowly and for goodness' sake don't sneeze. You may find it tidier to apply the metallic powders through the stencil cut-outs, pressing the card down to stop it seeping underneath. When you have powdered all the stencilled areas, leave it to set for an hour. Then carefully rub off anything that has settled on the varnished surface with a damp cloth. Metallic powder sticks very firmly over size. Tidy up edges with the original paint colour.

ABOVE *A small, all-over stencil taken from a fabric block, this can be built up to cover an entire piece (see p. 156).*

BELOW *Birds, flowers and butterflies – perennially popular stencil subjects, can be combined in all sorts of different ways.*

PENWORK

Penwork decoration can be done to great effect on quite a large scale as well as on small boxes, trays, frames, drawer fronts or inset panels and knick-knacks. On a large scale it is undoubtedly time consuming – it takes months to achieve some sensational effects – but the result might well be an heirloom. Sources for most of these black and white designs are traditionally engravings and pattern books of classical ornament, but the technique is open to all kinds of new interpretations.

Wood and metal are equally suitable surfaces to work on. A few coats of gesso (see p. 150) make an excellent base on both materials. Metal, however, should first be cleaned of all rust and given a coat of metal primer. The gesso should be sealed with white polish or orange shellac giving an ivory or straw-coloured base respectively.

The only equipment I use for penwork is indelible Indian ink and a selection of mapping pens, which give suitably fine lines. On a larger piece, pens with slightly broader nibs would be useful. Having chosen my design elements, for example a classical scene set in a decorative border (see p. 161), I rough it out on the surface (attempt one face of a box at a time) in fine pencil lines. Then I just leap in with my pen and ink, reproducing the original with a wealth of fine detail, shading and cross-hatching in the manner of old engravings. You may be a bit anxious at first about making mistakes, but practice soon makes for confidence. Mistakes can sometimes be very delicately wiped off with a cotton bud dipped in meths, or touched out with Tippex, but on the whole I think it looks better to try and incorporate them into the design. As one surface is completed, seal it with more white polish to protect it while you tackle the next. Lining is best done using Sally Kenny's easy method, that is, with scored 'tracks'.

For pieces which are liable to get wet, a clear eggshell varnish, applied with a varnish brush and rubbed down sensitively with wet-and-dry paper used with water, gives a very strong finish. Apply two coats of varnish before you begin rubbing down in case you cut back to the decoration.

SPECIAL EFFECTS (see pp. 168–9)

Sally Kenny is a young Australian decorative painter who started learning her trade early – her antique-dealer father asked her to 'have a go' at restoring pieces when she was still a child. Sally's boxes, shown here, are painted to show clients the range of her special effects. She spends many evenings happily experimenting on what were originally a job lot of crystallized fruit boxes. Marbling is her speciality and she stresses the importance of looking at real examples.

MALACHITE:

Materials

This is a very simple finish, though it may not look like it. The base is a commercial colour – Dulux Tourmaline Green – in a mid-sheen finish. The glaze is made up of 70% Ratcliffe Glaze tinted with viridian artists' oil colour (to which a speck of ultramarine and yellow ochre may be added for variety), and 30% white spirit. A little matt varnish will speed up the drying process.

Method

Coat the surface liberally with glaze and dab with a soft cotton cloth. Tear a piece of card from a Kleenex box or cereal carton and fold it, making a fuzzy, uneven edge along the fold line. Using this as a tool, bring it down gently in one corner of the surface and make characteristic malachite stripes, some straight and long, some round. Cover most of the area, making different-sized shapes. Spin a small, worn, stubby brush (No. 6) here and there to make small circles, and stipple in darker areas. Then soften the whole surface with a rag, radiating out from the centre and travelling in one direction to give movement to the shapes. When it has dried, apply varnish followed by French polish and then wax.

WALNUT:

Method

As for malachite, except that the finish is done with a brown glaze – burnt umber, black and a little burnt sienna – over a putty-coloured base. The shapes are defined with a piece of torn cardboard, and details are added in the same way as for malachite.

AGATE:

Method

Round a white centre, draw in lines with a thin, pointed brush in earth colours, ranging from raw sienna through burnt sienna to dark burnt umber and black. Agate shapes should never be left with ragged edges, but should be gently softened sideways at right angles to the striations. The white centre can have swirls spun with a stubby brush to represent crystallization.

ROSEWOOD GRAINING:

Method

Over a shell-pink eggshell base brush a smooth coat of glaze, tinted with burnt sienna, burnt umber and a touch of rose madder. Leave until the glaze is half-dry – just tacky enough to be moved by the brush – and then draw striped grain patterns across, dipping the brush tip into a mixture of burnt umber and black. The stripes will merge with the base paint as it dries. If you want a more tigerish effect, add black stripes when the first coat is dry. Finally, apply varnish, or French polish and wax.

NATIVE GOLD:

Method

A pale blue-grey base is dabbed with a variety of glaze colours – coral (made with white, lemon yellow and rose madder), pale green and light grey. Rag the glazes in order to soften the colours, and then let them dry. Paint the desired shapes in quick-drying gold size. Pick up crumpled scraps or 'skewings' of Dutch metal transfer leaf and dab them onto the wet size. Then pat flat with cotton wool. Using a little coloured varnish, vary the tones of the gold skewings, making some warm, some cool or dark. When dry, spatter all over with three tones of grey. The last coat of French polish can be spirited out and the surface burnished with steel wool.

RED AND GOLD:

Method

This finish must be done on a horizontal, level surface. The base should be a vivid poppy-red eggshell. The glaze (70% glaze to 30% white spirit) is tinted with vermillion, crimson and rose madder, and sponged on for a mottled effect. It should be softened slightly. Sprinkle copper, pale gold and silver metallic powders randomly into the wet glaze. Then, with a brush, drop a little white spirit carefully into the glaze. It will create roundels as it spreads. Emphasize with colour when the surface dries. Varnish and rub down.

LAPIS LAZULI:

Method

The ground should be gilded with Dutch metal transfer leaf. Mix up glazes in ultramarine, a little Indian red, mid-grey, raw sienna and white. Cover most of the ground with blue, leaving some vein-like areas. Then add white and grey veinings, some stippled white flecks and then soften a little. Add some well-thinned raw sienna, diluted copiously with white spirit so that it spreads gently. For variety, tap this on from a height. Let it dry, varnish it, and then apply French polish and burnish.

TORTOISESHELL:

Method

Using a sea sponge dab straw-coloured paint onto a white base to give a mottled effect. The colours Sally uses for markings are burnt umber, black, and burnt and raw sienna. She puts in the markings with a soft brush, beginning with the palest: largish patches of raw sienna, softened, are overlaid with warmer brown markings made with a little burnt sienna and burnt umber, overlapping some of the first patches. Soften. Over these still smaller markings are added in black mixed with burnt umber, keeping mostly within the previous patches. Some dark colour should be flicked on in the lighter areas. The whole surface is lightly softened to blur the shapes into each other, but not so much that the edges appear frayed. Sally created the white banding on her tortoiseshell box, which looks like ivory inlay, by sticking pin-striping straight onto the base coat before painting and finally French polishing the box. She then removed the striping, leaving a pale indented line. Polish once to seal.

BASIC SIENNA MARBLE:

Method

This finish has an orangey cast, 'like old clock faces'. It is painted on a white eggshell ground. Two tones of yellow are mixed, one using raw sienna and a touch of orange in basic glaze, the other cadmium and raw sienna, also in glaze. These colours are brushed on in irregular patches, leaving plenty of white showing. Pale mid-grey is applied here and there, and is then distinctly veined in a darker grey, the patches being outlined in the darkest tone using a swordliner. This is then softened out. Using grey to black, add darker veins across or through the previous veins. Using dead white glaze and scrumpled tissue paper, dab lightly over the marbling; then soften.

For variants on basic sienna, Sally might change the colours, using very pale yellows with more pronounced black veining, or she might alter the marble formation itself, going for an angular zig-zag effect 'like fifties formica'. Some sienna contains only pale-grey and white, plus a lot of quartz.

For finishing marble Sally likes to coat it with matt or eggshell varnish, and then just before this is quite dry, she rubs in French chalk (or household flour) which soaks up any remaining tackiness and takes on a soft shine when polished.

Sally stresses that the best confidence booster for novices attempting these special effects is to study small bits and pieces on the natural materials themselves, collected either from junk markets or from specialist shops.

SNOWFLAKE OBSIDIAN IN NEGATIVE:

Method

This needs to be done on a level horizontal surface. The white base is rubbed over with a mixture of 3 parts linseed oil to 1 part siccative, or dryer. Mix up your colour – black plus raw umber – into a little of the same mixture until it reaches the consistency of single cream, and then drop it on here and there. In the middle of these drops place a tiny amount of white spirit with the tip of a brush, and tilt the box so that the mixture spreads out to form coral or sunflower shapes. This finish may take two days to dry, according to Sally. She sometimes uses spray varnish or retouching varnish to speed up the drying process.

ROSEWOOD AND WALNUT CROSS-BANDING:

Method

Follow the method for malachite, but use a burnt umber or black glaze over a biscuit-coloured base.

Over any finish which might lift or seems fragile, Sally brushes on four coats of white shellac before moving onto the fadge and French polishing stages. In this way she can build up a good surface in a day.

ROSEMALING

Rosemaling is Norwegian for 'rose painting', a highly stylized and colourful floral decoration which seems to have originated in Scandinavia in the eighteenth century, spreading to Northern Europe and ultimately to the United States with the great wave of Scandinavian immigrants. Rosemaling is strongly regional in Norway, with different areas having their own characteristic colours and styles of execution: Telemark rosemaling is painted in an asymmetrical fashion with rococo 'croting' shapes – 'C's and 'S's – on a background of black, dark green or rusty red; Hallingdal rosemaling goes in for asymmetrical arrangements of roses in bold colours on a Parisian-blue ground; and Westlandet goes for a more folksy effect on a red ground. Rosemaling is enjoying a revival in Norway today, and I was lucky enough to meet Ginty Watson, who studied

Rosemaling, like most folk decoration, is built up of brushstrokes, flicked on in one movement. Repeat the shapes shown here, over and over again, until the process is unthinking and easy. If you practise on a surface sealed with varnish, it can all be wiped off again.

The spotty 'dalmatian' of paint finishes, Sally Kenny's snowflake obsidian in negative.

Fantasy finishes like these are wonderful in the right place. Gold leaf 'skewings' and metallic powders build up a jewel-like intensity together with richly-coloured glazes.

Two ways with sienna, one vivid, the other refined, plus a purely fantasy finish in tones of grey.

Malachite and a fake pietra dura *marble mosaic.*

A chic trio in shades of tawny: oyster-walnut on top of tortoiseshell on top of blond graining.

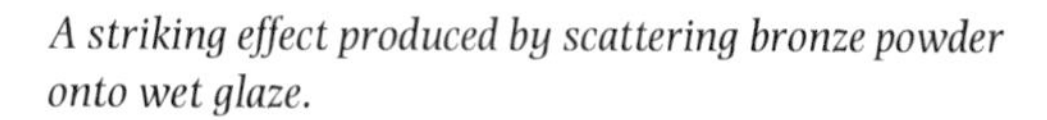

A striking effect produced by scattering bronze powder onto wet glaze.

the different regional techniques while she was living in Norway. A well as painting our hatbox (see p. 144), she told me how rosemaling is done in Norway today and her techniques are noted here for you to try.

Materials

You will need sable brushes in various sizes. Oil colours can be used almost straight from the tube, though some colours might need a little mixing or perhaps a little white spirit in order to dilute them.

The items to be decorated should be sandpapered in the usual way to get a smooth surface. You should wipe the piece over with linseed oil before you start to enable the colours to flow more smoothly. You learn as you paint, according to Ginty. 'Always paint with one hand resting on the other for extra control.' You are not supposed to draw the design in first, but a chalk circle helps to keep the design symmetrical. Rosemaling is all in the brushstrokes; the only way to get them flowing properly is practice. The design looks like nothing at all until you add the 'croting' – the outlining which goes on after you have put in the basic roses and flowers and leaves. Usually this is done in a creamy-yellow colour – white with cadmium or ochre – but sometimes black is used. For the shaded leaves, take up two colours on the brush, lighter on one side, darker on the other, so they blend together as you brush in the shape. In a warm place, the painting should dry overnight. To finish off, give it a coat of clear varnish.

Ginty paints small pieces, mostly, though she has done chests-of-drawers and bedside cupboards. Much as she enjoys this type of folk painting as a hobby, she says she has to be careful not to put roses everywhere. 'One or two things in a room is enough, otherwise it begins to look ridiculous.'

FERNWORK

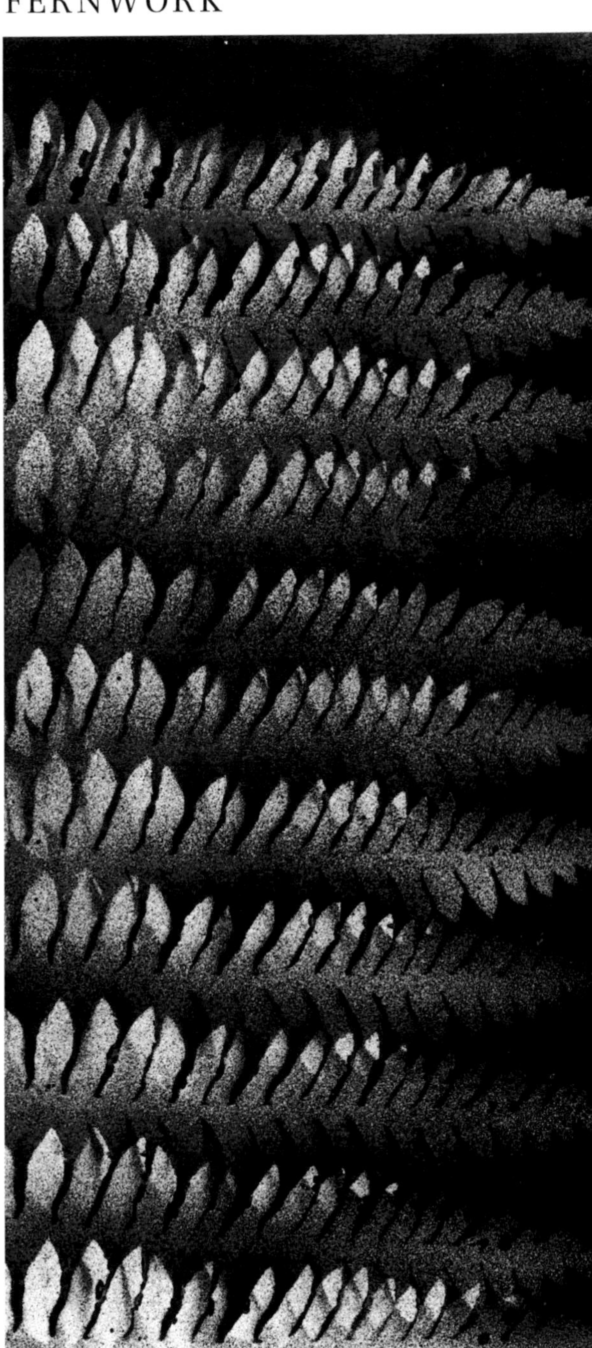

Moving a fern leaf along, and stippling, gives a leafy border like those on old papier maché trays.

FIREPLACES

Now that fireplaces, whose cheery blaze may well come from gas logs these days, have been re-instated as the natural focus of a room, people are looking for appropriate ways of re-vamping or rejuvenating fireplace surrounds. Overpainted marble or slate presents no problem that a quick coat of paint stripper cannot solve. But very often you are faced with something that is less adaptable to contemporary decorating ideas – heavy-looking surrounds of varnished oak, excellent examples of period joinery but lacking in charm, or cast-iron surrounds smothered in old paint. Sometimes, too, you inherit a reproduction surround, installed during the pine-with-everything phase in the seventies, which suddenly looks oddly out of place. Provided the fireplaces include the usual slips of marble, slate, iron or tiling round the grate (whose purpose is to resist the direct heat of the fire), wooden or iron surrounds can be given decorative finishes to make them fit in with updated colour schemes.

PORPHYRY:

A porphyry finish is much easier to do than it looks. It suits plain and chunky surrounds rather than fussy ones. Real porphyry is usually a rich dark claret to maroon colour – 'liver'-coloured – but the same spattering technique can be transposed to any strong colour successfully. I have seen it done with blues, greens and greys.

Method

The procedure with all the porphyry-type finishes, whatever the colour, is to begin by sponging on a flat oil-based paint, tinted to a tone darker than the colour you eventually want, over a flat white base. The sponging should be quite even, giving a mottled effect. Spattering in various colours is the next stage, which gives the vivacity of polished stone. Before attempting this you should mask off the surrounding area with newspaper and masking tape – spatters are apt to spread. The first coat of spatter paint should be a cream, or off-white colour, made by tinting the same flat white with a little yellow ochre and/or raw umber, and then thinning it with white spirit until it is quite fluid. Spatter this evenly over the sponged colour, just enough to lighten it by a couple of tones overall. For a straightforward porphyry the next spatter coat should be black, thinned in the same way, and applied less heavily but evenly over the entire surface. If you want a more dramatic effect, you could spatter first with a related but contrasting colour to your base colour – crimson on red, turquoise on blue, emerald on green. Flick this over lightly, just enough to create a lift in the overall tone, and then move on to the black spatters.

Finish with two or three coats of clear gloss polyurethane varnish for protection. The varnish can be lightly tinted with oil-colour if you feel like heightening the tone of the finish. The second coat of varnish, and any further coats, should be rubbed down with fine wire wool, or wet-and-dry paper, to smooth and dull the surface just a little. Sally Kenny finishes her fireplaces with wax and finest grade wire wool.

STONE STIPPLING:

Less formal than porphyry, this is a useful way of softening and lightening a fireplace surround to blend in with a cool modern interior.

Method

Depending on whether you want your stone to look grey or yellow, start with a pale grey or sandy-coloured base, tinted with flat oil paint or vinyl silk. Make up a basic glaze, using undercoat but not proprietary glaze, tinted with burnt umber, a touch of yellow ochre and a dot of black.

TOP LEFT *Its primitive style sympathetic to an all-Americana bedroom, this black-painted fireplace has been decoratively doodled in gold to simulate stylized marbling.*

BELOW LEFT *Cast iron can be picked out in contrasting paint colours, either richly pre-Raphaelite, or sweetly pastel, as here.*

TOP RIGHT *Taking its colour cue from the Fornasetti theme, a black and white fireplace – black, veined in white, for the pilasters, plain white gloss for the shelf on top.*

BELOW RIGHT *Inside a magnificent carved and gilded Portuguese frame, hand-painted Delft designs imitate old tiles. An idea that can be added to as time allows.*

Sponged supports in sludgy colours frame a vivid little landscape with figures in bright colours for a cottage-style room.

Paint it over the fireplace a section at a time, and while the glaze is wet pat it all over with a sponge to mottle it. Leave it to dry. Mix up a second batch of glaze, in a colder, stony shade, using Paynes grey and a little raw umber. This time use proprietary glaze instead of undercoat, and repeat the mottling process. When dry, varnish with two or three coats of eggshell or gloss clear varnish, but dull down the final coat with wet-and-dry paper or fine wire wool.

LIMING WITH WAX AND STAIN:

Oak, that problem wood that looks funereal when varnished and wonderful when blackened with age, is enjoying a revival. Our fashionable finish is an updated version of the limed effect produced in Vienna around the turn of the century by the Wiener Werkstätte, and later by firms like Heals in the twenties and thirties. Their solution to the coarse grain, characteristic of oak, was to fill it with a white paste filler. This did the double task of levelling the surface, so it could take a smooth polish, and turning the natural wood markings to decorative effect. The difference between the two approaches mentioned is that the Viennese stained the wood black first, against which the filler stands out dramatically, while the latter tended to bleach it so that the overall look was smoky-grey. Both look elegant and are good ways of re-styling varnished oak to fit in with current nostalgia.

Preparation

Your first task is to strip off the varnish, French polish or paint. Use paint stripper and scour with coarse wire wool until the wood is back to its natural biscuit shade. Then go over it in the direction of the grain with a wire brush. This opens up the grain markings to receive the filler.

Method

If you want the Viennese look, stain the oak with commercial black wood stain (Indian ink makes a plausible alternative). For the bleached version, use either an oxalic-based wood bleach (see suppliers index) or rub greyish-white paint into the wood. This is cheating, but gives much the same effect. When it has dried the wood should be sealed. This will prevent the liming sinking in anywhere except the scoured-out grain. Bleached shellac – often called white polish – does this quickly and efficiently. It is touch-dry in minutes, though it is best left for an hour or so to harden. When quite dry, apply the filler. Specialist stores sell a pasty white wax called liming wax for the purpose. This is simplicity itself to use. It should be rubbed on with a rag, first against the grain and then with the grain. Check to see that it has filled all the open grain markings. Polish it off with a soft cloth having allowed a little time for it to harden. The waxed finish can be lacquered or shellacked after overnight-drying to seal it and give the wood a sheen. This looks best on the bleached oak.

I prefer to fill black-stained wood with a standard filler, or gesso (see p. 150) diluted to a paint consistency and brushed on. Leave this for a few minutes, then wipe off firmly with a wet cloth, so that it remains only in the grain. This looks more dramatic on black wood because it dries very white. However, it must not be varnished or shellacked to seal it because that would make it transparent again. A light waxing is all it needs to protect it and seal in the stain, bringing it up to a dull shine.

It is worth experimenting with variants of this finish if you want to give oak furniture a new lease of life. The wood can be stained with colours other than black – dark green, red and grey, for example. But remember to seal it before liming so filler only enters the grain.

PICKING-OUT CAST IRON RELIEFS:

Victorian cast-iron fireplaces lend themselves ideally to the enjoyable game of picking-out their relief designs in various paint colours. Base your colour scheme on those richly coloured pieces of majolica or faience. Painted like this, a standard cast iron surround which you do not want to have sand-blasted (expensive if it has to be removed and then re-plastered in) becomes highly ornamental. It would look excellent in a room with a grandly printed wallpaper in the Morris style. Alternatively, in a simpler bedroom scheme, you could paint the surround in Wedgwood colours, chalky pastels with white (see my fireplace, p. 172).

Preparation

If the fireplace is already painted, and in reasonable shape, you need only fill in the chips with filler, apply a layer of undercoat and then paint as with any other surface. If, on the other hand, it is clotted with old paint, badly chipped and rusty, it might be better to remove the old paintwork. Mask off the wall, apply paint stripper with an old brush and then remove the softened paint with a scraper, coarse wire wool and a wire brush. Having cleaned it back to the metal, start by giving it a coat of anti-rust metal primer, then undercoat as above. Flat oil paint is a nice smooth paint for this sort of work (see suppliers index); otherwise use standard undercoat, tinted up, and varnish to seal.

Method

Mix your paint colours and apply them using pointed sable brushes for outlining the raised areas and a small standard brush or a filbert for filling in the background and larger areas. Varnish darker colour schemes with eggshell polyurethane and pale ones with extra pale, dead flat varnish. You can add a little gloss to this if you want a shine, although you should remember that Wedgwood pottery has a matt surface.

CRACKLEGLAZE

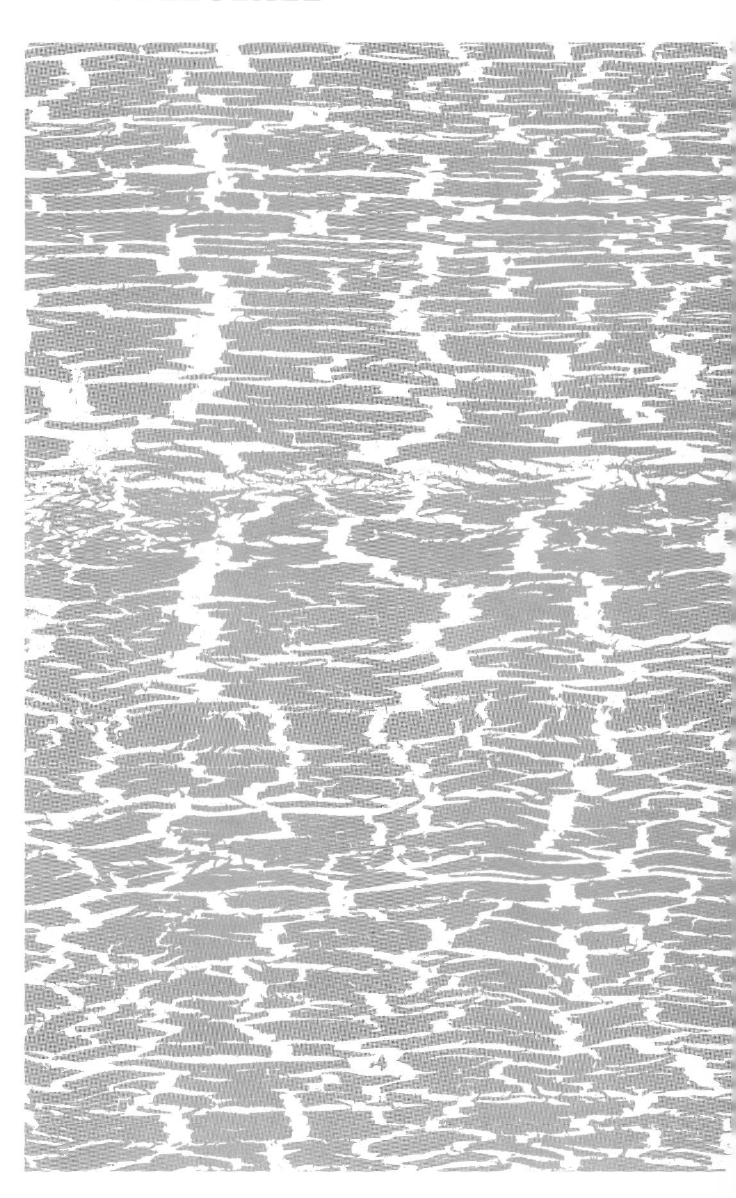

The effect of crackleglaze is dramatized when two strongly contrasting colours are used, black on white, red on black. There are various forms of special glazes; ours depends on using water-based paints. Alternatively, use pale colours to give a delicate porcelain finish (see p. 161).

7

THE SKILFUL ART OF

THE GREAT ILLUSIONISTS

THE PAINTED PRETENCE

The great surprise of the current decorative painting revival has been the demand for large-scale murals and trompe l'œil effects. Suddenly the wall-as-picture has become an international status symbol, and painters specializing in this area of the decorative arts find themselves summoned, like djinns, to paint jungle scenery round swimming pools in Aldershot, classical ruins on palace walls in Dubai, garlanded goddesses on ceilings in Paris or romantic landscapes in living-rooms in Miami. What clients are re-discovering is that skilful painting can supply whatever element seems lacking in their surroundings. Most coveted, it seems, is a look of romantic, patrician decay; the newer the penthouse, the more gently crumbling the painted 'rustication', complete with moss, cracks, lizards and carved escutcheons, defaced by time.

The teasing inconsequence of trompe l'œil is brilliantly demonstrated in this kitchen, where almost nothing is what it seems and wisps of string on painted nails, objects dangling out of drawers, are a cleaning lady's despair. Amateurs could have fun with the idea of trompe l'œil objects on cupboard doors. Another fashionable use for trompe l'œil is the addition of architectural details to flat walls, like this arched niche.

Stepping through the front door can land you anywhere from the Temple of Diana to a geisha house or Tippoo Sahib's travelling war tent. If the trompe l'œil artist was in puckish mood, unsuspecting visitors may find their coats sliding off painted coat hooks, illusory ten pound notes might peep out from under the carpet or appear swept into a pile on the hearth, cigarette packets on the table may mislead you into reaching for one, while painted mice scuttle into painted mouseholes. Paul and Janet Czainskis spend a few weeks in Scotland each summer adding yet another hallucinatory detail, such as a field-mouse clinging to a wheat stalk, a dragon-fly or dandelion, to an astonishing bedroom where the forces of nature seem to be fighting to gain admission through every painted crack and crevice, a *tour de force* of what admirers of the Gothick called 'horrid imagination'. Whatever this painted phantasmagoria may indicate about its patrons, it is all in a day's work for the artists who create them: 'Turps smells the same whether you're in Bangkok or Tuscany', as one of them put it.

Trompe l'œil work at the level on which Ian Cairnie, the Czainskis, Lincoln Taber and their colleagues operate, is technically highly skilled, and probably beyond most amateurs. Unless the painted mouse really 'deceives the eye' the joke misfires. On the other hand, a slightly primitive version of trompe l'œil can be decorative and witty in the right place. Painting the contents of cupboards on their doors, as in the Czainskis' example shown here, is an attractive way of reminding people where to stow things after washing-up. 'You use just about every trick there is to speed things up, it's not like conventional easel painting in that sense. Stencils, graining, stippling, anything is used that will help the illusion along.' Or, like Victoria Sharples, you can have fun painting alarm clocks and chamber pots on bedside-cupboard doors, and sheafs of trompe l'œil correspondence on the breakast tray. Small faked details like these are fun to paint, and add an amusing personal note. The only way to do them is to scale, with the objects in front of you so that you can reproduce them faithfully. Getting the shadows right is the secret of success, Paul Czainskis says, because it is shadow that gives the flat painted article a three-dimensional look. He will scrumple a ten pound note to create shadows before painting its portrait. Ian Cairnie lays stress on getting little details exactly right. 'If you are doing a trompe door, you need to take time over the knob, the keyhole and the hinges. If they look convincing you are halfway there.' When he painted a trompe window, framing a Claude Lorraine view, in a client's windowless hall, he took twice as long painting the glazing bars as the pastoral vista beyond.

One paint with which Owen Turville wants to experiment further, both for exterior and interior murals, is the German-made Keim paint, sold here to the trade by Mineral Protect Ltd. The principle behind the Keim paint was discovered over a century ago by Professor Keim who was looking for a paint with the lasting qualities of true fresco. The oldest Keim-painted surfaces are over a hundred years old and look pristine, so it looks as if he was successful. The Keim system uses natural earth oxide pigments which are painted onto a mineral substrate and fixed by a silicate binder; the chemical reaction forms a crystalline surface, which not only prevents colours fading but allows surfaces to breathe, ideal for damp walls or places with condensation problems. The only problem with Keim paint is that it cannot be applied over a previously painted surface, other than limewash. It can be used straight onto standard thistle plaster, however, or over concrete.

For mural painters Keim is made in a special formulation where the silicate binder is brushed on after the painting is complete. This allows changes to be made. The Keim system approaches the clear, luminous colour of true fresco. To achieve that colour quality over walls which are to be simply painted rather than 'muralised', the makers recommend using a combination method. Paint the walls first with white Granital, their exterior base, and then brush over a diluted colour mixed with half fixative, half water. It costs perhaps twice as much as a standard paint, but gives a freshness and subtlety of colour unattainable except by the laborious old fresco method, and will last virtually for ever.

At present Keim paints are largely used for restoration work, inside and out – the Queen Mother's house at Windsor has a Keim finish. Mineral Protect Ltd (see suppliers index) do not sell directly over the counter, but via architects and decorating firms, because they want to ensure that the paints are used over a properly prepared base of the right material.

Ashlar or painted stone work

It is something of a coup for us to be able to publish the first photographs of work by Paul and Janet Czainskis (see pp. 128–9), a highly talented young couple whose reputation has spread entirely by word of mouth. Paul painted the trompe stone-work in this tiny London hall using dry pigments – raw sienna, raw umber, white and vandyke brown – in stale beer, an old graining trick. To obviate brushmarks and achieve an air-brushed smoothness, he sponged the shading colours through a stencil, which allowed him to keep building up layers of watercolour until he got the effect he wanted. The highlights, or light edges of dressed stone, were done by wiping off the watercolour with a wet chamois to reveal the white base. Stencilling over in a paler colour obliterated the stencil ties, and the whole surface was finished in matt varnish.

Seeing is believing; there is something magical about transformations like these that appeals to the child in all of us. Paint can do so much for you if you just use a little 'paintability'. It can work miracles, and not only in this most spectacular form of decorative painting. Colour, texture and pattern can be yours – not only on the walls, but just about everywhere. All achieved with paint, and nothing but paint. I hope this book will stir your imaginations and provide the key to making your home a unique environment instead of just a 'painted box'.

RIGHT *This exercise in perspective, dated 1662 and painted by the Dutch painter Van Hoogstraeten, is a celebrated example of visual trickery, especially when seen through an enfilade of doorways as at Dyrham Park.*

FAR RIGHT *Graham Rust is one of the most full-blooded muralists around today, as evidenced in this rusticated hallway where the jungle seems to be taking over – notice the spectacular cracks.*

A trompe l'œil doorway uses a mixture of styles: grisaille for the architectural fantasy, and stunning realism for the odd painted details, like the monkey.

LEFT *More of the trompe l'œil painter's favourite witticisms for you to try – pillars and draperies.*

RIGHT *Caught in a beam of light, a flutter of brilliantly coloured trompe l'œil butterflies.*

"Owen Turville worked for many years with John Fowler, and has absorbed much of the Fowler wisdom about colour, together with a painterly handling of decorative techniques. What he would really like to do is paint landscapes; in the meantime large-scale murals provide an outlet, though like most Fowler-trained decorative artists he can turn his hand to anything from restoring antique furniture to painting flowers on cushions.

'I find Liquitex [acrylic] gesso makes a marvellous primer for murals. I paint straight onto it, using acrylics as a rule for the drying speed, though I sometimes finish a mural in oils. I usually prepare a fairly finished coloured sketch of the scheme for the client, so I work from that. I might transpose it onto the wall surface very accurately to scale, making a grid – black cotton fixed in place with Blu-Tack is a good way of marking out a grid and it can be removed as soon as you have blocked in the design. Sometimes, though, I might start by drawing a large rough sketch using chalks or charcoal – pencil has a way of coming through paint. But my

favourite means of drawing a preparatory sketch is with a brush. A brush makes thin and thick lines, almost carving out the design, and I have another brush dipped in white spirit as an eraser. I suppose if you were a beginner you could project a picture onto the wall and draw round it. If I'm drawing with the brush I

Contents

Welcome to *Wordly Wise 3000*®

You've been learning words since you were a tiny baby. At first, you learned them only by hearing other people talk. Now that you are a reader, you have another way to learn words.

Obviously, it's important to know what words mean, but lots of times, we think we can get away without knowing some of them as we read. This could cause a problem. Say you are reading the directions for a new game. You know most of the words in the sentence you're reading. Then you stop for a word you don't recognize:

> *Please do not touch the* blegmy *or your score will be lost.*

You ask yourself, "What is a *blegmy?*" At first you think, "Well, it's only one word." But then you think, "What is it that I'm not supposed to touch?" All of a sudden, knowing what that one word means is important!

Clearly, the more words you know, the better your understanding of everything you read. *Wordly Wise 3000* will help you learn a lot of words, but it can't teach you *all* the words you'll ever need. It can, however, help guide your learning of new words on your own.

How Do You Learn What Words Mean?

There are two main ways you learn what words mean: directly and indirectly.

You have to learn some words *directly*. You may study them for a class, look them up in a dictionary or glossary, or ask someone what they mean. You also learn word meanings *indirectly* by hearing and reading the words. In fact, the more you listen and read, the more words you'll learn. Reading books, magazines, and online can help build your vocabulary.

At school, you learn a lot of words directly. If you're using this book, you are learning words directly. You are reading the words, learning what they mean, and studying them. Then you are practicing them as you do the activities. Finally, you might even use them in your own writing or conversations. There is an old saying: "Use a word three times and it's yours." Three times might not be enough, of course, but the idea is right. The more you practice using a word, the better you understand it.

What Is "School Language"?

School language—or school words—are the words you find in the books you read, from novels to textbooks, and on tests. You read them online as you look up information. Your teacher uses these words to explain an important concept about math or reading. Some have to do with a particular topic, such as the building of the Great Pyramid in Egypt. Others are words for tasks you are being asked to do, such as *summarize.* These words are different from the kinds of words you use when you're hanging out with your friends or talking casually with your family. That's why you often need to study such words directly. In this book, these important words are underlined to help you focus on them.

Wordly Wise 3000 is designed to teach you some of the words you need to do well in school and on tests—and later on in your jobs. It will also help you learn how to learn more words. Remember, there is no single thing that will help you understand what you read as much as knowing word meanings will.

How Do You Figure Out Word Meanings?

What should you do when you come to a word and you think you don't know what it means?

Say It

First, say it to yourself. Maybe once you do this, it will sound like a word you *do* know. Sometimes you know a word in your head without knowing what it looks like in print. So if you match up what you know and what you read—you have the word!

Use Context

If this doesn't work, take the next step: look at the context of the word—the other words and sentences around it. Sometimes these can give you a clue to the word's meaning. Here's an example:

> *Mr. Huerta had great respect for his* opponent.

Say that you don't know what *opponent* means. Does Mr. Huerta have respect for his teacher? His mother? Then you read on:

> *The two players sat across from each other in the warm room. The chessboard was between them. Both looked as if they were concentrating very hard.*

Now you see that Mr. Huerta is taking part in a chess game. You know that in a chess game, one person plays another. So his *opponent* must be the person he is playing against. You reread the sentence using that meaning. Yes, that works. In this sentence, *opponent* means "someone you play against, or compete with."

Use Word Parts

If the context doesn't help, look at the parts of the word. Does it have any prefixes you know? How about suffixes? Or roots? These can help you figure out what it means. Look at this sentence:

> *Shania had the* misfortune *to hurt her arm right before the swim meet.*

If you don't know the meaning of *misfortune*, try looking at parts of the word. You might know that *fortune* means "luck." Maybe *mis-* is a prefix. You could look it up, or maybe you remember its meaning from studying prefixes in school. The prefix *mis-* means a few different things, but one of them is "bad." You try it out and reread the sentence using that meaning. It would certainly be bad luck, or a *misfortune,* to hurt your arm before a swim meet.

Look It Up

If saying the word or using context and word parts don't work, you can look it up in a dictionary—either a book or online reference—or a glossary.

Nobody knows the meaning of every word, but good readers know how to use these strategies to figure out words they don't know. Get into the habit of using them as you read, and you may be surprised at how automatic it becomes!

How Well Do You Know a Word?

It's important to know many words and to keep on learning more. But it's also important to know them well. In fact, some experts say that there are four levels of knowing a word:

1. I never saw/heard it before.
2. I've heard/seen it, but I don't know what it means.
3. I think it has something to do with…
4. I know it.*

Just because you can read a word and have memorized its definition, it doesn't mean that you know that word well. You want to know it so well that you know when to use it and when to use another word instead. One way to help deepen your knowledge of a word is to use a graphic organizer like the one below that tells about the word *portion.*

Concept of Definition Map

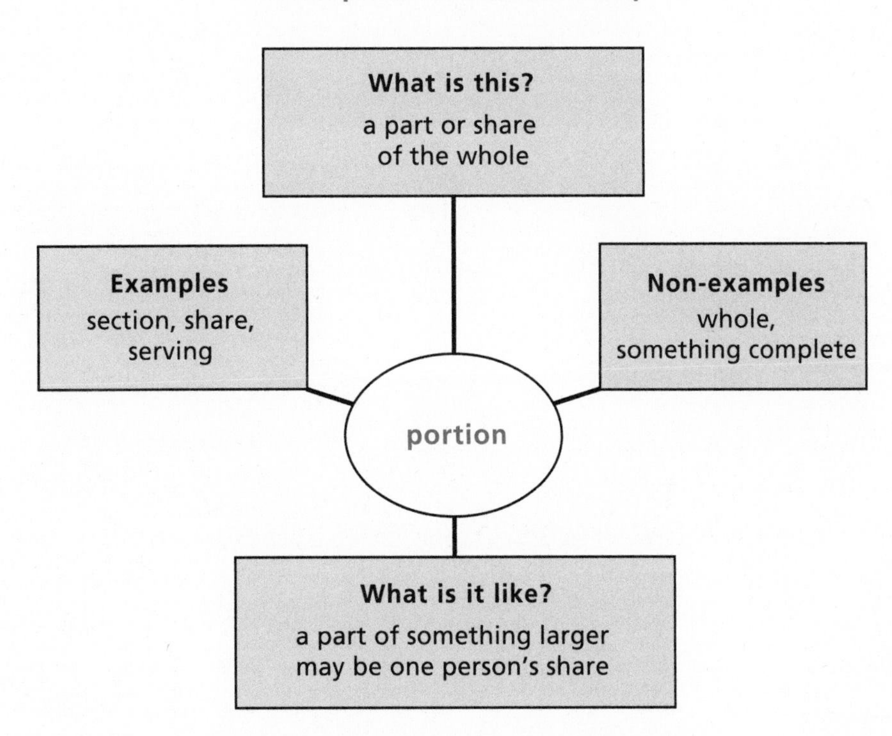

If you can fill in all the parts of this graphic organizer, you are well on your way to really knowing the word *portion*.

*Dale, E., & O'Rourke, J. (1986). *Vocabulary Building*. Columbus, OH: Zaner-Bloser.

Lesson
1
Word List

Study the definitions of the words. Then do the exercises that follow.

affection
ə fek′ shən

n. A fond or tender feeling.
Hugging is one way to show **affection.**

affectionate *adj.* Gentle and loving.
My cousin took my hand and gave it an **affectionate** squeeze.

appeal
ə pēl′

v. 1. To make an earnest request; to ask.
Three students **appealed** for more time to finish the work.

2. To be of interest to; to be attractive to.
This funny movie will **appeal** to children of all ages.

n. 1. An earnest request for help.
The letter contained an **appeal** for money to provide shelters for the homeless.

2. The power to attract or be of interest.
Neither the asparagus and onions nor the meatloaf had much **appeal.**

Appeal to your partner to hand you his or her pencil or pen.

clasp
klasp

v. To grasp or hold tightly.
The dancers **clasped** hands and circled the maypole.

n. 1. A strong grasp or hold.
The nurse gently removed the doll from the toddler's **clasp.**

2. Something, such as a hook or fastener, that holds two parts together.
The necklace has a **clasp** in the shape of a snake biting its tail.

conspicuous
kən spik′ yo͞o əs

adj. Easily or plainly seen.
His great height made him **conspicuous** in any crowd.

Tell your partner what you think is the most conspicuous thing in the classroom.

contribute
kən trib′ yo͞ot

v. 1. To give along with others who are giving.
I **contributed** a spinach salad to the potluck supper.

2. To have a part in bringing about.
Exercise **contributes** greatly to good health.

contribution *n.* (kän tri byo͞o′ shən) That which is given.
The museum sent a thank-you note for the fifty-dollar **contribution.**

contributor *n.* (kən trib′ yə tər) One who gives.
Contributors to the new theater received free tickets for opening night.

Share with your partner a cause or a charity you would like to be a contributor to, and discuss how you could contribute.

declare
dē klâr´

v. To make known; to state openly.
"I will not share a room with my sister anymore," she **declared.**

declaration *n.* (dek lə rā´ shən) A public statement.
The **declaration** read by the mayor stated that November was bicycle safety month.

Declare to your partner your feelings about your favorite movie.

eloquent
el´ ə kwənt

adj. Skilled at speaking or writing; having the power to move people.
Anne Frank's **eloquent** diary often moves readers to tears.

eloquence *n.* Skill at speaking or writing; the power to move people.
Dr. Martin Luther King Jr.'s **eloquence** made him a strong leader of the 1960s Civil Rights Movement.

exhibit
eg zib´ it

v. To show in public.
Local artists **exhibited** their paintings at the library.

n. An item or collection of items in a public show.
The most interesting **exhibit** in the museum was the dinosaur skeleton.

exhibition *n.* (ek sə bish´ ən) A large-scale public show.
Tickets for the **exhibition** of early automobiles go on sale next week.

Tell your partner what you might like to exhibit on a bulletin board or in a trophy case.

ferry
fer´ ē

n. A boat that carries people and goods back and forth across a stretch of water.
The **ferry** will stop running when the new bridge opens.

v. To move people or goods by boat across a stretch of water.
The boat owner who **ferried** us across the lake would not accept any payment.

immigrant
im´ ə grənt

n. A person who comes into a country to live there.
Many Polish **immigrants** settled in Chicago.

Discuss with your partner how immigrants make the United States special.

lofty
lôf´ tē

adj. 1. Very tall or high.
Lofty elm trees provided welcome shade along the streets.

2. Noble in feeling or ideals.
Ending world hunger in our lifetime is a **lofty** goal.

3. Showing a too-proud or superior attitude.
The **lofty** way the diner spoke to the waiter made me feel uncomfortable.

In a lofty way, describe for your partner how great your singing is.

pedestal
ped´ əs təl

n. A base or support on which something stands.
At the museum, I backed up to get a better view of the painting and almost knocked the sculpture off its **pedestal.**

persecute
pʉr´ sə kyo͞ot

v. To treat cruelly or harshly because of political, religious, or other differences.
The First Amendment to the United States Constitution does not allow anyone to be **persecuted** based on religious beliefs.

persecution *n.* (pur sə kyo͞o´ shən) The state or condition of being persecuted.
Hitler's **persecution** of the Jewish people led to the murder of millions of innocent people.

poverty
päv´ ər tē

n. The state of being poor.
The food stamp program was started to help feed families living in **poverty.**

unveil
un vāl´

v. 1. To remove a covering from.
The American Red Cross held a ceremony to **unveil** the portrait of its founder, Clara Barton.

2. To make known or reveal for the first time.
The police chief will **unveil** a plan to reduce street crime at today's meeting.

1A Finding Meanings

Choose two phrases to form a sentence that correctly uses a word from Word List 1. Then write the sentence.

1. (a) let that person go free. (c) treat that person badly.
   (b) To clasp someone is to (d) To persecute someone is to
   To persecute someone is to treat that person badly.
2. (a) If something is lofty, (c) it is hidden from view.
   (b) If something has appeal, (d) it has the power to attract.
   If something has appeal, it has the power to attract.
3. (a) To exhibit something is to (c) understand it fully.
   (b) To unveil something is to (d) reveal it for the first time.
   To uneil something is to reveal it for the first time.

4. (a) Poverty is
   (b) Eloquence is
   (c) a condition of poor health.
   (d) the state of being poor.

   Poverty is the state of being poor.

5. (a) To speak in an affectionate manner
   (b) To speak in a lofty manner
   (c) is to show a too-proud attitude.
   (d) is to show extreme shyness.

   To speak in a lofty manner is to show a too-proud attitude.

6. (a) a lever operated by the foot.
   (b) An exhibit is
   (c) a public showing.
   (d) A pedestal is

   An exhibit is a public showing.

7. (a) entry into a country to live there.
   (b) Eloquence is
   (c) skill at speaking or writing.
   (d) Affection is

   Eloquence is skill at speaking or writing.

8. (a) understand it.
   (b) hold it tightly.
   (c) To clasp something is to
   (d) To contribute to something is to

   To clasp something is to hold it tightly.

9. (a) ask that person for help.
   (b) To ferry someone is to
   (c) To appeal to someone is to
   (d) give comfort to that person.

   To appeal someone is to give comfort to that person.

10. (a) A pedestal is
    (b) A contribution is
    (c) a person traveling on foot.
    (d) something that is given.

    A contribution is something that is given.

affection
appeal
clasp
conspicuous
contribute
declare
eloquent
exhibit
ferry
immigrant
lofty
pedestal
persecute
poverty
unveil

1B Just the Right Word

Replace each phrase in bold with a single word (or form of the word) from the word list.

1. My parents were **people who came to live in this country** from Mexico.

2. The **boat that carries people across the river** leaves every hour on the hour.

3. The sundial, together with the **base on which it stands,** costs two hundred dollars.

4. There was a burst of applause when the artist **removed the covering from** her painting.

5. The president's **public statement** that the factory would not be closing was welcome news to the townspeople.

6. A heavy dessert would not **be of interest** to me after that big dinner.

7. The generosity of the teacher **was one of the things that led** to the success of the students.

8. The **powerful, moving words** of Abraham Lincoln's "Gettysburg Address" made a deep impression on me.

9. Their unusual way of dressing makes them **easy to notice** in a crowd.

10. I have nothing but **fond and tender feelings** for you all.

Applying Meanings

Circle the letter or letters next to each correct answer. There may be more than one correct answer.

1. Which of the following could be **unveiled?**
   (a) a statue
   (b) a cloud
   (c) a painting
   (d) a plan

2. Which of the following can be **declared?**
   (a) a winner
   (b) one's friends
   (c) one's love
   (d) a holiday

3. Which of the following can be **contributed?**
   (a) money
   (b) time
   (c) clothing
   (d) space

4. Which of the following could be **ferried?**
   (a) hopes
   (b) fears
   (c) people
   (d) cars

5. For which of the following might someone be subjected to **persecution?**
   (a) driving too fast
   (b) having political views
   (c) breaking into someone's home
   (d) practicing a religion

6. Which of the following would be **conspicuous?**
   (a) a lighthouse on a cliff
   (b) a pebble on the beach
   (c) a billboard by the roadside
   (d) a purple house

7. Which of the following could be **exhibited?**
   (a) pottery
   (b) days
   (c) uncertainty
   (d) coins

8. Which of the following could you say to give someone a clue that you are an **immigrant?**
   (a) "Math is my favorite subject."
   (b) "I have a dog."
   (c) "I plan to live in a new country."
   (d) "I have left my home country."

affection
appeal
clasp
conspicuous
contribute
declare
eloquent
exhibit
ferry
immigrant
lofty
pedestal
persecute
poverty
unveil

Word Study: Synonyms

Circle the two synonyms in each group of four words.

Synonyms are words that have the same or similar meanings.

1. tall	eloquent	hidden	lofty
2. understand	contribute	declare	state
3. show	return	exhibition	appeal
4. eloquent	moving	conspicuous	tired
5. contribute	request	return	appeal
6. fastener	base	poverty	pedestal
7. affectionate	fond	conspicuous	sad
8. persecution	anger	grasp	clasp
9. ferry	poverty	poor	unveil
10. clasp	immigrant	supply	fastener

Vocabulary in Context

Read the passage.

Lady Liberty

The Statue of Liberty is a symbol of freedom to people all over the world. Since 1886 it has welcomed **immigrants** who sail into New York harbor to begin a new life in the United States. Like many of them, Lady Liberty, as the statue is **affectionately** known, had to overcome some difficulties before reaching these shores.

The statue was a gift from the people of France to the people of the United States. It was given in honor of the friendship between the two countries and the one-hundredth anniversary of the American Revolution. But before the statue could be put in place, the people of the United States had to provide a **pedestal** for it at a cost of one hundred thousand dollars. That turned out to be no easy task. A fund-raising drive was launched and ran into immediate difficulties. Newspapers across the United States ridiculed the effort. They argued that because the French were sending over the statue, they should be the ones to pay the extra costs involved for the base.

Despite this opposition, the effort to raise the money continued. A forty-foot-high section of the right arm, with the hand **clasping** the torch of liberty, was sent to the United States. It was displayed at the 1876 Philadelphia **exhibition** marking the one-hundredth birthday of the United States. Visitors paid fifty cents to climb onto the balcony surrounding the torch. Many other fund-raising events were also held. But even after several years, **contributions** fell far short of the total needed. The future of the entire project seemed in doubt. Not until a newspaper **appeal** promised to print donors' names was the necessary money raised.

With the success of the project assured, the rest of the statue was finally shipped from France. It arrived in pieces packed in over two hundred wooden crates. The work of assembling it proceeded without further delay. A public holiday was **declared** on October 28, 1886, when the Statue of Liberty was at last **unveiled.** It was one of the largest gatherings ever in New York City. The island where the statue stands is called Liberty Island. It is reached by a short **ferry** ride from lower Manhattan. At just over 305 feet, the statue was the tallest structure in New York City. Though it is now dwarfed by the **lofty** skyscrapers of Manhattan, at the time it was the most **conspicuous** landmark in the city.

affection
appeal
clasp
conspicuous
contribute
declare
eloquent
exhibit
ferry
immigrant
lofty
pedestal
persecute
poverty
unveil

In the 1880s, people seeking a better life were flooding into the United States. They arrived at the rate of one million a year. Many of them came from Russia and Eastern Europe; they had been cruelly **persecuted** by their governments and were fleeing to safety. Others were escaping the **poverty** of their native lands in search of a more prosperous life in America.

The museum at the base of the statue contains a bronze tablet placed there in 1903. On it is a poem written twenty years earlier by Emma Lazarus, whose own family had fled Russia. The poem has captured the imagination of the American people and has become forever associated with the Statue of Liberty. It ends with these **eloquent** lines:

Give me your tired, your poor,
Your huddled masses yearning to breathe free,
The wretched refuse of your teeming shore;
Send these, the homeless, tempest-tost to me,
I lift my lamp beside the golden door!

▶ **Answer each of the following questions with a sentence. If a question does not contain a vocabulary word from the lesson's word list, use one in your answer. Use each word only once.**

1. What is the meaning of **lofty** as it is used in the passage?

____

____

2. What finally caused Americans to **contribute** the necessary funds?

____

____

3. What was done with the statue's arm in Philadelphia in 1876?

____

____

4. How can you tell that the author has a favorable opinion of Lazarus's poem?

____

____

5. What is the meaning of **appeal** as it is used in the passage?

____

____

6. Why were so many people able to attend the first showing of the statue?

7. What was the hope of people who came to America to escape the **poverty** of their homelands?

8. Why did the American people have to raise one hundred thousand dollars?

9. How is the torch of liberty supported by the statue?

10. How do visitors reach the Statue of Liberty?

11. What is the meaning of **unveil** as it is used in the passage?

12. Why do you think the United States has been called a nation of **immigrants?**

13. Why is the statue not such a **conspicuous** landmark as it once was?

14. Why would **persecuted** people want to come to the United States?

15. Do you think the people fleeing to the United States for safety in the 1880s felt **affection** for their governments? Why or why not?

affection
appeal
clasp
conspicuous
contribute
declare
eloquent
exhibit
ferry
immigrant
lofty
pedestal
persecute
poverty
unveil

Fun & Fascinating FACTS

- The Latin word for *foot* is *ped,* and several English words, such as *pedal* (a lever worked by the foot) and *pedestrian* (a person going on foot), come from it. Because a **pedestal** is a base that stands at the foot, or lowest part, of a statue, column, or similar object, you might think that *pedestal* comes directly from *ped.* Actually it comes from an Italian phrase, *pie di stallo,* which means "a foot (or lowest part) of a stall." Because the Italian word for *foot* comes from *ped,* it's correct to say that the English word *pedestal* also comes from it, but in a roundabout manner.

- An **immigrant** is a person who enters a country intending to live there. An *emigrant* is a person who leaves one country to settle in another. In the late nineteenth and early twentieth centuries, many people *emigrated* from Europe and arrived in the United States as *immigrants.*

- **Persecute** and *prosecute* are similar-sounding words that are sometimes confused even though they have quite separate meanings. To *persecute* someone is to make that person suffer because of political, religious, or other beliefs or characteristics.. To *prosecute* someone is to bring that person to trial for criminal acts.

1 Vocabulary Extension

exhibit

noun Something that is put in a public place where many people can see it.

verb To show something in a public place where many people can see it.

Academic Context

These sentences give clues to the meaning of **exhibit**.

*An art teacher often puts students' artwork on **exhibit** somewhere in the school.*

*A teacher might **exhibit** several good examples of students' writing each week on the board.*

Word Family

exhibition (noun)
exhibitor (noun)
exhibiting (verb)

Discussion & Writing Prompt

If you went to an **exhibit** about space at a museum, what would you see?

2 min. 1. Turn and talk to your partner or group.	3 min. 2. Write 2–4 sentences.
Use this space to take notes or draw your ideas.	Be ready to share what you have written.

Lesson 2

Word List

Study the definitions of the words. Then do the exercises that follow.

arrogant
ar´ ə gənt

adj. Showing too much pride in oneself.
You were **arrogant** to claim that you knew all the answers.

arrogance *n.* A feeling of too much pride in oneself.
Declaring that you are sure to win is another example of your **arrogance.**

Tell your partner how you react when a friend talks with arrogance.

boycott
boi´ kät

v. To join others in refusing to support an organization.
Customers plan to **boycott** that store if it continues to discriminate.

n. The act of boycotting.
The fans called off their **boycott** when the teams agreed to lower ticket prices.

campaign
kam pān´

n. 1. A series of actions intended to accomplish a goal.
Picking up litter was the first step in the **campaign** to clean up the town center.

2. A series of military actions in a particular area.
The Battle of the Bulge was part of the Allied **campaign** to invade Germany and end the war.

v. To take part in actions planned to accomplish a particular goal.
Students who wish to **campaign** for class office must submit petitions.

ceremony
ser´ ə mō nē

n. A formal event held in honor of a special occasion.
The bride and groom exchanged rings during the wedding **ceremony.**

custody
kus´ tə dē

n. 1. Control over and responsibility for care.
The stolen Picasso painting was returned to the **custody** of the Museum of Modern Art.

2. In the keeping of the police; in jail.
The police officer took the thief into **custody.**

degrade
dē grād´

v. To bring shame or disgrace upon.
By lying to cover up his cheating, Sam **degraded** himself even more.

degrading *adj.* Causing shame or disgrace.
Losing the trophy because one player cheated on a test was a **degrading** experience.

Discuss with your partner if being sent to the school principal's office is a degrading experience.

detain
dē tān´

v. To stop or hold; to keep from going on.
The hall monitor **detained** us until we could prove we had permission to leave the classroom.

extend
ek stend´

v. 1. To reach out.
The conductor **extended** her arms as a signal to the orchestra to be ready.

2. To offer.
I wish to **extend** my apologies for behaving so badly.

3. To make longer.
The exhibition was so popular that the museum decided to **extend** it by a week.

4. To stretch or spread outward from a certain point.
The property **extends** for a half mile beyond the river.

Extend your arms to the ceiling with your partner.

integrate
in´ tə grāt

v. To unite into a whole; especially to end the separation of people of different races.
In 1948, President Truman **integrated** the armed forces of the United States.

integration *n.* (in tə grā´ shən) The act of uniting or bringing together, especially people of different races.
The racial **integration** of public and private places has made our country better and stronger.

Talk to your partner about how you can help a new student integrate into the school.

segregate
seg´ rə gāt

v. To keep separate or apart.
Ranchers **segregate** sick animals from the herd to prevent diseases from spreading.

segregation *n.* (seg rə gā´ shən) The act of keeping separate or apart.
One of the goals of the Civil Rights Movement was to end racial **segregation** in the United States.

supreme
sə prēm´

adj. 1. The highest in rank or position.
The **supreme** commander was happy to retire after years of responsibility.

2. Of the greatest importance.
The sea captain's **supreme** mission was to get revenge on the white whale.

Tell your partner about a time you felt supreme happiness.

triumph trī´ əmf

n. 1. A noteworthy success.
Helen Keller's graduation from college was a **triumph.**

2. The joy that winning brings.
The dancer who was invited to audition shot a look of **triumph** at those who were not so lucky.

v. To win.
The winner of the national spelling bee **triumphed** over forty-nine other contestants.

triumphant *adj.* (trī um´ fənt) Joyful over a victory or success.
The **triumphant** skater was given a hero's welcome on her return from the Olympic Games.

vacate vā´ kāt

v. To make empty, as by leaving.
We will **vacate** the house at the end of June to make way for the people moving in.

Vacate your chair for five seconds, and then return to your seat and face your partner.

verdict vʉr´ dikt

n. 1. The decision reached at the end of a trial.
The jury looked grim as she announced the **verdict.**

2. A judgment or opinion.
The **verdict** on the new computer is that it does twice the work in half the time.

violate vī´ ə lāt

v. 1. To break, as a law or a promise.
Damien **violated** our teacher's trust by trying to cheat on the homework.

2. To treat in an improper or disrespectful way.
The vandals who **violated** the cemetery by knocking over gravestones had to restore it.

violation *n.* (vī ə lā´ shən) A breaking of or failing to keep something like a law or a promise.
Revealing the secret was a **violation** of your friend's trust.

Discuss with your partner what happens when you violate a school rule.

2A

Using Words in Context

Read the following sentences. If the word in bold is used correctly, write C on the line. If the word is used incorrectly, write I on the line.

1. (a) The woman claims to be able to **verdict** the future. ___
   (b) The jury came back after an hour with a **verdict** of "not guilty." ___
   (c) The **verdict** on the new restaurant is that it is amazing. ___
   (d) The **verdict** becomes soft as soon as you pop it. ___

2. (a) Selma **triumphed** in the 200- and 400-meter events. ___
   (b) We cheered for the **triumphant** team in the parade. ___
   (c) I was so sad, I covered my **triumphant** face with my hands. ___
   (d) The dog sniffed the **triumph** and then walked away. ___

3. (a) Throwing litter on the sidewalk is a **violation** of the law. ___
   (b) By early May, the rain has started to **violate.** ___
   (c) If one person is allowed to **violate** the rule, then everyone will want to. ___
   (d) Beautiful purple **violates** grew in the shade. ___

4. (a) The umbrella can be **extended** by pressing this button. ___
   (b) The forest **extended** for fifty miles. ___
   (c) The toddler **extended** her arms for a hug. ___
   (d) I **extended** to visit my aunt, but I kept putting it off. ___

5. (a) His **arrogant** remarks made the other students dislike him. ___
   (b) His confidence is sometimes mistaken for **arrogance.** ___
   (c) Your room will become **arrogant** if you don't clean it up. ___
   (d) The **arrogant** colors of the parrot are beautiful. ___

6. (a) Students should **vacate** the classroom if the fire alarm rings. ___
   (b) Tourists have **vacated** the beach by October. ___
   (c) **Vacate** the markers back in the box. ___
   (d) Farook and I **vacated** all the oranges. ___

7. (a) You need to **detain** an adult if you are out after ten. ___
   (b) Our teacher **detained** us after class to explain the homework more clearly. ___
   (c) We **detained** each other about the new movie that just came out. ___
   (d) Papa was **detained** at work and won't be home for dinner. ___

8. (a) All the teachers went to the graduation **ceremony.** ___
   (b) The **ceremony** is held every year to celebrate the first snow. ___
   (c) The girl raised the **ceremony** over her head and then threw it. ___
   (d) We ate too much **ceremony** at the party. ___

arrogant
boycott
campaign
ceremony
custody
degrade
detain
extend
integrate
segregate
supreme
triumph
vacate
verdict
violate

9. (a) Judging by the **supreme** look she gave me, Liu was not happy. ___
   (b) The ruler of the country calls himself the **supreme** leader. ___
   (c) The **supreme** prize at the carnival was given to Aaron. ___
   (d) The students grew more and more **supreme** in the sun. ___

10. (a) Luis's older brother will **campaign** for their father, who is running for mayor. ___
    (b) The **campaign** to provide free flu shots kicked off yesterday. ___
    (c) The Allied **campaign** against Nazi rule began in France on June 6, 1944. ___
    (d) The **campaign** in the mountains is difficult for hikers. ___

2B Making Connections

Circle the letter next to each correct answer. There may be more than one correct answer.

1. Which word or words go with *against* and *refuse?*
   (a) oppose (b) extend (c) boycott (d) vacate

2. Which word or words go with *jail?*
   (a) ceremony (b) custody (c) horizon (d) exhibit

3. Which word or words go with *shame?*
   (a) depend (b) degrade (c) detain (d) descend

4. Which word or words go with *bigger?*
   (a) integrate (b) extend (c) declare (d) expand

5. Which word or words go with *bring together?*
   (a) combine (b) segregate (c) integrate (d) unveil

6. Which word or words go with *joyful?*
   (a) conspicuous (b) triumphant (c) jubilant (d) arrogant

7. Which word or words go with *greatest?*
   (a) eloquent (b) supreme (c) degrading (d) superior

8. Which word or words go with *the law?*
   (a) pardon (b) verdict (c) triumph (d) violation

9. Which word or words go with *too much pride?*
   (a) enormous (b) plain (c) artificial (d) arrogant

10. Which word or words go with *keep apart?*
   (a) vacate (b) segregate (c) accommodate (d) isolate

Determining Meanings

Circle the letter next to each answer choice that correctly completes the sentence. There may be more than one correct answer.

1. The nation **extends**
   (a) from one ocean to another ocean.
   (b) greetings to the people of Japan.
   (c) to be the site of the next summer Olympic Games.
   (d) millions of people from all over the world.

2. The **segregation**
   (a) is supposed to make the sauce extra salty.
   (b) of Native Americans onto reservations by the U.S. government still affects people today.
   (c) is kept secret until the number is drawn.
   (d) of those who have the flu from those who don't will keep the flu from spreading.

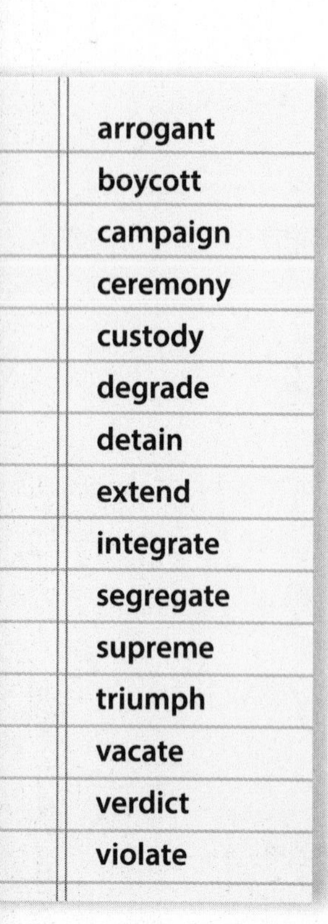

3. The **custody** of
   (a) the prisoner is the duty of the police officer.
   (b) the child is the responsibility of both parents.
   (c) the market likes to shop on Saturdays.
   (d) most teachers is that summer school is a good thing.

4. We **integrated**
   (a) the two grades for certain activities like gymnastics.
   (b) the new student into the school.
   (c) our friends into telling us the truth.
   (d) the light before we went to sleep.

5. The **campaign**
   (a) is rusty and needs to be replaced.
   (b) is filled with cherry trees.
   (c) to save water is almost finished.
   (d) is being led by a superior military.

6. We **vacated**
   (a) the classroom at the end of the day.
   (b) her hair to get out the tangles.
   (c) our home during the fire.
   (d) each book to keep them clean.

7. The **ceremonies**
   (a) reminded us that we have a lot to be grateful for.
   (b) were just under one hour each.
   (c) were found at the park under the slide.
   (d) at Arlington National Cemetery honor the memory of fallen soldiers.

8. We **boycotted**
   (a) the supermarket last month until they supplied clean fruit.
   (b) the company but didn't get what we wanted.
   (c) the team so the coach would be replaced.
   (d) almost two dollars.

2D Completing Sentences

Complete the sentences to demonstrate your knowledge of the words in bold.

1. The **supreme** leader in my classroom is

   ____ .

2. I believe there should be **integration** of

   ____ .

3. A **triumph** for me would be

   ____ .

4. If you **violate** the law, that means you

   ____ .

5. I would be happy to start a **campaign** to

   ____ .

6. A **verdict** is

   ____ .

7. The purpose of a **boycott** is to

   ____ .

8. Someone I might **detain** from entering my room is

   ____ .

9. A **ceremony** I have been to is

____.

10. Someone who is sick might be **segregated** in order to

____.

2E Vocabulary in Context

Read the passage.

The Mother of the Civil Rights Movement

Many people believe that the Civil Rights Movement in America began on December 1, 1955. On that date, an African American woman named Rosa Parks refused to **vacate** her seat on a Montgomery, Alabama, bus so that a white person could sit there. At the time, local laws unjustly allowed African American people to be treated as second-class citizens. Many hotels, restaurants, and even drinking fountains throughout the South were for white people only. And in Montgomery, the state capital of Alabama, as elsewhere throughout the South, city buses were **segregated**. The front ten seats were set aside for white people; African American passengers had to ride in the back.

As an active supporter of civil rights, Rosa Parks knew that this unequal treatment was unfair and **degrading.** She worked closely with an organization in Montgomery that promoted African American people. With the support of this group, Parks decided that it was time to resist. Though she usually walked home from her job in a Montgomery department store, on that winter evening, Parks took the bus. Soon all ten seats in the front of the bus were occupied by white people. When another white man got on, the driver told Parks and three others to give up their seats so that he could **extend** the "white people only" section. The three others gave up their seats, but Parks refused to move. The driver called the police, who took her into **custody.**

Parks was **detained** at the police station for three hours. When she was released, she was ordered to appear in court four days later. There she was found guilty and fined ten dollars. Her lawyers appealed the **verdict,** and the case slowly began making its way through the courts.

Meanwhile, the battle for civil rights was also being fought in the streets of Montgomery. African American people **boycotted** the city's buses. This

arrogant
boycott
campaign
ceremony
custody
degrade
detain
extend
integrate
segregate
supreme
triumph
vacate
verdict
violate

resulted in heavy losses to the company. An African American minister from Atlanta, Georgia, Dr. Martin Luther King Jr., found himself suddenly thrust into a position of leadership. Many white citizens felt that the boycotters were being **arrogant** in demanding equal treatment under the law. There were numerous outbreaks of violence. However, Dr. King preached a message of nonviolence. He urged his supporters never to use force even if they were attacked. The country was moved by his eloquence; they could no longer ignore the racial injustice that had been previously taken for granted. The **campaign** lasted 381 days. It ended on December 20, 1956, when the United States **Supreme** Court made a historic ruling that the Montgomery law violated the United States Constitution. The nation's highest court ordered the city's bus company to **integrate** its buses. In doing so, it sent a powerful message: African American people could no longer be treated as second-class citizens.

It was clear that the movement sparked by Rosa Parks had **triumphed** when Congress passed the 1964 Civil Rights Act. This law opened up public housing, schools, and employment to people of all races. In 1989, Parks was invited to attend **ceremonies** at the White House marking the twenty-fifth anniversary of its passage. In 2002, her former home in Montgomery was placed on the National Register of Historic Places. Rosa Parks died in 2005, but she will always be remembered as the mother of the Civil Rights Movement. Her hundredth birthday would have been February 4, 2013. To mark the date, the United States Postal Service created a Rosa Parks stamp, and later that month President Barack Obama unveiled a statue of her in the U.S. Capitol building.

▶ **Answer each of the following questions with a sentence. If a question does not contain a vocabulary word from the lesson's word list, use one in your answer. Use each word only once.**

1. How do you think African Americans were affected by the bus **boycott?**

____

____

2. What is the meaning of **extend** as it is used in the passage?

____

____

3. Why did Rosa Parks get home late on December 1, 1955?

____

____

4. What is the meaning of **custody** as it is used in the passage?

5. What did the **Supreme** Court rule in 1956?

6. How did **segregation** in the South affect African Americans?

7. What is the meaning of **campaign** as it is used in the passage?

8. How did local laws throughout the South **degrade** African Americans?

9. Why did some white people believe that the African American protesters in Montgomery were behaving **arrogantly?**

10. What was the **verdict** in Rosa Parks's first court case?

11. What was the result of the **integration** of Montgomery's buses?

12. What is the meaning of **triumph** as it is used in the passage?

13. What did those sitting next to Rosa Parks on December 1, 1955, do when they were told to move?

arrogant
boycott
campaign
ceremony
custody
degrade
detain
extend
integrate
segregate
supreme
triumph
vacate
verdict
violate

14. What are two things you might do if called upon to organize a **ceremony** honoring Rosa Parks?

____

____

15. What is the meaning of **violated** as it is used in the passage?

____

____

Fun & Fascinating FACTS

- Captain Charles Boycott ran the Irish estates of the Earl of Erne in the 1880s, a time of great poverty in Ireland. He refused to lower rents and threw those who couldn't afford to pay out of their homes. In an attempt to force him to change his harsh ways, the people of County Mayo banded together and refused to have any dealings with him. Servants would not work in his house, and shopkeepers would not supply him with goods. In a very short time the captain's name had entered the English language. To **boycott** someone or something is to join with others in refusing to have any dealings with that person or organization. The word soon spread to other languages and has the same meaning in French, German, Dutch, and Russian.

- The word **campaign** entered the English language from the Latin by way of the French. The Latin word for *field* is *campus*. Soldiers on active duty are sometimes said to be "in the field"; thus, a series of military actions in a particular area came to be called a *campaign*. The meaning of the word has been expanded so that it no longer refers only to a military course of action. We now have voter registration *campaigns,* antidrug *campaigns,* and *campaigns* to clean up our city streets and parks.

- The Latin word *integer* means "complete" or "whole," and whole numbers such as 1, 2, 3, and 4 are known as *integers*. The word **integrate** is formed from this Latin word; to be *integrated* is to be made *whole* or *complete*.

- The Latin word for a herd or flock is *grex* or *greg*. The word **segregate** is formed by combining this root with the Latin prefix *sed-* or *se-*, which means "apart from." To *segregate* a group is to keep it *apart from* the rest of the *flock*.

- A **verdict** is a decision reached at the end of a trial. The person who announces the *verdict* must speak the truth, as the word itself suggests. It comes from the Latin *dicere,* "to speak," and the Latin *verus,* "true."

Vocabulary Extension

integrate

verb To help a person or persons become part of a larger group.

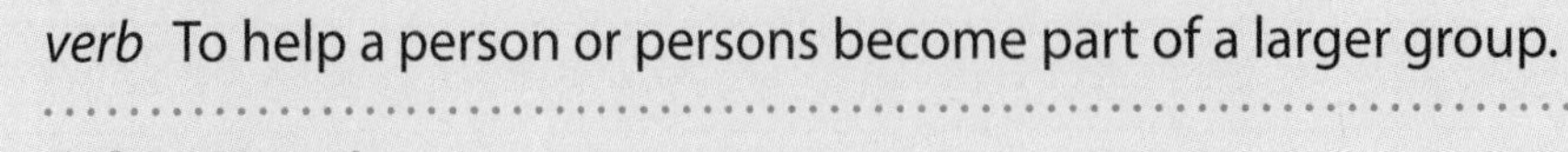

Other Meaning

verb To combine things or work together in a way that makes something better.

Word Family

dis**integrate** (verb)
integration (noun)
integrated (adjective)

Discussion & Writing Prompt

If someone moves to your town, how could you help them **integrate** into the community?

2 min.

1. Turn and talk to your partner or group.

Use this space to take notes or draw your ideas.

3 min.

2. Write 2–4 sentences.

Be ready to share what you have written.

Lesson 3

Word List

Study the definitions of the words. Then do the exercises that follow.

abundant ə bun´ dənt
adj. More than enough; plentiful.
If good weather continues, farmers can expect an **abundant** harvest.

abundance *n.* A great amount.
The Great Lakes are considered a national treasure because of the **abundance** of fresh water they contain.

arid âr´ id
adj. Having little or no rainfall; very dry.
Much of North Africa is **arid** land.

distinct di stiŋkt´
adj. 1. Not the same; different or separate.
Apples come in over two thousand **distinct** varieties.
2. Unmistakable; definite.
Chili peppers add a **distinct** flavor to this dish.

Talk to your partner in two distinct voices.

graze grāz
v. 1. To feed on growing grass.
A small herd of cows **grazed** in the meadow.
2. To touch lightly in passing.
The snowball **grazed** my cheek but didn't hurt me.

Show your partner how you graze your cheek with a piece of paper.

hectic hek´ tik
adj. Full of feverish activity, haste, or confusion.
After a **hectic** week of sightseeing, the tourists were glad to go home and relax.

horde hôrd
n. A large group or crowd, especially one on the move.
Hordes of swimmers head for the pool in summer.

humid hyo͞o´ mid
adj. Having a large amount of water or moisture in the air.
Residents of Hong Kong escape the hot, **humid** weather by going inside where it is cool and dry.

humidity *n.* (hyo͞o mid´ ə tē) The amount of moisture in the air.
The **humidity** was so high that the slightest activity made us sweat.

Describe to your partner how you feel in humid weather.

incredible in kred´ ə bəl
adj. Hard or impossible to believe.
It seems **incredible** that humans and stars are made of the same stuff.

inhabit
in hab´ it

v. To live in or on.
Millions of bison once **inhabited** the great plains of America.

inhabitant *n.* (in hab´ i tənt) A person or animal that lives in a certain place.
Many of the **inhabitants** of California were born somewhere else.

Tell your partner about the people who inhabit your home.

peninsula
pə nin´ sə lə

n. A piece of land, connected to a larger land mass, that juts out and is almost completely surrounded by water.
Bays along the Baja **peninsula** provide shelter for several kinds of whales.

rural
roor´ əl

adj. Of or relating to the country and the people who live there.
The villagers believe that a shopping mall has no place in a **rural** area.

sanctuary
saŋk´ cho͞o er ē

n. 1. A place of safety or shelter.
The neighboring country was a **sanctuary** to those who were being persecuted.

2. Protection offered by such a place.
The shelter offers **sanctuary** for stray animals.

Discuss with your partner places around your area that could be sanctuaries for those in need.

splendor
splen´ dər

n. Magnificence; brilliance of appearance.
The **splendor** of the palace at Versailles took our breath away.

splendid *adj.* Very impressive; magnificent.
The exhibition of American sculpture includes several **splendid** Brazilian statues.

Tell your partner about a splendid piece of music you listened to recently.

squalor
skwä´ lər

n. Filth; misery.
People lived in **squalor** after their homes were destroyed by the hurricane.

squalid *adj.* Dirty and unfit for living, especially as a result of neglect.
When their father climbed into the tree house, he was shocked at the **squalid** conditions and told them to clean it up before continuing to play.

Talk to your partner about whether your family would describe your room as "squalid."

terrain
tə rān´

n. 1. An area of land; a region.
After hiking for several days, we knew the **terrain** quite well.

2. The surface features of a region.
The mountainous **terrain** of western Colorado attracts skiers from all parts of the country.

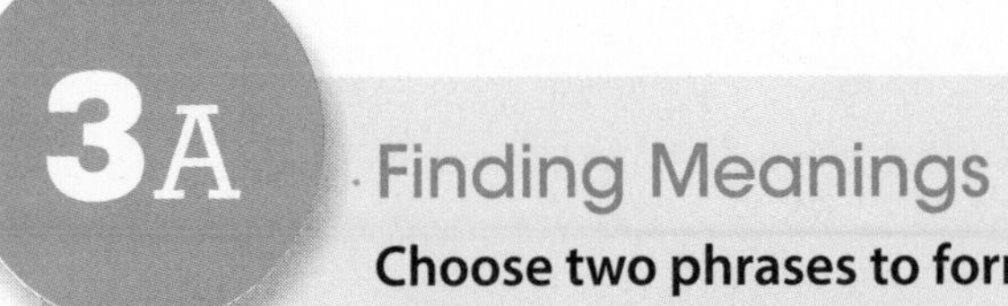

Finding Meanings

Choose two phrases to form a sentence that correctly uses a word from Word List 3. Then write the sentence.

1. (a) Squalid areas are those
   (b) with little rainfall.
   (c) Rural areas are those
   (d) away from large cities.

2. (a) a place where prisoners are held before trial.
   (b) land almost completely surrounded by water.
   (c) A sanctuary is
   (d) A peninsula is

3. (a) Something that is abundant is
   (b) hard to understand.
   (c) Something that is incredible is
   (d) hard to believe.

4. (a) dampness in the air.
   (b) Terrain is
   (c) Humidity is
   (d) the condition of being hot.

5. (a) A squalid building is
   (b) A splendid building is
   (c) one that is not lived in.
   (d) one that is dirty and neglected.

6. (a) A horde is
   (b) a place where one may find safety.
   (c) An abundance is
   (d) a large crowd on the move.

7. (a) A splendid change is
   (b) A distinct change is
   (c) one that goes unnoticed.
   (d) one that is unmistakable.

8. (a) Sanctuary is
   (b) the surface features of an area.
   (c) Terrain is
   (d) a lack of confidence in oneself.

____

____

3B Just the Right Word

Replace each phrase in bold with a single word (or form of the word) from the word list.

1. The Underground Railroad offered **a place of shelter** to enslaved people who were escaping to freedom.

2. The first ball from the pitcher **just barely hit** the batter's shoulder.

3. **Large numbers** of fans surrounded the stage door waiting for autographs.

4. Pitcairn Island has fewer than fifty **people who make their homes there.**

5. Her life was **full of feverish activity** because she had soccer practice every day and a big test coming up.

6. Mark Twain wrote mostly about **life away from the cities and towns of** America.

7. The sounds of a flute and a trombone are quite **different from each other,** so you can easily tell them apart.

8. Few crops can be grown where the land is **very dry and gets little rain.**

9. Monet's later paintings capture the **magnificent appearance** of his garden at Giverny.

10. Italy is a large **country that is almost completely surrounded by water.**

11. The rough **surface features of the land** made travel difficult.

12. Crops grow in **quantities that provide more than is needed** in such fertile soil.

Word List
abundant
arid
distinct
graze
hectic
horde
humid
incredible
inhabit
peninsula
rural
sanctuary
splendor
squalor
terrain

3C

Applying Meanings

Circle the letter or letters next to each correct answer. There may be more than one correct answer.

1. Which of the following animals **graze?**
   (a) crocodiles
   (b) sheep
   (c) horses
   (d) cats

2. Which of the following would you find in an **arid** region?
   (a) ponds
   (b) streams
   (c) snow
   (d) cactus plants

3. Which of the following are **abundant?**
   (a) fish in the sea
   (b) water in the desert
   (c) food at a feast
   (d) trees in a forest

4. Which of the following might be found in **hordes?**
   (a) tourists
   (b) ants
   (c) eagles
   (d) water

5. Which of the following might live in **splendor?**
   (a) a supreme ruler
   (b) a famous movie star
   (c) a coal miner
   (d) a person in custody

6. Which of the following places might be **hectic?**
   (a) a restaurant's kitchen
   (b) backstage on opening night
   (c) an airport over a holiday
   (d) a mall on a day in December

7. Which of the following might **inhabit** a tropical island?
   (a) ice sculptors
   (b) penguins
   (c) polar bears
   (d) monkeys

8. Which of the following could cause one to seek **sanctuary?**
   (a) fear
   (b) danger
   (c) happiness
   (d) safety

Word Study: Analogies

Circle the letter next to the pair of words that most nearly expresses the relationship of the pair of words in capital letters.

Analogies test your understanding of the relationship between pairs of words. Example:

HOT : COLD ::
(a) hungry : tired (c) soaked : wet
(b) light : heavy (d) blue : yellow

When we read the analogy we say, "Hot is to cold as ________ is to ________."

The relationship between HOT and COLD is that they are opposites, or antonyms. So, to find the answer, look for a pair of words that are also opposites. *Light* and *heavy* are opposites. None of the other pairs of words have this relationship. So, the correct answer is (b).

HINT! Keep antonyms in mind as you do this exercise.

1. HUMID : ARID ::
   (a) square : round (c) thirsty : hungry
   (b) sloppy : careless (d) wet : dry

2. SPLENDID : SQUALID ::
   (a) attractive : ugly (c) lofty : towering
   (b) loud : noisy (d) lonely : alone

3. POVERTY : WEALTH ::
   (a) love : marriage (c) age : beauty
   (b) sickness : health (d) affection : friend

4. ARROGANT : HUMBLE ::
   (a) cruel : kind (c) abundant : plentiful
   (b) hectic : eloquent (d) friendly : loving

5. AFFECTIONATE : HATEFUL ::
   (a) loud : noisy (c) afraid : terrified
   (b) colorful : bright (d) abundant : scarce

6. VACATE : OCCUPY ::
   (a) release : detain (c) appeal : demand
   (b) graze : touch (d) exhibit : show

abundant
arid
distinct
graze
hectic
horde
humid
incredible
inhabit
peninsula
rural
sanctuary
splendor
squalor
terrain

Vocabulary in Context

Read the passage.

Land of Contrasts

Thailand is a country about the size of France, with a population of over sixty-five million people. About fifty percent of the people live in **rural** areas, away from Bangkok, the nation's capital and its only major city. Tourism is the country's top industry. Every year visitors from all over the world vacation in Bangkok, but most of them leave without seeing the rest of this fascinating country. This is a pity, for Thailand is a land of startling contrasts. It is made up of four **distinct** regions.

The northwestern region is the least accessible part of the country because of its mountainous **terrain** and many forests. Tigers, leopards, bears, and monkeys **inhabit** the more remote areas. Deer and buffalo **graze** on the grasslands that cover the lower slopes of the mountains. One of the world's great wildlife **sanctuaries** is located near the city of Chiang Mai. Its population is only a small fraction of Bangkok's. The two most important industries in this part of the country are lumber and tin mining.

The northeastern part of Thailand is vastly different from the northwestern part. It is by far the poorest region. Few crops grow there because of its **arid** climate and barren soil. Poor highways and a lack of railroads add to its problems. This region has little industry, and most of its people live in poverty. Many have left the land hoping to find work in Bangkok.

The most prosperous region is the great central plain. There the soil is fertile and crops grow in **abundance.** Farmers produce enough rice to feed the people of Thailand and still have some for export. Other crops include cotton, sugar, corn, tobacco, and peanuts. Bangkok is located on the southern edge of the central plain. It is a modern city with huge luxury hotels that have sprung up in recent years to accommodate the ever-increasing **hordes** of tourists. Many of them visit Bangkok to explore its rich cultural history. Among the city's attractions are over four hundred Buddhist temples and numerous universities. There is also a huge Grand Palace where the rulers of Thailand once lived in luxury. Not all of the capital is **splendid,** though. Tourists seldom stray from the downtown area, with its many expensive shops and fine restaurants. But not far off are the more **squalid** parts of Bangkok. There the city's poor live in overcrowded conditions.

The fourth distinctive region is the southern part of the country. It reaches to the Malaysian **peninsula,** within five hundred miles of the equator. This part of Thailand is mostly tropical rainforest, with a **humid** climate and over two hundred inches of rain a year. It has an **incredible** variety of plant and animal life. For example, over one thousand different kinds of butterflies live there! It also has some of the finest beaches in the world to lure those tourists seeking a change from the **hectic** city life of Bangkok.

Visitors who spend a week or two in Bangkok may go home and tell their families and friends that they have seen Thailand. However, only those who have explored all four regions of the country can truly say, "I have seen Thailand."

▶ **Answer each of the following questions with a sentence. If a question does not contain a vocabulary word from the lesson's word list, use one in your answer. Use each word only once.**

1. What is the meaning of **terrain** as it is used in the passage?

____

____

2. Why would many people in Thailand be unaccustomed to city life?

____

____

3. Which parts of Bangkok would *not* be shown in tourist brochures?

____

____

4. Why have so many large new hotels been built in Bangkok?

____

____

5. Why would you expect daily life in Bangkok to be more **hectic** than in Chiang Mai?

____

____

6. How can you tell that no one in Malaysia lives far from the sea?

____

____

abundant
arid
distinct
graze
hectic
horde
humid
incredible
inhabit
peninsula
rural
sanctuary
splendor
squalor
terrain

7. What is one of the most **splendid** sights in Bangkok?

8. Why would Thailand's tropical rainforest be a good place to make a nature film?

9. What is the meaning of **distinct** as it is used in the passage?

10. Give an example of Thailand's **abundance** of animal life.

11. What is the meaning of **sanctuary** as it is used in the passage?

12. Which of the four regions of Thailand gets the least amount of rain? How do you know?

13. How many **inhabitants** does Thailand have?

14. Why would you be likely to sweat a lot in the rainforest?

15. What is the meaning of **graze** as it is used in the passage?

Fun & Fascinating FACTS

- **Horde** comes from the Polish word *horda,* which in turn came from the Turkish word *ordu,* meaning "military camp" or "army." Centuries ago, the Turkish Mongols swept across Asia and eastern Europe in vast numbers, conquering the people in those areas. The word *horde* came to mean "a large number [of people] on the move." Don't confuse this word with *hoard,* which is a noun and means "a hidden supply or store." *Hoard* is also a verb that means "to save and store away in a greedy or secret manner." *Horde* and *hoard* are homophones; they sound the same but have different meanings and spellings.

- The antonym of **rural** is *urban*. New York City is a large *urban* center; upper New York State, with its many farms and small towns, is mostly *rural*.

- In Latin, *sanctus* means "holy," and the original meaning of **sanctuary** is "a holy place." Churches, temples, and mosques were considered *sanctuaries;* people in trouble with the law could find protection in such places because officers of the law would not enter them. The word *sanctuary* came to mean "protection offered by being in a holy place," and its meaning was later extended to include any place that offers safety. A bird *sanctuary*, for example, offers protection to the birds that nest there.

abundant
arid
distinct
graze
hectic
horde
humid
incredible
inhabit
peninsula
rural
sanctuary
splendor
squalor
terrain

3 Vocabulary Extension

distinct

adjective Clearly different.

Word Family

distinction (noun)
distinctive (adjective)
distinctly (adverb)

Synonyms and Antonyms

Synonyms: different, unlike, non-identical
Antonyms: same, alike, identical

Discussion & Writing Prompt

Gasoline has a **distinct** smell. Give another example of something that has a **distinct** smell and describe what it smells like to you.

2 min. 1. Turn and talk to your partner or group.	3 min. 2. Write 2–4 sentences.
Use this space to take notes or draw your ideas.	Be ready to share what you have written.

Word List

Study the definitions of the words. Then do the exercises that follow.

aloft
ə lôft´

adv. Up in the air, especially in flight.
A strong breeze kept the kites **aloft.**

attain
ə tān´

v. 1. To reach; to arrive at.
Redwood trees **attain** heights of over three hundred feet.

2. To achieve.
DeShawn **attained** his goal of getting straight A's on his report card.

Tell your partner one thing you plan to do when you attain age eighteen.

buffet
bə fā´

n. 1. A piece of furniture with drawers and shelves for the storage and display of plates, dishes, and bowls.
This splendid antique **buffet** contains a valuable collection of china.

2. A meal laid out for guests to help themselves.
The abundance of food at the **buffet** allowed people to go back for second or third helpings.

v. (buf´ ət) To pound repeatedly; to batter.
High winds and waves **buffeted** the ship during the storm.

Show your partner what you would look like if you were being buffeted by the wind.

elude
ē lo͞od´

v. To escape by being quick or clever.
The mouse **eluded** the cat by slipping through a crack in the wall.

elusive *adj.* (ē lo͞o´ siv) 1. Hard to find or capture.
The **elusive** eagle flew above the pine trees before disappearing again.

2. Hard to explain or make clear.
Albert Einstein's connection between energy and the speed of light is too **elusive** for most nonscientists to grasp.

Discuss with your partner why math is elusive for some students.

flammable
flam´ ə bəl

adj. Able to catch fire easily.
Building materials must be fireproofed so they are not **flammable.**

hover
huv´ ər

v. To remain in place over an object or location.
Hummingbirds **hover** by beating their wings sixty times a second.

inflate
in flāt´

v. To fill with air or other gas.
Inflate your bike tires to the correct pressure.

Tell your partner what happens when you inflate a balloon too much.

jeopardy
jep´ ər dē

n. Danger.
Mountaineers who climb without partners put their lives in **jeopardy.**

jeopardize *v.* To put in danger of loss or injury.
Bikers **jeopardize** their safety by riding without a helmet.

Chat with your partner about whether you would jeopardize your life by skydiving or mountain climbing.

moor
moor

v. To hold in place with ropes or anchors.
After the sailors **moored** the boat to the dock, they went ashore.

mooring *n.* A place to which a boat or aircraft can be moored.
The hurricane tore many boats from their **moorings.**

plummet
plum´ ət

v. To fall suddenly toward the earth or to a lower level; to plunge.
We tried not to panic as the apartment elevator **plummeted** to the basement.

pollute
pə lo͞ot´

v. To make impure or dirty.
Teachers help keep your mind from being **polluted** by incorrect information.

pollution *n.* (pə lo͞o´ shən) The action of polluting; the state of being polluted.
The careless dumping of poisonous chemicals caused widespread **pollution** of the soil.

propel
prə pel´

v. To push or drive forward.
Two engines **propelled** the speedboat.

stationary
stā´ shə ner ē

adj. 1. Not moving.
A **stationary** bicycle is used for exercise.

2. Not changing.
The price of admission to the ballpark has remained **stationary** for the past couple of years.

Show your partner how you can be stationary for ten seconds.

superb
so͞o pʉrb´

adj. Of the highest quality; grand; splendid.
The view from the mountaintop was **superb.**

Tell your partner about a superb meal you ate recently.

swivel *n.* A fastening that allows any part joined to it to swing freely.
swiv´ əl This chair has a **swivel** that enables it to turn in a full circle.

v. To turn freely around a fixed point.
Owls can **swivel** their heads to look behind them.

4A Using Words in Context

Read the following sentences. If the word in bold is used correctly, write C on the line. If the word is used incorrectly, write I on the line.

aloft
attain
buffet
elude
flammable
hover
inflate
jeopardy
moor
plummet
pollute
propel
stationary
superb
swivel

1. (a) The price of pool admission will remain **stationary** for the summer. ___
   (b) We poured the **stationary** in the bowl. ___
   (c) Sometimes the dog runs, and sometimes it is **stationary.** ___
   (d) The bird was **stationary** for twenty minutes before it finally flew away. ___

2. (a) The **buffet** is made of oak and is two hundred years old. ___
   (b) Sudden gusts of wind **buffeted** the campers' tent. ___
   (c) Sanaa **buffeted** her shoes and went for a run. ___
   (d) The **buffet** had piles and piles of fruit. ___

3. (a) You **jeopardize** your safety when you stand up in a canoe. ___
   (b) In early May, **jeopardy** grew in the dirt next to our garage. ___
   (c) You **jeopardize** your cat when you let him roam around outside. ___
   (d) The **jeopardy** they were planning would probably fail. ___

4. (a) The sign says that the ocean is too **polluted** for swimming. ___
   (b) Smoke from the factory was a major cause of air **pollution.** ___
   (c) We may be able to reverse the **pollution** and make the pond clean again. ___
   (d) The patient became **polluted** after taking just a few steps. ___

5. (a) My skin feels **elusive** if I spend too much time in the sun. ___
   (b) The escaped dog **eluded** its owners for over a year. ___
   (c) Her name remained **elusive** until someone reminded me what it was. ___
   (d) The test score is **eluded** in your final grade. ___

6. (a) You can **attain** your goals if you work hard. ___
   (b) When you **attain** the age of eighteen, you can vote. ___
   (c) The blue whale can **attain** a length of a hundred feet. ___
   (d) I threw away the box but **attained** the ribbon and bow. ___

7. (a) Marya was a **superb** singer and won an audition for the local opera. ___
   (b) The Patels have a white rug in their **superb.** ___
   (c) The coffee from Jamaica is considered **superb.** ___
   (d) The most **superb** skateboard is the worst ever made. ___

8. (a) I **swiveled** the money from between the couch cushions. ___
   (b) Small children start to **swivel** if they don't get their own way. ___
   (c) The weather vane turns on its **swivel** if the wind changes direction. ___
   (d) Tell your sister to stop **swiveling** on the stool. ___

9. (a) My cousin **hovered** over me as I opened her gift. ___
   (b) The helicopter can **hover** in one place. ___
   (c) Is anyone **hovering** to see the movie tonight? ___
   (d) I got on my bike and **hovered** over to my friend's house. ___

10. (a) Sometimes my mom seems to be able to **propel** what I'm thinking. ___
    (b) Good grades **propelled** me closer to the honor roll. ___
    (c) Early aircraft **propelled** by steam engines were too heavy to fly. ___
    (d) I felt **propelled** to tell him that he had hurt my feelings. ___

4B Making Connections

Circle the letter next to each correct answer. There may be more than one correct answer.

1. Which word or words go with *reach?*
   (a) elude (b) attain (c) jeopardy (d) achieve

2. Which word or words go with *flying?*
   (a) hover (b) altitude (c) aloft (d) stationary

3. Which word or words go with *the best?*
   (a) superior (b) grasp (c) superb (d) elusive

4. Which word or words go with *higher?*
   (a) ascend (b) swivel (c) elevate (d) aloft

5. Which word or words go with *sailing?*
   (a) voyage (b) helm (c) flammable (d) moor

6. Which word or words go with *burning?*
   (a) abundant (b) flammable (c) elusive (d) stationary

7. Which word or words go with *food?*
   (a) extend (b) buffet (c) expand (d) inflate

8. Which word or words go with *falling?*
   (a) buffet (b) plunge (c) plead (d) plummet

9. Which word or words go with *movement?*
   (a) violate (b) propel (c) launch (d) catapult

10. Which word or words go with *danger?*
   (a) flammable (b) jeopardy (c) triumph (d) eloquence

Determining Meanings

Circle the letter next to each answer choice that correctly completes the sentence. There may be more than one correct answer.

- aloft
- attain
- buffet
- elude
- flammable
- hover
- inflate
- jeopardy
- moor
- plummet
- pollute
- propel
- stationary
- superb
- swivel

1. You **inflated**
   (a) the raft before we got in the water.
   (b) the tires because they needed more air.
   (c) the birthday balloons with helium.
   (d) your grandfather and kissed him on the cheek.

2. We were **buffeted**
   (a) by strong winds while out on the boat.
   (b) back and forth on the carnival ride.
   (c) with a banquet when we got back.
   (d) new scooters by my aunt and uncle.

3. They were **aloft**
   (a) in their hot-air balloon with the trees below them.
   (b) to see that both their names were on the list for the basketball team.
   (c) in the depths of the ocean.
   (d) on their first flight, and it was so much fun.

4. The Changs **moored**
   (a) next to a forty-foot sailboat.
   (b) their canoe to the dock and went ashore for a meal.
   (c) closer and closer to the rocks but luckily just missed them.
   (d) to a new apartment last year.

5. We began **plummeting** when
   (a) we ate dinner.
   (b) we heard the hilarious joke.
   (c) the elevator broke.
   (d) the roller coaster reached the highest point.

6. The **pollution**
   (a) in the oceans is caused by chemicals and trash.
   (b) in the air makes it hard to breathe.
   (c) of the lake should be easy to fix.
   (d) to the math problem is in the book.

7. The **swiveling**
   (a) globe can turn in a full circle.
   (b) chair is stuck and won't move.
   (c) grew louder as we swam farther into the pool.
   (d) that came out of his mouth shocked everyone.

8. Our **attainment**
   (a) reaches speeds of two hundred miles per hour.
   (b) of the hockey trophy makes me proud.
   (c) is flooded with water.
   (d) of the apples at the top of the tree means we can have a snack.

Completing Sentences

Complete the sentences to demonstrate your knowledge of the words in bold.

1. An **elusive** idea is one that is

   ____ .

2. One way you can put yourself in **jeopardy** is to

   ____ .

3. Something that can cause **pollution** is

   ____ .

4. To be a **superb** leader, you should

____.

5. A goal I would like to **attain** is

____.

6. My favorite item at a **buffet** is

____.

7. We need to be careful with **flammable** materials because

____.

8. Something that **swivels** is

____.

9. A **stationary** target is easy to hit because

____.

10. Something you can **inflate** is

____.

4E Vocabulary in Context

Read the passage.

aloft
attain
buffet
elude
flammable
hover
inflate
jeopardy
moor
plummet
pollute
propel
stationary
superb
swivel

A Different Way to Fly

Billboards standing along the highway are easily ignored, but a two-hundred-foot billboard floating across the sky grabs everyone's attention. That's why blimps are so attractive to advertisers with a product to sell or a message to communicate. But advertising is only one of the uses for a blimp.

Blimps can be moved easily to different locations at varying altitudes. This makes them useful for a variety of purposes. Scientists use blimps for collecting samples used in the study of air **pollution;** the United States Navy employs them for offshore patrols; and one was even used to search for the **elusive** Loch Ness monster, supposed to inhabit a lake in Scotland.

The main body of the blimp is a large bag, called the envelope. It is **inflated** with helium gas. The blimp stays **aloft** because helium is seven times lighter than air. Once inside the envelope, the helium is left there unless the blimp needs major repairs. After the envelope has been filled, a cabin called a gondola is attached under it; this is where the crew and passengers ride. It is also where the light panels used for advertisements are attached. Computer graphics provide a dazzling display of pictures and words that can't be matched by any billboard.

Blimps are **propelled** by two engines, one on each side, and can **attain** a top speed of about forty miles an hour. Although slow in comparison to airplanes, blimps can do something most planes cannot: They can stop and **hover** in midair. This ability enables them to provide a **stationary** platform for the television cameras covering sporting events, giving viewers a bird's-eye view of the action.

Blimps are not designed to take a **buffeting** from high winds, though. They usually can go up only when the air is calm. When not flying, they have to be **moored** by the front end to a tall mast on a truck specially equipped for this purpose. Plenty of space is needed because the blimp has to be free to **swivel** clear of the ground when the wind changes.

In some cities it is possible to buy a ticket and go on a sightseeing trip in a blimp; because blimps fly so slowly and at such a low altitude, those on board enjoy **superb** views of the ground below. You might wonder what would happen if the envelope got a small hole in it. Would the helium rush out, causing the gondola to **plummet** to the ground? Passengers need not worry about that; their lives would not be in **jeopardy** if such a thing happened. Why? The pressure of the air outside the envelope is greater than that of the helium inside. Because of that, the helium doesn't easily escape. And because helium is not **flammable,** there is no danger of the envelope's contents catching fire. Flying in a blimp is safe and enjoyable.

▶ **Answer each of the following questions with a sentence. If a question does not contain a vocabulary word from the lesson's word list, use one in your answer. Use each word only once.**

1. Give two reasons why helium is used to fill a blimp's envelope.

____

____

2. For how long does the blimp's envelope remain **inflated?**

____

____

3. What is the meaning of **elusive** as it is used in the passage?

____

____

4. What would happen to the gondola if it became separated from the envelope while the blimp was in flight?

5. What is the meaning of **stationary** as it is used in the passage?

6. How can blimps be of use in scientific studies of the air?

7. What is the purpose of the **swivel** to which a blimp is attached?

8. Why does a blimp need to be **moored** when not flying?

9. Why does a blimp's movement not depend on the direction of the wind?

10. What is the meaning of **attain** as it is used in the passage?

11. How could bad weather **jeopardize** a planned trip in a blimp?

12. Are engines essential to keep a blimp in the air? Why or why not?

13. Why do some advertisers think a blimp is a **superb** way to get their message across?

aloft
attain
buffet
elude
flammable
hover
inflate
jeopardy
moor
plummet
pollute
propel
stationary
superb
swivel

14. What is the meaning of **buffet** as it is used in the passage?

____

____

15. Why is a blimp useful as a platform for cameras for sporting events?

____

____

Fun & Fascinating FACTS

- The noun formed from the verb **inflate** is *inflation*. This word has a special meaning in economics. As wages and prices rise, a dollar no longer buys what it did earlier. A movie ticket once cost a quarter. What does it cost today? Twenty times as much? More? That's *inflation!*

- **Stationary** is an adjective and means "not moving." *Stationery* is a noun and means "writing materials such as paper, envelopes, pens, and pencils." These two words are connected as the following story tells. Centuries ago in London, people sold goods from stalls set up near the London law courts. Some were permitted to stay in one spot for a short time only and then had to move to a new location. Others had special licenses that allowed them to stay in one place; they were called *stationers* because they did not move. Many of these *stationary* stall holders sold writing materials to the people who worked in the law courts, and because they were called stationers, the writing materials they sold came to be called *stationery*.

  By the early 1800s, spelling became fixed in its present form. The two different meanings were indicated by different spellings. *Stationary* was the adjective form and meant "not moving." *Stationery* was the noun form and meant "writing materials."

  These two words are homophones; they have different meanings and spellings but are pronounced the same. It will keep you from confusing these two words if you remember the *a* is in the *adjective* form.

Vocabulary Extension

attain

verb To succeed in meeting a goal, especially after trying for a long time.

Academic Context

Hard work and excellent attendance will help you **attain** the best grades.

Context Clues

These sentences give clues to the meaning of **attain.**

*After many years of training, Ina was able to **attain** her goal of dancing with the city ballet company.*

*Kai worked hard to **attain** the position of student-council president.*

Discussion & Writing Prompt

Tell about one of your personal goals. How do you plan to **attain** it?

2 min. 1. Turn and talk to your partner or group.	3 min. 2. Write 2–4 sentences.
Use this space to take notes or draw your ideas.	Be ready to share what you have written.

Review

Crossword Puzzle Solve the crossword puzzle by studying the clues and filling in the answer boxes. The number after a clue is the lesson the word is from.

Clues Across

1. A request for help **(1)**
5. More than enough; plentiful **(3)**
8. To hold in place with ropes or anchors **(4)**
10. A fond or tender feeling **(1)**
11. To reach; to arrive at **(4)**
12. To grasp or hold tightly **(1)**
13. To break, as a law or promise **(2)**
16. Having a large amount of moisture in the air **(3)**
20. A large crowd **(3)**
21. To cause to suffer; to inflict hardship on **(1)**
22. People have a duty to ______ in an election.
23. To touch lightly in passing **(3)**
25. To make empty, as by leaving **(2)**
26. ______ and key
27. The 37th president of the United States
28. Responsibility for the care and control of **(2)**

Clues Down

2. To push or drive forward **(4)**
3. Very tall; high up **(1)**
4. To show in public **(1)**
6. To pound repeatedly; to batter **(4)**
7. Opposite of *dead*
9. Opposite of *to lower*
12. A series of actions to accomplish a goal **(2)**
14. Showing too much pride in oneself **(2)**
15. Unmistakable; definite **(3)**
17. To make known or show for the first time **(1)**
18. To stop or hold; to keep from proceeding **(2)**
19. Of or relating to the country **(3)**
20. Opposite of *there*
24. Having little or no rainfall; very dry **(3)**

Word List

Study the definitions of the words. Then do the exercises that follow.

antic an´ tik
n. (usually plural) A playful or funny act.
The **antics** of the clown made the crowd roar with laughter.

attire ə tīr´
n. Clothes, especially fine and expensive clothes.
One often needs special **attire** to be in a wedding party.
v. To dress up or be dressed up.
The designer **attired** the models in shirts and trousers for the fashion show.

captivate kap´ ti vāt
v. To please greatly; to win over by special charm.
The cast's superb acting **captivated** the audience.

Explain to your partner why an actor or a singer captivates you.

deft deft
adj. Quick and sure; skillful at handling.
A **deft** juggler can keep five or more objects in the air at one time.

diligent dil´ ə jənt
adj. Working with great care and effort.
Diligent students succeed in reaching their goals.

Tell your partner about a family member or a friend who is a diligent worker.

eclipse ē klips´
n. The total or partial hiding of one heavenly body by another.
An **eclipse** of the sun occurs when the moon passes directly in front of it.
v. To do or be better than; to outshine.
Her latest novel **eclipses** all her previous work.

Discuss with your partner how you feel when a friend's or family member's achievement eclipses yours.

evolve ē vôlv´
v. To develop and change gradually over time.
Scientists think that modern birds may have **evolved** from dinosaurs.
evolution *n.* (ev ə lo͞o´ shən) The changes that take place as something evolves.
The **evolution** of aircraft from the Wright brothers' flimsy plane to the modern jet airplane occurred over an incredibly short time.

Discuss with your partner how your thoughts about eating a good diet and exercising regularly might evolve as you get older.

innate in āt´
adj. Having from birth; occurring naturally rather than being learned.
The singer's **innate** musical ability showed itself at a very early age.

inscribe
in skrīb´

v. To write, print, or etch into as a permanent record.
Most of the gravestones were simply **inscribed** with the person's name, date of birth, and date of death.

inscription *n.* (in skrip´ shən) The act of inscribing or what is inscribed.
Coins of the United States bear the **inscription** *E Pluribus Unum*, a Latin phrase that means "Out of many, one."

posture
päs´ chər

n. The way one holds one's body; a pose or position.
You can improve your **posture** by throwing your shoulders back.

v. To assume a particular position, especially a pretended one.
They **postured** as my friends while secretly talking behind my back.

Take turns demonstrating examples of good and bad posture with your partner while sitting in your chairs.

shroud
shroud

n. 1. Something that covers or hides from view.
A **shroud** of mystery surrounds the couple's disappearance.

2. Cloth used to wrap a dead body before burial.
It used to be the custom to make a **shroud** from a long linen sheet dipped in melted wax.

v. To block from sight.
Dense fog on the river **shrouded** the tugboats.

stifle
stī´ fəl

v. 1. To cut off the air from; to smother.
Thick smoke **stifled** those who sat around the campfire.

2. To hold back; to check.
The spectators tried to **stifle** their yawns during the lengthy ceremony.

tentative
ten´ tə tiv

adj. Not fully worked out or final; hesitating or uncertain.
The deadline is **tentative** and may be extended.

Ask your partner if his or her plans for today after school are definite or tentative.

tranquil
traŋ´ kwil

adj. Calm; peaceful.
The sea was **tranquil** with no hint of the approaching storm.

tranquility *n.* (traŋ kwil´ ə tē) The state of being tranquil.
Many authors prefer writing during the **tranquility** of early morning before anyone else is up.

versatile
vʉr´ sə təl

adj. Able to do many different things or to be used in many different ways.
She is a **versatile** musician who can play eight instruments.

versatility *n.* (vʉr sə til´ ə tē) The state or condition of being versatile.
The tomato's **versatility** and distinct flavor make it a favorite of many cooks.

Chat with your partner about how a piece of paper can be a versatile item.

Finding Meanings

Choose two phrases to form a sentence that correctly uses a word from Word List 5. Then write the sentence.

1. (a) To evolve is to
   (b) To posture is to
   (c) pretend to a position one doesn't really hold.
   (d) remain in one position without moving.

____

____

2. (a) make fun of that person.
   (b) To attire someone is to
   (c) dress that person.
   (d) To captivate someone is to

____

____

3. (a) A deft move is one that
   (b) is made in an uncertain way.
   (c) is repeated over and over.
   (d) A tentative move is one that

____

____

4. (a) gradual change over time.
   (b) Tranquility is
   (c) the ability to do many things well.
   (d) Evolution is

____

____

5. (a) A diligent person is one who
   (b) engages in foolish or playful acts.
   (c) A versatile person is one who
   (d) makes an effort to exercise great care.

____

____

6. (a) To stifle someone is to
   (b) To eclipse someone is to
   (c) fill that person with joy.
   (d) cut off that person's supply of air.

____

____

7. (a) Versatility is
   (b) Tranquility is
   (c) the state of being at peace.
   (d) an unwillingness to change one's mind.

____

____

8. (a) Something that is inscribed is
   (b) carried out in secret.
   (c) written into a permanent record.
   (d) Something that is innate is

____

____

Word List
antic
attire
captivate
deft
diligent
eclipse
evolve
innate
inscribe
posture
shroud
stifle
tentative
tranquil
versatile

9. (a) a covering for a dead body.
   (b) An eclipse is
   (c) a silly or playful act.
   (d) A shroud is

____

____

10. (a) To be deft
    (b) is to be greatly pleased.
    (c) To be captivated
    (d) is to be held against one's will.

____

____

5B Just the Right Word

Replace each phrase in bold with a single word (or form of the word) from the word list.

1. The children's **playful acts** made their parents roar with laughter.

2. Your **ability to do so many things well** was what impressed me the most.

3. What is the correct **clothing that should be worn** for an awards banquet?

4. She **completely won over** the audience with her fine performance.

5. I admire the **very skillful** way you handled what could have been an embarrassing situation.

6. When is the next **time that the earth will pass directly between the sun's position and that** of the moon?

7. My aunt's exceptional vigor was **present from the time of her birth;** even as an infant she was active and strong.

8. Your backache is probably caused by your poor **way of holding your body.**

9. The bride **struggled to hold back** a giggle when the nervous bridegroom dropped the ring during the ceremony.

10. A thick fog **hid from sight everything that was in** the harbor.

Applying Meanings

Circle the letter or letters next to each correct answer. There may be more than one correct answer.

1. Which of the following can be **versatile?**
   (a) a tool
   (b) a date in history
   (c) a performer
   (d) a thank-you note

2. Which of the following is a piece of **attire?**
   (a) a vest
   (b) a walking stick
   (c) a hat
   (d) a pair of gloves

3. Which of the following might be an **antic?**
   (a) tickling someone
   (b) robbing someone
   (c) making funny faces
   (d) turning cartwheels

4. Which of the following could be **tentative?**
   (a) a movement
   (b) a suggestion
   (c) a proposal
   (d) a triumph

5. Which of the following have **evolved?**
   (a) plants
   (b) human beings
   (c) animals
   (d) automobiles

6. On which of the following might you find an **inscription?**
   (a) a pedestal
   (b) the front of a building
   (c) the inside cover of a book
   (d) an exhibit in a museum

7. Which of the following would you expect to be **tranquil?**
   (a) a hectic chase
   (b) a sanctuary
   (c) a rural scene
   (d) a rose garden

8. Which of the following is a **posture?**
   (a) sitting slumped over
   (b) dressing up
   (c) standing up with arms crossed
   (d) standing with bent knees

antic
attire
captivate
deft
diligent
eclipse
evolve
innate
inscribe
posture
shroud
stifle
tentative
tranquil
versatile

Word Study: Synonyms and Antonyms

Each group of four words contains either two synonyms or two antonyms. Circle that pair. Then circle the S if they are synonyms or the A if they are antonyms.

1. outshine	eclipse	vacate	posture	S	A
2. skillful	deft	humid	innate	S	A
3. tranquil	hidden	peaceful	versatile	S	A
4. exchange	purify	pollute	propel	S	A
5. swivel	charge	inflate	turn	S	A
6. hectic	distinct	rural	calm	S	A
7. squalid	diligent	versatile	magnificent	S	A
8. superb	splendid	distinct	enormous	S	A
9. danger	buffet	terrain	jeopardy	S	A
10. propel	detain	pollute	persecute	S	A

Vocabulary in Context

Read the passage.

A Born Artist

To exhibit one's work at the Smithsonian Institution in Washington, D.C., would be a high point in any artist's career; to receive such an honor at the age of fourteen is truly remarkable. Yet that was the age of the Chinese painter Wang Yani when her paintings were given their first American showing there in 1989. Hundreds of thousands of visitors came and were **captivated** by her pictures of animals, birds, and landscapes. And in the Smithsonian's Sackler Gallery, audiences were able to watch as Yani, barefoot and **attired** casually in shirt and denim shorts, walked on stage. With **deft** strokes of the brush, she produced works of art right before their eyes. She did so with total concentration, seemingly unaware of the onlookers.

If fourteen seems a young age to receive so much attention, consider this: Yani's first exhibition, in her native China, was held when she was four! She has been working **diligently** at her art since the age of two; that was when Wang Shi Chiang first became aware of his daughter's interest in painting. Himself a well-known artist, he encouraged Yani by providing her with large sheets of paper, ink, and brushes. These are the traditional materials of Chinese painting. He never gave her a lesson and also discouraged her teachers at school from doing so. He believed such instruction would only **stifle** her imagination and prevent her from expressing her feelings freely. His faith in his daughter's **innate** talent was fully justified by her early success. In fact, Wang Yani's fame soon **eclipsed** her father's fame.

Yani's first subjects were monkeys. She became fascinated with their **antics** after a visit to the local zoo. She has painted hundreds of pictures of them. One of her favorites is thirty feet long and took her just four hours to complete. It shows 112 monkeys in various **postures,** each with a different expression.

As she grew older, she became more **versatile** and began painting other creatures such as birds, horses, and lions. Later, her style **evolved.** She broadened her range of subjects to include trees, flowers, and, especially, landscapes. Her interest in landscapes is not surprising, because Yani lives in a region of great natural beauty in southern China, with gently rolling hills, clear streams, and ancient temples. Not far away are the famous cone-shaped Guilin mountains. The mountains are often **shrouded** in mist and are a favorite subject of the young painter. Yani paints what she feels about what she

- antic
- attire
- captivate
- deft
- diligent
- eclipse
- evolve
- innate
- inscribe
- posture
- shroud
- stifle
- tentative
- tranquil
- versatile

sees rather than simply what she sees. In her paintings of the mountains, she tries to capture the feeling of **tranquility** that she experienced while visiting the scene.

She often begins by spilling ink onto the paper, a method known as *po-mo*. She follows this with a few **tentative** strokes. Then she proceeds rapidly until the painting is completed, often in less than half an hour. Yani often includes an **inscription** in Chinese characters as part of a painting. A typical one reads, "Autumn is a withering season for the trees, but the animals are happy."

By the time she was sixteen, Yani had painted more than ten thousand pictures. Today, as an adult, she is still painting. Her work continues to grow and change. She finds new ideas in nature and in the changing world around her. She also finds them through singing and dancing. These are skills that she feels have helped with her painting. In a good painting, according to a Chinese saying, "the brush sings and the ink dances."

▶ **Answer each of the following questions with a sentence. If a question does not contain a vocabulary word from the lesson's word list, use one in your answer. Use each word only once.**

1. Why do you think Yani was able to produce more than ten thousand paintings by the time she was sixteen?

____

____

2. Why do you think Yani's first brushstrokes are sometimes made in a **tentative** manner?

____

____

3. What feeling does Yani capture in her paintings of the Guilin mountains?

____

____

4. What subject **captivated** Yani when she was very young?

____

____

5. What ability is required in order to enjoy the **inscription** on a painting by Yani?

____

____

6. What is the meaning of **stifle** as it is used in the passage?

7. How can you explain Yani's ability to paint when she was so young and had never received any lessons?

8. What is the meaning of **posture** as it is used in the passage?

9. Has Yani always worn traditional Chinese **attire** when appearing in public?

10. How does Yani demonstrate her **versatility** in painting?

11. What is the meaning of **eclipse** as it is used in the passage?

12. Why would you expect a painting done by Yani when she was six years old to be different from one done when she was sixteen?

13. How does Yani's style of working enable her to finish a painting in such a short time?

antic
attire
captivate
deft
diligent
eclipse
evolve
innate
inscribe
posture
shroud
stifle
tentative
tranquil
versatile

14. What kind of monkeys' **antics** do you think Yani found amusing?

15. What is the meaning of **shroud** as it is used in the passage?

Fun & Fascinating FACTS

- The Latin word *natus* means "born" and forms the root of several English words. **Innate** qualities are those that seem to have been with a person since birth. *Prenatal* care is that given to a mother before the birth of her child. To be a *native* of a particular place means that one was born in that place.

- Old English was the language spoken in England between 500 and 1200 CE. A number of its words have survived, often with changed spellings and slightly altered meanings to become part of modern English. **Shroud** is such a word; it comes from *scrud,* an Old English word for a loose article of clothing that covered most of the body. The dead would usually be buried wearing the scrud they had worn in life, and in time the word, changed to *shroud,* came to mean "a covering for a dead body." As a verb it came to mean "to hide from sight" or "to cover."

5 Vocabulary Extension

evolve

verb To change gradually over a period of time.

Academic Context

In school, you may have learned how methods of transportation have evolved over time.

Word Family

evolution (noun)
evolutionary (adjective)
evolving (adjective)

Discussion & Writing Prompt

*As part of its **evolution,** the rose plant developed thorns on its stems to protect it from animals that would eat it.*

Based on this sentence, write the definition of **evolution** and then use it in a new sentence of your own.

2 min. 1. Turn and talk to your partner or group.	3 min. 2. Write 2–4 sentences.
Use this space to take notes or draw your ideas.	Be ready to share what you have written.

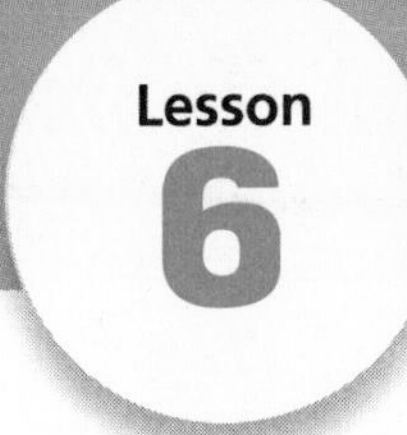

Word List

Study the definitions of the words. Then do the exercises that follow.

apparel
ə per´ əl

n. The things that are worn by a person; clothing.
Partygoers dressed in their finest **apparel** for New Year's Eve.

appreciate
ə prē´ shē āt

v. 1. To see the worth or quality of.
I **appreciate** handmade gifts my friends made for me.

2. To increase in value.
The baseball card I bought for three dollars has **appreciated** to five dollars in just one year.

Share with your partner what you appreciate most in your life.

continuous
kən tin´ yo͞o əs

adj. Going on without stopping.
The **continuous** flow of traffic makes it impossible to cross the street here.

dissolve
di zälv´

v. 1. To make or become liquid.
Sugar **dissolves** easily in warm water.

2. To bring or to come to an end.
The members agreed to **dissolve** the chess club.

Tell your partner how you would feel if an important friendship dissolved.

domesticate
dō mes´ ti kāt

v. To tame; to bring plants or animals under human control.
Some people claim that they can **domesticate** skunks and that they make good pets.

domesticated *adj.* Brought under human control; tamed or cultivated.
The carrot is a **domesticated** form of a plant called Queen Anne's lace.

Talk to your partner about whether it helps or hurts wild animals when humans try to domesticate them.

emerge
ē mʉrj´

v. 1. To come into view; to appear.
A large brown bear **emerged** from the cave.

2. To become known.
The truth did not **emerge** until the trial was under way.

Describe to your partner what you think would be the most frightening creature to emerge from the sea.

fiber
fī′ bər

n. 1. A thin, threadlike part of animal hair or plant tissue; also, an artificial thread that resembles this.
Cotton, wool, and rayon **fibers** can all be spun into yarn to make cloth.

2. An arrangement of body cells that forms muscles and nerves.
Red meat is made up of muscle **fiber.**

3. A food substance that provides bulk but is not digested.
Beans and whole grains are good sources of **fiber** in one's diet.

function
fuŋk′ shən

v. To serve a purpose.
This couch also **functions** as a bed.

n. 1. The special purpose something is used for.
One **function** of a dictionary is to define words.

2. An important ceremony or gathering.
Following tonight's **function** to honor the retiring teachers, there will be a buffet.

Explain to your partner the function of an item on your desk or table.

hatch
hach

v. 1. To come or to bring forth from an egg.
A little yellow chick **hatched** last night.

2. To think up.
The children **hatched** a plot to scare their parents.

n. A small opening with a door or cover.
The **hatch** on the main deck flew open when the ship hit a reef.

inhibit
in hib′ it

v. To prevent from doing something or to prevent from happening.
Oil **inhibits** the formation of rust on metal.

inhibited *adj.* Held back because of shyness.
Inhibited people don't make friends easily.

Discuss with your partner how seatbelts help inhibit injuries in car accidents.

minute
mī no͞ot′

adj. Very small; tiny.
A **minute** speck of dust in one's eye can be very annoying.

motion
mō′ shən

n. 1. Movement.
The **motion** of the train almost put me to sleep.

2. A suggestion on which members at a meeting must vote.
The **motion** to end further discussion was defeated by a show of hands.

v. To signal.
The shop owner **motioned** for the shoppers to come in.

motionless *adj.* Not moving; stationary.
The bus remained **motionless** in the morning traffic jam.

sheathe shēth

v. To cover with something that protects.
Metal workers will **sheathe** the ship's bottom with copper plates.

shed shed

v. 1. To lose; to give up.
Cats **shed** hair in the summer.

2. To cause to flow.
The family **shed** tears of joy when they heard their lost dog had been found.

3. To throw off water without letting it soak through.
A raincoat should **shed** water.

4. To send out or give off.
The full moon **shed** a bright light.

transfer trans′ fər

v. To move, carry, send, or change from one person or place to another.
Transfer your notes to a fresh notebook.

n. 1. The act of transferring.
After moving his data to a new hard drive, Oscar received a message that said, "The **transfer** is complete."

2. A ticket used for transferring from one bus or train to another.
A **transfer** from the subway allows riders to continue by bus without paying an additional charge.

Transfer your pencil to your partner's desk, and then return it to your own.

6A Using Words in Context

Read the following sentences. If the word in bold is used correctly, write C on the line. If the word is used incorrectly, write I on the line.

1. (a) We had to **shed** our way up the mountain in freezing cold. ___
   (b) Latisha **shed** her last tear and then cleared her throat. ___
   (c) The new information **sheds** light on an old mystery. ___
   (d) Huang had a whole **shed** of reasons to explain Nick's behavior. ___

2. (a) Sugar **dissolves** quickly in hot tea. ___
   (b) The club was **dissolved** when the members dropped out. ___
   (c) I **dissolved** to get a summer job instead of going to camp. ___
   (d) The brick was **dissolved** onto the wall. ___

3. (a) The groundhog **emerged** when it crawled back into its hole. ___
   (b) Out of the darkness, the figure of a man **emerged.** ___
   (c) As the facts began to **emerge,** we knew there was trouble. ___
   (d) The submarine could stay **emerged** underwater for days. ___

4. (a) The bike is starting to **function,** so I need a new one. ___
   (b) The **function** is being held to award the volleyball team. ___
   (c) What if someone invented a car that also **functions** as an airplane? ___
   (d) The machine has several different **functions.** ___

5. (a) I **appreciate** the help you gave me. ___
   (b) You can **appreciate** around the pool. ___
   (c) The new restaurant is perfect for people who **appreciate** spicy food. ___
   (d) The old toy my parents bought me for ten dollars has now **appreciated** to one hundred dollars! ___

6. (a) We opened the **hatch** to let in some fresh air. ___
   (b) The hen sits on the eggs until they **hatch.** ___
   (c) We **hatched** an idea to convince the teacher to cancel the quiz. ___
   (d) The drawing of a monkey was **hatched** in ink. ___

7. (a) The safety patrol **motioned** to us to not cross the street yet. ___
   (b) I felt so much happy **motion** when my baby sister was born. ___
   (c) The **motion** for the school to take part in the city fair was voted down. ___
   (d) Any **motion** in the room sets off the alarm. ___

8. (a) Our **transfer** kept us from climbing the hill. ___
   (b) Can you **transfer** your books to another table? ___
   (c) After a short bus ride, we **transferred** to the ferry. ___
   (d) The novel has been **transferred** into many different languages. ___

9. (a) A **continuous** stream of students kept the principal busy. ___
   (b) If the patient becomes **continuous,** give him some juice to sip. ___
   (c) A **continuous** supply of fresh water came from the village well. ___
   (d) The twins exchanged **continuous** looks when their mother found the spilled paint. ___

10. (a) We **inhibit** an apartment on the top floor. ___
    (b) An **inhibited** person usually does not like to talk to new people. ___
    (c) The spray **inhibits** the growth of weeds in the playground. ___
    (d) Emiliano **inhibited** no sign that he was tired after the race. ___

apparel
appreciate
continuous
dissolve
domesticate
emerge
fiber
function
hatch
inhibit
minute
motion
sheathe
shed
transfer

Making Connections

Circle the letter next to each correct answer. There may be more than one correct answer.

1. Which word or words go with *increase?*
   (a) function (b) escalate (c) appreciate (d) transfer

2. Which word or words go with *without stopping?*
   (a) transfer (b) domesticate (c) continuously (d) fiber

3. Which word or words go with *boat?*
   (a) eclipse (b) hatch (c) voyage (d) vessel

4. Which word or words go with *movement?*
   (a) ceremony (b) accelerate (c) soar (d) motion

5. Which word or words go with *tame?*
   (a) inhibit (b) domesticate (c) captivate (d) brace

6. Which word or words go with *food?*
   (a) consume (b) edible (c) fiber (d) inhibit

7. Which word or words go with *protect?*
   (a) hatch (b) sheathe (c) minute (d) attain

8. Which word or words go with *size?*
   (a) minute (b) vast (c) diligent (d) mammoth

9. Which word or words go with *prevent?*
   (a) emerge (b) inhibit (c) stifle (d) vacate

10. Which word or words go with *clothing?*
    (a) threadbare (b) apparel (c) attire (d) dense

Determining Meanings

Circle the letter next to each answer choice that correctly completes the sentence. There may be more than one correct answer.

1. The **functional**
   (a) elevator has been working nonstop for five years.
   (b) cheese turned moldy.
   (c) toaster is broken.
   (d) parts of the bike are worth keeping.

2. **Inhibiting**
   (a) yourself by not speaking makes you seem shy.
   (b) how much water you give the flowers will keep them from blooming.
   (c) your sleep will make you more awake.
   (d) the forest are a huge number of deer.

3. Stop **shedding**
   (a) the time if you have nothing to do.
   (b) the door so loudly.
   (c) on the couch, you silly dog!
   (d) so many tears and try to laugh instead.

4. Ari **transferred**
   (a) to the wrong subway line.
   (b) his phone from his left pocket to his right pocket.
   (c) into a polite young man around his grandparents.
   (d) his stereo from his bedroom to the basement.

5. The **fiber**
   (a) must be shown to the security guard before you can go in.
   (b) that many people prefer for cloth is bamboo.
   (c) told the truth this time.
   (d) in whole-wheat flour is good for you.

6. Something **emerged**
   (a) out of the fog and then disappeared again, right in front of me!
   (b) from the report that was not good.
   (c) me that the story wasn't true.
   (d) from the ocean that looked like a large lizard.

apparel
appreciate
continuous
dissolve
domesticate
emerge
fiber
function
hatch
inhibit
minute
motion
sheathe
shed
transfer

7. The **domestication** of
   (a) the poisonous weed into a household plant is going to be hard to do.
   (b) dogs began thousands of years ago.
   (c) the dancer is stiff and sore.
   (d) pasta should be sprinkled with cheese.

8. Try **dissolving**
   (a) the code before you can read the secret message.
   (b) the vitamins in orange juice to hide the taste.
   (c) the characters on the sign before we go any farther.
   (d) the sugar in water to make syrup.

Completing Sentences

Complete the sentences to demonstrate your knowledge of the words in bold.

1. A quality I **appreciate** in others is

   ____.

2. I might feel **inhibited** if

   ____.

3. If you **sheathe** something, that means you

   ____.

4. The main **function** of a toaster is

   ____.

5. **Apparel** is a fancy word for

   ____.

6. An animal that would probably be hard to **domesticate** is

   ____.

7. Something **minute** in my classroom is

   ____.

8. I wish the school board would pass a **motion** to

   ____.

9. If a length of string is **continuous,** that means it

   ____.

10. A food that has **fiber** is

    ____.

Vocabulary in Context

Read the passage.

The Story of Silk

"As soft as silk" we say, and with good reason, for silk is among the softest and finest of all fabrics. But where does silk come from? The silkworms that produce it come mainly from China, where they have been **domesticated** for thousands of years by silk farmers. According to legend, a Chinese empress known as the Lady of Si-ling began the cultivation of silkworms in 2640 BCE. The practice then spread from China to other regions. Silk-producing areas today include Japan, Korea, India, Thailand, and Brazil.

The story of silk begins when the female moth lays its eggs, up to five hundred of them at a time; they are **minute,** each smaller than the head of a pin. The eggs are stored in a cool place to **inhibit** their growth until the silk farmer is ready to use them. At that time they are **transferred** to a heated container called an incubator. Twenty days later, tiny silkworms start to **hatch.**

At this stage of its life, a silkworm does just one thing: It eats. And it eats just one thing—the leaves of the mulberry tree. A silkworm eats **continuously,** and it grows bigger and bigger until it seems ready to burst out of its skin. Then it stops eating, and it remains **motionless** for about a day—a sign that it will soon **shed** its old skin and replace it with a new one. The shedding occurs four times altogether. When fully grown, at about six weeks, the silkworm has increased its size seventyfold. It now stops eating and prepares to enter the next stage of its life.

To accomplish this, the silkworm first **sheathes** itself in a cocoon. The cocoon is a kind of protective shell made from silk thread that the silkworm produces from a part of its body called the spinneret. During the three weeks it spends inside the cocoon, the silkworm turns into a fully grown moth. It has no teeth, so it cannot eat its way out; instead, it produces a liquid that **dissolves** the silk, making a hole in the cocoon. Then it slowly pulls itself through the hole. Once it has **emerged** from the cocoon, it is free to stretch its wings, although they serve no useful **function.** Centuries of careful breeding have resulted in the silk moth's wings being so feeble that it cannot fly.

apparel ✓
appreciate ✓
continuous
dissolve ✓
domesticate
emerge ✓
fiber
function ✓
hatch ✓
inhibit
minute ✓
motion
sheathe
shed ✓
transfer

Most silkworms, however, do not survive to become moths. The few that do are used for breeding. The farmer takes the rest while still in their cocoons and heats them in an oven to kill them. The silk, which is up to a mile long, is then carefully unwound from the cocoon by machines. It can then be spun and woven into cloth. The silk cloth is used to make men's and women's **apparel,** as well as upholstery, sheets, curtain materials, and even carpets.

Silk is the strongest of all natural **fibers,** and it is also light in weight, warmer than cotton, rayon, or linen, and wrinkle resistant. These qualities, together with its incredible softness, make it highly desirable to those who **appreciate** the finer things in life.

▶ **Answer each of the following questions with a sentence. If a question does not contain a vocabulary word from the lesson's word list, use one in your answer. Use each word only once.**

1. What is the meaning of **hatch** as it is used in the passage?

The silkworms hatched, or came/broke out of its egg.
(To come of bring forth from an egg)

2. What are coats, dresses, scarves, and shirts?

Coats, dresses, scarves, andshirts are all apparel.

3. What is the meaning of **emerge** as it is used in the passage?

The silkworms came into view from the cocoon.

4. Why is a cocoon that produces a live silk moth useless for making silk cloth?

~~Their wings~~ The cocoon will be dissolved. ~~of the~~

5. What is the meaning of **function** as it is used in the passage?

Their wings served no useful purpose.
Purpose

6. Why does the incubator used by the silk farmer not need to be large?

The silkworms' eggs are minute.

7. What do you think causes the silkworm's size to increase so rapidly?

The silkworm eats continuously.

8. What is the meaning of **shed** as it is used in the passage?

To lose or to give off. (up?)

9. What is the Chinese empress, the Lady of Si-ling, known for?

(domesticated) Lady Si-Ling was known for her domesticating silkworms. cultivated

10. How does the silkworm protect itself while it changes into a moth?

They Sheathes itself to form a cocoon.

11. What does the silk farmer do with cocoons not needed for breeding purposes?

transffered into oven to be killed. ~~Silk farmers inhibits the worms by burning it.~~

12. What effect does a cool temperature have on the growth of the silk moth's eggs?

The eggs are stored in a cool place to inhibit their growth.

13. How can one tell that a silkworm has outgrown its old skin and will shed it?

The silkworms are motionless when it is ready to shed.

14. What is the meaning of **appreciate** as it is used in the passage?

To see the worth or quality of.

15. What do silk, rayon, and wool have in common?

~~Fiber~~ Silk, rayon, and wool have fiber in common.

- apparel ✓
- appreciate ✓
- continuous ✓
- dissolve ✓
- domesticate ✓
- emerge ✓
- fiber ✓
- function ✓
- hatch ✓
- inhibit ✓
- minute ✓
- motion ✓
- sheathe ✓
- shed ✓
- transfer ✓

Fun & Fascinating FACTS

- **Continuous** means "going on without stopping." *Continual* means "happening over and over again." When a telephone rings *continuously,* it does so without stopping, perhaps because no one answers and the person calling does not hang up. When a telephone rings *continually,* it starts to ring again as soon as one call ends, and this goes on repeatedly for some time.

- To **sheathe** something is to cover it for protection. A *sheath* is a case that fits over something, such as the blade of a knife. Note that *sheathe* rhymes with *breathe* and *sheath* rhymes with *teeth.*

- The adjective **minute** is pronounced mī nōōt´. A *minute* amount is one that is very small. The noun *minute* is pronounced min´ it. (There are sixty *minutes* in an hour.)

6 Vocabulary Extension

emerge

verb 1. To appear.

2. To become known, especially after being hidden or secret.

Word Family

emergence (noun)
emergent (adjective)
emerging (adjective)

Context Clues

These sentences give clues to the meaning of **emerged.**

*After it **emerged** from its chrysalis, the butterfly rested for a while before flying away.*

*New clues **emerged** about the location of Rami's lost puppy.*

Discussion & Writing Prompt

How might you feel if you **emerge** from your bed in the middle of the night?

2 min. 1. Turn and talk to your partner or group.	3 min. 2. Write 2–4 sentences.
Use this space to take notes or draw your ideas.	Be ready to share what you have written.

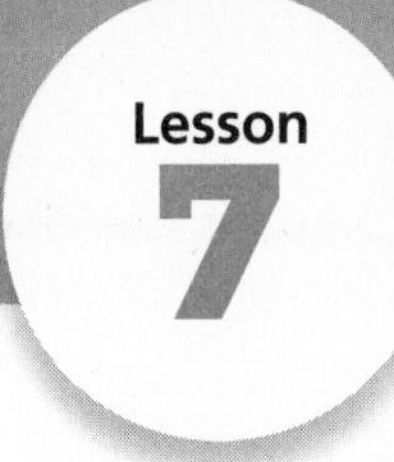

Word List

Study the definitions of the words. Then do the exercises that follow.

brawl
brôl

n. A rough, noisy fight.
Teachers walk the halls between classes to prevent **brawls** between students.

v. To fight noisily.
Players who **brawl** have to sit out the next game.

casual
kazh´ o͞o əl

adj. 1. Not planned.
Several friends got together for a **casual** meeting after the movie.

2. Not regular; occasional.
I have a **casual** job doing errands for my uncle when he needs me.

3. Suitable for everyday use; comfortable.
The store sells **casual** apparel for the beach.

Tell your partner the difference between being a regular exerciser and a casual exerciser.

constant
kän´ stənt

adj. 1. Not changing.
When I ride my bike, I try to maintain a **constant** speed.

2. Loyal; faithful.
The farmer's **constant** companion is an affectionate dog.

3. Without a pause; unending.
A small child requires **constant** attention.

Discuss with your partner how important it is to be a constant friend to someone who is having problems.

excel
ek sel´

v. To do well; to be better or greater than others.
Jackie Robinson **excelled** as both a fielder and a batter.

exhaust
eg zôst´

v. 1. To use up.
Lost on the mountain, the climbers **exhausted** their supplies after two days.

2. To tire out.
A ten-mile hike will **exhaust** most people.

n. The waste gases from an engine; *also*, the system that pumps out such waste gases.
The muffler is often the first part of the **exhaust** to wear out.

Chat with your partner about why someone traveling in the desert should be careful not to exhaust the water supply.

hardy
här′ dē

adj. Able to survive under bad conditions; tough.
Sage is a **hardy** plant that can be left outside during the winter.

mediocre
mē dē ō′ kər

adj. Of low to medium quality; barely passable.
Mediocre grades make it difficult to get into a good college.

monotonous
mə nät′ n əs

adj. Always the same; not varying; boring.
Making photocopies is **monotonous** work.

monotony *n.* Lack of variety resulting in boredom.
Switching chores with my brother helps relieve the **monotony** of housework.

Tell your partner how you could make a monotonous chore, such as washing the dishes or vacuuming, more fun.

originate
ə rij′ ə nāt

v. To bring or come into being.
The custom of sending Valentine cards **originated** in the 1800s.

origin *n.* (ôr′ ə jin) A beginning or coming into being.
What is the **origin** of the story that alligators live in the New York sewers?

punctuate
puŋk′ cho͞o āt

v. 1. To add marks such as commas and periods to writing to make the meaning clear.
Choose the best way to **punctuate** this sentence.

2. To interrupt from time to time.
Claps of thunder **punctuated** the evening.

punctuation *n.* (puŋk cho͞o ā′ shən) The use of marks such as commas and periods in writing.
Using a comma instead of a semicolon is a common error in **punctuation.**

Discuss with your partner what it sounds like when fireworks punctuate the night.

ravenous
rav′ ə nəs

adj. 1. Very hungry.
The skaters were **ravenous** because they'd skipped lunch.

2. Eager for whatever satisfies one's needs or wants.
To be **ravenous** for praise shows a lack of confidence in oneself.

realistic
rē ə lis′ tik

adj. 1. Closely resembling real life.
This video game has very **realistic** race-car sounds.

2. Aware of things as they are; practical.
Running a Saturday car wash is a **realistic** way for the club to raise money.

Talk to your partner to decide if it is realistic to expect to meet your favorite music star at the grocery store.

soothe
so͞oth

v. 1. To make calm and relaxed.
The principal tried to **soothe** the angry students by promising to consider their demands.

2. To relieve soreness; to make less painful.
Calamine lotion will **soothe** a sunburn.

stampede
stam pēd´

n. A sudden rush of animals or people, usually caused by fear.
A breeze carried the lion's scent to the antelope and began a **stampede** of the herd.

v. To take part in a stampede.
The crowd **stampeded** for the exit when someone yelled, "Fire!"

veteran
vet´ ər ən

n. 1. A person who has served in the armed forces.
Veterans in their uniforms marched in the Memorial Day parade.

2. A person with much experience.
The director is a **veteran** who has been with the dance company from its beginning.

adj. Experienced.
We were fortunate to have several **veteran** musicians in our band.

Tell your partner about something you are a veteran at doing, such as mowing lawns or playing the violin.

7A Finding Meanings

Choose two phrases to form a sentence that correctly uses a word from Word List 7. Then write the sentence.

1. (a) a person who has much experience.
   (b) A veteran is
   (c) a sudden rush of frightened animals.
   (d) A brawl is

____

____

2. (a) A realistic offer is one that
   (b) is made in a joking manner.
   (c) A casual offer is one that
   (d) seems to make a lot of sense.

____

____

3. (a) A stampede is
   (b) a rope used by cowboys.
   (c) a rough and noisy fight.
   (d) A brawl is

4. (a) Monotony is
   (b) markings that make the meaning of writing clearer.
   (c) Punctuation is
   (d) a state of very great hunger.

5. (a) To stampede cattle is to
   (b) cause them to rush off in a panic.
   (c) To soothe cattle is to
   (d) put them out to feed on grass.

6. (a) A monotonous inspection
   (b) A casual inspection
   (c) is one that is thorough.
   (d) is one made without much thought.

7. (a) To exhaust someone is to
   (b) help that person relax.
   (c) forget about that person.
   (d) To soothe someone is to

8. (a) To excel at something is to
   (b) bring it to a sudden end.
   (c) To originate something is to
   (d) do it better than others.

brawl
casual
constant
excel
exhaust
hardy
mediocre
monotonous
originate
punctuate
ravenous
realistic
soothe
stampede
veteran

7B Just the Right Word

Replace each phrase in bold with a single word (or form of the word) from the word list.

1. He doesn't seem to be very **aware of how things really are** when he talks about his future plans.

2. The speech was **interrupted a number of times** by bursts of applause from the audience.

3. To spend winters in Alaska you need to be **tough enough to withstand difficult conditions.**

4. The tornado caused a **panic in which everyone rushed** away from the store's windows.

5. It takes a **person with years of experience as a** chef to run a smoothly functioning restaurant kitchen.

6. After being away for so long, the travelers were **very eager** for news from home.

7. By the time our supply of firewood was **used up,** warm weather had arrived.

8. A hot bath will **ease the soreness of** your aching muscles.

9. Some teenagers prefer clothes that are **suitable for everyday wear.**

10. The math homework is **boring because it lacks variety.**

11. Who **first came up with** the idea of growing plants in water?

12. Once set, the speed of the escalator was **fixed and did not change.**

7C Applying Meanings

Circle the letter or letters next to each correct answer. There may be more than one correct answer.

1. Which of the following are **casual** clothes?
   (a) blue jeans
   (b) an evening gown
   (c) a dark blue suit
   (d) a track suit

2. Which of the following help musicians **excel?**
   (a) watching television
   (b) practicing every day
   (c) listening to their teachers
   (d) having innate ability

3. Which of the following might you say about an idea you thought was **mediocre?**
   (a) "This is an okay idea."
   (b) "This is a very bad idea."
   (c) "This is a fantastic idea!"
   (d) "This is an impressive idea!"

4. Which of the following would a **ravenous** person want to do?
   (a) eat
   (b) relax
   (c) sleep
   (d) exercise

5. Which of the following could **stampede?**
   (a) ants
   (b) a herd of cows
   (c) a horde of shoppers
   (d) a row of trees

6. Which of the following **punctuate** a piece of writing?
   (a) sentences
   (b) commas
   (c) adjectives
   (d) question marks

7. Which of the following could be **monotonous?**
   (a) a voice
   (b) a car trip
   (c) a nightmare
   (d) a triumph

8. Which of the following might take part in a **brawl?**
   (a) newborns
   (b) hockey players
   (c) a herd of cattle
   (d) demonstrators at a rally

brawl
casual
constant
excel
exhaust
hardy
mediocre
monotonous
originate
punctuate
ravenous
realistic
soothe
stampede
veteran

7D Word Study: Word Parts

Complete each sentence with a word from a previous lesson. Use the explanation in parentheses to help you.

1. To ______________________ to something is to give along with others. (The word is formed from the prefix *con-*, which means "with," together with a root formed from the Latin word *tribuere,* which means "to grant or give.")

2. A(n) ______________________ speaker is one who reaches out and moves an audience with the power of spoken language. (The word is formed from the Latin prefix *e-*, which means "out," together with a root formed from the Latin word *loqui,* which means "to speak.")

3. ______________________ are people who leave their homeland and settle in another country. (The word is formed from the prefix *im-*, which means "in," together with a root formed from the Latin word *migrare,* which means "to depart.")

4. To ______________________ different elements is to bring them together into a whole. (The word is formed from the Latin word *integrare,* which means "to make whole.")

5. A(n) ______________________ story is one that is hard to believe. (The word is formed from the Latin prefix *in-*, which means "not," together with a root formed from the Latin word *credere,* which means "to believe.")

6. ______________________ qualities are those that a person is born with. (The word is formed from the Latin prefix *in-*, which means "in" as well as "not," together with a root formed from the Latin word *natus,* which means "born.")

7. The ______________________ Court is the highest court in the land. (The word is formed from the Latin word *supremus,* which means "highest.")

8. ______________________ conditions are those unfit for living because of dirt and other unhealthy conditions. (The word is formed from the Latin word *squalus,* which means "filthy.")

9. A(n) ______________________ is a decision reached at the end of a trial. (The word is formed from the roots of two Latin words, *verus,* which means "truth," and *dicere,* which means "to say.")

10. ______________________ animals live near or in people's homes. (The word is formed from the Latin *domus,* which means "home.")

7E Vocabulary in Context

Read the passage.

Home, Home on the Range

People may think they know all about the cowboys of the Wild West from watching westerns. But Hollywood movies do not give a very **realistic** picture of the life cowboys really led. Cowboy movies are **punctuated** throughout by gunfire, but real cowboys were mostly **mediocre** shots. Cowboys seldom had reason to draw their guns; they carried them mostly for display. However, they did **excel** at riding and roping steers. These were the essential skills for men whose job was handling cattle.

Although you would not know it from the movies, about a third of all cowboys were African American or Latino. In fact, the first cowboys came from Mexico. They were called *vaqueros*, from the Spanish word *vaca*, which means "cow." The vaqueros contributed to the English language many of the words we associate with the Wild West, including *sombrero*, *mustang*, and *rodeo*.

Following the end of the Civil War in 1865, the vaqueros' numbers swelled with **veterans** who headed west to work on cattle ranches. Many were African Americans who found a greater degree of freedom in lands that were just opening up to settlement. The rodeo offered them an opportunity to prove their worth. One of the earliest performers was an African American cowboy named Nat Love. Love was born in Tennessee as an enslaved person in 1854. As a boy of fifteen, he worked as a trail hand out of Dodge City. There he learned the riding and roping skills that made him a star of the rodeo. Perhaps the most famous rodeo performer was Bill Pickett, star of the Miller Brothers' Wild West Show. Pickett was the first African American admitted to the National Cowboy Hall of Fame.

Westerns usually show the cowboys in town having a good time. But the lives of the real cowboys were quite **monotonous.** Days were spent mostly working on the range. At that time, cowboys drove the cattle along trails that **originated** in Texas, where most of the cattle ranches were located. The trails ended in Kansas City, Abilene, or Dodge City. From there the cattle were shipped east on the recently built railroads.

Cowboys found **casual** employment as trail hands for these great cattle drives. A drive covered hundreds of miles and lasted up to three months. Cowboys were in the saddle from sunup to sundown as they herded the moving cattle. They kept a string of mustangs, the **hardy** wild ponies that

brawl
casual
constant
excel
exhaust
hardy
mediocre
monotonous
originate
punctuate
ravenous
realistic
soothe
stampede
veteran

roamed the plains, and changed to fresh mounts several times a day. Working hard in the open air made the cowboys **ravenous.** When the evening sun went down, they were too **exhausted** to do anything but eat and sleep. Cowboys took turns during the night keeping a **constant** watch over the cattle. Whenever they seemed restless, the cowboys would **soothe** them by singing softly. Any loud noise or sudden movement could panic the herd and start a **stampede.** Then several thousand frantic cattle would suddenly charge off into the darkness with the hastily awakened cowboys in pursuit.

When the hands were paid at the end of the trail, they headed into town to spend their money. Those were the times when **brawls** might erupt. It was then that a cowboy's life was most likely to resemble what we see in the movies.

▶ **Answer each of the following questions with a sentence. If a question does not contain a vocabulary word from the lesson's word list, use one in your answer. Use each word only once.**

1. What is the meaning of **exhausted** as it is used in the passage?

____

____

2. Why did cowboys on the trail need to be especially alert during a thunderstorm?

____

____

3. How might western movies be made more **realistic?**

____

____

4. When do you think a cowboy might find himself locked up in the town jail?

____

____

5. Why were mustangs especially suitable for work on the cattle drives?

____

____

6. What is the meaning of **punctuate** as it is used in the passage?

____

____

7. Why do you think movies don't give an accurate picture of cowboys' lives?

8. Were most cowboys good shooters?

9. What is the meaning of **casual** as it is used in the passage?

10. What is the **origin** of *sombrero* and *mustang?*

11. Why do you think roping steers was a popular feature of the rodeo?

12. What is the meaning of **soothe** as it is used in the passage?

13. What do you think would be a welcome sight to **ravenous** cowboys?

14. How did the end of the Civil War affect the Wild West?

15. What is the meaning of **constant** as it is used in the passage?

brawl
casual
constant
excel
exhaust
hardy
mediocre
monotonous
originate
punctuate
ravenous
realistic
soothe
stampede
veteran

Fun & Fascinating **FACTS**

- The noun form of the verb **exhaust** is *exhaustion*. (Several runners collapsed from *exhaustion* at the end of the race.) The adjective form is *exhausted*. (The *exhausted* rowers collapsed over their oars as they crossed the finish line.) A different adjective formed from this word is *exhaustive,* which means "thorough" or "complete." (After an *exhaustive* search, the missing book was found under the sofa.)

- *Medi* means "middle" or "halfway" in Latin, and *ocris* means "mountain." These two words are combined to form the adjective **mediocre,** which means "halfway up the mountain." To be *mediocre* is to be neither very good nor very bad, neither at the top nor at the bottom.

- Don't confuse **veteran** with *veterinarian,* a person qualified to give medical treatment to animals. Both words are sometimes shortened to *vet*.

Vocabulary Extension

constant

adjective 1. Happening all the time.

2. Not changing.

3. Loyal.

Malik likes riding his bike at a ***constant*** *high speed through the park.*

Academic Context

In math, you may learn that a **constant** number is a number that has a fixed value.

Synonyms and Antonyms

Synonyms: stable, steady, unchanging

Antonyms: unstable, unpredictable, changing

Discussion & Writing Prompt

Why does a new puppy or a new baby need **constant** attention?

2 min. 1. Turn and talk to your partner or group.	3 min. 2. Write 2–4 sentences.
Use this space to take notes or draw your ideas.	Be ready to share what you have written.

Word List

Study the definitions of the words. Then do the exercises that follow.

accompany
ə kum′ pə nē

v. 1. To go along with; to be together.
Thunder often **accompanies** lightning.

2. To play a musical instrument for or with.
The pianist offered to **accompany** the singer.

Tell your partner about two foods that often accompany each other, such as beans and rice.

beneficial
ben ə fish′ əl

adj. Being of use; helpful; favorable.
A balanced diet is **beneficial** to one's health.

Discuss with your partner about how working hard at a sport can be beneficial to how well you play.

captive
kap′ tiv

n. One that is held prisoner.
The **captives** were closely guarded.

adj. Unable to escape or get away.
The hospital patients provided a **captive** audience for the comedian.

captivity *n.* (kap tiv′ i tē) The state of being held against one's will; loss of freedom.
The giant panda is thriving in **captivity.**

convenient
kən vēn′ yənt

adj. Suitable for one's needs; making life easier or more comfortable.
The bus stop is **convenient** because it's close to my house.

convenience *n.* Anything that makes life easier or more comfortable.
We appreciated the central air-conditioning and other **conveniences** of the apartment.

ecstasy
ek′ stə sē

n. A strong feeling of emotion, especially joy.
Fans screamed in **ecstasy** when their idol appeared on stage.

ecstatic *adj.* (ek stat′ ik) Full of or causing ecstasy.
The winners were **ecstatic** when the judges read the names.

expanse
ek spans′

n. A wide, open area or surface; a stretch.
Wheat grows on the broad **expanse** of the Kansas prairie.

expedition
ek spə dish´ ən

n. 1. A long journey by a group to explore or do battle.
The **expedition** into the Brazilian rain forest lasted nearly a year.

2. A group that makes such a journey.
The **expedition** was attempting to find the origin of the Nile.

Share with your partner three places in the world where you'd go on an expedition.

inept
in ept´

adj. 1. Clumsily or awkwardly expressed; not suitable for the occasion.
That **inept** remark you made upset those who overheard it.

2. Lacking in skill or ability.
An **inept** handler damaged the contents of the crate.

Chat with your partner about how you could make up for an inept comment you made to a friend.

interpret
in tʉr´ prət

v. 1. To translate into another language.
A native Parisian was hired to **interpret** the French minister's remarks for the audience.

2. To explain the meaning of.
Josef offered to **interpret** the dream.

3. To understand in one's own way.
The coach **interpreted** my absence from the team meeting as a lack of commitment to the team.

Talk to your partner about how you might interpret a person's feelings by looking at the person's face.

invaluable
in val´ yo͞o ə bəl

adj. Too valuable to measure; priceless.
The students' help in organizing the boycott was **invaluable.**

linger
liŋ´ gər

v. To be slow in leaving or going away.
The students **lingered** in the hall, reluctant to go out into the cold.

retrieve
rē trēv´

v. 1. To get back; to recover.
Campers can **retrieve** their lost items from the lost and found.

2. To find and bring back.
The puppy **retrieves** sticks the children throw in the pond.

Hide your pencil near your desk and ask your partner to try to retrieve it from its hiding place.

skirmish
skûr´ mish

n. A minor fight or battle.
Apart from a few **skirmishes,** both sides kept the cease-fire that had been agreed to.

v. To take part in such a fight.
The two sides began to **skirmish** before the major battle.

supplement
sup´ lə mənt

n. Something added to make up for something missing.
Those who eat a well-balanced diet probably do not need vitamin **supplements.**

v. To add to.
I **supplement** my allowance with earnings from a paper route.

Discuss with your partner an activity you could do on your own to supplement the education you receive at school.

territory
ter´ ə tôr ē

n. 1. A particular area of land.
A dog will defend its **territory.**

2. A land area under control of a particular group or government.
The island of Guam is a **territory** of the United States.

8A Using Words in Context

Read the following sentences. If the word in bold is used correctly, write C on the line. If the word is used incorrectly, write I on the line.

1. (a) Aseem apologized for barging in and said he didn't mean to **interpret** me. ___
   (b) The teacher's remarks were **interpreted** as being friendly. ___
   (c) Ming-na's silence was **interpreted** as anger. ___
   (d) She spoke Arabic, so she was able to **interpret** for the travelers. ___

2. (a) The Sunday comics **supplement** comes with the local newspaper. ___
   (b) **Supplement** will be served at five. ___
   (c) Yong's mom **supplemented** his lunch with a bag of nuts and raisins. ___
   (d) We **supplemented** the time by reading and playing games. ___

3. (a) I once made an **inept** attempt to learn juggling. ___
   (b) An **inept** runner should probably not try out for track. ___
   (c) Grab the **inept** tomatoes off the table. ___
   (d) The team played an **inept** game because they were out of practice. ___

4. (a) The family has been **accompanying** bread for two hundred years. ___
   (b) The violinist **accompanied** the singer in her recital. ___
   (c) A young child needs to be **accompanied** by an adult when traveling. ___
   (d) The fish was **accompanied** by a fresh salad. ___

5. (a) Nakala is **retrieved** that she found her favorite shirt. ___
   (b) We tried to **retrieve** the kite that got stuck in a tree. ___
   (c) You can't **retrieve** the message after it has been sent. ___
   (d) We were **retrieved** to hear that the package had arrived safely. ___

6. (a) We were told to keep our backpacks with us at all **invaluable** times. ___
   (b) A rare book is an **invaluable** addition to the library. ___
   (c) Santos won the Most **Invaluable** Player award. ___
   (d) The support given to the team by the fans was **invaluable.** ___

7. (a) Arizona was a **territory** until it became a state in 1912. ___
   (b) The cat walked slowly around its **territory** and stared at the dog. ___
   (c) Pamela pressed the soft **territory** to her face. ___
   (d) Much United States **territory** was stolen from Native Americans. ___

8. (a) An astronaut **expedition** to Mars is still many years in the future. ___
   (b) The **expedition** reached the South Pole in 1911. ___
   (c) This baseball card could be worth a lot of **expeditions.** ___
   (d) My **expedition** is that we won't win the football game. ___

9. (a) My mom always has **skirmishes** with my brother about how late he can stay out. ___
   (b) The two sides **skirmished** all night. ___
   (c) We were **skirmished** after the long drive. ___
   (d) I **skirmished** with the idea of going but then decided to stay. ___

10. (a) I kept a list of all our **expanses,** including movies and snacks. ___
    (b) An **expanse** of grass stretched for miles over the hills. ___
    (c) The vast **expanse** of the universe is filled with planets and stars. ___
    (d) I **expanse** that we will need to wear winter coats tomorrow. ___

accompany
beneficial
captive
convenient
ecstasy
expanse
expedition
inept
interpret
invaluable
linger
retrieve
skirmish
supplement
territory

Making Connections

Circle the letter next to each correct answer. There may be more than one correct answer.

1. Which word or words go with *easier?*
   (a) mediocre (b) convenient (c) ravenous (d) captive

2. Which word or words go with *loss of freedom?*
   (a) course (b) accompany (c) bondage (d) captive

3. Which word or words go with *helpful?*
   (a) prefer (b) linger (c) interpret (d) beneficial

4. Which word or words go with *happiness?*
   (a) supplement (b) bliss (c) ecstasy (d) monotony

5. Which word or words go with *slow?*
   (a) linger (b) accompany (c) supplement (d) saunter

6. Which word or words go with *clumsily done?*
   (a) retrieve (b) bungle (c) convenient (d) inept

7. Which word or words go with *wide-open spaces?*
   (a) captivity (b) expanse (c) territory (d) supplement

8. Which word or words go with *language?*
   (a) linger (b) translate (c) skirmish (d) interpret

9. Which word or words go with *battle?*
   (a) expanse (b) skirmish (c) victim (d) supplement

10. Which word or words go with *priceless?*
    (a) invaluable (b) inept (c) inhibit (d) beneficial

Determining Meanings

Circle the letter next to each answer choice that correctly completes the sentence. There may be more than one correct answer.

1. Livvy **accompanied**
   (a) the famous pianist with her violin.
   (b) her sister to the store.
   (c) a deep breath and closed her eyes.
   (d) very hard to find the tickets, but they were nowhere to be found.

2. The **convenience**
   (a) of your best friend also being your neighbor is great.
   (b) of riding a bike to school is much better than waiting a long time for the bus.
   (c) on the top shelf was hard to reach.
   (d) of living next to the grocery store is almost too good to believe.

3. We **lingered**
   (a) with our friends for so long that we almost missed our bus.
   (b) to eat lunch, but were too busy.
   (c) the red and blue paint together to make purple.
   (d) in the doorway, waiting for the rain to stop.

4. Oona **retrieved**
   (a) the broken light bulb with a new one, right?
   (b) her books from her locker at school.
   (c) that she would tell her friend the truth.
   (d) the baseball and threw it to the pitcher.

5. They **ecstatically**
   (a) greeted their grandma as she stepped off the train.
   (b) found an old letter that made them cry.
   (c) jumped out the door and ran toward the pool.
   (d) wore masks to keep from getting the flu.

6. **Captivity**
   (a) awaited the lost dog when it was caught.
   (b) surrounded the ships as they drew closer to shore.
   (c) increased during the night and disappeared in the morning.
   (d) is best for the wild horse because its injury needs to be taken care of.

accompany
beneficial
captive
convenient
ecstasy
expanse
expedition
inept
interpret
invaluable
linger
retrieve
skirmish
supplement
territory

7. The **supplements**
   (a) make our cat's fur shiny and help her shed less.
   (b) are probably on the bottom shelf behind the napkins.
   (c) may help him heal more quickly.
   (d) might ache if you lean on them too long.

8. We **interpreted**
   (a) the student's words into Spanish.
   (b) his clumsiness to mean he had never played soccer.
   (c) our way across the driveway on two skateboards.
   (d) at least three ways of getting to school from the gym.

Completing Sentences

Complete the sentences to demonstrate your knowledge of the words in bold.

1. An **expedition** is a

____.

2. It would be **beneficial** to me if

____.

3. One **convenience** for me is

____.

4. I would be **inept** if I tried to

____.

5. Something that is **invaluable** might be

____.

6. I might **linger** after a party if

____.

7. Today someone **accompanied** me to

____.

8. A **skirmish** is a

____.

9. If an animal is born in **captivity,** that means

____.

10. I would be **ecstatic** if

____.

Vocabulary in Context

Read the passage.

Sacagawea's Great Adventure

Imagine being snatched from your family and friends as a young teenager and taken far from home to be sold into slavery. That was the fate of Sacagawea, a Shoshone chief's daughter. The Shoshone people occupied what is now central Idaho on the western slopes of the Rocky Mountains. Sacagawea was taken **captive** in 1799 during a **skirmish** with a Hidatsa raiding party. She was then carried off to their village on the banks of the Missouri river, seven hundred miles to the east, in what is now North Dakota. It must have been a terrifying experience for the young girl. But because of her kidnapping and the events that followed it, she became part of United States history. This is her story.

After she had been kidnapped, Sacagawea was sold to a French Canadian named Charbonneau who lived in the Hidatsa village; she became his wife when she was only fifteen years old. In 1804 the Lewis and Clark **expedition** arrived at the village. Its purpose was to explore routes to the Pacific coast and report back to the United States government. Having set out from St. Louis six months earlier, its leaders decided that the Hidatsa village would be a **convenient** place to spend the winter. Because they knew they would be passing through Shoshone **territory,** they hired Charbonneau. He spoke the Shoshone language and could **interpret** for them. They decided that even though she had just had a baby, Sacagawea should also **accompany** them. Her presence with the baby would demonstrate to the Shoshone that the expedition's intentions were peaceful.

In April 1805 the party set out, traveling in canoes up the Missouri river. Sacagawea, her baby strapped to her back, proved to be an **invaluable** member of the team. She collected roots and berries to **supplement** the food stocks. She was also able to add to the medical supplies, for she knew which plants had a **beneficial** effect when someone fell ill. One day, Charbonneau's **inept** handling of the canoe overturned it, and some important records would have been lost had Sacagawea not **retrieved** them. Because of such acts, Sacagawea earned the respect of Lewis and Clark.

When they finally reached Shoshone country, Sacagawea had an **ecstatic** reunion with her brother, who was now a Shoshone chief. However, there was little time for her to **linger** among her own people. The expedition had to reach the Pacific before winter made travel impossible.

accompany
beneficial
captive
convenient
ecstasy
expanse
expedition
inept
interpret
invaluable
linger
retrieve
skirmish
supplement
territory

In mid-November the expedition reached the West Coast. There Sacagawea gazed for the first time at the vast **expanse** of the Pacific Ocean, of which she had heard stories since childhood. In March of 1806 the expedition began the return journey and reached the Hidatsa village in mid-August. Sacagawea remained there with her husband and child while the rest of the party continued east. Her great adventure was over. She had done things that must have been beyond her wildest dreams only two years before. She had been reunited with her brother, whom she had never expected to see again, and she had seen the Great Water. Although she had no way of knowing this, she had also earned for herself an honored place in history.

▶ **Answer each of the following questions with a sentence. If a question does not contain a vocabulary word from the lesson's word list, use one in your answer. Use each word only once.**

1. What were Lewis and Clark looking for six months after leaving St. Louis?

____

____

2. What is the meaning of **inept** as it is used in the passage?

____

____

3. How is it made clear that Sacagawea did not go willingly with the Hidatsa?

____

____

4. What is the meaning of **retrieve** as it is used in the passage?

____

____

5. What does the author indicate might have been the most striking feature of the Pacific Ocean for Sacagawea?

____

____

6. What is the meaning of **interpret** as it is used in the passage?

____

____

7. For how long was Sacagawea with the **expedition?**

8. Why was Sacagawea able to **supplement** the party's medical supplies?

9. What did the Shoshone do when they encountered the Hidatsa raiding party?

10. Why did Lewis and Clark believe that the presence of Sacagawea's baby might have a **beneficial** effect on the expedition?

11. What is the meaning of **territory** as it is used in the passage?

12. Why was Sacagawea **ecstatic** when she met the Shoshone chief?

13. How do you think Lewis and Clark felt about Sacagawea?

14. What is the meaning of **accompany** as it is used in the passage?

15. Do you think Sacagawea was eager to leave her brother?

accompany
beneficial
captive
convenient
ecstasy
expanse
expedition
inept
interpret
invaluable
linger
retrieve
skirmish
supplement
territory

Fun & Fascinating FACTS

- *Translate* and **interpret** have similar meanings; both mean to take words of one language and express them in another. *Translate* is the broader term and covers both written and spoken language. A speaker's words can be *translated* as they are being uttered; a book can be *translated* from one language into another. *Interpret* is a narrower term and is generally used to refer only to spoken words being expressed in another language.

- A person who has had a frightening experience while in a plane might express relief at being back on *terra firma* after the plane has landed. The Latin for *land* is *terra,* and the phrase *terra firma* means "solid ground." The Latin *terra* occurs in several English words; among them are *terrain* (Word List 3) and **territory,** an area of land. The term *territory* is applied to those parts of the United States that have some form of self-government but have not been admitted to the Union as states. Guam and American Samoa are *territories.*

8 Vocabulary Extension

interpret

verb 1. To translate into another language.

2. To explain the meaning of something.

Word Family

interpretation (noun)
interpreter (noun)
mis**interpret** (verb)

Context Clues

These sentences give clues to the meaning of **interpret.**

*The woman was hired by the hospital to **interpret** for the patients who used sign language.*

*Can someone help me **interpret** the meaning of this paragraph? I don't understand it.*

Discussion & Writing Prompt

An **interpreter** is a person who can translate one language into another language. Why are **interpreters** important?

2 min.	3 min.
1. Turn and talk to your partner or group.	2. Write 2–4 sentences.
Use this space to take notes or draw your ideas.	Be ready to share what you have written.

Review

Crossword Puzzle Solve the crossword puzzle by studying the clues and filling in the answer boxes. The number after a clue is the lesson the word is from.

Clues Across

1. To move from one place to another **(6)**
6. One-twelfth of a foot
9. Clothes **(5)**
10. A small opening with a door or cover **(6)**
11. A small body of water
13. To bring under human control **(6)**
15. To write as a permanent record **(5)**
16. To come out of **(6)**
20. Of use; helpful **(8)**
22. A person with much experience **(7)**
23. To serve a purpose **(6)**
24. Not present
25. To change gradually over time **(5)**

Clues Down

2. A playful or funny act **(5)**
3. To cover or hide from sight **(5)**
4. To get back; to recover **(8)**
5. A sudden rush of frightened animals **(7)**
6. Present from birth **(5)**
7. A place where one could find sanctuary
8. To lose or give up **(6)**
12. To be in no hurry to leave **(8)**
14. To bring or come into being **(7)**
17. To make a movement of the hand or arm **(6)**
18. Worn so that one may see better
19. Suitable for everyday use; comfortable **(7)**
21. To do better than others **(7)**
22. What people do in elections

Word List

Study the definitions of the words. Then do the exercises that follow.

accumulate
ə kyōōm´ yōō lāt

v. To increase in number or amount; to pile up, collect, or gather.
An inch of snow **accumulated** overnight.

Identify for your partner something that has accumulated in your classroom over the year.

aggravate
ag´ rə vāt

v. 1. To make worse.
The skater **aggravated** an old knee injury when she fell.

2. To anger or annoy.
That loud rock music from the club **aggravates** the neighbors.

aggravation *n.* (ag rə vā´ shən) 1. Annoyance; exasperation.
My **aggravation** increased as the noisy construction continued outside my window.

2. A source of annoyance or exasperation.
Deer and rabbits are a continuous **aggravation** to rural gardeners.

Discuss with your partner whether going to a rock concert will help or aggravate a headache.

conserve
kən sʉrv´

v. To save by using carefully.
Lower speed limits help **conserve** gasoline.

conservation *n.* (kän sər vā´ shən) The saving or protection of something through careful use.
A plan for the **conservation** of water during the drought was unveiled at the town meeting.

contaminate
kən tam´ i nāt

v. To harm by contact with something undesirable.
Chemicals spilled last year continue to **contaminate** the lake.

contamination *n.* (kən tam i nā´ shən) The act of or result of contaminating.
Salt used on the roads in winter could lead to the **contamination** of the river.

Tell your partner why you would or would not want to swim in a creek that has been contaminated with garbage.

diminish
di min´ ish

v. To make or become smaller or less; to reduce.
The popcorn we ate after school **diminished** our hunger.

Talk to your partner for fifteen seconds, letting the sound of your voice diminish until you are silent.

drastic
dras´ tik

adj. Severe; extreme.
Criminals receive **drastic** punishment in this new novel.

extravagant
ek strav´ ə gənt

adj. Spending, costing, or using more than is required.
Shawn's buying lunch for everyone was an **extravagant** thing to do.

extravagance *n.* 1. The quality of being wasteful or spending more than is necessary.
Emma's **extravagance** in early adulthood led to poverty later.

2. A thing that costs more than one can afford.
I admit the team jacket was an **extravagance,** but I couldn't resist buying it.

frugal
fro͞o´ gəl

adj. Careful in spending or using something.
The bill for the splendid wedding ceremony shocked my **frugal** relatives.

impurity
im pyo͞or´ ə tē

n. Something that is harmful or dirty.
Filtering removes the **impurities** from water.

peril
per´ əl

n. Danger; something that is dangerous.
The sailor understood the **peril** involved in a solo crossing of the Atlantic Ocean.

imperil *v.* (im per´ əl) To place in danger.
A bad driver's ineptness **imperils** the passengers.

perilous *adj.* (per´ ə ləs) Dangerous.
An expedition into enemy territory could be **perilous.**

perpetual
pər pech´ o͞o əl

adj. Lasting or seeming to last forever or for a long time; continuous.
A **perpetual** rain has been falling for nine days.

resource
rē´ sôrs

n. 1. A supply that can be used when there is a need.
Coal and lumber are natural **resources.**

2. Skill in dealing with difficult situations.
The teacher trusted us to be left to our own **resources** when she stepped outside to take a phone call.

resourceful *adj.* (rē sôrs´ fəl) Able to deal with difficult problems.
A **resourceful** person will triumph over difficulties.

Chat with your partner about the resources for learning that are available in your school.

substitute
sub´ stə to͞ot

v. To replace one thing or person for another.
Cooks sometimes **substitute** lemon for vinegar in salad dressing.

n. Something or someone that replaces another.
Luis will be the **substitute** in case another player is injured in the soccer match.

adj. Acting in place of someone or something else.
The **substitute** teacher tolerated the class's antics.

Talk to your partner about whether you have ever wanted to substitute what you ate at lunch for something else.

sustain
sə stān´

v. 1. To keep up; to support.
Their firm belief that they would be rescued **sustained** them.

2. To suffer; to undergo.
The driver of the wrecked car **sustained** serious injuries.

Tell your partner if you have ever sustained a bad cut or scrape, and explain how it occurred.

vital
vīt´ l

adj. 1. Necessary for continued life or prosperity.
Clean water is **vital** for our health.

2. Full of lively spirit.
Nelson Mandela's **vital** personality enabled him to survive years of imprisonment without bitterness.

3. Of the greatest importance.
It is **vital** that you make a decision immediately.

Finding Meanings

Choose two phrases to form a sentence that correctly uses a word from Word List 9. Then write the sentence.

1. (a) a source of annoyance.
   (b) An extravagance is
   (c) a source of danger.
   (d) An aggravation is

   ____

   ____

2. (a) that make a bad situation worse.
   (b) that are extreme in nature.
   (c) Drastic measures are those
   (d) Frugal measures are those

   ____

   ____

3. (a) a gradual increase over time.
   (b) Contamination is
   (c) Conservation is
   (d) contact with something harmful.

____

____

4. (a) a way of politely saying no.
   (b) A substitute is
   (c) something that is harmful or dirty.
   (d) An impurity is

____

____

5. (a) to increase its amount.
   (b) to spend it wastefully.
   (c) To conserve wealth is
   (d) To accumulate wealth is

____

____

6. (a) A substitute player is one who
   (b) suffers an injury.
   (c) A vital player is one who
   (d) replaces another one.

____

____

7. (a) never seem to end.
   (b) Diminished demands are those that
   (c) seem reasonable.
   (d) Perpetual demands are those that

____

____

8. (a) Something that is perilous is
   (b) very dangerous.
   (c) quite harmless.
   (d) Someone who is resourceful is

____

____

9. (a) A resource is something
   (b) that requires attention.
   (c) An extravagance is something
   (d) that costs more than one can easily afford.

____

____

Just the Right Word

Replace each phrase in bold with a single word (or form of the word) from the word list.

1. Many students **had to suffer through** heat exhaustion after the race.

2. Carmella's mother did not approve of Carmella's **wasteful spending of large amounts of money.**

3. The new bottled water was recalled because it contained many **dirty and harmful substances.**

4. A thick layer of dust had **gathered little by little** on top of the piano.

5. A cook who is **careful not to waste anything** can make interesting dishes from leftovers.

6. The pain started to **become less severe** after a few days.

7. Our **abilities to deal with difficult situations** were tested to the maximum when our raft was propelled into dangerous rapids.

8. She seems so **full of lively spirit** that one forgets she is sick.

9. The stage manager faced many **things that bothered or annoyed her** in trying to be ready for opening night.

10. By driving recklessly, you **placed in real danger** the lives of your passengers.

11. **Very severe** changes are needed to make sure the lunchroom serves healthy food.

12. Unwashed hands can easily **bring dirt into contact with** food products.

13. The **careful use and saving** of water is extremely important on a long expedition.

accumulate
aggravate
conserve
contaminate
diminish
drastic
extravagant
frugal
impurity
peril
perpetual
resource
substitute
sustain
vital

9C Applying Meanings

Circle the letter or letters next to each correct answer. There may be more than one correct answer.

1. Which of the following would **conserve** water?
   (a) watering the lawn less often
   (b) taking fewer showers
   (c) turning the faucet off while brushing one's teeth
   (d) fixing a leaky faucet

2. Which of the following would **diminish** one's freedom?
   (a) being held captive
   (b) having one's driver's license taken away
   (c) being sent to jail
   (d) being released from prison

3. Which of the following are **vital** in a democracy?
   (a) voting in elections
   (b) advertising on television
   (c) learning about presidential candidates
   (d) spending a lot of money on campaigns

4. Which of the following might a **frugal** person do?
   (a) save used string
   (b) buy expensive presents
   (c) compare prices
   (d) travel by plane

5. Which of the following are natural **resources?**
   (a) water
   (b) lumber
   (c) air
   (d) coal

6. Which of the following are **substitutes** for sugar?
   (a) honey
   (b) artificial sweeteners
   (c) chocolate
   (d) milk

7. Which of the following are needed to **sustain** life?
   (a) oxygen
   (b) food
   (c) water
   (d) education

8. Which of the following might **aggravate** a sore throat?
   (a) eating something cold
   (b) coughing
   (c) screaming
   (d) shouting

Word Study: Synonyms and Antonyms

Each group of four words contains either two synonyms or two antonyms. Circle that pair. Then circle the S if they are synonyms or the A if they are antonyms.

1. necessary	safe	drastic	vital	S	A
2. aggravate	linger	accumulate	annoy	S	A
3. impurity	expanse	peril	danger	S	A
4. substitute	replace	diminish	skirmish	S	A
5. extravagant	frugal	drastic	lengthy	S	A
6. resourceful	continuous	perpetual	anxious	S	A
7. increase	sustain	diminish	compete	S	A
8. waste	shed	conserve	soothe	S	A
9. extreme	resourceful	realistic	drastic	S	A

accumulate
aggravate
conserve
contaminate
diminish
drastic
extravagant
frugal
impurity
peril
perpetual
resource
substitute
sustain
vital

Vocabulary in Context

Read the passage.

Water, Water, Everywhere

What sets our planet apart from all the others? Pictures from space show Earth to be the blue planet. Its color comes from the water that covers about three quarters of its surface. To the best of our knowledge, ours is the only planet that can **sustain** life, and water is the reason. You'd think we would treat something so **vital** to our lives as a valuable gift. Sadly, that has not been the case. Except during times of drought, when we realize how precious it is, water is something we take very much for granted.

The water that makes up Earth's rivers, oceans, and lakes is always in motion. As it is warmed by the sun, water evaporates into the air. The vapor forms clouds, leaving behind the **impurities** that were dissolved in the water. As the vapor cools, it forms water droplets that eventually fall as rain. The rainfall **accumulates** in Earth's different bodies of water. There it is heated by the sun and evaporates once more. This process is known as the water cycle. It has gone on **perpetually** since it started—about five hundred thousand years after Earth was formed. The water cycle is nature's way of keeping Earth's supply of water clean. For billions of years it worked well. However, with the growth of industry and the increase in population over the past two hundred years, the situation has changed **drastically.**

The standard of living that Americans enjoy exceeds anything our ancestors dreamed of. But the conveniences of daily life that we are accustomed to have been obtained at a terrible price. In our eagerness to make progress, we have **contaminated** our rivers, oceans, and lakes by emptying the raw sewage from our toilets into them. We have **aggravated** the problem by allowing chemical pesticides and fertilizers used on crops to run off into our water supplies. We have also dumped poisonous chemicals into landfills so that in many places the water lying under the ground **imperils** the health of those who eventually drink it. As a result, the amount of clean water is **diminishing.**

Human beings have often demonstrated how **resourceful** they can be when there are problems to be solved. When we run out of something we need, we can usually find something else to take its place; however, there is no **substitute** for water. We have to learn to **conserve** this precious liquid as though our lives depend on it—because they do. An **extravagant** person is sometimes said to "spend money like water." Now, however, the time has come for us to learn to be **frugal** and spend our water as carefully as a penny-pincher spends money.

▶ **Answer each of the following questions with a sentence. If a question does not contain a vocabulary word from the lesson's word list, use one in your answer. Use each word only once.**

1. What are three things that can **contaminate** water?

2. What is the meaning of **aggravate** as it is used in the passage?

3. What three ways can you think of to practice water **conservation?**

4. What is the meaning of **substitute** as it is used in the passage?

5. What happens to the quantity of clean water as water pollution increases?

6. What is the meaning of **vital** as it is used in the passage?

7. What remains after the **impurities** have been removed from water?

8. How would you describe the taking of twenty-minute showers during a drought?

9. Why is water our most precious natural **resource?**

accumulate
aggravate
conserve
contaminate
diminish
drastic
extravagant
frugal
impurity
peril
perpetual
resource
substitute
sustain
vital

10. What happens when poisonous chemicals **accumulate** in landfills?

___

___

11. How would you describe your use of water if you turn off the faucet when you brush your teeth?

___

___

12. How can drinking from water that comes from the earth under a landfill affect a person's health?

___

___

13. How would you describe an order that restricted families to only one gallon of water a day?

___

___

14. What is the meaning of **sustain** as it is used in the passage?

___

___

15. Has the water cycle ever stopped since it began, and how does the passage tell you this?

___

___

Fun & Fascinating **FACTS**

- To *preserve* something is to keep it from being harmed or used up. To **conserve** something is to use it carefully and without waste.

- When **substitute** is used as a verb, it is always followed by the preposition *for*. You *substitute* one thing *for* another.

Vocabulary Extension

substitute

verb To replace one thing or person for another.

noun Something or someone that replaces another.

Academic Context

If your usual teacher is absent, another teacher will **substitute** for the day.

Discussion & Writing Prompt

If you wanted to make your lunch healthier, what could you **substitute** for French fries, a hamburger, and a soda? Why?

2 min. 1. Turn and talk to your partner or group.	3 min. 2. Write 2–4 sentences.
Use this space to take notes or draw your ideas.	Be ready to share what you have written.

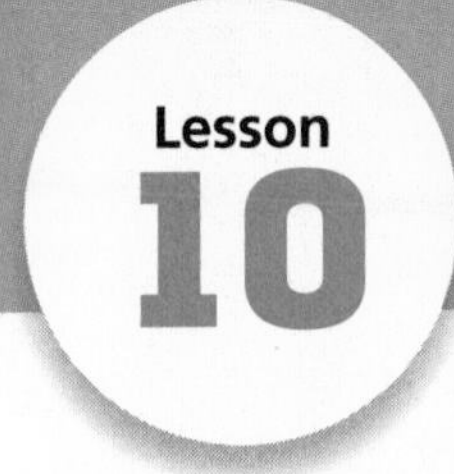

Word List

Study the definitions of the words. Then do the exercises that follow.

anticipate
an tis´ ə pāt

v. 1. To look forward to; to expect.
We **anticipated** having a good time at the party.

2. To be aware of and to provide for beforehand.
The teacher **anticipated** their questions by explaining the assignment thoroughly.

Tell your partner what you are anticipating doing this weekend.

bankrupt
baŋk´ rupt

adj. 1. Unable to pay one's debts and freed by law from doing so.
The store owner was **bankrupt** after the business failed.

2. Left without any worth or value.
Kylie was **bankrupt** of ideas for the project.

v. To leave without worth or value.
His extravagances **bankrupted** him.

brief
brēf

adj. Short; not long-lasting.
The guests had time for just a **brief** visit, so they did not linger when it was time to leave.

v. To give a short explanation or set of instructions to.
An assistant **briefed** the mayor before the debate.

n. A statement giving the main points in a case, for use in a court of law.
The attorney glanced at her **brief** before addressing the judge.

Think of a brief sentence and say it to your partner.

brisk
brisk

adj. 1. Quick; active.
The runners kept up a **brisk** pace at the start of the race.

2. Stimulating; refreshing.
The **brisk** wind blowing off the ocean felt good.

budget
buj´ ət

n. A plan for spending money during a certain period.
The extravagant dinner caused the family to overspend their weekly food **budget.**

v. To plan the use of carefully.
A part-time job may affect your schoolwork unless you **budget** your time.

compete
kəm pēt´

v. To try to win against others.
Five students **competed** for first prize.

competition *n.* (käm pə tish´ ən) 1. The act of trying to win against others.
Competition to get into a good college can be fierce.

2. A contest.
The team entered the **competition** even though it had little chance of winning.

competitor *n.* (käm pet´ i tər) One who competes against others.
Six **competitors** entered the race.

complicate
käm´ pli kāt

v. To make difficult.
An extra guest may **complicate** the seating arrangements.

complicated *adj.* Not easy or simple; having many different parts.
The instructions are so **complicated** that no one could figure them out.

Chat with your partner about silly ways to complicate brushing your teeth.

effect
ə fekt´

v. To make happen.
The new principal will **effect** many changes.

n. A result.
The medicine I took for my headache had no **effect.**

effective *adj.* (ə fek´ tiv) 1. Bringing about the desired result.
Gargling with salt water is an **effective** treatment for a minor sore throat.

2. In operation; active.
A new dress code was **effective** the day school opened.

3. Making a strong and favorable impression.
People are likely to remember what an **effective** speaker says.

Talk to your partner about actions you could take to effect a change in school rules.

err
er

v. To be wrong or to do wrong.
I **erred** when I accused you of lying.

error *n.* (er´ ər) A mistake.
Errors in punctuation are easily corrected.

erroneous *adj.* (ər rō´ nē əs) Mistaken; wrong.
The facts are correct, but the conclusion is **erroneous.**

factor
fak´ tər

n. Something that contributes to a result.
Paying attention and studying diligently are two **factors** in getting good grades.

Share with your partner what factors you keep in mind when you buy new shoes.

fad fad

n. Something that is very popular for a short time, then forgotten.
Ankle bracelets were the **fad** one summer.

gripe grīp

v. 1. To complain.
The children always **gripe** about having to get up early.

2. To annoy or irritate.
Crowded streets **gripe** the traveling public.

n. A complaint.
Too much homework and too few lunch choices were two of the students' **gripes.**

Gripe to your partner about one thing you dislike about your town.

knack nak

n. A special talent or skill; ability to do something easily.
My mother has a **knack** for making friends wherever she goes.

leisure lē´ zhər

n. Free time not taken up with work.
My father's sixty-hour work week allows little time for **leisure.**

leisurely *adj.* Slow; relaxed.
The friends strolled at a **leisurely** pace through the park.

unique yo͞o nēk´

adj. The only one of its kind.
The platypus, a mammal that lays eggs, is **unique** among animals.

Tell your partner something that makes you a unique person.

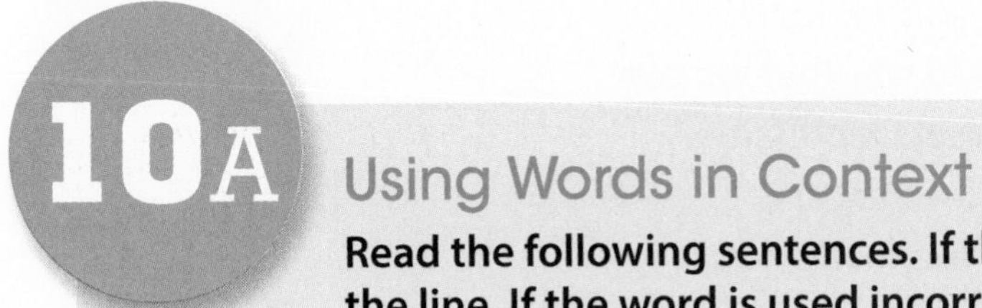

10A Using Words in Context

Read the following sentences. If the word in bold is used correctly, write C on the line. If the word is used incorrectly, write I on the line.

1. (a) Dinner is at six, so please get **effective** for it. ___
   (b) The new coach plans to **effect** some changes on the team. ___
   (c) The rule was **effective** immediately. ___
   (d) The tea I drank for the flu had the desired **effect.** ___

2. (a) For a **brief** moment, I thought I was dreaming. ___
   (b) The mayor was **briefed** on the earthquake that night. ___
   (c) The lawyer took her **brief** to the courthouse. ___
   (d) We **briefed** a sigh of relief when we made it through the snow. ___

3. (a) When my little brother starts to get **erroneous,** I tell him to be quiet. ___
   (b) It is **erroneous** to say that a kitten is a baby dog. ___
   (c) There is an **error** in the book. ___
   (d) I **erred** to the top of the hill. ___

4. (a) The **competition** for the spelling bee is intense. ___
   (b) Over two hundred nations **compete** in the Olympic Games. ___
   (c) She was a **competitor** who hated to lose. ___
   (d) I **competed** that we had only one slice of bread left. ___

5. (a) Four teams **anticipated** in the finals. ___
   (b) We **anticipated** a few problems, but nothing serious happened. ___
   (c) They **anticipated** that a lot of people would be at the carnival. ___
   (d) I **anticipated** the cat down from the tree. ___

6. (a) Jana started her day with a **brisk** cold shower. ___
   (b) His **brisk** personality did not make him very popular. ___
   (c) Why **brisk** the floor if it's already clean? ___
   (d) You need plenty of **brisk** to win the game. ___

7. (a) The instructions were very **complicated,** so I wrote them down. ___
   (b) Cheyenne **complicates** things more than they need to be. ___
   (c) The teacher **complicated** that the students did a great job on the homework. ___
   (d) Josiah was **complicated** for having the highest grade on the test. ___

8. (a) The weather will be a **factor** in whether we play. ___
   (b) Several **factors** led to the Great Depression. ___
   (c) The **factors** make the parts for the cars. ___
   (d) You can't **factor** if you want me to like you. ___

9. (a) My mom said my **leisure** was crooked. ___
   (b) My **leisure** time is spent reading. ___
   (c) We took a **leisurely** walk through the park. ___
   (d) Crack open the **leisure** so we can see what's inside. ___

10. (a) Tiana **griped** because she was in a bad mood. ___
    (b) My **gripe** is that we have too much schoolwork to do. ___
    (c) The **gripes** are picked in October before it gets too cold. ___
    (d) The teacher listened to our **gripes** and promised to make some changes. ___

anticipate
bankrupt
brief
brisk
budget
compete
complicate
effect
err
factor
fad
gripe
knack
leisure
unique

Making Connections

Circle the letter next to each correct answer. There may be more than one correct answer.

1. Which word or words go with *money?*
   (a) bankrupt (b) motion (c) budget (d) fad

2. Which word or words go with *short?*
   (a) brisk (b) brief (c) minute (d) elusive

3. Which word or words go with *mistake?*
   (a) rouse (b) compete (c) err (d) bungle

4. Which word or words go with *look forward to?*
   (a) effect (b) ancestor (c) anticipate (d) brisk

5. Which word or words go with *successful?*
   (a) brief (b) complicated (c) effective (d) erroneous

6. Which word or words go with *complain?*
   (a) restrict (b) gripe (c) fad (d) knack

7. Which word or words go with *talent?*
   (a) ability (b) budget (c) knack (d) factor

8. Which word or words go with *sports?*
   (a) linger (b) compete (c) challenge (d) complicate

9. Which word or words go with *the only one?*
   (a) erroneous (b) solitary (c) effective (d) unique

10. Which word or words go with *fashion?*
    (a) apparel (b) fad (c) attire (d) factor

Determining Meanings

Circle the letter next to each answer choice that correctly completes the sentence. There may be more than one correct answer.

1. His **uniqueness**
   (a) makes him special.
   (b) comes from his sense of humor.
   (c) always hurts when he bends his arm.
   (d) looks like he spent a lot of time on it.

2. A **leisurely**
   (a) piece of paper is very light.
   (b) girl tried to finish her book as fast as she could.
   (c) meal can take an hour or more.
   (d) afternoon may be spent resting.

3. **Factors**
   (a) that might make you late are bad weather and traffic.
   (b) get bigger the more you try to stop them.
   (c) are formed at the end of rainbows.
   (d) such as who can come to your birthday party are important for planning.

4. **Fads**
   (a) in space are made of dust and gas.
   (b) are things that are briefly popular.
   (c) burrowed into the dirt to escape the predator.
   (d) that summer involved rolling up your pants.

5. A **complicated**
   (a) design involving different shapes was chosen for the wall.
   (b) plot makes it hard to follow what's happening in the movie.
   (c) glass of water sat on the table.
   (d) person is very simple and easy to understand.

6. The **budgets**
   (a) were let out of the cage to fly around the room.
   (b) left me with ten extra dollars each week.
   (c) were set in August for the new school year.
   (d) had a crack in it that was easy to repair.

anticipate
bankrupt
brief
brisk
budget
compete
complicate
effect
err
factor
fad
gripe
knack
leisure
unique

7. **Bankruptcy**
   (a) left Mr. Simon unable to pay anyone back.
   (b) frustrated the owner's dreams of expanding her store.
   (c) creates flowers that attract bees.
   (d) in bones can make them break more easily.

8. I **briskly**
   (a) ran a mile in gym class.
   (b) poured the syrup slowly onto the waffle.
   (c) tiptoed up the stairs so I wouldn't wake anyone.
   (d) chased my sister up and down the street during a game of tag.

Completing Sentences

Complete the sentences to demonstrate your knowledge of the words in bold.

1. I would win a **competition** in

   ______________________________ .

2. An **effective** way to get a good night's sleep is to

   ______________________________ .

3. An example of an **error** in punctuation might be

   ______________________________ .

4. A company is **bankrupted** when

   ______________________________ .

5. A **factor** that might make me run home after school is

   ______________________________ .

6. Something I **anticipate** about tomorrow is

   ______________________________ .

7. A **fad** I know about is

   ______________________________ .

8. Something I **gripe** about is

   ______________________________ .

9. **Complicated** math problems make me feel

   ______________________________ .

10. A **budget** is

    ______________________________ .

Vocabulary in Context

Read the passage.

Fun and Games

Have you ever invented a new game or toy? Lots of people have, and most of them would tell you that it's not all fun and games. In fact, inventing and producing games is a very serious business.

Many of those who have tried to interest a company in their inventions have a common **gripe:** Most companies will not consider an idea from someone unknown to them. Companies prefer to deal only with established inventors with whom they have developed a long-term relationship. These veteran inventors have a **knack** for thinking up ideas—lots of them—for new toys and games. Just as important, they are willing to spend the time to develop their ideas. Only then do they take their new game or toy to a company and try to sell it.

Toys and games are big business. People may complain that they have less **leisure** time than they used to, but today they spend far more money on ways to fill this time. Billions of dollars are spent this way in the United States alone each year. Toy stores do a **brisk** business in the weeks between Thanksgiving and the end of the year. They can **anticipate** selling more toys and games in this one period than in the entire rest of the year! Companies **compete** to meet the enormous demand by engaging in a perpetual search for new products. These companies aren't interested in warmed-over ideas from previous years; they are looking for something **unique.**

Originality may be the main consideration, but companies must also keep other **factors** in mind when deciding which games or toys to produce. First, the cost of producing a new product is very important; the less **complicated** the toy or game is, the cheaper it will be to make. Companies also take into account the age of the children for whom the toy or game is intended; if it is easy to understand, then younger children will be able to play it. The result is an increase in the number of likely buyers. Finally, the larger companies with big advertising **budgets** must ask whether they can make an **effective** television commercial for the new product.

Producing a new toy or game is risky, but the rewards can be great. If a company **errs** by putting a lot of money into a new toy or game that fails to sell, the company can go **bankrupt.** If it is successful, on the other hand, everyone is ecstatic. Even success is not without risks. Should a game or toy

anticipate
bankrupt
brief
brisk
budget
compete
complicate
effect
err
factor
fad
gripe
knack
leisure
unique

catch on, the maker may not be in a position to meet the sudden demand. By the time the factory is able to turn out the items, the **fad** may have died down. Then the company is left with tens of thousands of items it cannot sell.

In fact, most toys and games do have **brief** lives, but there are always exceptions. Monopoly has been a popular game for more than eighty years. Over 250 million Monopoly games have been sold. Of course, only a handful of lucky inventors create highly successful new toys or games and become millionaires. But inventors are natural optimists. That is why there is no shortage of newcomers eager to break into this high-stakes business.

▶ **Answer each of the following questions with a sentence. If a question does not contain a vocabulary word from the lesson's word list, use one in your answer. Use each word only once.**

1. Why are large companies able to advertise heavily on television?

____

____

2. How long do most toys and games remain popular?

____

____

3. Why might a toy-store owner **gripe** about a severe storm in December?

____

____

4. Is the belief that one can get rich by inventing games an **erroneous** one? Why or why not?

____

____

5. What is the meaning of **brisk** as it is used in the passage?

____

____

6. What happens when more and more companies get into the games business?

____

____

7. What are some ways you spend your **leisure** time?

8. Why would it be incorrect to call Monopoly a **fad?**

9. What is the meaning of **anticipate** as it is used in the passage?

10. What kind of toy or game usually appeals to very young children?

11. What is the meaning of **effective** as it is used in the passage?

12. Why is the decision to make a new toy not a quick and easy process for a company?

13. What does a person need in order to be a successful games inventor?

14. What is the meaning of **bankrupt** as it is used in the passage?

15. What is the most important thing that games companies look for when considering a game?

anticipate
bankrupt
brief
brisk
budget
compete
complicate
effect
err
factor
fad
gripe
knack
leisure
unique

Fun & Fascinating FACTS

- **Effect** is a verb and means "to make happen." It is also a noun and means "a result." *Affect* is a verb and means "to cause a change in." (The bus strike will *affect* our travel plans.) It also means "to pretend to have." (He *affected* a British accent when in England because he didn't want to sound like a tourist.)

- **Unique** means "the only one of its kind." It is incorrect to say that something is "very *unique*" or "most *unique*"; if something is the *only* one of its kind, it cannot be compared to something else.

- In addition to meaning "something that contributes to a result," **factor** is also a term used in mathematics, where it has two separate but related meanings.

  A **factor** is one of two or more numbers that divide a given number without a remainder: 2, 3, and 5 are *factors* of 30, as are 5 and 6, 3 and 10, and 2 and 15.

  A *factor* is also the number of times a given number is increased or decreased. A population that goes from 2 million to 6 million has increased by a *factor* of 3.

Vocabulary Extension

effect

noun A result.

Academic Context

Understanding cause and **effect** is an important reading skill.

Word Family

effective (adjective)
effectively (adverb)
effectiveness (noun)

Discussion & Writing Prompt

What are the **effects** of a thunderstorm?

2 min. 1. Turn and talk to your partner or group.	3 min. 2. Write 2–4 sentences.
Use this space to take notes or draw your ideas.	Be ready to share what you have written.

Word List

Study the definitions of the words. Then do the exercises that follow.

abbreviate
ə brē´ vē āt

v. To shorten by leaving out certain parts.
Main Street can be **abbreviated** to Main St.

abbreviation *n.* (ə brē vē ā´ shən) The result of abbreviating.
Mr. Smith is the accepted **abbreviation** for Mister Smith.

appropriate
ə prō´ prē ət

adj. Suitable or right for the purpose.
Sandals are not **appropriate** footwear for hiking.

v. (ə prō´ prē āt) To set aside for a particular purpose.
Congress **appropriates** money for various programs.

Discuss with your partner some behaviors that are not appropriate in the classroom but are appropriate in the park.

exclude
eks klo͞od´

v. To leave out; to keep from being a part of.
The gym teacher **excluded** everyone who could not run a mile from the advanced gym class.

Talk to your partner about how you would feel if you were excluded from a party you really wanted to attend.

fanciful
fan´ si fəl

adj. 1. Not based on reason; unrealistic.
One inventor came up with a **fanciful** scheme to turn water into gasoline.

2. Not real; imaginary.
For the costume party, some of the children dressed up as ghosts, goblins, and other **fanciful** creatures.

futile
fyo͞ot´ l

adj. Certain to fail; hopeless or useless.
Before giving up, we made several **futile** attempts to retrieve the car keys that had fallen into the lake.

grudge
gruj

n. A feeling of resentment.
Rosa held a **grudge** against her friends because of the way they treated her brother.

v. To be unwilling to give.
Do you **grudge** me this food when you see how ravenous I am?

grudging *adj.* Done or said with reluctance.
Everyone knew that such a **grudging** apology could not be sincere.

inspire
in spīr´

v. To fill with emotion or great excitement.
Einstein's discoveries **inspired** me to become a scientist.

inspiration *n.* (in spər ā´ shən) The power to affect the mind or the emotions; anything that has this effect.
The sight of leaves falling was the **inspiration** for this poem.

Tell your partner about someone—a famous person or someone you know—who has inspired you to be a better person.

majority
mə jôr´ ə tē

n. 1. The greater number or part; more than half.
The **majority** of teachers at this school live in town.

2. The amount by which one number of votes is greater than another.
The vote was 97 to 91, a **majority** of six.

With your partner, count the number of students in the room and then figure out how many students would make up a majority.

persevere
pʉr sə vir´

v. To refuse to give up despite difficulties.
The workers **persevered** through the blizzard until the house for the needy family was complete.

perseverance *n.* Continued efforts in spite of difficulties.
With **perseverance,** you can overcome extravagance and stick to a budget.

Tell your partner about someone you know who has persevered in a tough situation.

possess
pə zes´

v. 1. To have or to own.
The children **possess** three pairs of shoes.

2. To get power or control over.
Fear **possessed** them as they entered the haunted house.

possession *n.* (pə zesh´ ən) 1. The act of owning or holding.
The family recipe book is in my grandmother's **possession.**

2. The thing that is held or owned.
The immigrants arrived with all their **possessions** in a few suitcases.

Show your partner how many pencils you possess.

prejudice
prej´ ə dis

n. An opinion or strong feeling formed without careful thought or regard to the facts.
Her **prejudice** against tomatoes keeps her from trying many delicious dishes.

v. To cause to have such a feeling.
A student's casual attire should not **prejudice** a store owner against him or her.

prejudiced *adj.* Having such a feeling.
One cannot expect a fair verdict from a **prejudiced** judge.

Tell your partner about any foods you have a particular prejudice against.

resolute rez´ ə lo͞ot — *adj.* Determined not to give in; unyielding.
The shelter was **resolute** about finding good homes for the kittens.

sneer snēr — *v.* To look down on with scorn; to mock or insult by words or manner.
"That was the most mediocre acting I've ever seen," someone **sneered.**

n. A scornful look; a mocking or insulting remark.
I didn't let my companion's **sneers** diminish my enjoyment of the local artists' exhibition.

unanimous yo͞o nan´ ə məs — *adj.* Without any disagreement.
The motion passed by a **unanimous** vote of 57 to 0.

unanimity *n.* (yo͞o nə nim´ ə tē) The condition of being unanimous.
The committee voted 12 to 0 in a rare display of **unanimity.**

unruly un ro͞o´ lē — *adj.* 1. Badly behaved.
An **unruly** child in a restaurant can be very annoying to the other diners.

2. Hard to control.
This hair spray might help keep your **unruly** hair in place.

Finding Meanings

Choose two phrases to form a sentence that correctly uses a word from Word List 11. Then write the sentence.

1. (a) be without it.
   (b) To appropriate money is to
   (c) To possess money is to
   (d) set it aside for a purpose.

   ____

   ____

2. (a) An inspiration is
   (b) a mocking or insulting remark.
   (c) A sneer is
   (d) an opinion held without regard to the facts.

   ____

   ____

3. (a) more than half.
   (b) A majority is
   (c) A prejudice is
   (d) a number that is too large to be counted.

   ____

   ____

4. (a) who is easily upset.
   (b) who behaves badly.
   (c) An unruly person is one
   (d) A resolute person is one

___

___

5. (a) Perseverance is
   (b) the expectation that things will improve.
   (c) Inspiration is
   (d) the power to affect one's emotions.

___

___

6. (a) An abbreviation is
   (b) A possession is
   (c) a thought that is shared.
   (d) a thing that is owned.

___

___

7. (a) A grudge is
   (b) Unanimity is
   (c) a feeling of resentment.
   (d) a feeling of helplessness.

___

___

8. (a) An abbreviation is
   (b) Perseverance is
   (c) a shortened form of a word.
   (d) an incorrectly pronounced word.

___

___

9. (a) a lack of caring.
   (b) Unanimity is
   (c) complete agreement.
   (d) Futility is

___

___

abbreviate
appropriate
exclude
fanciful
futile
grudge
inspire
majority
persevere
possess
prejudice
resolute
sneer
unanimous
unruly

Just the Right Word

Replace each phrase in bold with a single word (or form of the word) from the word list.

1. Greed **got power over** them and led to their downfall.
2. I soon discovered that asking my parents if I could stay out later was **a waste of my time.**
3. How do you **write the shortened form of** the word *adjective?*
4. The idea that the stork brings a new baby is **one that does not seem very reasonable.**
5. The decision was **made with everyone in agreement.**
6. Thoughtful people do not let **opinions formed without regard for the facts** affect their judgment.
7. I believe they **parted unwillingly with** the dollar they gave to the Red Cross.
8. The club is for teenagers only, and adults are **not allowed to be members of it.**
9. Only by **a firm refusal to give up** can you hope to succeed.
10. Do not **direct your scornful remarks** at things you don't understand.
11. Some people like to wear jeans, but they aren't always **suitable for the occasion.**
12. I think you're making a mistake, but I see you are quite **determined not to change your mind** about going.
13. The thrill of flying for the first time **had a great effect on me and caused** me to want to be a pilot.

Applying Meanings

Circle the letter or letters next to each correct answer. There may be more than one correct answer.

1. Which of the following can be **possessed?**
   (a) a pair of shoes
   (b) a knack
   (c) a rainbow
   (d) courage

2. Which of the following would be **futile?**
   (a) proving that 1+1= 3
   (b) appealing a verdict
   (c) counting to a million
   (d) boycotting a business

3. Which of the following is a **majority?**
   (a) one-half
   (b) three-quarters
   (c) one-third
   (d) all but one

4. Which of the following groups **exclude** even numbers?
   (a) 1, 3, 5, 7, 9
   (b) 1, 3, 3, 5, 7, 9
   (c) 1, 3, 7, 9
   (d) 1, 2, 3, 4, 5, 6

5. Which of the following statements show **prejudice?**
   (a) "Americans are rude."
   (b) "Men don't have feelings."
   (c) "Women have too many feelings."
   (d) "All politicians are liars."

6. Which of the following are **appropriate** at a funeral?
   (a) antics
   (b) weeping
   (c) flowers
   (d) brawling

7. Which of the following might cause a person to **persevere?**
   (a) laziness
   (b) ambition
   (c) fear
   (d) greed

8. Which of the following would be **unruly** behavior?
   (a) brushing a friend's hair
   (b) reading books
   (c) pulling a friend's hair
   (d) throwing books

abbreviate
appropriate
exclude
fanciful
futile
grudge
inspire
majority
persevere
possess
prejudice
resolute
sneer
unanimous
unruly

Word Study: Prefixes

The Greek prefix *mono-* and the Latin prefix *uni-* both mean "one." Match each definition with the correct word chosen from the list. Write each word in the space provided.

unilateral	**unicycle**	**monotone**	**monologue**
unique	**monolith**	**uniform**	**monorail**

1. Attire in which any one person looks like all the rest ______________________
2. A train system with just one rail ______________________
3. Being the only one of its kind ______________________
4. A cycle with just one wheel ______________________
5. A dramatic speech given by one person ______________________
6. A sound that stays on one note ______________________
7. Affecting only one of two or more sides ______________________
8. A single large stone, standing alone ______________________

Vocabulary in Context

Read the passage.

Elizabeth Blackwell, M.D.

In the early 1800s, a woman in the United States had few rights. She was not allowed to vote; that would not happen for a hundred years. She was not allowed to own property, and if she married, everything she **possessed** became the property of her husband. And if she wanted to work, she soon learned that careers in medicine or law were not considered **appropriate** for women; only men were admitted to medical or law schools. Most people regarded this as a perfectly normal state of affairs, but Elizabeth Blackwell was not one of them.

Born in England in 1821, Blackwell came to America as a young girl with her parents. Later, when she expressed a desire to become a doctor, her parents and friends told her to put aside such **fanciful** ideas because it would be **futile** for her to try to get into medical school. But Blackwell was **resolute** in her determination. She studied medicine privately and began applying to medical schools. Despite one rejection after another, she **persevered.**

One of the places to which she applied was the Geneva Medical School in western New York, now part of Syracuse University. The professors there were just as **prejudiced** as those at other medical schools and were quite ready to reject her application. However, in the belief that a **majority** would be against Blackwell's admission, they decided to let the students vote. Just to be sure, they ruled that a single *no* vote would **exclude** her. To the professors' surprise, the students **unanimously** voted *yes.* Blackwell later found out that they had done it as a joke. That had no effect on the result, however, and the professors **grudgingly** accepted her as a student.

In 1847, Elizabeth Blackwell became the first woman in America to be admitted to medical school. Life in the classroom, however, was uncomfortable for her at first. Some students found it amusing to throw paper darts at her, touch her hair, and make offensive remarks about her in her presence. Blackwell responded to the **sneers** and bullying with a dignified silence, and the **unruly** behavior soon ended, to the relief of the more serious students. Blackwell worked hard, earned the respect of the faculty, and received high marks in all her courses. She graduated at the top of her class on January 23, 1849.

abbreviate
appropriate
exclude
fanciful
futile
grudge
inspire
majority
persevere
possess
prejudice
resolute
sneer
unanimous
unruly

Not only had Blackwell become a Doctor of Medicine with the right to put the **abbreviation** *M.D.* after her name, she had also entered the history books as the first woman in the United States to do so. Her younger sister Emily followed in Elizabeth's footsteps, and she also became a doctor. Together they established the New York Infirmary for Women and Children. During the Civil War, Blackwell trained nurses to tend the wounded. Most of all, her courage in challenging tradition **inspired** other women and opened up the medical profession to them. By the end of the century, over seven thousand women were practicing medicine in the United States.

▶ **Answer each of the following questions with a sentence. If a question does not contain a vocabulary word from the lesson's word list, use one in your answer. Use each word only once.**

1. What effect did Blackwell's life and career have on other women?

____

____

2. What is the relationship of the letters *N.Y.I.W.C.* to the New York Infirmary for Women and Children?

____

____

3. How much property was a woman required to turn over to her husband when she married?

____

____

4. How were women **excluded** from the political process during Blackwell's lifetime?

____

____

5. Why do you think so few women demanded changes in the way they were treated?

____

____

6. Why might Blackwell's desire to become a doctor have shocked some people?

7. What is the meaning of **fanciful** as it is used in the passage?

8. How did Blackwell feel when she encountered obstacles to becoming a doctor?

9. Why do you think Blackwell's applications to medical schools were rejected?

10. How was Blackwell's **perseverance** rewarded?

11. What is the meaning of **unruly** as it is used in the passage?

12. Why did the professors insist that the vote on Blackwell's admission be **unanimous?**

13. What is the meaning of **majority** as it is used in the passage?

14. How did the male students at Geneva Medical School bully Blackwell?

15. How did the professors' feelings about Blackwell as a student change over time?

abbreviate
appropriate
exclude
fanciful
futile
grudge
inspire
majority
persevere
possess
prejudice
resolute
sneer
unanimous
unruly

Fun & Fascinating FACTS

- **Majority** takes a plural form of the verb if the emphasis is on individual members. (The *majority* of my friends are planning to go to college when they graduate.) If the emphasis is on the group, *majority* takes a singular form. (The *majority* of the human race is still living in poverty.)

  An associated word is *minority,* which means "the lesser number or part; less than half." (Most students take the school bus, but a *minority* walk or ride bicycles to school.)

- The Latin verb *judicare* means "to judge." By combining the root from *judicare* with the Latin prefix *pre-*, which means "before," we form the word **prejudice.** To *judge* the merits of a case *before* having all the facts is to show *prejudice.*

- Two Latin words, *unus* (one) and *animus* (mind) combine to form the word **unanimous.** When people are *unanimous* about something, they are of *one mind*, which means that they all agree.

11 Vocabulary Extension

appropriate

adjective Correct for a situation or purpose.

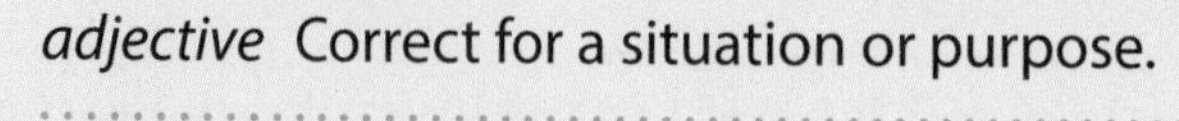

Academic Context

In school, it is important to act in an **appropriate** way, including how you behave in the classroom and how you treat others.

Word Family

appropriately (adverb)
appropriateness (noun)
in**appropriate** (adjective)
in**appropriate**ly (adverb)

Discussion & Writing Prompt

What is **appropriate** behavior when you are in a library?

2 min. 1. Turn and talk to your partner or group.	3 min. 2. Write 2–4 sentences.
Use this space to take notes or draw your ideas.	Be ready to share what you have written.

Lesson 12

Word List

Study the definitions of the words. Then do the exercises that follow.

abandon
ə ban´ dən

v. 1. To give up by leaving in a time of danger.
The captain gave the order to **abandon** the ship when it began to sink.

2. To lose or give up completely.
The trapped miners refused to **abandon** hope of rescue.

3. To withdraw help or support from one in need.
The city had to **abandon** its plan for low-income housing because the budget for it was not approved.

Discuss with your partner what could be hiding in an abandoned house.

adversary
ad´ vər ser ē

n. An enemy or opponent.
France and Germany were **adversaries** in two world wars but now enjoy friendly relations.

baffle
baf´ əl

v. To confuse; to prevent from understanding.
Alice was **baffled** by their inappropriate behavior and didn't know how to respond.

blunder
blun´ dər

n. A stupid or careless mistake.
The mayor's rude comment was a major **blunder** that cost him the election.

v. 1. To make such a mistake.
The chess champion **blundered** when she failed to protect her knight from her opponent's bishop.

2. To move in a clumsy or careless way.
The Sheriff of Nottingham **blundered** into the trap Robin Hood had set for him.

Share with your partner how you would feel if you made a blunder that caused your team to lose a game.

colossal
kə läs´ əl

adj. Very big; enormous.
The **colossal** size of the Great Wall is what impressed the tourists most.

detect
dē tekt´

v. To discover something not easily noticed.
The witness did not **detect** anything unusual that day.

Chat with your partner about what you would do if you detected someone cheating on a test.

haul
hôl

v. To pull or carry with effort.
We **haul** the boat out of the water every winter.

n. 1. The amount caught or taken at one time.
The crew was delighted with the large **haul** of fish today.

2. The distance traveled or to be traveled.
It's a long **haul** into town.

overpower
ō vər pou´ ər

v. To get the better of; to defeat.
The spider **overpowered** the insect caught in its web.

Describe to your partner a smell that can overpower every other smell.

rejoice
rē jois´

v. To be very happy.
Family members **rejoiced** when they heard that members of the Mount Everest expedition had returned safely.

Tell your partner whether you rejoice when the school week ends or when the school week begins.

scoff
skôf

v. To mock; to ridicule.
People once **scoffed** at the idea of space travel.

sentinel
sen´ ti nəl

n. One who keeps watch or guards a point of entry.
Sentinels were posted to warn of the enemy's approach.

siege
sēj

n. The surrounding of a place in order to force it to surrender.
The **siege** of Leningrad by the German army lasted from 1941 to 1944.

sinister
sin´ is tər

adj. Suggesting or leading to evil or harm.
The villain's **sinister** words, "I'll be back!" sent shivers down our spines.

Look at your partner in a sinister way.

victor
vik´ tər

n. The winner in a contest or struggle.
The **victors** of the semifinal competition will meet in the finals tomorrow.

victorious *adj.* (vik tôr´ ē əs) Successful in a contest or battle.
The **victorious** debate team was honored at a ceremony attended by the mayor.

woe wō *n.* 1. Deep distress or misery.
The students' **woe** was evident as they were led off to the principal's office.

2. Trouble; misfortune.
The country's **woes** cannot be cured overnight.

woeful *adj.* 1. Full of woe; unhappy.
Those fleeing the country told a **woeful** tale of persecution by its rulers.

2. Very bad; wretched.
The pilot made a **woeful** error in judgment by trying to land in dense fog.

Look at your partner in a woeful way.

12A Using Words in Context

Read the following sentences. If the word in bold is used correctly, write C on the line. If the word is used incorrectly, write I on the line.

1. (a) The climber **blundered** in the fog and almost fell. ___
   (b) When the player dropped the ball, it was a **blunder** that cost them the game. ___
   (c) Forgetting how to solve the math problem on the test was a major **blunder.** ___
   (d) The pirates buried their **blunder** in a secret location. ___

2. (a) We **hauled** the tiles onto the roof and started working. ___
   (b) The **haul** of the ship was made of plywood. ___
   (c) The gold miners took their monthly **haul** into town and sold it for cash. ___
   (d) The seven inches of rain yesterday was the largest **haul** of the year. ___

3. (a) The **woeful** look on his face made me think something was wrong. ___
   (b) She sat down and told me all about her **woes.** ___
   (c) Texting while driving shows a **woeful** lack of concern for other drivers. ___
   (d) "I won't **woe** you with my problems," my grandma said when I asked how she was. ___

4. (a) The sprinter **abandoned** his time for the one-hundred-meter race to ten seconds. ___
   (b) Buildings that were **abandoned** in the past are now being restored. ___
   (c) He **abandoned** his cozy home and went out into the snow. ___
   (d) When people **abandon** their pets, they often end up in shelters. ___

5. (a) Lupe was **scoffed** that her name had been left off the list. ___
   (b) My friends **scoffed** at me when I said I could climb the wall. ___
   (c) Xavier **scoffed** his opponent into thinking he was about to quit. ___
   (d) Queen Isabella of Spain did not **scoff** at Columbus's plan to find the New World. ___

6. (a) When we reached the gate, we were **baffled** as to what to do next. ___
   (b) The ship **baffled** its way through stormy seas and ten-foot waves. ___
   (c) The secret code **baffled** the experts who tried to break it. ___
   (d) The **baffle** broke out when someone started laughing. ___

7. (a) The students **rejoiced** when it was time for recess. ___
   (b) The broken fan was easily **rejoiced.** ___
   (c) She **rejoiced** when she found out her grade on the project. ___
   (d) We **rejoice** our muscles with regular exercise. ___

8. (a) The **sentinels** guarding the palace wore fancy uniforms. ___
   (b) Geese were used as **sentinels** by the Romans to warn of an attack. ___
   (c) The plants are grown in long **sentinels** three feet apart. ___
   (d) The **sentinels** in the pasta tasted like tomatoes. ___

9. (a) The teacher **detected** the student for lying. ___
   (b) Doctors are learning to **detect** diseases before you get sick. ___
   (c) My mom left England fifteen years ago, but I can still **detect** a British accent. ___
   (d) The mother duck **detected** her ducklings from the storm. ___

10. (a) We decided to have a **siege** at my house on the last day of school. ___
    (b) The **siege** was made of iron that was heated and then beaten into shape. ___
    (c) The **siege** of Troy ended when the Greeks forced their way into the city. ___
    (d) The **siege** of Leningrad by the German army lasted for 872 days. ___

abandon
adversary
baffle
blunder
colossal
detect
haul
overpower
rejoice
scoff
sentinel
siege
sinister
victor
woe

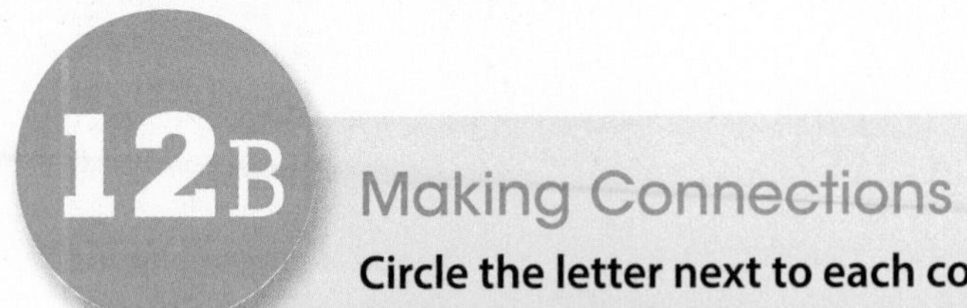

Making Connections

Circle the letter next to each correct answer. There may be more than one correct answer.

1. Which word or words go with *happiness?*
   (a) abandon (b) baffle (c) rejoice (d) jubilation

2. Which word or words go with *make fun of?*
   (a) ridicule (b) scoff (c) jeer (d) woe

3. Which word or words go with *sad?*
   (a) forlorn (b) melancholy (c) sinister (d) woeful

4. Which word or words go with *enemy?*
   (a) woe (b) adversary (c) error (d) opponent

5. Which word or words go with *large?*
   (a) gigantic (b) colossal (c) mammoth (d) sinister

6. Which word or words go with *winning?*
   (a) sinister (b) triumphant (c) victorious (d) woeful

7. Which word or words go with *mistake?*
   (a) haul (b) blunder (c) error (d) bungle

8. Which word or words go with *scary?*
   (a) complicated (b) monstrous (c) colossal (d) sinister

9. Which word or words go with *war?*
   (a) baffle (b) siege (c) skirmish (d) campaign

10. Which word or words go with *defeat?*
    (a) overpower (b) overdue (c) overthrow (d) scoff

Determining Meanings

Circle the letter next to each answer choice that correctly completes the sentence. There may be more than one correct answer.

1. The **victorious**
   (a) chess player proudly accepted her trophy.
   (b) grows mostly in the cracks of sidewalks.
   (c) rumors were spread by an enemy.
   (d) athletes paraded down Main Street after the championship.

2. We are **hauling**
   (a) loudly to make sure people hear us.
   (b) the suitcases up three flights of stairs tomorrow.
   (c) the song in front of the whole class.
   (d) the nets from the ocean when they fill up with fish.

3. The **sentinels**
   (a) let us through after we gave the password.
   (b) fell asleep while on duty.
   (c) went on for two days until the sun finally came out.
   (d) build nests twenty feet from the ground.

4. I **detected**
   (a) the smell of something burning.
   (b) that something was wrong with the computer.
   (c) myself against harm while we camped.
   (d) something moving in the bushes.

5. There was an **adversarial**
   (a) look in his eye as he stepped onto the soccer field.
   (b) relationship between me and my cousin.
   (c) feeling in the air when we started to play.
   (d) stone on the ground that almost looked like a diamond.

6. A **colossally**
   (a) gray mouse ran through the hole in the door.
   (b) mammoth statue of four presidents is carved into Mount Rushmore.
   (c) enormous wave soaked the sunbathers.
   (d) dumb mistake made me fail the test.

abandon
adversary
baffle
blunder
colossal
detect
haul
overpower
rejoice
scoff
sentinel
siege
sinister
victor
woe

7. We were **baffled**
   (a) across the hall and into a small classroom with no windows.
   (b) when we were told it would snow on the first day of summer.
   (c) by strong winds as we walked home from the park.
   (d) by the riddle and had to look up the answer.

8. I **abandoned**
   (a) my bike when I got a flat tire and had to walk home.
   (b) any thoughts of winning when our star player twisted her ankle.
   (c) myself in the basement when the tornado struck.
   (d) my way to Mexico with my family.

Completing Sentences

Complete the sentences to demonstrate your knowledge of the words in bold.

1. I would **rejoice** if

   ____ .

2. I **scoff** at the idea that

   ____ .

3. A **woeful** situation makes you feel

   ____ .

4. I might have a **sinister** look if

   ____ .

5. Something you might **abandon** is

   ____ .

6. To **overpower** your pessimistic thoughts, you could

   ____ .

7. It's good manners for a **victor** to

   ____ .

8. I admit I'm sometimes **baffled** by

   ____ .

9. An example of a **colossal** animal is

   ____ .

10. It's hard to **detect** something if

    ____ .

Vocabulary in Context

Read the passage.

The Trojan Horse

Many captivating tales have come down to us from ancient Greece. They tell of great heroes, of goddesses and gods, and of stirring adventures. One of the best-known stories concerns the Trojan Horse. It began when Helen, wife of the Greek king Menelaus, was kidnapped and taken to the city of Troy.

The Greeks assembled a mighty fleet and sailed across the Aegean Sea in pursuit. After landing their army near Troy, they began laying **siege** to the city, the home of the Trojans. Although many battles were fought outside the city's thick, high walls, the Trojans kept their **adversaries** at bay, so the Greeks were unable to force their way inside.

The war dragged on for ten long years. Then one day the Trojan **sentinels** saw the Greeks sail away! Further investigation revealed that the Greeks had **abandoned** their camp. The delighted Trojans at once declared the war over and themselves **victorious.** One thing **baffled** them, though. The Greeks had left behind an enormous wooden horse. What was it for? The Trojans finally decided that their enemies had left it as a gift to the gods.

Cassandra, a member of the Trojan royal family, warned the citizens of Troy that the wooden horse was a trick intended to bring about the destruction of their city. The Trojans, however, **scoffed** at her warning. They saw nothing **sinister** in the "gift" left by the Greeks, and they joyfully **hauled** the wooden horse through the gates and into the city. It could not have been otherwise. Some years before, Apollo, one of the gods of Mount Olympus, had fallen in love with Cassandra and had given her the ability to predict the future. But when she failed to return his love, Apollo spitefully declared that when she made a prediction, no one would believe her.

The people of Troy **rejoiced** far into the night. They were too busy enjoying themselves to pay close attention to the **colossal** wooden horse in their midst. They failed to examine it closely enough to **detect** the heavily armed Greek soldiers huddled inside, waiting for the right moment. At last the celebrations came to an end as the Trojans grew sleepy and one by one began to slumber. A stillness fell over the city. All seemed tranquil within Troy's walls.

Then a concealed hatch in the wooden horse opened, and the Greek soldiers emerged, dropping silently to the ground. They quickly **overpowered** the Trojan guards and opened the city gates to admit the rest of the Greek

- abandon
- adversary
- baffle
- blunder
- colossal
- detect
- haul
- overpower
- rejoice
- scoff
- sentinel
- siege
- sinister
- victor
- woe

soldiers, who had only pretended to sail away and were now hiding outside. The Trojans paid a terrible price for their **blunder.** Their city was destroyed, and many of its people perished; the rest of the **woeful** inhabitants, including Cassandra, were taken into captivity. As for Helen, according to the most popular version of the story, she returned to Greece with Menelaus, and they lived happily ever after.

▶ **Answer each of the following questions with a sentence. If a question does not contain a vocabulary word from the lesson's word list, use one in your answer. Use each word only once.**

1. Why were the Greeks and the Trojans **adversaries?**

____

____

2. What is the meaning of **woeful** as it is used in the passage?

____

____

3. How long did the **siege** last?

____

____

4. What is the meaning of **abandoned** as it is used in the passage?

____

____

5. What did the Trojans think when they first saw the large wooden horse?

____

____

6. What **blunder** did the Trojans make?

____

____

7. How were the Greek soldiers able to hide inside the wooden horse?

____

____

8. Why was it necessary for the Greeks inside the horse to remain quiet?

____

____

9. How might the Trojans have **hauled** the wooden horse into the city?

____

____

10. Might the Trojans have seen anything **sinister** if they had looked more closely at the wooden horse?

____

____

11. Why did the Trojans **scoff** at Cassandra's warning?

____

____

12. What might have happened if the Trojans had **overpowered** the Greek soldiers as they emerged from the wooden horse?

____

____

13. Who should have been keeping watch on the wooden horse?

____

____

14. Why was the Trojans' **rejoicing** premature?

____

____

15. What was the outcome of the Trojan War?

____

____

abandon
adversary
baffle
blunder
colossal
detect
haul
overpower
rejoice
scoff
sentinel
siege
sinister
victor
woe

Fun & Fascinating FACTS

- One of the Seven Wonders of the ancient world was a huge statue of the sun god Helios, erected at the entrance of the harbor at Rhodes, one of the Greek islands. The statue was called the Colossus of Rhodes and stood there for about sixty years until it was destroyed by an earthquake in 224 BCE.

  The word *colossus* came to be applied to anything that is very large. That is why the United States is sometimes called "the *Colossus* of the North" by people of South and Central America. **Colossal** is the adjective form of this word.

- The ancient Romans regarded the left side as unlucky. Soothsayers, people who were believed to have the power to foretell the future, looked upon signs that appeared on the left as evidence of misfortune. Because the Latin word for "left" is **sinister,** it is easy to see how the word came to have its present meaning.

- **Haul** and *hall* are homophones, words that sound alike but have different meanings and spellings. A *hall* is (1) a large room held for public meeting, (2) a passageway providing access to rooms along it, and (3) an entrance room in a building.

12 Vocabulary Extension

detect

verb To discover something that is usually hard to notice.

Academic Context

In science class, you may **detect** something during an experiment. When you read a mystery book, you may **detect** a detail about a character that allows you to solve the mystery.

Word Family

detection (noun)
detective (noun)
detector (noun)

Discussion & Writing Prompt

How might you **detect** that there is a fire in a building?

2 min. 1. Turn and talk to your partner or group.	3 min. 2. Write 2–4 sentences.
Use this space to take notes or draw your ideas.	Be ready to share what you have written.

Lessons 9–12

Review

Hidden Message In the boxes provided, write the words from Lessons 9 through 12 that are missing in each of the sentences. The number after each sentence is the lesson the word is from. When the exercise is finished, the shaded boxes will spell some lines from a poem by John Greenleaf Whittier, perhaps the most popular American poet of the nineteenth century.

1. The swimmers stopped for a(n) _____ rest before finishing the workout. (10)
2. The _____ of students at that school go on to college. (11)
3. A larger force should be able to _____ a smaller one. (12)

4. All your friends _____ at your success. (12)
5. Don't _____ at the idea until you hear the details. (12)

6. I have a(n) _____ for being able to play any instrument. (10)
7. The boycott of the airline may _____ travel plans on this holiday weekend. (10)
8. Their lives were in constant _____ from the bad storms. (9)

9. The young fan's hopes were crushed when he saw the singer _____ at the gift he offered. (11)
10. You will _____ the injury by not taking care of it. (9)
11. We didn't mean to _____ anyone from the trip, but the car seats only five people. (11)

12. Their look of _____ told me they had lost the game. (12)
13. Players who are _____ have a good chance of making the team. (11)
14. The antics of _____ students disrupted the meeting. (11)
15. Not anticipating the likelihood of an oil spill was a serious _____ . (12)
16. The principal promised _____ changes to make the food choices better in the lunchroom. (9)

17. The internet is one ______ when researching for a project. (9)
18. Here's a trick that would ______ even a magician. (12)

19. The moon causes the ______ motion of the tides. (9)
20. The ______ in the debate receives a gold medal. (12)
21. The kindergarteners' talk of marriage is just a(n) ______ idea. (11)
22. Their ______ is that they don't get enough time for tests. (10)
23. To say that all people with poor posture are lazy shows ______. (11)
24. Are you going to ______ in the long jump? (10)

25. A bad back caused Ashley to ______ the goal of being a cheerleader. (12)
26. I do not ______ them any success they have had. (11)

27. Talking during a movie is not ______ behavior. (11)
28. The country's leader was a powerful ______. (12)
29. The decision of the five judges was ______. (11)

30. Sad to say, our efforts to save the beached whale were ______. (11)
31. Cracks will ______ the value of old photographs. (9)
32. You can ______ *New York City* to *N.Y.C.* (11)

33. Nature ______ the poet to write her best poems. (11)
34. The hula hoop was the greatest ______ of the 1960s. (10)
35. Did I ______ a note of anger in your voice? (12)
36. The ______ allows ten dollars a day for food. (10)
37. You ______ if you think you can attain those goals with mediocre grades. (10)
38. The president does not ______ unlimited power. (11)
39. You can ______ margarine for butter in the recipe. (9)

40. The exhausted swimmers could not ______ such a fast pace any longer. **(9)**

41. Any ______ in the baby food can cause illness. **(9)**

42. Earth is ______ in its ability to support life. **(10)**

43. The pirate's ______ smile made them shudder. **(12)**

H

44. To succeed at auditions, dancers must ______ even when they are exhausted and ravenous. **(11)**

45. Landing people on Mars will be a(n) ______ undertaking. **(12)**

46. We ______ energy by moving as little as possible. **(9)**

47. Lead from the pipes will ______ the water. **(9)**

48. Speed was a(n) ______ in the team's success. **(10)**

49. Dirt will ______ if the rooms are not cleaned often. **(9)**

50. I ______ going to camp in July this year. **(10)**

51. A(n) ______ person throws very little away. **(9)**

H

52. The ______ at the gate saw us approach the fort. **(12)**

53. A tow truck had to ______ the wrecked car to the dump. **(12)**

54. It is ______ that all flammable materials be removed from the school. **(9)**

55. Taking limousines everywhere seems very ______. **(9)**

56. Grandfather spends most of his ______ time in the garden. **(10)**

57. Taking a(n) ______ walk every day is beneficial. **(10)**

58. What ______ does television have on a child's mind? **(10)**

59. After a ten-month ______, the city surrendered. **(12)**

60. The company went ______ when it failed to make a profit. **(10)**

Lesson

13

Word List

Study the definitions of the words. Then do the exercises that follow.

adapt
ə dapt´

v. 1. To change to fit new conditions.
Whales were once land animals but **adapted** well to life in the ocean.

2. To make changes in something to make it useful.
The students **adapted** the unused closet into a small library.

adaptation *n.* (ad ap tā´ shən) 1. A changing to fit new conditions.
Adaptation to a full school day takes a while for some first graders.

2. Something that is changed from something else.
The musical *Annie* is an **adaptation** of an old-fashioned comic strip.

Discuss with your partner if you are someone who can handle adaptation or if you prefer for nothing to change.

deplete
dē plēt´

v. To use up.
Unless we are frugal, we will **deplete** our savings by the end of March.

efficient
ə fish´ ənt

adj. Producing results without waste.
Tube lights are more **efficient** than light bulbs.

fatigue
fə tēg´

n. A feeling of tiredness from work or exercise.
Although overcome with **fatigue,** the runner persevered to the finish line.

v. To make or become tired.
Since my illness, even light work **fatigues** me.

Pretend for your partner that you feel fatigue.

gait
gāt

n. The way a person or animal moves on foot.
A horse's **gait** changes as it goes from a walk to a trot.

glare
glār

v. 1. To shine with a strong, harsh light.
The bright sun **glared** off the icy snowbanks, making it difficult to see.

2. To stare angrily at.
The store manager **glared** at me when I toppled the stack of books.

n. 1. A strong, blinding light.
The **glare** from oncoming cars is diminished if drivers dim their headlights.

2. An angry stare.
I ignored my adversary's **glare,** which I interpreted as an attempt to scare me.

glaring *adj.* 1. Shining with a harsh, brilliant light.
There was no shade from the **glaring** summer sun in the open fields.

2. Very obvious.
The teacher detected a **glaring** error in the math problem.

Write a word for your partner that contains a glaring spelling error.

habitat hab´ i tat

n. The place or type of place where a plant or animal is normally found.
The **habitat** of the saguaro cactus is the desert of southwest Arizona.

oblivious ə bliv´ ē əs

adj. Not aware of.
The audience was **oblivious** to everything except the actor's inspired performance.

oblivion *n.* A state of forgetting or being forgotten.
These songs sank into **oblivion** after the band that recorded them broke up.

Discuss with your partner whether using a cell phone would make you oblivious to everything going on around you.

outmoded out mōd´ əd

adj. No longer needed or fashionable.
The coming of the railroad made the stagecoach an **outmoded** way to travel.

prominent präm´ ə nənt

adj. 1. Projecting; standing out.
Mount Rushmore is a **prominent** feature of the Black Hills in South Dakota.

2. Very easy to see; easily noticed.
Pinocchio's **prominent** nose grew even longer every time he told a lie.

3. Famous; well known.
The accident victim asked a **prominent** lawyer for advice.

Talk to your partner about which of your feelings is most prominent when you first wake up.

quench kwench

v. 1. To put out; to extinguish.
Not even reading three books on the subject could **quench** his interest in the mysterious stories about the haunted house.

2. To satisfy with a liquid.
Water **quenches** a thirst better than a sweetened soda drink.

rigor
rig´ ər

n. (often plural) 1. A condition that makes life difficult.
The orange tree couldn't survive the **rigors** of a Canadian winter.

2. Strictness or severity.
The police chief enforced the law with **rigor.**

rigorous *adj.* 1. Severe; extreme.
The team was put through a **rigorous** exercise program that included a daily eight-mile run.

2. Thorough; complete.
This **rigorous** thirty-day course of study has students speaking Italian effortlessly.

Chat with your partner about why people must pass a rigorous physical test to become firefighters.

sear
sēr

v. 1. To wither; to dry up.
A long drought, as well as heat, can **sear** grass.

2. To burn the surface of with sudden heat.
Cooks **sear** steak to help retain the juices.

transport
trans pôrt´

v. To carry or move from one place to another.
A large truck **transports** sets and costumes for the acting company.

n. (trans´ pôrt) The act of carrying from one place to another.
The company will arrange for the **transport** of the goods by rail.

Discuss with your partner the best way to transport a birthday cake from someone's kitchen to the school.

wend
wend

v. To travel; to go on one's way.
It took two weeks to **wend** our way over the mountain pass.

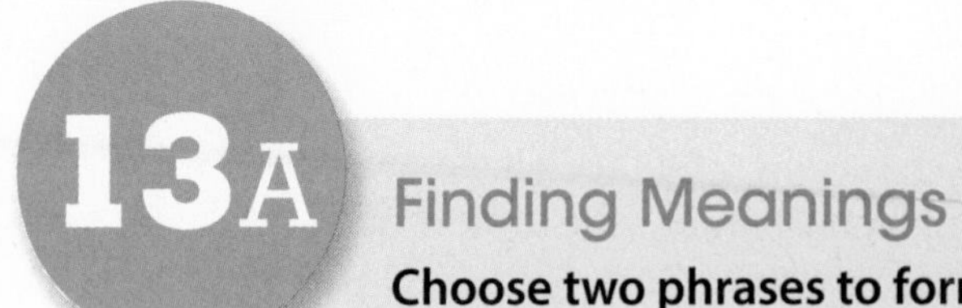

Finding Meanings

Choose two phrases to form a sentence that correctly uses a word from Word List 13. Then write the sentence.

1. (a) a state of uncertainty.
   (b) a feeling of tiredness.
   (c) Oblivion is
   (d) Fatigue is

2. (a) A glaring error is one
   (b) to which no one pays attention.
   (c) A rigorous rule is one
   (d) that should be obvious to anyone.

3. (a) a feeling of worry or concern.
   (b) Oblivion is
   (c) Adaptation is
   (d) a total lack of awareness.

4. (a) is in a rundown condition.
   (b) A prominent building is one that
   (c) stands out from those around it.
   (d) An efficient building is one that

5. (a) Transport is
   (b) a change to fit a new condition.
   (c) An adaptation is
   (d) a breaking down of something into its parts.

6. (a) A gait is
   (b) a slight burn.
   (c) an angry stare.
   (d) A glare is

7. (a) To sear something is to
   (b) burn its surface.
   (c) To quench something is to
   (d) store it for later use.

8. (a) An animal's gait is
   (b) its sense of smell.
   (c) An animal's habitat is
   (d) the way it walks.

9. (a) is thorough and complete.
   (b) is carried out carelessly.
   (c) A rigorous test is one that
   (d) An outmoded test is one that

____

____

10. (a) a change in manner.
    (b) A habitat is
    (c) the place a plant naturally grows.
    (d) Transport is

____

____

13B Just the Right Word

Replace each phrase in bold with a single word (or form of the word) from the word list.

1. If we aren't careful, we will **completely use up** the water we brought on the hike.
2. Even a short walk **causes a feeling of tiredness to come over** my old dog.
3. Animals that do not **make changes to fit new conditions** fail to survive.
4. The mighty Mississippi **moves along** its way to the sea.
5. The Empire State Building is a **well-known and easily spotted** landmark in New York City.
6. **The carrying of goods to where they have to go** is the responsibility of the shipping department.
7. The **harsh and brilliant light** of the welding torch almost blinded me.
8. The lemur's **natural home and the place where it is normally found** is Madagascar.
9. The children can **have a drink to satisfy** their thirst at the water fountain.
10. A tune-up will help an engine be **able to work properly while using less energy.**

adapt
deplete
efficient
fatigue
gait
glare
habitat
oblivious
outmoded
prominent
quench
rigor
sear
transport
wend

11. The method you propose is **no longer in use because a better one has been discovered.**

12. Penguins are well suited to the **harsh conditions** of the Antarctic.

13C Applying Meanings

Circle the letter or letters next to each correct answer. There may be more than one correct answer.

1. Which of the following could be **transported?**
   (a) animals
   (b) terrain
   (c) veterans
   (d) supplies

2. Which of the following is **outmoded?**
   (a) a fashion model
   (b) the nineteenth century
   (c) gaslight
   (d) silent movies

3. Which of the following can be **quenched?**
   (a) a sneer
   (b) a campfire
   (c) thirst
   (d) plans

4. Which of the following could be **adapted?**
   (a) a method
   (b) a baby
   (c) a tool
   (d) a book

5. Which of the following can be **depleted?**
   (a) resources
   (b) savings
   (c) supplies
   (d) clouds

6. Which of the following might **glare?**
   (a) a spotlight
   (b) a radio
   (c) an angry person
   (d) light reflected in a mirror

7. Which of the following can be **rigorous?**
   (a) a fitness program
   (b) an inspection
   (c) a climate
   (d) a blunder

8. Which of the following is a **gait?**
   (a) a posture
   (b) a gallop
   (c) a limp
   (d) a haul

Word Study: Similar Meanings

Sometimes words have such similar meanings that it is easy to confuse them. Read the pairs of sentences. Then choose the word that best completes each sentence.

transport / carry

1. I saw Mom ____________________ the baby upstairs.

2. A jet was waiting to ____________________ the important papers to the president.

oblivious / unaware

3. I was ____________________ of the fact that Mars has an atmosphere.

4. My dog Dickens was happily running around, ____________________ to his surroundings.

woe / misery

5. Cries of ____________________ came from the people who had watched their houses slide down into the ocean.

6. I was in such ____________________ that I had to call the dentist about my toothache.

blunder / mistake

7. I made a ____________________ when I wrote down the address.

8. The candidate's major ____________________ cost him the election.

peril / danger

9. The child was in ____________________ of slipping on the ice.

10. The Argonauts faced each new ____________________ with steadfast courage.

gripe / complain

11. I told the sales clerk that I would ____________________ to the manager.

12. People ____________________ at having to stand in line at airports.

conserve / save

13. Buying your ticket on the Internet will ____________________ you time.

14. Modern houses are built to ____________________ heat and lower fuel costs.

adapt
deplete
efficient
fatigue
gait
glare
habitat
oblivious
outmoded
prominent
quench
rigor
sear
transport
wend

diminish / reduce

15. I will ____________________ the amount of fat I use in that recipe by one half.

16. The winds did not ____________________ until after midnight.

captive / prisoner

17. The ____________________ was released by the rebels after six months.

18. Each ____________________ in the county jail is awaiting trial.

origin / beginning

19. I turned back to the ____________________ of the story.

20. Do you know the ____________________ of the word *boycott?*

Vocabulary in Context

Read the passage.

The Ship of the Desert

Picture a long line of camels **wending** its way slowly across the skyline. This sight was once a common one in the North African and Arabian deserts. The animals are dromedaries, the kind of camel most familiar to people in the West. The Bedouins, the migrant people of the Arabian and Sahara deserts, call the dromedary "the ship of the desert." This creature has **transported** goods and people over some of the most arid regions in the world for thousands of years.

Bearing its burden patiently, and seemingly **oblivious** to hunger and thirst, the dromedary can keep up a steady, plodding **gait** over great distances. It can travel fifty miles a day for up to five days without showing signs of **fatigue.** When it reaches water, it **quenches** its thirst by drinking as much as fifteen gallons at a time. When food is not available, it lives on the fat stored in its hump. The hump is not filled with water as some people think. The dromedary's hump fills out and is quite **prominent** when the animal is well fed; it gets smaller as the fat stored inside is **depleted.**

The dromedary is very well **adapted** to life in the desert. Its broad feet do not sink into soft sand. It can close its nostrils completely during sandstorms while protecting its eyes with double rows of eyelashes. The dromedary is comfortable in the **searing** heat of the desert. It will stretch out in the full **glare** of the noonday sun even though shade may be available. The dromedary is capable of carrying up to six hundred pounds on its back. It knows its limits, though. If given too heavy a burden, it will obstinately refuse to budge until the load is lightened.

Closely related to the dromedary is the Bactrian camel. Its **habitat** is the cold desert regions of Siberia in central Asia. The Bactrian camel is smaller and sturdier than the dromedary. It has shorter legs and is covered with long, shaggy hair. Its coat protects it from the **rigorous** Siberian climate. But the most obvious difference between the two types of camel is their humps. The dromedary has a single hump; the Bactrian camel has two. Although both kinds have been domesticated for thousands of years, the Bactrian camel, unlike its cousin, is still found in the wild.

To the Bedouins and the migrant people of central Asia, the dromedary and Bactrian camel are much more than beasts of burden. Their hair provides wool for making clothes and carpets; their hides can be used to make tents and footwear; they can be milked like cows; and their meat, which tastes like veal or beef, forms an important part of these peoples' diets.

In spite of their great versatility, both kinds of camels are becoming **outmoded** means of transportation. Four-wheel-drive vehicles are more **efficient;** they can travel faster and further and carry heavier loads. That long line of camels wending its way across the Arabian desert is disappearing from the modern world. Like the American wagon train that headed west in the 1800s, it may someday be seen only in the movies.

adapt
deplete
efficient
fatigue
gait
glare
habitat
oblivious
outmoded
prominent
quench
rigor
sear
transport
wend

▶ **Answer each of the following questions with a sentence. If a question does not contain a vocabulary word from the lesson's word list, use one in your answer. Use each word only once.**

1. Why are camels called beasts of burden?

____

____

2. How has the use of camels as beasts of burden been affected by four-wheel-drive vehicles?

___

___

3. Name one way four-wheel-drive vehicles are more **efficient** than camels.

___

___

4. What is the **habitat** of the dromedary?

___

___

5. Why might it be advisable to wear sunglasses in the North African desert?

___

___

6. Why can the North African desert at noon be an uncomfortable place for humans?

___

___

7. What is the meaning of **adapted** as it is used in the passage?

___

___

8. How did the Bedouins once travel across the desert?

___

___

9. Why do you think dromedaries do not bother to seek shade?

___

___

10. What is the meaning of **prominent** as it is used in the passage?

___

___

11. What would a shrunken hump on a dromedary tell you about the animal?

___

___

12. What is the meaning of **quenches** as it is used in the passage?

____

____

13. What sort of weather might one expect in Siberia's **rigorous** climate?

____

____

14. How do dromedaries move across the desert?

____

____

15. How might a dromedary be affected if made to travel more than fifty miles a day?

____

____

adapt
deplete
efficient
fatigue
gait
glare
habitat
oblivious
outmoded
prominent
quench
rigor
sear
transport
wend

Fun & Fascinating FACTS

- **Adapt** means "to change in order to fit new conditions" or "to make changes in, so as to be of use." *Adopt* means "to take into one's family." (Childless couples often would like to *adopt* a child.) *Adopt* also means "to take and use as one's own." (The English writer Mary Ann Evans *adopted* the name George Eliot because women novelists were not taken seriously in mid-nineteenth-century England.) *Adapt* and *adopt* can be confused because their meanings overlap slightly. It is possible to *adopt* someone else's idea and then *adapt* it so as to improve it or use it for a different purpose.

- A **gait** is a manner or way of walking. A person in a hurry may walk with a fast *gait*. A sailor, used to being on a ship, may walk with a rolling *gait*.

  A *gate* is a hinged door in a fence or wall. The words *gait* and *gate* are homophones.

- Don't confuse **oblivious** with *obvious,* which means "easy to see or understand." (The answers to the questions were *obvious* to anyone who had read the book.)

  Oblivious always has either *of* or *to* after it. (I was *oblivious* of the danger. The principal remained *oblivious* to the need for change.)

- **Fatigue** is a French word that comes from the Latin verb *fatigare,* which means "to tire." *Fatigue* has been taken into English with its spelling and pronunciation unchanged.

  This word has two other meanings, which are used in the military. *Fatigue* is domestic duty performed by people in the military; *fatigues* are special clothing worn by military personnel while performing these tasks and while in the field.

13 Vocabulary Extension

transport

verb To carry or move from one place to another.

noun The act of carrying from one place to another.

Word Family

transportable (adjective)
transportation (noun)
transporter (noun)

Word Parts

The prefix *trans-* means "through" or "across." The root *port* means "carry."
So, *transport* can mean "carry across."
What are some other words with the prefix *trans-* or the root *port?*

Discussion & Writing Prompt

What types of **transportation** do students use to get to and from your school each day?

2 min. 1. Turn and talk to your partner or group.	3 min. 2. Write 2–4 sentences.
Use this space to take notes or draw your ideas.	Be ready to share what you have written.

Word List

Study the definitions of the words. Then do the exercises that follow.

benevolent
bə nev′ ə lənt

adj. Wanting to do good; kind.
A **benevolent** employee paid for the team's Little League uniforms.

Tell your partner about a benevolent person you know, such as a nice neighbor or a helpful coach.

consent
kən sent′

v. To agree; to allow to happen.
The judges **consented** to hear the case.

n. Permission; approval.
Students need a parent's **consent** to go on the field trip.

Discuss with your partner whether your principal would consent to letting students go home early today.

discreet
di skrēt′

adj. Showing care or wisdom in what one says or does.
The counselor made **discreet** inquiries into the student's past.

discretion *n.* (di skresh′ ən) The ability to handle matters wisely.
The English teacher left the choice of books to our **discretion.**

engross
en grōs′

v. To take up one's complete attention.
The puzzle so **engrossed** me that I lost track of time.

engrossing *adj.* Taking up one's complete attention.
The **engrossing** conversation made everyone oblivious to the ringing doorbell.

esteem
e stēm′

v. To think highly of; to respect.
Historians **esteem** Eleanor Roosevelt for her human rights work.

n. Respect; high regard.
The players credit their success to the great **esteem** they feel for their coach.

esteemed *adj.* Highly regarded.
An **esteemed** member of the community was the unanimous choice to head the task force on housing.

Tell your partner about a person you greatly esteem.

exaggerate
eg zaj′ ər āt

v. To describe something as larger or greater than it really is.
Some donors **exaggerate** the value of their contributions to the campaign.

exaggeration *n.* (eg zaj ər ā′ shən) Something that is exaggerated.
Saying that your baseball-card collection is worth thousands of dollars is quite an **exaggeration.**

extensive ek sten´ siv

adj. 1. Covering a large area.
Central Park is an **extensive** green expanse in the middle of Manhattan.

2. Ambitious; far-reaching.
The team made **extensive** preparations for the Himalayan expedition.

Talk with your partner about the most extensive park you have visited.

fantastic fan tas´ tik

adj. 1. Almost unbelievable.
The guests on the talk show told a **fantastic** tale of being followed by creatures from outer space.

2. Unusual; odd.
Spectators saw the most **fantastic** costumes at the Mardi Gras parade.

intrigue in trēg´

v. 1. To fascinate.
The way stage magicians do their tricks **intrigues** me.

2. To plot in a secret way; to scheme.
Benedict Arnold **intrigued** against his own country to help the British.

n. (in´ trēg) A secret plot or scheme.
Mary Queen of Scots was beheaded when Elizabeth I learned of her **intrigues** against the throne.

marvel mär´ vəl

n. A wonderful or amazing thing.
The Amazon River is one of the great **marvels** of nature.

v. To be filled with wonder or amazement.
The world **marveled** at the pictures of astronauts walking on the moon.

marvelous *adj.* 1. Causing wonder; astonishing.
It would be **marvelous** if we made contact with intelligent life elsewhere in the universe.

2. Of the highest quality; splendid.
The school play has a **marvelous** part for a versatile actor.

mission mish´ ən

n. 1. A special or important task or assignment.
The ambassador's **mission** was to arrange a meeting with the prime minister.

2. A group sent on an important assignment.
The **mission** from Israel agreed to resume the peace talks.

Discuss with your partner the main mission teachers have.

opportunity äp ər tōō´ nə tē

n. 1. A time that is right for doing something.
Isabella was waiting for the **opportunity** to talk to her mother alone.

2. A chance for getting ahead.
This job offers plenty of **opportunity** for a diligent young person.

Share with your partner an opportunity you once had to go somewhere fun.

relinquish
rē liŋ´ kwish

v. To let go; to give up.
The little boy who found the lost puppy didn't want to **relinquish** it.

Relinquish your book to your partner.

tyrant
tī´ rənt

n. A ruler or person who has complete power and uses it in cruel or unjust ways.
The **tyrant** lived in splendor while his people lived in squalor.

tyranny *n.* (tir´ ə nē) Rule by a tyrant.
Joseph Stalin's **tyranny** over the people of the Soviet Union did not end until his death in 1953.

vanquish
vaŋ´ kwish

v. To defeat utterly and completely; to overcome.
Success quickly **vanquishes** fear.

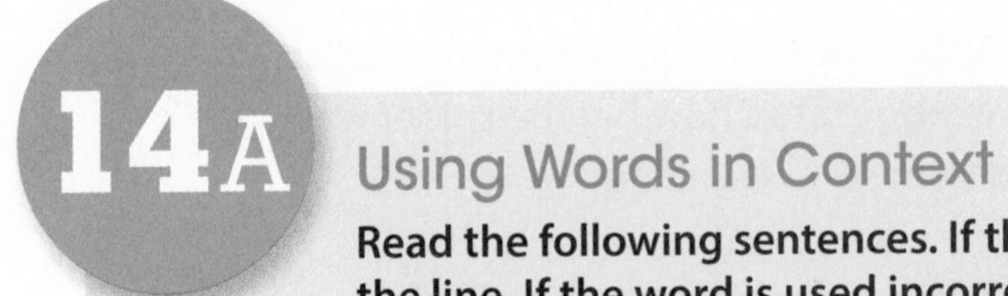

Using Words in Context

Read the following sentences. If the word in bold is used correctly, write C on the line. If the word is used incorrectly, write I on the line.

1. (a) The pigeons pecked at the **marvels** on the ground at the park. ___
   (b) Many believe the cell phone to be a **marvelous** invention. ___
   (c) The eighty-foot blue whale is one of the **marvels** of nature. ___
   (d) The crew grew more and more **marvelous** as conditions worsened. ___

2. (a) Many **esteemed** Barack Obama for his social policies as president. ___
   (b) Students hold the respectful and intelligent teacher in high **esteem.** ___
   (c) Einstein was an **esteemed** member of the scientific community. ___
   (d) The plumber **esteemed** that the repairs would cost a hundred dollars. ___

3. (a) Scientists have **vanquished** many life-threatening diseases. ___
   (b) A coat of **vanquish** will make your floors sparkle. ___
   (c) Bruno **vanquished** his fear of heights by going skydiving. ___
   (d) The painting **vanquished** without a trace and was never found. ___

4. (a) It would **relinquish** me greatly if you could help me study. ___
   (b) The team that lost the game **relinquished** the trophy gracefully. ___
   (c) Josef finally **relinquished** my hand. ___
   (d) A hot meal and a good night's sleep **relinquished** us. ___

5. (a) I am **intrigued** by dinosaurs and want to learn more. ___
   (b) A group of students **intrigued** all the way to the bus. ___
   (c) We were **intrigued** by the spider spinning its web. ___
   (d) The painting was just too interesting, so I had to take another **intrigue.** ___

6. (a) We couldn't find the **mission** in the sandbox, so we gave up. ___
   (b) The **mission** to rescue the cat in the tree was successful. ___
   (c) A **mission** to Mars in the next century is on NASA's agenda. ___
   (d) He tripped on the **mission** sticking out of the ground. ___

7. (a) Ping Ho took every **opportunity** to practice on the basketball court. ___
   (b) The **opportunity** to go up in a blimp was too good to be missed. ___
   (c) Where others saw a problem, Sanji saw an **opportunity.** ___
   (d) My shoe fell into the **opportunity** and was never seen again. ___

8. (a) Randy was able to **exaggerate** himself from other people. ___
   (b) Mika **exaggerated** when she said she had made a hundred dollars. ___
   (c) My sister admitted that she **exaggerated** how big the spider was. ___
   (d) The fence was **exaggerated** from six to eight feet. ___

9. (a) I was **engrossed** in reading my notes when lightning struck. ___
   (b) Once the money is **engrossed,** you will never see it again. ___
   (c) The novel is so **engrossing;** you should read it! ___
   (d) Everyone was **engrossed** by the news about the royal wedding. ___

10. (a) Indrajit's account of her adventures got more **fantastic** with each telling. ___
    (b) The novel is filled with odd characters and **fantastic** situations. ___
    (c) Houses in this part of town are selling for **fantastic** prices. ___
    (d) The TV show was so **fantastic,** I fell asleep. ___

benevolent
consent
discreet
engross
esteem
exaggerate
extensive
fantastic
intrigue
marvel
mission
opportunity
relinquish
tyrant
vanquish

Making Connections

Circle the letter next to each correct answer. There may be more than one correct answer.

1. Which word or words go with *give up?*
   (a) forsake (b) abdicate (c) esteem (d) relinquish

2. Which word or words go with *like a lot?*
   (a) cherish (b) esteem (c) exaggerate (d) baffle

3. Which word or words go with *wonderful?*
   (a) fantastic (b) discreet (c) colossal (d) marvelous

4. Which word or words go with *defeat?*
   (a) conquer (b) consent (c) vanquish (d) overpower

5. Which word or words go with *interesting?*
   (a) sinister (b) benevolent (c) fascinating (d) engrossing

6. Which word or words go with *ruler?*
   (a) dictator (b) sentinel (c) tyrant (d) mission

7. Which word or words go with *large area?*
   (a) consent (b) expanse (c) extensive (d) interpret

8. Which word or words go with *keep a secret?*
   (a) victorious (b) fantastic (c) discreet (d) marvelous

9. Which word or words go with *kindness?*
   (a) compassionate (b) extensive (c) benevolent (d) discreet

10. Which word or words go with *agree?*
    (a) exaggerate (b) consent (c) rejoice (d) vanquish

Determining Meanings

Circle the letter next to each answer choice that correctly completes the sentence. There may be more than one correct answer.

1. She **esteemed**
   (a) Martin Luther King Jr. for leading the Civil Rights movement in the 1960s.
   (b) all those who give their time to charity.
   (c) that the price of the purse was too much.
   (d) ahead in the race, while others lagged behind.

2. It's an **exaggeration**
   (a) to say she made a million dollars before she was eighteen.
   (b) that was kept hidden from me until the holidays.
   (c) of the water in the fountain that is causing the problem.
   (d) that got more complicated every time I heard him say it.

3. The **mission**
   (a) was to win more than half the votes.
   (b) to bring the friends back together was a success.
   (c) ran past us and knocked us over.
   (d) from Russia stayed at a hotel in Harlem for the "green energy" meetings.

4. Some great **opportunities**
   (a) always look best in sunlight.
   (b) can be found at school.
   (c) can pass you by if you don't take risks.
   (d) are listed in the newspaper article about summer jobs.

5. The **tyrannical**
   (a) Roman emperor would listen to no one.
   (b) six-stringed instrument is played like a banjo.
   (c) dancers spun across the stage.
   (d) dictator was replaced by someone even worse.

6. An **extensively**
   (a) detailed search failed to find the missing ring.
   (b) hilly area has been set aside for a skateboard park.
   (c) Spanish coin was found in the cave.
   (d) researched project is certain to be successful.

benevolent
consent
discreet
engross
esteem
exaggerate
extensive
fantastic
intrigue
marvel
mission
opportunity
relinquish
tyrant
vanquish

7. **Engrossed**
   (a) across the page were the letters RSVP.
   (b) by his disgusting behavior, I left the room in a hurry.
   (c) in my book, I didn't hear the knock at the front door.
   (d) in my studies, I had little time for fun.

8. A **benevolently**
   (a) evil act is one intended to do harm.
   (b) kind ruler is loved and respected.
   (c) bad story is hard to finish reading.
   (d) generous uncle always has gifts for his nieces.

14D Completing Sentences

Complete the sentences to demonstrate your knowledge of the words in bold.

1. You should use **discretion** when

   ____.

2. It's an **exaggeration** if I say that

   ____.

3. It would be **fantastic** if

   ____.

4. My **mission** after school today is to

   ____.

5. If I had the **opportunity** to go anywhere I wanted, I would go

   ____.

6. If you give your **consent** to do something, that means

   ____.

7. One way to **vanquish** fear is to

   ____.

8. A **tyrant** is

   ____.

9. If I were on a desert island, the one thing I wouldn't **relinquish** is

   ____.

10. One of the things that I **marvel** at is

   ____.

Vocabulary in Context

Read the passage.

The Travels of Marco Polo

One of the most **engrossing** travel books ever written is over seven hundred years old. *The Travels of Marco Polo* is a true account of a young Venetian's adventurous life. Although it was written so long ago, you can probably find a copy of it on the shelves of your neighborhood library.

Marco Polo was only seventeen when his adventures began. In the year 1271, he left his native Venice for the Chinese court of Kublai Khan, the absolute ruler of most of Asia. He accompanied members of his family who were employed in the service of Kublai Khan. They were now returning to China after a visit home. The journey took the Venetians four years.

The immense Mongol empire of Kublai Khan had been founded fifty years earlier by the emperor's grandfather, Genghis Khan. One of the most feared **tyrants** in history, Genghis Khan had **vanquished** most of his challengers in Asia. Kublai Khan, by contrast, was a wise and **benevolent** ruler. He soon determined that Marco Polo was an exceptionally intelligent young man. Marco Polo was **discreet** as well. He could be trusted with information that the emperor hesitated to share with others at the court. Furthermore, because Marco Polo planned to return to Venice later, he was unlikely to **intrigue** against the emperor. For these reasons, Kublai Khan trusted Marco Polo as his ambassador to travel **extensively** throughout Asia, carrying out important **missions.**

After seventeen years Marco Polo grew homesick; he yearned for his native Venice. However, he could not depart without the emperor's permission. Kublai Khan held his young advisor in high **esteem** and had rewarded him with significant positions in his court. Naturally, he was reluctant to **relinquish** the services of such a valued friend and adviser. But finally the emperor gave his **consent.** In 1295, after a journey that lasted three years, Marco Polo arrived back in Venice.

He soon became a celebrated figure because of the stories he related of his travels. Many of his Venetian listeners thought he must be **exaggerating.** The things he claimed seemed to be too **fantastic** to be believed. But, in fact, Marco Polo was telling the truth. He had observed creatures with huge jaws and sharp teeth that could swallow a person whole (crocodiles); he had seen

benevolent
consent
discreet
engross
esteem
exaggerate
extensive
fantastic
intrigue
marvel
mission
opportunity
relinquish
tyrant
vanquish

black stones that, when ignited, burned with a great heat (coal); and he had witnessed many other **marvels.**

Three years after his return, Marco Polo was taken prisoner when hostilities broke out between Venice and Genoa, both Italian city-states. The year he spent in captivity gave him the **opportunity** to dictate his travel adventures to a fellow prisoner. The book that eventually resulted became one of the most popular and widely translated literary works ever written. For hundreds of years, it has been entertaining readers all over the world.

▶ **Answer each of the following questions with a sentence. If a question does not contain a vocabulary word from the lesson's word list, use one in your answer. Use each word only once.**

1. Do you think Kublai Khan was **esteemed** by his subjects? Why or why not?

____

____

2. How would you describe the size of the territory Kublai Khan ruled?

____

____

3. How did Ghengis Khan establish his empire?

____

____

4. Why was there no appeal against any of Genghis Khan's rulings?

____

____

5. Would it be accurate to say that Marco Polo traveled all over the world? Why or why not?

____

____

6. How did Kublai Khan demonstrate his **benevolence** toward Marco Polo?

____

____

7. What was the purpose of Marco Polo's travels through Asia?

8. Was Marco Polo free to return to Venice whenever he chose?

9. How might a less **discreet** person than Marco Polo have behaved at court?

10. What is the meaning of **fantastic** as it is used in the passage?

11. Why would Kublai Khan trust a foreigner like Marco Polo to work for him?

12. Why did Marco Polo want to **relinquish** his position in Kublai Khan's court?

13. What is the meaning of **opportunity** as it is used in the passage?

14. Why did crocodiles and coal seem like **marvels** to the Venetians?

15. Why do you think Marco Polo's book remains in print after 700 years?

benevolent
consent
discreet
engross
esteem
exaggerate
extensive
fantastic
intrigue
marvel
mission
opportunity
relinquish
tyrant
vanquish

Fun & Fascinating FACTS

- The antonym of **benevolent** is *malevolent*. A *malevolent* person is someone who wishes to do evil to others.

- In Roman times, as indeed throughout history, when sailors headed *toward port* after a long voyage, they could at last look forward to having an **opportunity** to do all the things they had been unable to do while living in cramped fashion on board a small boat. The word *opportunity* suggests this; it is formed from the Latin prefix *ob-*, which means "to" or "toward" (*ob-* changes to *op-* before the letter *p*) and *portum,* which means "a port."

14 Vocabulary Extension

consent

noun Permission; approval.

verb To agree; to allow to happen.

Academic Context

Before you are allowed to participate in after-school activities, your parent or guardian must give their **consent.**

Context Clues

These sentences give clues to the meaning of **consent.**

*My mom gave her **consent** to let me go to the zoo with my friends.*

*Mr. Velasquez would not **consent** to having the birthday party at his house.*

Discussion & Writing Prompt

Think about an activity that you do after school. What is it, and does it require **consent** from your parent or guardian?

2 min. 1. Turn and talk to your partner or group.	3 min. 2. Write 2–4 sentences.
Use this space to take notes or draw your ideas.	Be ready to share what you have written.

Word List

Study the definitions of the words. Then do the exercises that follow.

analyze
an´ ə līz

v. To break down into separate parts in order to study.
Experts who **analyze** auto accidents say that one of the major causes is a distracted driver.

analysis *n.* (ə nal´ ə sis) An examination of the whole in order to examine its various parts.
Chemical **analysis** of the rock showed that it contained uranium.

Analyze the lines on the palm of your hand and compare them to your partner's.

apprehensive
ap rē hen´ siv

adj. Worried or uneasy about what might happen.
Talk about another war made us **apprehensive.**

apprehension *n.* Worry about what might happen; dread.
The community was filled with **apprehension** as the hurricane approached.

Chat with your partner about why some people feel apprehension when they hear thunder.

coincide
kō in sīd´

v. 1. To be in the same place or occur at the same time.
Graduation day **coincides** with Akeesha's birthday.

2. To be exactly the same; to agree.
My skills **coincide** with the job description.

coincidence *n.* (kō in´ si dəns) Occurrences that seem to be related but are connected only by chance.
It's just a **coincidence** that the roommates have the same last name.

Discuss with your partner whether it is a coincidence that the two of you are working together.

compose
kəm pōz´

v. 1. To make by combining.
Concrete is **composed** of cement, sand, and water.

2. To create or write, as a poem or a song.
The singer and songwriter **composes** music that draws from many cultures.

3. To quiet or calm.
Compose yourself before you get up to speak.

disk
disk

n. Any thin, circular object.
The checkers pieces were plastic **disks.**

envelop
en vel´ əp

v. To hide or cover on all sides.
Darkness **enveloped** the town when the electric power station shut down.

exist eg zist´ *v.* 1. To be real.
Did the lost world of Atlantis really **exist?**

2. To be found; to occur.
Many scientists believe that life must **exist** elsewhere in the universe.

3. To stay alive.
Living things cannot **exist** without water.

Talk to your partner about something you wish existed, like a unicorn or a superpower.

extraordinary ek strôrd´ n er ē *adj.* Very unusual; remarkable.
When the hockey team won the Olympic gold medal, it was an **extraordinary** achievement.

fuse fyōōz *v.* To join together by or as if by melting.
Heat from the fire had **fused** the metal parts into a solid piece.

fusion *n.* (fyōō´ zhən) A fusing or joining together.
An alloy is made by the **fusion** of two or more different metals.

mere mēr *adj.* Nothing more than; only.
It is a **mere** half mile into town.

revolve rē välv´ *v.* To go around something in a circle; to turn around in a circle.
The rim of a wheel **revolves** around its hub.

Make one of your hands revolve around your other hand for your partner.

scale skāl *n.* 1. Any of the hard, thin plates that cover fish and certain reptiles.
Remove the **scales** from the fish before you cook it.

2. A series of musical notes that go higher and higher or lower and lower.
The chorus members sang a few **scales** to warm up their voices.

3. An instrument for measuring weight.
The doctor told the patient to get on the **scale** so she could check his weight.

4. The way size on a map or model compares with the size of the thing it stands for.
This map has a **scale** of one inch to a mile.

5. A series of steps, degrees, or stages.
The Richter **scale** measures the amount of energy released by an earthquake.

v. To climb or climb over.
The raccoons had to **scale** a high wall to enter the garden.

Share with your partner whether you would want to scale a mountain, and explain why.

solar *adj.* Of or having to do with the sun.
sō´ lər A **solar** eclipse occurs when the moon passes directly in front of the sun.

trace *n.* 1. A very small amount.
trās The **traces** of lead found in the water will not jeopardize the health of those who drink it.

2. A mark or sign left behind by someone or something.
The book claims that many ships entering the Bermuda Triangle have disappeared without a **trace.**

v. 1. To follow the trail or tracks of; to locate.
We **traced** our lost dog as far as Fifth Street before we caught up to him.

2. To copy by following the lines of a drawing through thin paper.
I carefully **traced** the map for my report.

Talk to your partner with a trace of fatigue in your voice.

velocity *n.* Rate of movement; speed.
və läs´ ə tē The **velocity** of a pitcher's fastball can exceed 90 miles per hour.

15A Finding Meanings

Choose two phrases to form a sentence that correctly uses a word from Word List 15. Then write the sentence.

1. (a) An extraordinary idea is one (c) A mere idea is one
(b) that one keeps to oneself. (d) that is very unusual.

____

____

2. (a) cover it completely. (c) To analyze something is to
(b) send it through the mail. (d) To envelop something is to

____

____

3. (a) To be a mere child is to be (c) nothing more than a child.
(b) To be a composed child is to be (d) a child in fiction rather than real life.

____

____

4. (a) a thin, circular object. (c) A scale is
(b) a mark left behind by something. (d) A trace is

____

____

5. (a) A composed witness is one (c) who does not get upset.
(b) who is obviously lying. (d) An apprehensive witness is one

____

____

6. (a) A disk is (c) A scale is
(b) a series of musical notes. (d) the highest point.

____

____

7. (a) worry about what might happen. (c) sadness over events of the past.
(b) Apprehension is (d) Fusion is

____

____

8. (a) the path of an object in space. (c) any thin, circular object.
(b) A disk is (d) A coincidence is

____

____

9. (a) Analysis is (c) Fusion is
(b) putting words to music. (d) a breaking down of the whole into its parts.

____

____

10. (a) To exist is to (c) To coincide is to
(b) keep happening over and over. (d) be real rather than imaginary.

____

____

analyze
apprehensive
coincide
compose
disk
envelop
exist
extraordinary
fuse
mere
revolve
scale
solar
trace
velocity

Just the Right Word

Replace each phrase in bold with a single word (or form of the word) from the word list.

1. I became **worried about what might have happened** when I didn't hear from you.

2. On a **series of steps** numbered from one to ten, the judges rated the performance a seven.

3. Extreme heat and pressure caused the metal plates to **join together as a single sheet.**

4. A microscope revealed **very small amounts** of bacteria in the water.

5. The moon **travels in a circular path** around Earth once every 27.3 days.

6. About a hundred pairs of condors still **are to be found** in the wild in the United States.

7. Mozart began **creating musical works** when he was five years old.

8. Some of the energy that provides my house with electricity is **from the sun.**

9. To find the **speed at which something travels,** you need to know distance traveled and time taken.

10. Because our birthdays **occurred on the same day,** we decided to throw a party together.

Applying Meanings

Circle the letter or letters next to each correct answer. There may be more than one correct answer.

1. Which of the following can be **analyzed?**
   (a) rock samples
   (b) the causes of the Vietnam War
   (c) blood
   (d) the length of the day

2. Which of the following could be **traced?**
   (a) the outline of a peninsula
   (b) a family history
   (c) a long-lost relative
   (d) a missing letter

3. Which of the following might **revolve?**
   (a) a door
   (b) a planet
   (c) a pedestal
   (d) a tree

4. Which of the following would be **extraordinary?**
   (a) a parrot that talks
   (b) a fish that walks
   (c) a fourteen-year-old college student
   (d) a twenty-foot sandwich

5. Which of the following **exist** today?
   (a) tyrants
   (b) unicorns
   (c) feelings
   (d) dinosaurs

6. Which of the following is a **disk?**
   (a) a coin
   (b) a softball
   (c) a dollar bill
   (d) the full moon's appearance

7. Which of the following can be **composed?**
   (a) a dream
   (b) a person
   (c) a reply
   (d) a poem

8. Which of the following could be **scaled?**
   (a) terrain
   (b) a fence
   (c) poverty
   (d) a ladder

analyze
apprehensive
coincide
compose
disk
envelop
exist
extraordinary
fuse
mere
revolve
scale
solar
trace
velocity

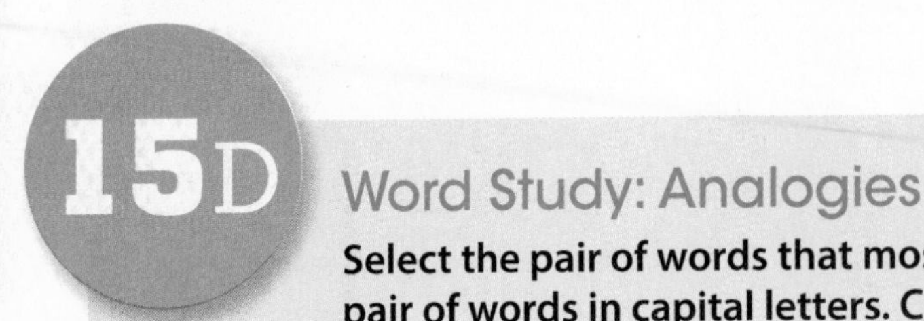

Word Study: Analogies

Select the pair of words that most nearly expresses the relationship of the pair of words in capital letters. Circle the letter next to the pair you choose.

HINT! Look for (1) a greater or lesser degree of the same condition; (2) the relationship of the part to the whole; or (3) the relationship between one part of speech and another.

1. SKIRMISH : BATTLE ::
   (a) trial : verdict
   (b) dispute : brawl
   (c) sword : shield
   (d) lion : tamer

2. APPREHENSIVE : TERRIFIED ::
   (a) possess : relinquish
   (b) tired : hungry
   (c) pleased : ecstatic
   (d) inhibited : bold

3. ERROR : BLUNDER ::
   (a) pain : agony
   (b) woe : tears
   (c) decision : unanimity
   (d) mistake : correction

4. HAPPY : ECSTATIC ::
   (a) joyful : mediocre
   (b) hungry : ravenous
   (c) skilled : inept
   (d) conspicuous : hidden

5. VALUABLE : INVALUABLE ::
   (a) fake : real
   (b) proud : arrogant
   (c) shy : quiet
   (d) soothing : irritating

6. SCALE : FISH ::
   (a) pounds : weight
   (b) feather : bird
   (c) stream : river
   (d) fly : plane

7. COAT : ATTIRE ::
   (a) paint : brush
   (b) shoes : socks
   (c) envelope : stationery
   (d) jacket : pants

8. SOLAR : SUN ::
   (a) bright : star
   (b) cold : ice
   (c) blue : sky
   (d) tyrannical : tyrant

9. BENEVOLENT : BENEVOLENCE ::
   (a) beneficial : benefit
   (b) weary : traveler
   (c) clever : mind
   (d) inept : skill

10. ANALYZE : ANALYSIS ::
   (a) coincide : chance
   (b) exist : creature
   (c) inhibit : inhibition
   (d) measure : velocity

15E

Vocabulary in Context

Read the passage.

Our Brightest Star

The sun has always occupied a unique place in the human imagination; indeed, in many societies throughout history it was worshiped as a god. The Colossus of Rhodes, one of the Seven Wonders of the ancient world, was a gargantuan statue of the sun god Helios. People once believed that the sun **revolved** around Earth, which was considered the center of the universe. They also believed that eclipses of the sun could cause hazardous conditions on Earth. This belief perhaps resulted from the **coincidence** of an earthquake or volcanic eruption occurring during an eclipse.

We know now that both of these beliefs are false. In fact, one of the most **extraordinary** things about the sun is that it is a perfectly ordinary star. It is no different from billions of other stars scattered throughout the universe. Of course, it is significant to us because without its energy, life on Earth could not **exist.** But the sole reason Earth receives more heat and light from the sun than from the other billions of similar stars is that the sun is so close to us. It is a **mere** ninety-three million miles away.

Light travels at a **velocity** of 186,000 miles per second. Light from the sun takes only eight minutes to reach Earth. Light from Proxima Centauri, the next closest star, takes over four years to reach us. If we imagine the sun diminished to the size of an orange, Earth on this same **scale** would be twenty-six feet from the sun. Earth would be only marginally bigger than the period that ends this sentence. Proxima Centauri would be over thirteen hundred miles away!

Human beings no longer worship the sun, but they do study it. Eclipses of the sun provide a superb opportunity for doing this. **Solar** eclipses occur when the moon passes directly in front of the sun and blocks out its direct light. Astronomers eagerly await solar eclipses, although they have a brief duration. In photographs taken at such times the sun appears as a black **disk** surrounded by tremendous flames leaping from its surface. These flames can be photographed only during an eclipse. They can attain a height of 120,000 miles. That is almost half the distance from Earth to the moon.

By **analyzing** the sun's light, scientists discovered the main elements that make up the sun. They found that the sun is **composed** almost entirely of hydrogen. It contains a much smaller amount of helium and minute **traces** of

- analyze
- apprehensive
- coincide
- compose
- disk
- envelop
- exist
- extraordinary
- fuse
- mere
- revolve
- scale
- solar
- trace
- velocity

other elements as well. The sun's interior is about 150,000 times hotter than boiling water. It is hot enough that hydrogen atoms **fuse** and are transformed into helium atoms, giving off energy as they do so. This energy reaches Earth in many forms; the two most familiar to us are heat and light.

By comparing the sun to other stars, scientists can estimate the age of the sun, for stars are born, reach middle age, and eventually die. We know that our sun is approximately five billion years old, which is middle-aged for a star. When it eventually uses up its entire supply of hydrogen, it will start to die. With no more fuel to burn, it will start to cool, getting larger and larger as it does so. It will finally become so enormous that it will **envelop** the planets closest to it, including our own Earth. However, there is no reason for anyone to be **apprehensive;** it will be five billion years before the sun terminates our planet.

▶ **Answer each of the following questions with a sentence. If a question does not contain a vocabulary word from the lesson's word list, use one in your answer. Use each word only once.**

1. Why might the sun have made ancient peoples **apprehensive?**

____

____

2. How might ancient peoples have felt about an eclipse of the sun?

____

____

3. With which two forms of **solar** energy are we most familiar?

____

____

4. What is the meaning of **exist** as it is used in the passage?

____

____

5. What is the relationship of Earth's movement to the sun?

____

____

6. Why do you think the author says that the sun is a **mere** 93 million miles away?

____

____

7. What is the meaning of **traces** as it is used in the passage?

8. How fast does light travel?

9. What happens to hydrogen atoms at very high temperatures?

10. How do scientists know what the sun is made of?

11. What is the meaning of **scale** as it is used in the passage?

12. Is the eruption of a volcano during an eclipse related to the eclipse?

13. How does the sun appear during a total eclipse?

14. What is the meaning of **composed** as it is used in the passage?

15. How large will the sun get when it starts to expand?

analyze
apprehensive
coincide
compose
disk
envelop
exist
extraordinary
fuse
mere
revolve
scale
solar
trace
velocity

Fun & Fascinating FACTS

- An *envelope* (än´ və lōp) is a folded paper cover for a letter. Don't confuse this word with the verb **envelop** (en vel´ əp) which means "to cover completely."

- **Disk** is sometimes spelled *disc*. Both are correct, but *disk* is the more usual spelling.

- To **revolve** is to move in a circular path around another object. The moon, for example, takes one month to *revolve* around Earth. To *rotate* is to turn around an axis* or central point. Earth *rotates* once around its axis every twenty-four hours. Confusion arises because these two words are sometimes used interchangeably. A *revolving* door, for example, *rotates* around a central axis.

- Three of the many meanings of **scale** have quite different origins. From the Old French word *escale*, meaning "shell," comes the word for the thin, hard plates found on fishes. The Latin word *scala*, meaning "ladder," gives us the verb that means "to climb." And an old Scandinavian word *skal*, meaning "bowl," gives us our word for an instrument for measuring weight. *Scales* once had two large pans, one for weights and the other for whatever was being weighed.

- The adjective **solar** means "having to do with the sun." Adjectives having to do with other heavenly bodies include the following: *lunar*, "having to do with the moon"; *Martian*, "having to do with Mars"; *Venusian*, "having to do with Venus"; and *Jovian*, "having to do with Jupiter."

  Both the noun *Jupiter* and the adjective *Jovian* come from the Roman names for the chief god of Mount Olympus; he is sometimes referred to as Jupiter and sometimes as Jove.

* An axis is an imaginary straight line around which an object turns. Earth's axis is an imaginary line joining the North and South poles.

Vocabulary Extension

analyze

verb To break down into separate parts in order to study.

Academic Context

In science class, you may do an experiment and then **analyze** the results.

Word Family

analysis (noun)
analytical (adjective)
analyst (noun)

Discussion & Writing Prompt

*The **analyst** determined that the disease is spread by mosquitoes.*

Based on this sentence, write the definition of **analyst** and then use it in a new sentence of your own.

2 min.

1. Turn and talk to your partner or group.

Use this space to take notes or draw your ideas.

3 min.

2. Write 2–4 sentences.

Be ready to share what you have written.

Lesson **16**

Word List

Study the definitions of the words. Then do the exercises that follow.

awe
ô

n. A feeling of fear or nervous wonder and respect.
The view of Earth from space filled the astronauts with **awe.**

v. To fill with awe.
The immensity of the whale breaking the surface **awed** the passengers on the boat.

awesome *adj.* Causing feelings of awe.
The herd of stampeding buffalo was an **awesome** sight.

catastrophe
kə tas´ trə fē

n. Something that causes great loss and suffering; a terrible disaster.
The earthquake was a **catastrophe** that claimed thousands of victims.

collide
kə līd´

v. To come together with great force.
The two skaters were injured when they **collided** on the ice.

collision *n.* (kə lizh´ ən) The act of colliding.
The **collision** occurred because neither of the drivers was paying attention.

Chat with your partner about what astronauts could do if an asteroid were on a collision course with Earth.

consequence
kän´ sə kwens

n. 1. A result or outcome.
Receiving a scolding was the **consequence** of my rude behavior.

2. Importance.
The matter was of no **consequence** and was soon forgotten.

Remind your partner what the consequences are for students who turn in work late.

deceive
dē sēv´

v. To cause to believe something that is not true.
The Wizard of Oz tried to **deceive** Dorothy by pretending to perform real magic.

deceptive *adj.* (dē sep´ tiv) Intended to or likely to deceive or mislead.
Watch the mongoose carefully because its harmless appearance is **deceptive.**

deception *n.* (dē sep´ shən) An act of deceiving.
He pretended he didn't know my brother, and it was not until later that I discovered his **deception.**

Talk to your partner about how deception hurts the people who are lied to.

fatality
fə tal´ ə tē

n. A death resulting from an accident or a disaster.
Fortunately there were no **fatalities** when the train ran off the track.

improvise im´ prə vīz

v. 1. To compose or perform without preparation.
The actors occasionally **improvise** a scene based on suggestions from the audience.

2. To make do with whatever is on hand.
The kids at the slumber party **improvised** a tent from bed sheets.

Discuss with your partner how you could improvise a board game using paper and colored pencils.

loom lo͞om

n. A machine or device for weaving cloth.
These blankets were woven on a small hand **loom.**

v. 1. To appear in a sudden and frightening way.
A sinister figure **loomed** out of the darkness, scaring us half to death.

2. To get close.
As election day **loomed,** both parties scrambled for votes.

Chat with your partner about the types of things that loom in the dark in ghost stories.

lull lul

v. To cause to relax.
The sound of the ocean **lulled** us to sleep.

n. A temporary calm or quiet period.
There was usually a **lull** at the restaurant between the end of lunch and the start of the dinner rush.

placid plas´ id

adj. Calm and peaceful.
The wind suddenly picked up, ruffling the **placid** surface of the lake.

predicament prē dik´ ə mənt

n. A difficult or trying situation.
Running out of gas at night on a deserted road put the travelers in a **predicament.**

priority prī ôr´ ə tē

n. The state or condition of being before another in importance or time.
Chandra's first **priority** was to clean her room before her friends came over.

Tell your partner your top three priorities for summer vacation.

reinforce rē in fôrs´

v. To increase or strengthen.
Telling frightened children that there is nothing to worry about only **reinforces** their fear.

reinforcements *n. pl.* Extra people such as soldiers or police sent to provide help.
The soldiers were told to hold the fort until **reinforcements** arrived.

Discuss with your partner how you could help reinforce the teacher's rules about speaking during class.

stern
stʉrn

n. The rear part of a boat.
The front of the boat rose out of the water when everyone rushed to the **stern.**

adj. Unpleasantly severe.
The judge's **stern** expression suggested she was about to hand down a heavy sentence.

treacherous
trech´ ər əs

adj. 1. Not to be trusted.
A **treacherous** sentinel let the enemy pass through the gate.

2. Actually dangerous while seeming to be safe.
Hidden rocks make this part of the river **treacherous.**

16A Using Words in Context

Read the following sentences. If the word in bold is used correctly, write C on the line. If the word is used incorrectly, write I on the line.

1. (a) As the day of our departure **loomed,** we grew more and more nervous. ___
   (b) The ferry **loomed** out of the fog and came to a stop at the dock. ___
   (c) The **loom** takes cotton fibers and turns them into cloth. ___
   (d) Mateo disgraced himself by acting like a **loom** at the party. ___

2. (a) My friend sat in the **stern** of the boat while I rowed. ___
   (b) I took hold of the **stern** and spun it into the air. ___
   (c) The woman was given a **stern** warning by the judge. ___
   (d) The **stern** look on my mother's face told me I was in trouble. ___

3. (a) The gentle rumbling of the ship's engine **lulled** us to sleep. ___
   (b) The people were **lulled** into excitement. ___
   (c) My dad couldn't **lull** anymore, so we went out to eat. ___
   (d) There was a **lull** in the storm, so we decided to return home. ___

4. (a) My best friend's **deception** made me sad. ___
   (b) The Trojans were **deceived** into thinking the wooden horse was a gift. ___
   (c) Messages were sent and **deceived** by mail. ___
   (d) The company got caught using **deceptive** methods to sell its products. ___

5. (a) The judge **collided** that neither person was to blame for the accident. ___
   (b) The **collision** between the soccer players made everyone gasp. ___
   (c) The Andromeda galaxy will **collide** with our galaxy in four billion years. ___
   (d) The neighbors took up a **collision** for the family who lost their home. ___

6. (a) Reading about the ancient and beautiful Aztec society fills me with **awe.** ___
   (b) The hikers were **awed** by the beautiful view of the mountains. ___
   (c) A frozen waterfall must be an **awesome** sight. ___
   (d) We **awed** that my friends were probably right to quit the team. ___

7. (a) When the speaker's notes got mixed up, she had to **improvise.** ___
   (b) The sailors **improvised** a sail from whatever they could find. ___
   (c) The actors forgot their lines, so they began to **improvise.** ___
   (d) Tanis will **improvise** the food with her for the party. ___

8. (a) Uncle Ang is usually in a **placid** mood after his nap. ___
   (b) The ocean was **placid** for the first three days of our trip. ___
   (c) The can is filled with **placid** trash and needs to be emptied. ___
   (d) I felt so **placid,** I almost couldn't stop myself from screaming. ___

9. (a) A **priority** of the U.S. Postal Service is delivering the mail promptly. ___
   (b) The campers' first **priority** was putting up their tent. ___
   (c) Finding the best doctor for their baby was a **priority** for the new parents. ___
   (d) The **priority** was built in the 1200s and stood for seven centuries. ___

10. (a) The **catastrophe** fell fifty feet down the side of the mountain. ___
    (b) It would be a major **catastrophe** if a large meteorite struck Earth. ___
    (c) We cannot prevent every **catastrophe,** but we can try to prepare for them. ___
    (d) She couldn't believe the **catastrophe** she heard about on the news. ___

awe
catastrophe
collide
consequence
deceive
fatality
improvise
loom
lull
placid
predicament
priority
reinforce
stern
treacherous

Making Connections

Circle the letter next to each correct answer. There may be more than one correct answer.

1. Which word goes with *cloth?*
   (a) lull (b) loom (c) lumber (d) limb

2. Which word goes with *bad news?*
   (a) misfortune (b) disaster (c) reinforcements (d) catastrophe

3. Which word goes with *death?*
   (a) humid (b) fatality (c) consequence (d) lull

4. Which word goes with *difficult situation?*
   (a) awe (b) priority (c) predicament (d) loom

5. Which word goes with *support?*
   (a) relinquish (b) reinforce (c) improvise (d) sustain

6. Which word goes with *result?*
   (a) consequence (b) collision (c) effect (d) deception

7. Which word goes with *dishonest?*
   (a) collide (b) deceive (c) treachery (d) betray

8. Which word goes with *strict?*
   (a) deceptive (b) severe (c) stern (d) placid

9. Which word goes with *peaceful?*
   (a) deceptive (b) placid (c) treacherous (d) tranquil

10. Which word goes with *wonder?*
    (a) priority (b) awe (c) consequence (d) catastrophe

Determining Meanings

Circle the letter next to each answer choice that correctly completes the sentence. There may be more than one correct answer.

1. The **treacherously**
   (a) dangerous part of the trail is coming up, so be careful.
   (b) sinister man spread rumors against the government.
   (c) tiny stone is so small it won't hurt anything.
   (d) soft pillow is perfect for a good night's sleep.

2. We **reinforced**
   (a) the fence by fixing all the holes and replacing some of the posts.
   (b) the team with two top new players to make sure we would win the game.
   (c) the students that tomorrow would be a holiday.
   (d) our bones by drinking milk.

3. You should **prioritize**
   (a) all the cooked carrots because they're delicious.
   (b) saying thank you to the host of the birthday party before you go home.
   (c) your little sister's safety over going wherever you want.
   (d) finishing your homework, and then you can talk on the phone.

4. The **collisions**
   (a) of the ocean waves against the shore were beautiful.
   (b) make me so sleepy every time I eat them.
   (c) can be planted in the soil if they're watered immediately afterward.
   (d) of the comets over the last couple of days could be seen at night.

5. The **placidness** of
   (a) the clanging bell in my ear woke me up.
   (b) the lake looked inviting on such a hot day.
   (c) the tempting smells in the kitchen made my mouth water.
   (d) her mood made us all calm and relaxed.

6. The **consequences**
   (a) can be very bad if you fail every test.
   (b) of ignoring the rules won't be good.
   (c) at the top of the building were made of copper.
   (d) of people watching too much TV are still not fully understood.

awe
catastrophe
collide
consequence
deceive
fatality
improvise
loom
lull
placid
predicament
priority
reinforce
stern
treacherous

7. The number of **fatalities**
   (a) where climbers can spend the night has doubled in the past year.
   (b) scored in the last minute helped us win.
   (c) resulting from the earthquake is not yet known.
   (d) caused by people texting while driving is increasing.

8. **Improvisation**
   (a) can be fun if you're comfortable with abandoning the script.
   (b) during band practice can help you play better.
   (c) on the website will be a good resource for your report.
   (d) will be from June 1 through September 1.

Completing Sentences

Complete the sentences to demonstrate your knowledge of the words in bold.

1. **Placid** people might make friends easily because

   ____.

2. My top **priority** in school is

   ____.

3. If you **reinforce** a wall, that means you

   ____.

4. Parents might be **stern** when

   ____.

5. If someone **deceived** me, I would

   ____.

6. Something that **lulls** me to sleep is

   ____.

7. I would be **awed** by

   ____.

8. One **consequence** of a tornado might be

   ____.

9. It would be a **catastrophe** if

   ____.

10. One **predicament** I remember having is

    ____.

Vocabulary in Context

Read the passage.

The "Unsinkable" *Titanic*

On the night of April 14, 1912, in the Atlantic Ocean about 360 miles off the coast of Newfoundland, the *Titanic* blazed with lights. It was headed for New York, four days out from England on its very first voyage. Almost nine hundred feet long, it was the biggest passenger ship afloat. Its steel hull, the main body of the ship, had been **reinforced** with a second hull fitted inside it. Because of this safety feature, the *Titanic* was believed to be unsinkable—a belief that **lulled** everyone on board into a false sense of security. Their trust was to have tragic **consequences.**

Although the sea looked **placid** that night, its appearance was **deceptive.** The *Titanic*, in fact, was in **treacherous** waters. In 1912 there was no radar to warn of an approaching object. So when a huge iceberg suddenly **loomed** out of the darkness, there was little time to act. The *Titanic* made a desperate attempt to avoid a **collision,** but it was too late. The ship's right side struck the iceberg. Both its inner and outer hull were ripped open below the waterline. Water began pouring in, flooding the front of the ship. Because it was 11:40 p.m., many of the passengers were sleeping or getting ready for bed. The slight bump, which was all they felt, caused no alarm.

When Captain Edward Smith received a report of the damage, he knew at once that a **catastrophe** had occurred. He realized that his "unsinkable" ship could stay afloat for little more than an hour or two. Even as he gave the order to abandon ship, he faced a terrible **predicament:** There were not enough lifeboats for everyone on board. Furthermore, there had been no practice drills. Crew members were confused because there were no clear orders from their superiors.

There would have been enough time to **improvise** rafts, but in the panic that followed as passengers and crew were alerted, no attempt was made to do so. Women and children were given **priority** as the crew hastily prepared the lifeboats. In the confusion, many of the boats were lowered into the water half empty. That night there were fifteen hundred **fatalities,** and only seven hundred survived. Among the dead was the captain, who chose to go down with his ship. Another was Ida Straus of New York, who is remembered for gallantly refusing a place in one of the lifeboats to stay with her husband.

- awe
- catastrophe
- collide
- consequence
- deceive
- fatality
- improvise
- loom
- lull
- placid
- predicament
- priority
- reinforce
- stern
- treacherous

Those fortunate enough to have escaped in the lifeboats were filled with **awe** as they witnessed the final moments of the *Titanic.* The ship's bow sank first, leaving the **stern** sticking out high above the water. Then its lights suddenly went out. At 2:20 a.m., less than three hours after striking the iceberg, the great ship slid silently beneath the waves.

▶ **Answer each of the following questions with a sentence. If a question does not contain a vocabulary word from the lesson's word list, use one in your answer. Use each word only once.**

1. Why is a **collision** with an iceberg unlikely to occur today?

___

___

2. Why must the *Titanic* have seemed an **awesome** sight to people from passing ships who saw it at nighttime before it hit the iceberg?

___

___

3. What was the purpose of the *Titanic's* inner hull?

___

___

4. Why were those on board not apprehensive about possible danger?

___

___

5. What is the meaning of **treacherous** as it is used in the passage?

___

___

6. How were those keeping watch **deceived** by the sea's appearance that night?

___

___

7. What is the meaning of **loom** as it is used in the passage?

___

___

8. How serious was the damage caused by the accident?

9. Why might the passengers have remained **placid** when the *Titanic* first struck the iceberg?

10. What was the **predicament** that Captain Smith found himself in?

11. What is the meaning of **improvise** as it is used in the passage?

12. Which passengers left the sinking ship first?

13. What happened to Ida Straus?

14. Why would passengers who remained on board have tried to go to the rear of the boat?

15. What might have been an important **consequence** of the loss of the *Titanic?*

awe
catastrophe
collide
consequence
deceive
fatality
improvise
loom
lull
placid
predicament
priority
reinforce
stern
treacherous

Fun & Fascinating FACTS

- The Vikings were a warlike people who lived over a thousand years ago in what is now Norway, Denmark, and Sweden. They were superb boat builders and sailors, and they traveled in their famous longboats as far as Greenland and the northern shores of North America. The language they spoke is called Old Norse, and the English words *steer* and **stern** both come from the Old Norse word *stjorn,* which means "to steer." The two words are connected because the *stern* is the rear of a boat, the place from which the vessel is *steered.*

- The *stem* is the front end of a ship; it is a wooden or metal part to which the sides of the vessel are attached, rather as leaves are attached to the stem of a plant. To inspect a boat "from *stem* to *stern*" is to examine every part of it.

- The noun form of the verb **collide** is *collision*. A *collision course* is one that is being followed by moving objects that will result in their *colliding* unless there is a change of course by either or both. (The small two-seater plane was on a *collision course* with a large jetliner.)

16

Vocabulary Extension

priority

noun The thing that is most important and needs attention before anything else.

Things to Do
1. Study for test!
2. Call Grandma
3. Play video games

Academic Context

Your first **priority** during a test may be to answer all the questions you immediately know the answers to.

Idioms and Phrases

top priority (most important thing):
Fixing the leaky roof was the ***top priority.***

high priority (very important thing):
Hiring new teachers became a ***high priority.***

get your priorities straight (to focus on what is truly important):
After goofing off and getting poor grades, Lacy decided to ***get her priorities straight.***

Discussion & Writing Prompt

What is your **top priority** when you get home from school today?

2 min. 1. Turn and talk to your partner or group.	3 min. 2. Write 2–4 sentences.
Use this space to take notes or draw your ideas.	Be ready to share what you have written.

Lessons 13–16 Review

Crossword Puzzle Solve the crossword puzzle by studying the clues and filling in the answer boxes. The number after a clue is the lesson the word is from.

1				2								3		4	5		6	
7				8			9								10			
11		12								13								
				14														
															15			16
17								18					19					
												20				21		
22	23																	
													24		25			
							26											
27																		
					28								29					

Clues Across

1. Very unusual; remarkable **(15)**
4. An angry stare **(13)**
8. Calm and peaceful **(16)**
10. A machine for weaving cloth **(16)**
11. A condition that makes life difficult **(13)**
13. A wonderful or amazing thing **(14)**
14. To be real rather than imaginary **(15)**
15. To go on one's way **(13)**
17. Great respect **(14)**
18. Any thin, circular object **(15)**
20. Of, or having to do with, the sun **(15)**
22. An event that causes great loss and suffering **(16)**
24. Related to *brother*
26. To go around something in a circle **(15)**
27. "As American as ______ pie"
28. To cause to believe what is untrue **(16)**
29. A ruler who uses power in a cruel way **(14)**

Clues Down

2. Worried; uneasy about what might happen **(15)**
3. Happening once a year
5. To cause to relax **(16)**
6. To open again
7. A very small amount **(15)**
9. A synonym for *money*
12. The way a person or animal moves on foot **(13)**
13. Opposite of *hit*
16. Showing care in what one says or does **(14)**
18. To use up **(13)**
19. To agree; to allow to happen **(14)**
21. Animal similar to but larger than a mouse
23. To change to fit new conditions **(13)**
25. To wither; to dry up **(13)**

Word List

Study the definitions of the words. Then do the exercises that follow.

corrode
kə rōd´
v. To eat or wear away by degrees, usually by chemical action.
Exposure to the weather can **corrode** unprotected metal surfaces.

corrosion *n.* (kə rō´ zhən) The process or the result of corroding.
Metal bridges must be painted frequently to prevent **corrosion.**

Tell your partner something you have seen that had corrosion, such as an old bicycle.

debris
də brē´
n. 1. Broken, scattered remains.
Debris from buildings damaged by the hurricane littered the streets.

2. Litter; rubbish.
It took city workers all day to clean up the **debris** from the rock concert held in the park.

elated
ē lāt´ əd
adj. Happy and excited; overjoyed.
The **elated** winners jumped up and down.

elation *n.* (ē lā´ shən) A feeling of great joy and excitement.
The news that she had won a Nobel prize was greeted with **elation** by members of her family.

Share with your partner something that would fill you with elation.

exploit
eks´ ploit
n. A brave or daring act; an adventure.
The spy wrote a book about her **exploits.**

v. (ek sploit´) 1. To make full use of; to utilize.
Windmills **exploit** wind power to produce electricity.

2. To use in a selfish way; to take unfair advantage of.
Unions try to protect workers from employers who might **exploit** them.

Discuss with your partner whether it's a good idea, while doing work at school, to exploit your friend because she's good at math.

leeway
lē´ wā
n. An extra amount of time or space that allows some freedom.
The wide channel gives boats entering the harbor plenty of **leeway.**

miniature
min´ ē ə chər

adj. On a small scale.
A **miniature** railroad for young children ran through the park.

n. 1. A very small copy.
This **miniature** of a 1922 car is only six inches long but is complete in every exterior detail.

2. A small painting, especially a portrait.
The locket holds a **miniature** of the poet's great-grandmother.

mobile
mō´ bēl

n. An artistic structure with parts that move easily.
A huge **mobile** hangs in the National Gallery of Art in Washington, D.C.

adj. (mō´ bəl) Easily moved.
The actors travel with a **mobile** set when the play goes on tour.

Tell your partner about a mobile restaurant you have seen, such as a food cart.

onset
än´ set

n. A start or a beginning.
The **onset** of winter was marked by a steep temperature drop.

ooze
o͞oz

n. Soft, watery mud, as at the bottom of a lake or the sea.
Our feet sank into the **ooze** as we waded across the shallow pond.

v. To leak out slowly.
Sap **oozed** from the deep gash in the trunk of the tree.

pathetic
pə thet´ ik

adj. 1. Causing feelings of pity or sorrow.
The newly arrived refugees told a **pathetic** story of persecution by their tyrannical rulers.

2. Held in low esteem; arousing scorn.
The team's performance so far this season has been **pathetic.**

preliminary
prē lim´ i ner ē

adj. Coming at the beginning; coming before the main event or activity.
The band director made a few **preliminary** remarks before the concert began.

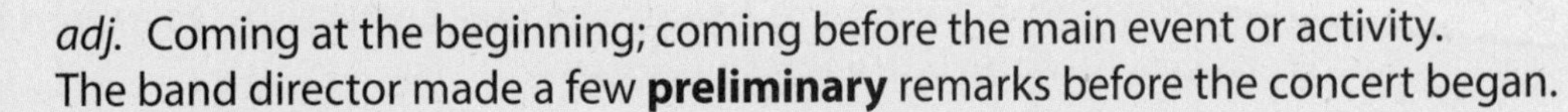

Describe to your partner your preliminary preparation before a physical activity.

quest
kwest

n. A hunt or search.
The expedition set out on a **quest** for the lost treasure of Montezuma.

restrain
rē strān´

v. To hold back; to keep under control.
The catcher tried to **restrain** the angry batter, but a brawl quickly erupted.

restraint *n.* 1. A holding back or keeping under control.
You showed great **restraint** in not defending yourself when you were unfairly attacked.

2. Something used to control or hold in check.
The dog wriggled out of the **restraint** and ran after the ball.

Chat with your partner about how you might restrain yourself if you get angry at someone.

salvage
sal´ vij

v. To save from destruction or loss.
Salvage what you can from the wreckage.

n. Property saved from loss or destruction.
Goods from the burned building were sold off cheaply as **salvage.**

scour
skour

v. 1. To clean by scrubbing hard.
We **scoured** the pots and pans until they gleamed.

2. To search thoroughly.
Detectives **scoured** the area but failed to find any clues.

Tell your partner about a time you scoured your room looking for a lost item.

Finding Meanings

Choose two phrases to form a sentence that correctly uses a word from Word List 17. Then write the sentence.

1. (a) To be exploited
   (b) To be elated
   (c) is to be annoyed.
   (d) is to be overjoyed.

____

____

2. (a) Salvage from a flood
   (b) is property saved from destruction.
   (c) Debris from a flood
   (d) is the soft mud it leaves behind.

____

____

3. (a) take unfair advantage of that person.
   (b) To restrain someone is to
   (c) save that person from harm or death.
   (d) To exploit someone is to

____

____

4. (a) A mobile is
   (b) something that is no longer made.
   (c) A miniature is
   (d) a small model of a larger object.

____

____

5. (a) Debris is
   (b) broken remains scattered about.
   (c) Ooze is
   (d) high, thin, scattered clouds.

____

____

6. (a) A quest is
   (b) an exact copy done on the same scale.
   (c) A mobile is
   (d) a work of art that moves.

____

____

7. (a) sneering at those less fortunate.
   (b) Corrosion is
   (c) Restraint is
   (d) keeping oneself under control.

____

____

8. (a) A quest for something is
   (b) a search for it.
   (c) The onset of something is
   (d) a reason for it.

____

____

9. (a) a gradual wearing away.
   (b) a thorough cleaning.
   (c) Leeway is
   (d) Corrosion is

____

____

10. (a) A pathetic account
    (b) is one that is complete.
    (c) is one that arouses pity.
    (d) A preliminary account

____

____

Just the Right Word

Replace each phrase in bold with a single word (or form of the word) from the word list.

1. Volunteers agreed to pick up the **garbage scattered on the ground** after the Fourth of July picnic.

2. This is all we managed to **save from destruction** when the house flooded.

3. I saw oil **leaking slowly** from the crack in the pipe.

4. Grandmother's latest **act of daring** was skydiving on her seventieth birthday.

5. These reports are **still in the early stages** and may have to be revised later.

6. The locket contained a **very small picture** of Abigail Adams.

7. "You are **held in very low esteem,**" she sneered when she found out about his deception.

8. The dog's **harness that is intended to hold it back** is made of heavy nylon straps.

9. At the **first sign** of a cold, I go to bed and get plenty of rest.

10. We have to be at the bus stop in fifteen minutes, which gives us very little **time to do anything else.**

11. **Thoroughly clean** the pots with steel wool until they shine.

corrode
debris
elated
exploit
leeway
miniature
mobile
onset
ooze
pathetic
preliminary
quest
restrain
salvage
scour

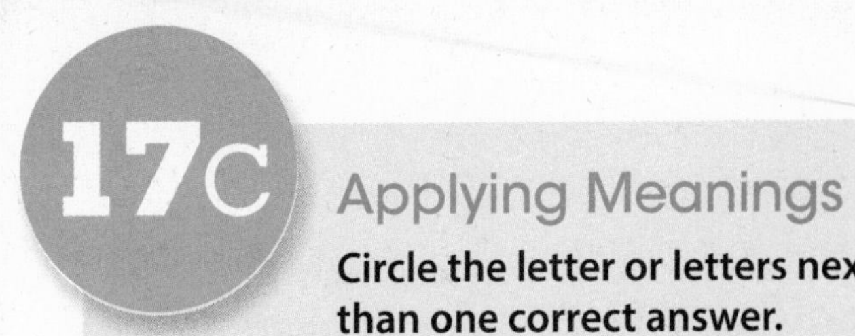

17C Applying Meanings

Circle the letter or letters next to each correct answer. There may be more than one correct answer.

1. Which of the following might **ooze?**
   (a) sap from a tree
   (b) rain from the sky
   (c) oil from an engine
   (d) blood from a wound

2. Which of the following can be **corroded?**
   (a) water
   (b) air
   (c) iron
   (d) soil

3. Which of the following would give a person **leeway?**
   (a) extra time
   (b) extra work
   (c) extra space
   (d) extra responsibility

4. In which of the following places might one find **debris?**
   (a) the scene of a train wreck
   (b) a picnic area
   (c) a battlefield
   (d) a bottle of water

5. Which of the following can be **mobile?**
   (a) a lamp post
   (b) a telephone
   (c) an army unit
   (d) a home

6. Which of the following might be considered an **exploit?**
   (a) a climb up Mount Everest
   (b) a trip into the city
   (c) a daring rescue attempt
   (d) a serious illness

7. Which of the following might be cause for **elation?**
   (a) obtaining a mediocre test score
   (b) becoming bankrupt
   (c) witnessing a catastrophe
   (d) finding a lost pet

8. Which of the following might be **scoured?**
   (a) a greasy frying pan
   (b) a dusty camera lens
   (c) a dirty floor
   (d) an area being searched

Word Study: Synonyms and Antonyms

Each group of four words contains either two synonyms or two antonyms. Circle that pair. Then circle the *S* if they are synonyms or the *A* if they are antonyms.

1. final	unique	preliminary	mobile	S	A
2. start	display	ooze	onset	S	A
3. tiny	pathetic	miniature	rigorous	S	A
4. mobile	elated	perpetual	stationary	S	A
5. corrosive	placid	pitiful	pathetic	S	A
6. elation	restraint	joy	surprise	S	A
7. search	leeway	siege	quest	S	A
8. release	exploit	restrain	discover	S	A
9. save	salvage	corrode	collide	S	A
10. use	exploit	arrange	scour	S	A

corrode
debris
elated
exploit
leeway
miniature
mobile
onset
ooze
pathetic
preliminary
quest
restrain
salvage
scour

17E

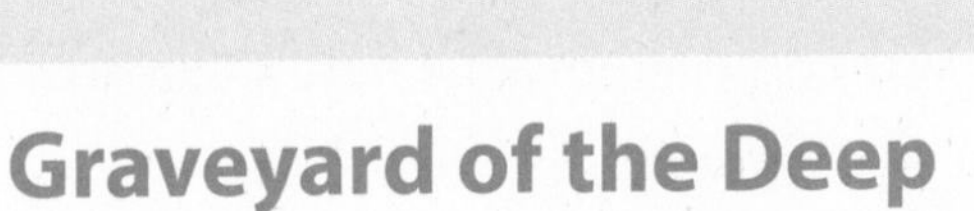

Vocabulary in Context

Read the passage.

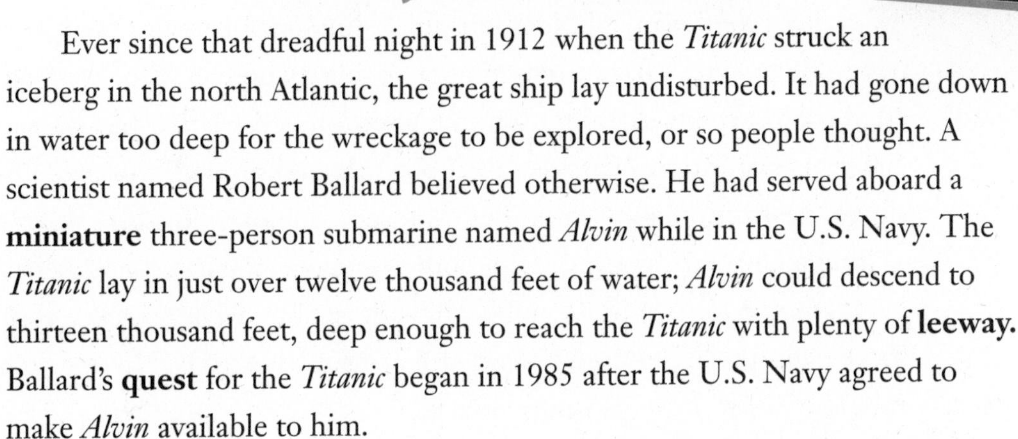

Graveyard of the Deep

Ever since that dreadful night in 1912 when the *Titanic* struck an iceberg in the north Atlantic, the great ship lay undisturbed. It had gone down in water too deep for the wreckage to be explored, or so people thought. A scientist named Robert Ballard believed otherwise. He had served aboard a **miniature** three-person submarine named *Alvin* while in the U.S. Navy. The *Titanic* lay in just over twelve thousand feet of water; *Alvin* could descend to thirteen thousand feet, deep enough to reach the *Titanic* with plenty of **leeway.** Ballard's **quest** for the *Titanic* began in 1985 after the U.S. Navy agreed to make *Alvin* available to him.

Ballard had only an approximate location for where the *Titanic* had gone down. He knew he would have to **scour** an area several miles across to have any hope of actually finding the wreckage. Before he could use *Alvin*, he needed to make a **preliminary** search using video cameras operated by remote control from a surface ship. These **mobile** cameras were mounted on a sled that was dragged along the bottom on a thirteen-thousand-foot cable.

Crew members aboard the surface ship studied the pictures from the deep on a television screen. For days the pictures showed nothing but the mud at the bottom of the ocean, and the crew grew increasingly bored. Then suddenly, pictures of scattered **debris** on the ocean floor appeared. But was it from the *Titanic* or from some other ship? When a large ship's boiler came into view, the crew members were **elated.** They recognized it from photographs and knew they had found the *Titanic.*

Because the **onset** of winter made further operations dangerous, Ballard waited until the following year to resume his search. This time he took *Alvin.* From inside the tiny submarine, Ballard explored the wreck up close. The ship's hull had broken into two parts that landed right-side up, almost half a mile apart. Both parts had settled in sixty feet of **ooze** and could never be pulled clear. No one would ever raise the *Titanic.*

Over a two-week period, *Alvin* made a total of eleven descents. Ballard's most anxious moments came during his second dive when he landed on the main deck. The wooden planks that had once covered it had all been eaten away, and there was a chance that the badly **corroded** metal plates would collapse as *Alvin* settled on them. Were they to do so, *Alvin* could become entangled between decks. A return to the surface would be impossible and there would be no way for the crew of the surface ship to attempt a rescue. Those aboard the tiny submarine held their breaths, then let out sighs of relief. The metal plates had held.

Ballard took many photographs, including one of a pair of empty shoes lying side by side, a **pathetic** reminder of those who had died. He made no attempt to **salvage** anything from the wreck. In a book that he later wrote about his **exploit,** he expressed the hope that other expeditions would show similar **restraint.** Sad to say, other explorers did not follow his example. Within a few years, gold coins and other valuable objects from the *Titanic* were being offered for sale to the public. The great ship itself, however, tomb to more than fifteen hundred people, will remain where it is. No one will ever raise the *Titanic* from its watery grave.

▶ **Answer each of the following questions with a sentence. If a question does not contain a vocabulary word from the lesson's word list, use one in your answer. Use each word only once.**

1. What was the outcome of Ballard's **quest?**

____

____

2. What was special about Ballard's **exploit** compared with those who came after him?

____

____

3. How would you describe the ocean floor in the area where the *Titanic* sank?

____

____

4. What is the meaning of **scour** as it is used in the passage?

____

____

5. Why is there very little room aboard *Alvin?*

____

____

corrode
debris
elated
exploit
leeway
miniature
mobile
onset
ooze
pathetic
preliminary
quest
restrain
salvage
scour

6. What did Ballard have to do before he could begin the main search?

____

____

7. Why did **mobile** cameras have to be used to look for the wreck?

____

____

8. How much **leeway** did Ballard have using *Alvin* to reach the wreck?

____

____

9. What ended the monotony of the crew members who were studying the television screen?

____

____

10. How might those studying the television screen have expressed their **elation** when the ship's large boiler came into view?

____

____

11. What effect does seawater have on metal?

____

____

12. Why did Ballard not continue his search immediately after finding the wreckage of the *Titanic?*

____

____

13. What is the meaning of **restraint** as it is used in the passage?

____

____

14. What did later expeditions **salvage** from the *Titanic?*

____

____

15. What is the meaning of **pathetic** as it is used in the passage?

____

____

Fun & Fascinating FACTS

- **Debris** is a French word brought unchanged into English. It comes from the French verb *debriser,* "to break into pieces."

- The word **miniature** comes from the Latin *miniare,* which means "to color in." Before printing was invented, books were written one page at a time with pens and ink. Pictures in them, usually quite small, were painted by hand. The word *miniature* came to mean "a very small picture." Its meaning was later extended to mean anything very small, especially a small portrait or a small copy or model of a larger object.

corrode
debris
elated
exploit
leeway
miniature
mobile
onset
ooze
pathetic
preliminary
quest
restrain
salvage
scour

17 Vocabulary Extension

restrain

verb To control something by holding it back.

Word Family

restrainable (adjective)
restrained (adjective)
restraint (noun)
un**restrain**ed (adjective)

Context Clues

These sentences give clues to the meaning of **restrain.**

I was so entranced by the painting that my friend had to ***restrain*** *me from touching it.*

Yoshi held the leash tight to ***restrain*** *the excited dog from jumping on his friend.*

Discussion & Writing Prompt

Seatbelts are used to **restrain** passengers in moving vehicles. Why are these **restraints** important?

2 min. 1. Turn and talk to your partner or group.	3 min. 2. Write 2–4 sentences.
Use this space to take notes or draw your ideas.	Be ready to share what you have written.

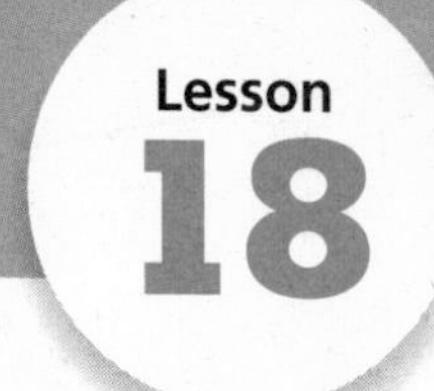

Word List

Study the definitions of the words. Then do the exercises that follow.

abroad
ə brôd´

adv. Away from one's own country.
Mark Twain wrote humorous stories of his travels **abroad.**

anguish
aŋ´ gwish

n. Extreme pain of the body or mind.
I felt **anguish** when no one turned up for the vote to protect the forest.

v. To suffer extreme doubts or uncertainties.
Jess **anguished** over whether to tell his teacher that he had seen someone cheating.

commence
kə mens´

v. To start; to begin.
The school year **commences** on September 9.

Commence talking to your partner and then stop.

commend
kə mend´

v. 1. To speak of with approval; to praise.
The teacher **commended** the students who excelled on the test.

2. To put in the care of.
A burial at sea usually ends with the words, "We **commend** this body to the deep."

controversy
kän´ trə vʉr sē

n. A public dispute that arouses strong feelings.
The plan to build a new power station in an unspoiled rural area created **controversy.**

controversial *adj.* (kän trə vur´ shəl) Causing controversy.
The school board's **controversial** decision to extend the school year was approved by a majority of one.

Discuss with your partner how people might feel when they talk about a controversial issue.

cordial
kôr´ jəl

adj. Sincerely warm and friendly.
The guests received a **cordial** welcome at the party.

dissent
di sent´

v. To disagree.
Only one senator **dissented** when the vote was taken.

n. The expression of a difference of opinion.
There was **dissent** from students over the school board's decision to increase testing.

Ask your partner if he or she would agree or dissent if a vote were held to ban school football teams.

earnest
ʉr´ nəst

adj. Serious and important; not light and playful.
The tornado victim's **earnest** appeal for help could not be ignored.

elicit
ē lis´ it

v. To draw out or to cause.
The fiery speech **elicited** an angry response from the crowd.

Elicit an answer from your partner to this question: Who is your favorite singer?

exhilaration
eg zil ə rā´ shən

n. Excitement; a state of elation.
The baseball fans showed their **exhilaration** by running onto the field and carrying the players off on their shoulders.

exhilarating *adj.* (eg zil´ ə rāt iŋ) Exciting; stimulating.
The high point of our day at the fair was the **exhilarating** ride on the roller coaster.

exhilarate *v.* (eg zil´ ə rāt) To excite; to cause to feel lively.
The sound of a big brass band never fails to **exhilarate** the crowds.

Tell your partner about an exhilarating experience you have had.

genuine
jen´ yo͞o in

adj. 1. Real; being what it seems to be.
This is a **genuine** diamond, not a fake.

2. Honest; sincere.
As a result of the successful boycott, the company made a **genuine** effort to stop polluting the groundwater.

hoax
hōks

n. An act intended to fool or deceive others.
We knew the player's injury was a **hoax** when he jumped to his feet and laughed at us.

v. To fool; to play a trick on.
Alisha believed she had won first prize until she learned that her friends had **hoaxed** her.

manipulate
mə nip´ yo͞o lāt

v. 1. To operate using the hands, especially in a skillful way.
The deft players **manipulated** the controls of the video game with incredible speed.

2. To control in a secret or unfair way.
Real friends don't **manipulate** each other into doing things that are wrong.

Chat with your partner about how you would feel if a friend was trying to manipulate you into skipping school.

recount
rē kount´

v. To give a detailed account of.
The judge asked the witness to **recount** what happened just before the accident.

n. (rē´ kount) A second count, as of the vote in an election.
The candidate who lost by only three votes immediately demanded a **recount.**

Recount for your partner what you did last weekend.

skeptic
skep´ tik

n. A person who is not easy to convince unless positive proof is offered.
When it comes to astrology, my cousin remains a **skeptic.**

skeptical *adj.* Showing doubt or an unwillingness to believe.
I gave the inept dancer a **skeptical** look when he offered to teach me to tango.

skepticism *n.* (skep´ tə siz əm) An attitude of doubt or disbelief.
The statement that the test didn't really matter was greeted with **skepticism.**

18A Using Words in Context

Read the following sentences. If the word in bold is used correctly, write C on the line. If the word is used incorrectly, write I on the line.

abroad
anguish
commence
commend
controversy
cordial
dissent
earnest
elicit
exhilaration
genuine
hoax
manipulate
recount
skeptic

1. (a) The jury was **manipulated** into voting "guilty" by the treacherous lawyer. ___
   (b) The clown **manipulated** the balloons into all kinds of animal shapes. ___
   (c) Six **manipulated** by five equals thirty. ___
   (d) American bison once **manipulated** the prairie in huge herds. ___

2. (a) A **recount** changed the result of the voting. ___
   (b) Yoshiko **recounted** to her mother her reasons for staying home from school. ___
   (c) This month we learned to **recount** the names of all the U.S. presidents in order. ___
   (d) I told my uncle I was **recounting** on his help with my homework. ___

3. (a) The candidate's **earnest** speech convinced many people to vote for her. ___
   (b) We made an **earnest** effort to win the game, but we failed. ___
   (c) We were too **earnest** to sleep, so we drank some hot chocolate. ___
   (d) I never know when Andreas is joking and when he is being **earnest.** ___

4. (a) Their **dissent** soon turned into a loud argument. ___
   (b) I **dissented** deeper and deeper into the cave. ___
   (c) Parents expressed their **dissent** at the meeting by raising their hands. ___
   (d) Two of us **dissented** to the library on our bikes. ___

5. (a) Mehar wrote a note on a piece of colored **hoax.** ___
   (b) We were **hoaxed** into thinking we were going to be on TV. ___
   (c) We discovered the **hoax** and told the teacher. ___
   (d) We made our way across fields of **hoax** to the top of the hill. ___

6. (a) We gave **cordial** smiles to everyone as they arrived. ___
   (b) The **cordial** holding the rod snapped, and we lost the fish. ___
   (c) Most of the entries in her journal were **cordial** thoughts about her friends. ___
   (d) Britain and France maintained **cordial** relations during this period. ___

7. (a) My joke **elicited** laughter from my friend. ___
   (b) The magician **elicited** an apple from a top hat. ___
   (c) The farmers around here **elicit** mostly sheep. ___
   (d) Try to **elicit** intelligent questions when you talk to a group. ___

8. (a) If the signature is **genuine,** this old letter could be worth a lot of money. ___
   (b) If his offer of help had been **genuine,** I would have accepted. ___
   (c) A **genuine** Stradivarius violin sells for tens of millions of dollars. ___
   (d) I was not **genuine** to his plans. ___

9. (a) Snowboarding for the first time was **exhilarating.** ___
   (b) My bike **exhilarated** down the hill. ___
   (c) I **exhilarated** the air from my lungs. ___
   (d) The **exhilaration** of the crowd could be heard from the parking lot. ___

10. (a) I was **skeptical** when Zayid said he could get us in for free. ___
    (b) The judges were **skeptical** that Maya could beat the record. ___
    (c) There was a lot of **skepticism** about whether the snowstorm would turn into a blizzard. ___
    (d) I keep a spare **skeptical** just in case I run out. ___

Making Connections

Circle the letter next to each correct answer. There may be more than one correct answer.

1. Which word goes with *give details about?*
   (a) manipulate (b) obscure (c) recount (d) dissent

2. Which word goes with *sincere?*
   (a) earnest (b) cordial (c) vast (d) genuine

3. Which word goes with *fool?*
   (a) hoax (b) commend (c) deceive (d) collide

4. Which word goes with *excite?*
   (a) commend (b) exhilarate (c) manipulate (d) rouse

5. Which word goes with *friendly?*
   (a) affectionate (b) skeptical (c) cordial (d) earnest

6. Which word goes with *dispute?*
   (a) commence (b) hoax (c) catastrophe (d) controversy

7. Which word goes with *start?*
   (a) commend (b) originate (c) recount (d) commence

8. Which word goes with *approve?*
   (a) manipulate (b) commend (c) jest (d) applaud

9. Which word goes with *pain?*
   (a) anguish (b) controversy (c) priority (d) torment

10. Which word goes with *far from home?*
    (a) abroad (b) jeopardy (c) predicament (d) dissent

abroad
anguish
commence
commend
controversy
cordial
dissent
earnest
elicit
exhilaration
genuine
hoax
manipulate
recount
skeptic

18C Determining Meanings

Circle the letter next to each answer choice that correctly completes the sentence. There may be more than one correct answer.

1. The **skeptical**
   (a) person is always optimistic about the future.
   (b) piece of toast tastes great with butter and jam.
   (c) voice in your head will tell you that lottery tickets are a waste of money.
   (d) mother was surprised when her son actually cleaned his room.

2. I am **commencing**
   (a) dancing lessons on Tuesday.
   (b) eating lunch after I wash my hands.
   (c) the engine by pressing this button.
   (d) that you weren't too happy to see me.

3. The **controversial**
   (a) book was in the news almost every day this week.
   (b) rule was put into effect on March 1.
   (c) air was bitterly cold.
   (d) skin on my right hand is always dry.

4. The **manipulation**
   (a) in a flower is what attracts bees.
   (b) of a person is done by betraying his or her trust.
   (c) on the floor was so shiny you could see your reflection.
   (d) of puppets can be achieved by pulling on their strings.

5. Martina **elicited**
   (a) juice from the lemons by squeezing them.
   (b) the grapes into raisins by drying them.
   (c) information from various sources by going online.
   (d) praise from her parents when she made the volleyball team.

6. We **anguished**
   (a) over silly things we shouldn't have worried about.
   (b) the tomatoes and carrots and added them to the soup.
   (c) the guest room so that everything was nice for Aunt Celia.
   (d) over whether we should mention his lost dog to him.

7. I **recounted**
   (a) onto the bed and slept for twelve hours.
   (b) to my dad what had happened to the broken TV.
   (c) the story to anyone who would listen.
   (d) the ball all the way down the hill.

8. The **hoaxes**
   (a) started as a joke and then got out of hand.
   (b) involved a large number of people.
   (c) had been nailed to the wall to hang the painting.
   (d) were cruel, and hurt people's feelings.

Completing Sentences

Complete the sentences to demonstrate your knowledge of the words in bold.

1. I think it would be **exhilarating** to

____.

2. Something that fills me with **skepticism** is

____.

3. Doctors should be **commended** for

____.

4. To **dissent** means to

____.

5. If I were going **abroad,** I would go to

____.

6. A **controversial** issue is something that

____.

7. I would **commence** planning for a picnic by

____.

8. If I'm asked to **recount** a story, that means I

____.

9. I would give a **cordial** welcome to

____.

10. A **hoax** is

____.

abroad
anguish
commence
commend
controversy
cordial
dissent
earnest
elicit
exhilaration
genuine
hoax
manipulate
recount
skeptic

Vocabulary in Context

Read the passage.

Journey to the Soviet Union

A war without battles! What kind of war is that? Answer: the Cold War. It was fought between the Soviet Union and the United States, and it lasted from 1945 to 1990. Each side had more than enough weapons to destroy the other if the Cold War turned hot. Fear was in the air. People built bomb shelters in their homes, and at school children were taught what to do if the country came under attack. Most people accepted that this was just the way it was. Not Samantha Smith, a fifth grader from Maine, who **anguished** over the possibility of nuclear war and decided to do something about it. In 1983, she wrote a letter to the leader of the Soviet Union containing an **earnest** plea for the two superpowers to settle their differences peacefully.

She waited several months before her letter **elicited** a reply, which came in the form of a mysterious phone call. A man speaking with a strong Russian accent thanked her for her letter and told her she would be receiving a written reply within a few days. Samantha was not sure that the phone call was **genuine;** she thought that it might be a **hoax** by one of her father's friends. Although her father denied it, Samantha remained **skeptical.** Her doubts were ended, however, when an envelope from the Soviet embassy in Washington was delivered to her home in Maine. Inside it was a **cordia**l letter from Yuri Andropov, the Soviet leader, who thanked her for taking the trouble to write and expressed a concern similar to her own about the threat of nuclear war. The letter also included an invitation to Samantha and her parents to visit the Soviet Union.

Samantha found herself famous overnight. She appeared on national television, and she was written about in magazines. Not everyone agreed that her visit to the Soviet Union would be desirable, though. People nationwide were soon discussing the issue. Those who supported her **commended** her for what she was doing and praised her as an example to young people everywhere. Those who **dissented** from this view believed that she should decline the invitation and stay home; they thought that she was being **manipulated** by the Communists, who would use her visit for their own purposes. Samantha ignored the **controversy** swirling about her, and in July 1983, accompanied by her parents, she went to the Soviet Union.

She had never been **abroad** before, and she found the experience **exhilarating.** On her return she wrote a book called *Journey to the Soviet Union*, in which she **recounts** everything that happened during her visit. She was also invited to costar in a television series. Her life at that point must have seemed like a fairy tale, and all because of a letter she had written.

With the collapse of communism in the Soviet Union in 1991, the threat of nuclear war was greatly reduced. Unfortunately, Samantha did not live to see this event. In 1985, shortly after she had **commenced** filming the new television series, she and her father died in a plane crash. During her short life, Samantha accomplished a great deal. She showed that if a young person, even one in elementary school, is willing to make her voice heard, the world will sometimes listen.

Answer each of the following questions with a sentence. If a question does not contain a vocabulary word from the lesson's word list, use one in your answer. Use each word only once.

1. Was Samantha's visit to the Soviet Union her first trip out of the United States?

___

___

2. How does the passage make clear that Samantha was a concerned citizen?

___

___

3. Do you think Samantha is to be **commended** for writing the letter? Why or why not?

___

___

4. Why do you think the Soviet leaders took Samantha's letter seriously?

___

___

5. What does Samantha's show of **skepticism** tell you about her?

___

___

abroad
anguish
commence
commend
controversy
cordial
dissent
earnest
elicit
exhilaration
genuine
hoax
manipulate
recount
skeptic

6. What is the meaning of **genuine** as it is used in the passage?

7. When did Samantha realize that the phone call she had received was not a **hoax?**

8. What kind of response to her letter did Samantha receive?

9. Why did Samantha's letter **elicit** so much attention?

10. Why was Samantha's planned trip **controversial?**

11. What is the meaning of **manipulated** as it is used in the passage?

12. Did everyone agree that Samantha's trip to the Soviet Union was a good idea? Why or why not?

13. When did Samantha's trip to the Soviet Union **commence?**

14. What is the meaning of **recounts** as it is used in the passage?

15. How do you think Samantha must have felt about appearing in a television series?

Fun & Fascinating FACTS

- The Latin word for *heart* is *cor* and forms the root of the adjective **cordial.** The heart was once believed to be the place where the emotions were located, and this is still reflected in our language. If someone speaks "from the heart," that person is being honest and sincere. Similarly, a *cordial* greeting is one that is *heart*warming.

- Don't confuse the verb **elicit,** which means "to draw out" or "to cause," with the adjective *illicit,* which means "illegal" or "forbidden." (A person selling illegal goods is engaging in an *illicit* activity.)

- An antonym of **dissent** is *assent*. To *dissent* from a decision that is made is to express one's disagreement with it. To *assent* to a decision is to agree with it and to voice one's approval.

abroad
anguish
commence
commend
controversy
cordial
dissent
earnest
elicit
exhilaration
genuine
hoax
manipulate
recount
skeptic

18 Vocabulary Extension

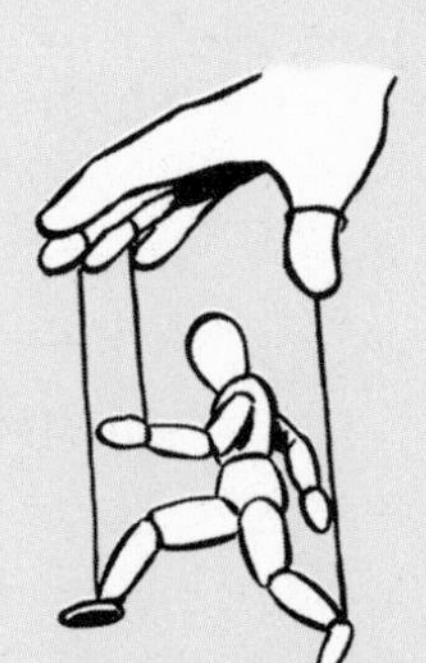

manipulate

verb 1. To control in a way that is unfair.

2. To skillfully handle something.

Word Family

manipulative (adjective)
manipulation (noun)
manipulator (noun)

Word Parts

The root *man* means "hand." Two other words with this root are *manager* and *manicure*. Can you think of any other words with the root *man*?

Discussion & Writing Prompt

The king thought he came up with the new law by himself, but one of his advisors was a master ***manipulator.***

Based on this sentence, write the definition of **manipulator** and then use it in a new sentence of your own.

2 min. 1. Turn and talk to your partner or group.	3 min. 2. Write 2–4 sentences.
Use this space to take notes or draw your ideas.	Be ready to share what you have written.

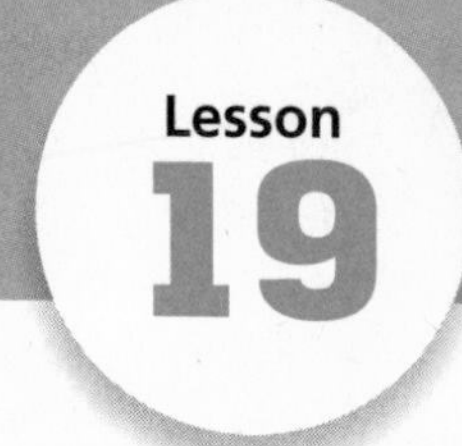

Word List

Study the definitions of the words. Then do the exercises that follow.

breach
brēch

n. 1. An opening made by battering.
Water poured through the **breach** in the dam.

2. A breaking or being broken.
Your attempts to manipulate your roommate are what caused the **breach** in your friendship.

v. 1. To break through.
The eager spectators **breached** the barriers along the parade route.

2. To fail to keep; to break.
Not telling the truth **breaches** the agreement you made.

Talk to your partner about what could happen when a river breaches its banks and flows into a nearby town.

clammy
klam´ ē

adj. Cold and damp.
The speaker was so nervous his hands were **clammy** with sweat.

construct
kən struckt´

v. To build; to make by fitting the parts together.
We **constructed** the tree house from pieces of scrap lumber.

construction *n.* (kə n struk´ shən) 1. The act of building.
The mason salvaged used bricks for the **construction** of the walk.

2. Something that is built.
The Great Pyramid is an extraordinary **construction.**

Chat with your partner about something you would love to construct, like a castle or an airplane.

elaborate
ē lab´ ə rət

adj. Having great detail; done with much care.
The **elaborate** meal took hours to prepare.

v. (ē lab´ ə rāt) To give more details.
Could you **elaborate** on the plan so that the student contributors can get a better understanding of it?

Think of a great day you had recently, and elaborate about it to your partner.

fragrant
frā´ grənt

adj. Having a pleasant smell.
We awoke to the **fragrant** aroma of freshly baked bread.

fragrance *n.* A sweet or pleasant smell.
The **fragrance** of her perfume lingered after she had departed.

furnish fûr´ nish

v. 1. To equip with what is needed; to supply.
The parents' club **furnished** most of the money for the art project.

2. To put furniture into.
The children **furnished** their room with bunk beds and matching dressers.

furnishings *n. pl.* Articles of furniture for the home or office.
Most of the **furnishings** in my grandparents' house are genuine antiques.

haven hā´ vən

n. A place of safety; a sanctuary.
The local school was a **haven** for those made homeless by the hurricane.

install in stôl´

v. 1. To put in place or set up.
We want to **install** a large skylight over the kitchen sink.

2. To place into office.
The members will **install** their new president at the next meeting.

Discuss with your partner something that could be installed in the school gym or the cafeteria to make school more enjoyable.

massive mas´ iv

adj. Very large and solid; heavy.
A **massive** meteorite collided with the Mexican coast sixty-five million years ago, making a crater nearly two hundred miles across.

repel ri pel´

v. 1. To drive away.
To **repel** mosquitoes, use this spray before going out in the woods.

2. To throw off; to shed.
A good raincoat is treated to **repel** water.

3. To disgust.
Cruelty to animals **repels** me.

repellent *n.* Something that repels.
This **repellent** is supposed to keep cats off the furniture.

adj. 1. Able to repel.
My slicker is both water **repellent** and warm.

2. Disgusting.
The way movies glorify violence is **repellent** to many people.

Talk to your partner about actions you should not take because they might repel your friends.

restore
ri stôr´

v. 1. To give back.
The police **restored** the stolen goods to the rightful owners.

2. To bring back to the original condition.
A good polishing will **restore** the shine to the brass candlesticks.

restoration *n.* (res tər ā´ shən) 1. The bringing back to the original condition.
The association began the **restoration** of George and Martha Washington's home in 1858.

2. The thing that is brought back to its original state.
Many of the buildings at Williamsburg are **restorations** from colonial America.

Tell your partner why it is important to restore historic buildings.

retaliate
ri tal´ ē āt

v. To return an injury, usually in the same way.
When my friend hid my bat, I **retaliated** by hiding her softball mitt.

retaliation *n.* (ri tal ē ā´ shən) The act of retaliating.
Should anyone attack UN peacekeeping troops, **retaliation** will be swift and certain.

Discuss with your partner why you should or should not retaliate if someone calls you a name.

stench
stench

n. A bad smell.
The **stench** of rotting fish drove the investigators away from the dock.

strew
strōō

v. To scatter.
The wind **strewed** papers all over the yard.

vicinity
və sin´ ə tē

n. The nearby or surrounding area.
Is there a library in the **vicinity** of your home?

Finding Meanings

Choose two phrases to form a sentence that correctly uses a word from Word List 19. Then write the sentence.

1. (a) A haven is
   (b) a high wall to keep out enemies.
   (c) A breach is
   (d) an opening made by breaking through.

____

____

2. (a) vacate it on an agreed date.
   (b) To restore a building is to
   (c) To construct a building is to
   (d) bring it back to its original condition.

____

____

3. (a) To be in the vicinity is to be
   (b) aware of what is going on.
   (c) To be clammy is to be
   (d) close by.

____

____

4. (a) To elaborate is to
   (b) make no further effort.
   (c) provide more details.
   (d) To retaliate is to

____

____

5. (a) build it.
   (b) To furnish a room is to
   (c) To construct a room is to
   (d) put it to its intended use.

____

____

6. (a) Retaliation is
   (b) the act of breaking through.
   (c) Fragrance is
   (d) the returning of an injury.

____

____

7. (a) To furnish things
   (b) is to supply them.
   (c) is to take them apart.
   (d) To strew things

____

____

8. (a) is to hide it.
   (b) To install something
   (c) To repel something
   (d) is to fix it in place.

____

____

9. (a) A stench is
   (b) A haven is
   (c) a sneering remark.
   (d) a bad smell.

____

____

10. (a) A fragrance is
(b) something that is put to regular use.
(c) A repellent is
(d) something that drives things away.

___

___

Just the Right Word

Replace each phrase in bold with a single word (or form of the word) from the word list.

1. Although only a few miles across, a neutron star can be as **tremendously full of matter** as the sun.

2. Rosa remembered the **pleasantly sweet smell** of the honeysuckle in her grandparents' garden.

3. You **failed to keep** my trust when you wouldn't stand up for me.

4. Prejudice of any kind is **so unpleasant that it is disgusting** to decent people.

5. A small inlet was the only **place of safety** for boats during the storm.

6. Kanye had thought that a snake's skin would feel **cold and damp,** but it felt quite dry.

7. Many of these colonial houses have been **brought back to their original condition** by prominent builders.

8. Garbage was **spread about here and there** all over the sidewalk from the overturned trash cans.

9. The ad for the furniture store said you can **obtain all the furniture you need for** three rooms for under $1,000.

10. When she broke her promise to me, I **got back at her** by telling all her friends what she had done.

breach
clammy
construct
elaborate
fragrant
furnish
haven
install
massive
repel
restore
retaliate
stench
strew
vicinity

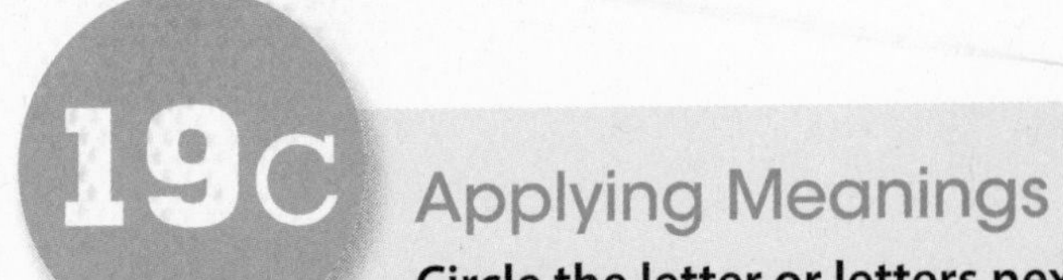

Applying Meanings

Circle the letter or letters next to each correct answer. There may be more than one correct answer.

1. Which of the following might be **fragrant?**
   (a) garbage
   (b) a glass ornament
   (c) flowers
   (d) perfume

2. Which of the following could be **installed?**
   (a) new members
   (b) firewood
   (c) smoke detectors
   (d) a fireplace

3. Which of the following might have a **stench?**
   (a) roses
   (b) garbage
   (c) spoiled milk
   (d) rotten eggs

4. Which of the following could be **elaborate?**
   (a) a ceremony
   (b) a hoax
   (c) an exhibit
   (d) a grain of sand

5. Which of the following can be **breached?**
   (a) a hoax
   (b) a wall
   (c) a contract
   (d) a friendship

6. Which of the following can be **restored?**
   (a) a fireplace
   (b) confidence
   (c) a painting
   (d) fatigue

7. Which of the following can be **repelled?**
   (a) an attack
   (b) a person
   (c) dogs
   (d) water

8. Which of the following can be **furnished?**
   (a) a room
   (b) an opportunity
   (c) supplies
   (d) anguish

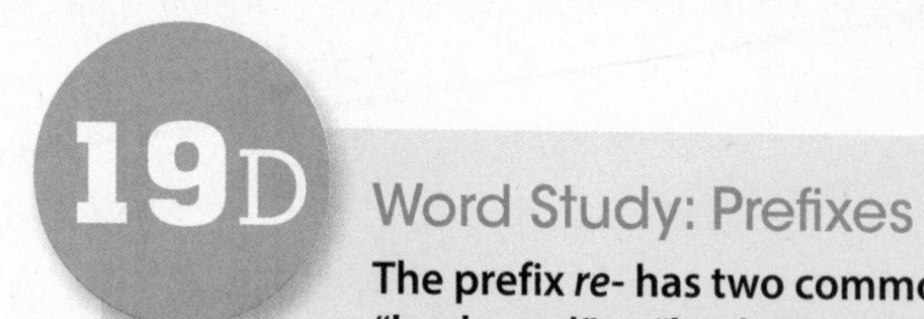

19D Word Study: Prefixes

The prefix *re-* has two common meanings. It can mean "again," or it can mean "backward" or "back." Match each definition with the correct word from the list. Write each word in the space provided.

restrain	**relive**	**refill**	**reread**
revise	**recall**	**return**	**revive**

1. To know again what one knew before ____________________
2. To hold back by force or force of will ____________________
3. To bring back to a former state or place ____________________
4. To fill again after being emptied ____________________
5. To look over again and make changes ____________________
6. To experience events again in your mind ____________________
7. To bring back to a lively state ____________________
8. To go over material in a book again ____________________

breach
clammy
construct
elaborate
fragrant
furnish
haven
install
massive
repel
restore
retaliate
stench
strew
vicinity

Vocabulary in Context

Read the passage.

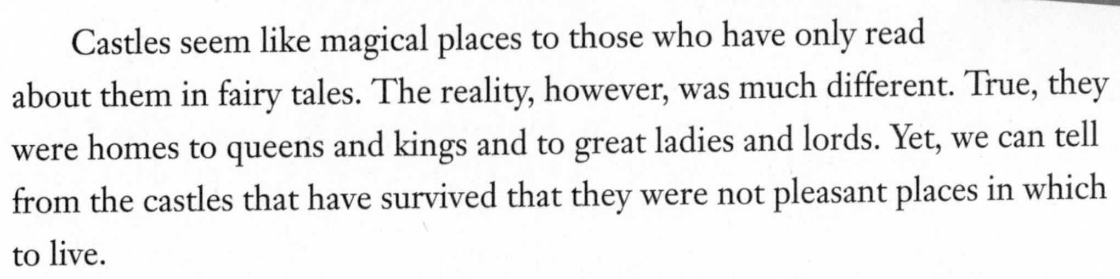

The Great Age of Castles

Castles seem like magical places to those who have only read about them in fairy tales. The reality, however, was much different. True, they were homes to queens and kings and to great ladies and lords. Yet, we can tell from the castles that have survived that they were not pleasant places in which to live.

Their outside walls were made of **massive** blocks of stone and were up to twenty feet thick. Living inside such thick stone walls must have felt like living in a cave. The rooms inside the castle were often **clammy.** In the winter, icy drafts blew through the narrow, glassless windows. In the heat of summer, the **stench** from the animals kept inside the castle, as well as from the unwashed bodies of the people, would have been overpowering. **Fragrant** herbs were used to mask the smells; one of the servants' jobs was to **strew** them on the castle floors.

The great age of castle building was the seven-hundred-year period from around 800 to 1500. Castles built at the beginning of this period were fairly simple wooden **constructions.** These have long since disappeared. The ones built later were made of stone and were much more **elaborate.** They had many private rooms and splendid **furnishings.** There was a great hall where banquets were held and visitors were greeted and entertained.

The main reason for building a castle was to provide a sanctuary in times of danger. The castle protected not only those who made their homes inside its walls but also those who lived in the **vicinity.** They could move inside the castle grounds if a hostile army approached. An attacking army had first to cross the moat, a wide, deep trench filled with water that surrounded the castle. Then the attackers had to scale the high, outside walls on ladders or platforms. Those defending the castle could **retaliate** by shooting arrows at them or by dropping rocks or pouring boiling liquids on them. If the attackers were **repelled,** they might begin a siege. The purpose of a siege was to starve the defenders into surrendering. It could last for many months before one side or the other gave up.

When gunpowder came into use around 1500, cannons could **breach** even the thickest walls. Castles were no longer the **havens** they had once been. Many were abandoned and fell into ruin, but a number of them are still standing. In some cases their modern owners have **restored** them and made them more comfortable for today's occupants by **installing** modern plumbing and electricity. Many castles are open to the public as museums or luxury hotels. Today you can enjoy some of the bygone magic of castles by visiting castles in Germany, particularly along the Rhine River, and in Great Britain.

▶ **Answer each of the following questions with a sentence. If a question does not contain a vocabulary word from the lesson's word list, use one in your answer. Use each word only once.**

1. What were the two main functions of castles?

____

____

2. What is the meaning of **construction** as it is used in the passage?

____

____

3. What would be the advantage of building castles near stone quarries?

____

____

4. Why are castles today more convenient and comfortable places to live in?

____

____

5. How did the building of castles evolve over the centuries?

____

____

6. Why would buying a ruined castle not appeal to a person of modest means?

____

____

7. How might a modern owner make a castle's rooms less **clammy?**

____

____

8. What **furnishings** might you find in the great hall of a castle?

____

____

breach
clammy
construct
elaborate
fragrant
furnish
haven
install
massive
repel
restore
retaliate
stench
strew
vicinity

9. What quality would have been valued in herbs grown in the castle gardens?

____

____

10. What difference would bathing regularly have made in the living conditions of the castle's inhabitants?

____

____

11. What use was made of the herbs grown in the castle gardens?

____

____

12. When might a castle have become overcrowded?

____

____

13. What is the meaning of **repelled** as it is used in the passage?

____

____

14. Name two ways that a castle's inhabitants could **retaliate** if attacked.

____

____

15. What is the meaning of **breach** as it is used in the passage?

____

____

Fun & Fascinating FACTS

- The adjective formed from the verb **construct** is *constructive,* which means "helpful" or "useful." Its antonym is *destructive,* which means "damaging" or "unhelpful." *Constructive* criticism is intended to be helpful; *destructive* criticism can be damaging to a person's self-confidence.

- *Mass* is the noun from which the adjective **massive** is formed. *Mass* is the amount of matter in a body. It is separate from weight, which is a measure of how strongly gravity is pulling on the object. A spaceship in orbit has a great deal of mass but weighs nothing because gravity is not pulling it to Earth. Even a relatively small boulder contains a great deal of mass. A blimp, on the other hand, although it may be many times larger, contains very little mass; it is *enormous* but not *massive.*

  Massive is also used in a figurative sense to describe something large in comparison with what is usual (a *massive* amount of ketchup; a *massive* blood clot causing a stroke).

breach
clammy
construct
elaborate
fragrant
furnish
haven
install
massive
repel
restore
retaliate
stench
strew
vicinity

19 Vocabulary Extension

construct

verb To build.

Word Family

construction (noun)
constructive (adjective)
constructively (adverb)
re**construct** (verb)
re**construct**ive (adjective)

Word Parts

The root *struct* means "build."
Another word with this root is *structure*. What are some other words with the root *struct?*

Discussion & Writing Prompt

A child uses building blocks to **construct** a toy house. What materials can **construction** workers use to **construct** a real house? What is your home **constructed** of?

2 min.

1. Turn and talk to your partner or group.

Use this space to take notes or draw your ideas.

3 min.

2. Write 2–4 sentences.

Be ready to share what you have written.

Lesson

20

Word List

Study the definitions of the words. Then do the exercises that follow.

bluster
blus´ tər

v. To talk in a loud and bullying manner.
"It's none of your business," he **blustered** when asked why he had stolen the money.

n. Loud, boastful or threatening talk or commotion.
They can talk tough, but their **bluster** doesn't scare me.

blustering *adj.* Blowing loudly and violently.
The **blustering** winds buffeted the ferry as it crossed the lake.

council
koun´ səl

n. A group of people who meet to decide or plan something, give advice, or make laws.
Members of the town **council** are elected for a two-year term.

Discuss with your partner how a student council is a useful school group.

dwell
dwel

v. 1. To live or reside.
How long did you **dwell** in the house where you were born?

2. To keep thinking about.
It does no good to **dwell** on past mistakes.

dwelling *n.* A house or home.
The only difference between one **dwelling** and the next was the color of the doors and shutters.

Chat with your partner about why it is not helpful to dwell on past regrets.

exterminate
ek stʉr´ mi nāt

v. To kill or destroy completely.
The hardware store sells products to **exterminate** ants and cockroaches.

fee
fē

n. A fixed sum of money charged.
The admission **fee** for the art museum is five dollars.

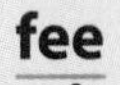

Talk to your partner about whether ticket fees for events such as the school play or band recitals are too high.

garment
gär´ mənt

n. Any piece of clothing.
These delicate **garments** should be washed by hand.

infest
in fest´

v. To overrun in a way that causes harm or annoyance.
Drastic measures are needed to deal with rats that **infest** the neighborhood.

insist
in sist´

v. To take a stand and hold firmly to it.
Her parents **insist** that she vacate her room so the walls can be scoured and painted.

insistent *adj.* (in sis´ tənt) Unyielding; firm.
The bird-watcher was **insistent** that everyone visit the bird sanctuary.

Tell your partner about something your family is insistent that you do each day, such as making your bed or walking the dog.

paltry
pôl´ trē

adj. Very small and worthless; hardly worth considering.
Five dollars may seem a **paltry** sum today, but in 1914 it was a day's wage for an automobile worker.

peculiar
pi kyo͞ol´ yər

adj. 1. Odd; strange.
It seems **peculiar** that such a frugal person would give everyone extravagant gifts.

2. Limited to a person, country, group, or thing.
Koalas are **peculiar** to Australia.

Work with your partner to think of a food peculiar to the United States.

rash
rash

n. 1. A breaking out of red spots on the skin.
This ointment will soothe the baby's **rash.**

2. A series of outbreaks.
A **rash** of storms disturbed the area right after Labor Day.

adj. Too hasty or reckless.
I regretted the **rash** statements I made while I was angry.

revenge
rē venj

n. 1. The desire to return harm for harm done.
Revenge for past wrongs was the only thing on their minds.

2. The act of paying back wrong done.
"I'll have my **revenge,**" said the victim of the hoax.

v. To get even for a wrong done; to retaliate.
The Sheriff of Nottingham swore to **revenge** the raids made by Robin Hood.

Discuss with your partner whether revenge or forgiveness is the right reaction when your feelings have been hurt.

rodent
rōd´ nt

n. An animal with sharp teeth for gnawing.
Small **rodents** such as gerbils and hamsters are popular pets.

adj. Of or relating to rodents.
The **rodent** droppings in the attic were a sign of mice.

swarm swôrm *v.* To move in large numbers.
Soccer fans **swarmed** into the stadium for the final game of the series.

n. A large, moving crowd or mass.
The bees emerged from the hive in a dense **swarm.**

Tell your partner about a place where there are swarms of people.

vat vat *n.* A large container such as a tub or barrel used for holding liquids.
Olive oil is stored in these large **vats.**

20A Using Words in Context

Read the following sentences. If the word in bold is used correctly, write C on the line. If the word is used incorrectly, write I on the line.

bluster
council
dwell
exterminate
fee
garment
infest
insist
paltry
peculiar
rash
revenge
rodent
swarm
vat

1. (a) The player was **insisted** by the referee for hitting someone with his elbow. ___
   (b) Aunt Winona was **insistent** that we stay for lunch. ___
   (c) Uncle Bao **insisted** on paying the restaurant bill. ___
   (d) The attic of the old house was **insisted** with wasps. ___

2. (a) The people on the west side **dwell** in very expensive homes. ___
   (b) At ninety, Mr. Torres **dwells** on the past and loves to talk about old times. ___
   (c) In a shady **dwell** by the river, they found a gold nugget. ___
   (d) A **dwelling** at the bottom of the mountain provided shelter. ___

3. (a) A **swarm** of locusts landed on the field. ___
   (b) People **swarmed** into town from all directions for the big event. ___
   (c) Priyansh was able to **swarm** his way out of a tricky predicament. ___
   (d) A **swarm** of meteors lit up the sky last night around midnight. ___

4. (a) Tropical beaches are **peculiar** to Antarctica. ___
   (b) The duck-billed platypus is **peculiar** to Australia. ___
   (c) The pitcher adopts a **peculiar** grip on the ball before releasing it. ___
   (d) Dirt is a **peculiar** thing to grow a flower in. ___

5. (a) The thick **council** swirled around their legs as they walked. ___
   (b) The seven-member **council** meets every Wednesday. ___
   (c) The **council** voted to stop street parking during the blizzard. ___
   (d) My brother took the **council** up to his room and fell asleep on it. ___

6. (a) Without realizing it, Camilla had **blustered** into a trap. ___
   (b) The candidate **blustered** that he alone could fix everything. ___
   (c) The two friends **blustered** down the hill on the sled. ___
   (d) The **blustering** storm spread across three states. ___

7. (a) Each exquisite **garment** was made of silk. ___
   (b) The first **garments** worn by early humans were made of animal skins. ___
   (c) She wore elaborate **garments** for the ceremony. ___
   (d) **Garments** of flowers were hung around the necks of the dancers. ___

8. (a) Their desire for **revenge** was so strong, they could think about nothing else. ___
   (b) The medieval knight **revenged** his father's death. ___
   (c) The students **revenged** to their tests when the teacher turned her back to them. ___
   (d) The children **revenged** each other with gifts they had made themselves. ___

9. (a) A **rash** of crime happened the night the power went out. ___
   (b) The doctor looked at the **rash** on my arm and said not to worry about it. ___
   (c) His predicament was caused by the **rash** things he said. ___
   (d) The **rash** tomatoes grew on the vine in the sunshine. ___

10. (a) Be careful, or you may become **infested** with the flu. ___
    (b) Our cat keeps the house from being **infested** by mice. ___
    (c) I put the bread in the oven to **infest.** ___
    (d) Ladybugs can **infest** homes on sunny days in the fall. ___

20B Making Connections

Circle the letter next to each correct answer. There may be more than one correct answer.

1. Which word goes with *house?*
   (a) residence (b) council (c) dwelling (d) sentinel

2. Which word goes with *very small?*
   (a) minute (b) paltry (c) genuine (d) meager

3. Which word goes with *odd?*
   (a) bluster (b) stern (c) benevolent (d) peculiar

4. Which word goes with *kill?*
   (a) infest (b) slay (c) bluster (d) exterminate

5. Which word goes with *money?*
   (a) budget (b) hoax (c) fee (d) loom

6. Which word goes with *container?*
   (a) fee (b) vat (c) garment (d) cask

7. Which word goes with *clothing?*
   (a) outskirts (b) attire (c) apparel (d) garment

8. Which word goes with *hasty?*
   (a) paltry (b) rash (c) curious (d) placid

9. Which word goes with *harm?*
   (a) infest (b) improvise (c) reinforce (d) contaminate

10. Which word goes with *rat?*
    (a) antic (b) council (c) rodent (d) rural

bluster
council
dwell
exterminate
fee
garment
infest
insist
paltry
peculiar
rash
revenge
rodent
swarm
vat

Determining Meanings

Circle the letter next to each answer choice that correctly completes the sentence. There may be more than one correct answer.

1. Thiago **insisted**
   (a) in planting the tree because of the garden.
   (b) that we go to the swim meet with him.
   (c) on getting a dog when he turned twelve.
   (d) quickly all the way to the museum.

2. The **fee**
   (a) included a free beverage.
   (b) was paid to the lawyer before she accepted the case.
   (c) caught us by surprise because the forecast had predicted no storms.
   (d) is reduced for children under twelve.

3. We **exterminated**
   (a) the bugs in the attic.
   (b) the water before we poured it.
   (c) sunshine through the window.
   (d) rats from three different locations.

4. He began **blustering**
   (a) very quietly across the room in his socks.
   (b) when his friends told him to be quiet.
   (c) about how I never listen to him.
   (d) politely and told them how happy he was.

5. **Swarms**
   (a) of ants showed up at the picnic.
   (b) of protesters made their way to the White House gates.
   (c) of money were needed to care for such a large family.
   (d) of bees accompany their queen on her first flight.

6. The **vats**
   (a) of olive oil were kept in the farmhouse basement.
   (b) aren't meant to hold anything but liquid.
   (c) can be made of wood or metal.
   (d) measure the depth of the water in lakes.

7. She wanted **revenge**
   (a) to drink because she was freezing.
   (b) in her room to help her study.
   (c) for the terrible thing her best friend had said to her.
   (d) on the movie theater that had kicked her out.

8. **Rodents**
   (a) were hard to drive on at night.
   (b) gnawed their way through the door into the library.
   (c) eat many things, including grass, grains, and other plants.
   (d) such as rats are intelligent and can make very good pets.

Completing Sentences

Complete the sentences to demonstrate your knowledge of the words in bold.

1. If I could **dwell** anywhere in the world, I would choose

______________________________.

2. I pay a **fee** for

______________________________.

3. My favorite **garment** is

______________________________.

4. Someone who **blusters** probably feels

______________________________.

5. One thing I always **insist** on is

______________________________.

6. One of the most **peculiar** things I've ever seen was

______________________________.

7. If you are **rash** about something, that means

______________________________.

8. A **paltry** meal might be

______________________________.

9. I would be afraid of a **swarm** of

______________________________.

10. If you **exterminate** something, that means you

______________________________.

bluster
council
dwell
exterminate
fee
garment
infest
insist
paltry
peculiar
rash
revenge
rodent
swarm
vat

Vocabulary in Context

Read the passage.

The Pied Piper of Hamelin

Rats!
They fought the dogs, and killed the cats,
And bit the babies in the cradles,
And ate the cheeses out of the ***vats,***
*And licked the soup from the cooks' own ladles . . .**

There was no doubt that the people of Hamelin faced a very serious predicament. Their town was **infested** with rats, and the furry, beady-eyed **rodents** had grown so aggressive that they had invaded the townspeople's cellars, their kitchens, and even their bedrooms. There wasn't a **dwelling** in town that wasn't teeming with rats. The people threatened to run the mayor out of town unless he did something about the problem. The mayor promised to eliminate the rats; he vowed to **exterminate** every rat in town; he **blustered** that not a rat would survive his assault. But what could he do? Nothing except organize meetings with his **council** to discuss various ways of solving the problem. And the unpleasant truth was that neither he nor anyone else had the faintest idea what to do.

Suddenly a man dressed in a most **peculiar** fashion appeared at the meeting; his quaint **garments** drew hostile stares and rude comments from the townspeople.

His queer long coat from heel to head
Was half of yellow and half of red.

The stranger in the pied coat promised to rid the town of its rats by luring them away with the music from his pipe for a **fee** of one thousand guilders. The mayor was jubilant and replied instantly that this was too **paltry** a sum for performing such an assignment. He promised to compensate the piper no less than the amount of fifty thousand guilders!

Everyone followed as the Pied Piper stepped into the street. He raised his pipe to his lips and commenced playing. Over the sound of the music an unearthly noise could be heard.

And the muttering grew to a grumbling;
And the grumbling grew to a mighty rumbling;
And out of the houses the rats came tumbling.

Rats **swarmed** from the houses and into the streets, following the Pied Piper as he led them out of town while playing his tune. When they came to the river Weser, the rats plunged in and perished.

The people of Hamelin were most grateful to the Pied Piper and rang every bell in town to celebrate the occasion, but the mayor was now having second thoughts about the payment he had promised. He convinced himself that he had been **rash** to offer fifty thousand guilders. He now thought a mere fifty guilders would be more than sufficient. When the Pied Piper **insisted** on being paid in full, the mayor taunted him.

You threaten us, fellow? Do your worst,
Blow your pipe there 'til you burst!

As his **revenge**, the Pied Piper led away all the village's children, who were never seen or heard from again.

* *The rhymes are quotations from Robert Browning's poem "The Pied Piper of Hamelin," a fanciful story about a town in Germany.*

Answer each of the following questions with a sentence. If a question does not contain a vocabulary word from the lesson's word list, use one in your answer. Use each word only once.

bluster
council
dwell
exterminate
fee
garment
infest
insist
paltry
peculiar
rash
revenge
rodent
swarm
vat

1. Why were the inhabitants of Hamelin probably afraid to enter their homes?

____

____

2. Were any homes in the town free of rats?

____

____

3. What was the mayor's problem in dealing with the town's **rodents?**

____

____

4. What was aggravating the town's cheese makers?

____

____

5. Where did the Pied Piper make his offer to get rid of the rats?

6. Why did the Pied Piper's **garments** arouse so much interest among the townspeople?

7. How much did the Pied Piper say he would charge for getting rid of the rats?

8. What did the mayor first think of the amount of money the Pied Piper requested?

9. Why do you think it was **rash** of the mayor to offer fifty thousand guilders to the Pied Piper?

10. What did the astonished townspeople see when the Pied Piper began to play?

11. How did the Pied Piper **exterminate** the rats?

12. How did the mayor behave when the Pied Piper rejected the fifty guilders?

13. What is the meaning of **peculiar** as it is used in the passage?

14. Why do you think the Pied Piper **insisted** on being paid in full?

15. In what way does the passage end on a sinister note?

____

____

Fun & Fascinating FACTS

- Low German was the language spoken in northern Germany for several centuries up to around 1500. The word for *rag* in that language is *palte,* and the adjective *paltrig* means "ragged."

  Paltrig passed into English as **paltry.** Something ragged is of little value, so it is easy to see how *paltry* came to mean "worthless."

- *Avenge* and **revenge** are similar in meaning. A person can both *avenge* a wrong and *revenge* a wrong. There is a difference that should be noted, however.

  Avenge suggests striking back at a wrongdoer in order to obtain justice. Hamlet, in the play of the same name, is called upon to *avenge* his father's murder by killing his uncle, who had committed the crime. Hamlet takes no satisfaction from his action, which he feels has been forced upon him.

- *Revenge* carries the suggestion of striking back at a wrongdoer for the personal satisfaction it brings. Note that *revenge* is both a verb and a noun. *Avenge* is a verb only.

- A **council** is a group of people that meets to decide or plan something, give advice, or make laws. A town *council* may be the ruling body of a town. A president may appoint a *council* to look into an issue and offer advice. Students may elect a student *council* to govern their affairs. People who are members of a *council* are called *councillors.*

  Counsel is advice or opinion. When one is faced with seemingly unsolvable problems, it may be advisable to seek *counsel.* A person who gives *counsel* as a profession is called a *counselor.*

bluster
council
dwell
exterminate
fee
garment
infest
insist
paltry
peculiar
rash
revenge
rodent
swarm
vat

20 Vocabulary Extension

fee

noun A fixed amount of money that is paid so you can do something.

Academic Context

Students often have to pay school **fees** to cover the cost of supplies for certain classes, such as art or science.

Discussion & Writing Prompt

What are some services that charge a **fee?** Which service or services have you or your family paid a **fee** for?

2 min. 1. Turn and talk to your partner or group.	3 min. 2. Write 2–4 sentences.
Use this space to take notes or draw your ideas.	Be ready to share what you have written.

Review

Hidden Message In the boxes provided, write the words from Lessons 17 through 20 that are missing in each of the sentences. The number after each sentence is the lesson the word is from. When the exercise is finished, the shaded boxes should spell out some well-known words from the pen of Sir Walter Scott, the Scottish novelist and poet.

1. The _____ started over a ban on rock groups. (18)

2. Shoppers _____ into the malls every December. (20)
3. Her efforts to impress people seemed _____. (17)
4. Their story of winning a million dollars was a(n) _____. (18)
5. The peasants emptied the _____ that held the yellow dye. (20)

6. Lavender is a delightfully _____ herb. (19)

7. Be _____ if something sounds too good to be true. (18)
8. The child's forehead became _____ because of a fever. (19)
9. The scoundrel swore to take _____ on the investigator who tried to thwart him. (20)
10. The death of their pet caused them great _____. (18)
11. Bald eagles are _____ to North America. (20)
12. The villagers _____ in simple huts built of pine logs. (20)
13. _____ from the explosion was scattered widely. (17)

W

14. The island is a(n) _____ of peace in a troubled world. (19)
15. The council would like you to _____ on your outline for the concert. (19)

16. Don't _____ your dirty clothes all over the floor. (19)
17. The principal will _____ those students for doing such a fine job. (18)

18. This _____ will last a long time if washed by hand. **(20)**

19. The locket held a(n) _____ portrait of her mother. **(17)**

20. A(n) _____ boulder that had rolled onto the road was blocking our way and couldn't be moved. **(19)**

21. Blood began to _____ from the cut on my hand. **(17)**

W

22. The cars left no _____ for the bus to pass. **(17)**

23. The recent _____ of burglaries has the residents worried. **(20)**

24. Their _____ for knowledge about their ancestors led them abroad. **(17)**

25. Please _____ them with the information they request. **(19)**

26. The doctor's _____ was eighty dollars. **(20)**

27. _____ tests will indicate whether more extensive tests are needed. **(17)**

28. The salt air will soon _____ the metal. **(17)**

29. Insecure people sometimes _____ to hide their fears. **(20)**

30. My parents _____ that I do my homework before watching television. **(20)**

31. The fan's letters to the movie star failed to _____ a reply. **(18)**

W

32. The assembler will expertly _____ the controls. **(18)**

33. The fabric this tent is made of will _____ water. **(19)**

34. An honest person will not _____ an agreement. **(19)**

35. There was not time to _____ all my adventures. **(18)**

36. It took two years to _____ the new hospital wing. **(19)**

37. The lost dog was last seen in the _____ of the bus station. **(19)**

38. The only way to make these pots shine is to _____ them. **(17)**

39. Three jurors say they will _____ from the majority vote. **(18)**

40. Try to _____ yourself from yelling on the last day of school. **(17)**
41. I had never been _____ until my trip to Africa. **(18)**

42. The substitute teacher was given a(n) _____ welcome by the students. **(18)**
43. We made a(n) _____ attempt to find the owner. **(18)**
44. The town _____ has the power to raise taxes. **(20)**
45. Squirrels belong to the _____ family. **(20)**
46. He didn't _____ when angered because of his self-control. **(19)**
47. Were the survivors able to _____ anything from the fire? **(17)**
48. The painting may be _____, but the experts seem skeptical. **(18)**

Pronunciation Key

Symbol	Key Words
a	c**a**t
ā	**a**pe
ä	c**o**t, c**a**r
â	be**a**r
e	t**e**n, b**e**rry
ē	m**e**
i	f**i**t
ī	**i**ce, f**i**re
ō	g**o**
ô	fall, f**o**r
oi	**oi**l
ʊ	l**oo**k, p**u**ll
ōō	t**oo**l, r**u**le
ou	**ou**t, cr**ow**d
u	**u**p
ʉ	f**u**r, sh**i**rt
ə	**a** in **a**go
	e in ag**e**nt
	i in penc**i**l
	o in at**o**m
	u in circ**u**s

Symbol	Key Words
b	**b**ed
d	**d**og
f	**f**all
g	**g**et
h	**h**elp
j	**j**ump
k	**k**iss, **c**all
l	**l**eg, bott**le**
m	**m**eat
n	**n**ose, kitte**n**
p	**p**ut
r	**r**ed
s	**s**ee
t	**t**op
v	**v**at
w	**w**ish
y	**y**ard
z	**z**ebra
ch	**ch**in, ar**ch**
ŋ	ri**n**g, dri**n**k
sh	**sh**e, pu**sh**
th	**th**in, tru**th**
th	**th**en, fa**th**er
zh	mea**s**ure

A stress mark ´ is placed after a syllable that gets a primary stress, as in **vocabulary** (vō kab´ yə ler ē).